PABAY

Pabay

AN ISLAND ODYSSEY

CHRISTOPHER
A.WHATLEY

BIRLINN

In loving memory of my Aunt Margaret (1928–2005)
and Uncle Len (1919–74)

First published in Great Britain in 2019 by
Birlinn Ltd
West Newington House
10 Newington Road
Edinburgh
EH9 1QS

www.birlinn.co.uk

ISBN: 978 1 78027 579 6

British Library Cataloguing-in-Publication Data
A catalogue record for this book is available on request from the British Library.

Typeset by Hewer Text UK Ltd, Edinburgh

Printed and bound by Gutenberg Press, Malta

Contents

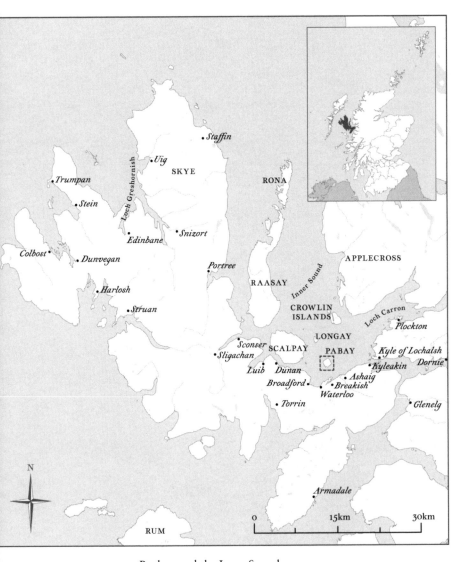

Paybay and the Inner Sound

List of Plates

Between pp. 164 and 165

Rock shelter, Pabay
Broadford pier, *c.* 1958
Pabay jetty, *c.* 1958
Pabay, jetty end, *c.* 1958
Egg collecting, Pabay, *c.* 1958
Len Whatley, packing live chicks, Pabay, mid-1950s
Lias rock strata, Ob Lusa-Ardnish, Breakish
Pabay, great trap dyke
MV *Coruisk*, Pabay, *c.* 1960
Pabay stamps, 1964 and 1965
Len, Alison and Michael, and *Klepper* sailing canoe, 1966
Len and Stuart Whatley, and kiln, early-1960s
Len Whatley, making pots, Edinbane Pottery, 1973
Edinbane Pottery, 2007
Stuart Whatley, throwing a large jug, 2008
Gotland and other sheep, Pabay farmyard, mid-1970s
Storm harbour, Pabay, mid-1980s
Margaret (Whatley) Mackinnon, Dunhallin Crafts, late 1990s
Pabay track and buildings, 2018

Between pp. 198 and 199

Margaret Whatley, and daughter, on boat for Pabay, 1950
Pabay, view of cottage and farmstead, *c.* 1951
Len, Margaret, Anthea, Stuart and Rachel, Pabay, 1952
Pabay, ploughing, 1951
Pabay, seaweed collecting, 1952
First threshing, 1952
'Lord Ivac of Cape Wrath'
Nissen hut construction, 1952
Nissen hut, after fire, 1958
Len Whatley, knitwear designing, Pabay, *c.* 1961

Between pp. 246 and 247

Hugh Miller, stonemason, 1843
Archibald Geikie, geologist, 1850s
Pabay ammonite
Contemporary engraving, Pabay ammonite (1828)
The *Sea Otter*, 1951
Sea Otter, wrecked, 1952
Landing craft, the *Jacqueline J*, Broadford, 1953
The DUKW, 1955
Len Whatley and others, boat refurbishment, Pabay, 1965

Introduction

I'm writing this by the window of a house at the sea front in Stein, a settlement on the western side of Skye's Waternish peninsula. Out over the water, at the edge of the bay, are three small uninhabited islands that from here appear to merge into one. All grass-topped, the nearest, at the seaward end of Loch Dunvegan, is Isay; the others are Mingay and Clett. Beyond them is the Little Minch, the stretch of sea that separates Skye from the Outer Hebrides. Lining the horizon lies North Uist, the last-named readily identified by the long triangular shape of Eaval, at over 1,130 feet (347 metres) its highest hill.

Islands mesmerise and intrigue me. They have since I was a very young boy. One in particular, the subject of this book.

I bought Isay Cottage a few years ago. As a Scottish historian, I rather liked the idea of spending time writing in a terrace that dated back to 1790, when the British Fisheries Society decided to lay out a fishing village here. Stein – known to the Society as Lochbay – was one of two villages planned by the Dumfriesshire-born civil engineer Thomas Telford.

Stein, however, was not one of Telford's successes. The Fisheries Society hoped Lochbay would become one of the finest fishing ports in Europe, a sophisticated town of interlocking crescents and squares. It hardly got off the drawing board.

But from the earliest days Stein boasted an inn, although at first it was a temporary establishment. The Stein Inn nowadays is one of the busiest on Skye. When the staff are in the mood, it is one of the best. Sometimes, the very best.

One warm summer's afternoon almost fifty years ago, towards the end of a gentle family walk to nearby Coral Beach north of Dunvegan, my cousin Stuart and I decided to go further and clamber round the steep coastal promontory of Cnoc Mòr Ghrobain that separates Loch Dunvegan from Stein's Loch Bay. The plan was for my father to pick us up from Fairy Bridge, four miles up the road from Stein. The terrain was rough, and we were longer than anticipated. A stickler for punctuality, my father had driven off. As this was long before mobile phones, we had to wait somewhere obvious and hope someone would come and collect us. The Stein Inn made sense. It was nearby, and we were hot and tired. As both of us had turned eighteen, we could even have a pint. It was then that Stein began to work its magic. And not only the beer. Over the following years I came back, with friends, family, my two wives (in sequence, with several years in between), and children; with its low ceilings, unplastered, rough-hewn, but stoutly built stone walls, open fire and generously portioned, unpretentious bar meals, it breathed warmth, and welcome.

But there was something else that took me to Stein.

It was partly an act of homage to the couple who first led me here. They were my Uncle Len and Aunt Margaret. After spending almost twenty remarkable years trying to make a living on the island of Pabay, off the coast of Skye's south-eastern corner, they had just sold up and moved to the village of Edinbane, some six or seven miles from Stein. It was Len who had suggested the expedition to Coral Beach.

My connection with Stein became even closer some years later. My uncle had died, and Auntie Margaret (as I then knew her) was now remarried. She had left Edinbane, to live first in a caravan and then a croft house along the road to the west of Stein. This was at the far end of Hallin, the unevenly strung-out line of houses that sit beneath the hilltop dun that gives the settlement its name.

Whenever I could, I visited the wee craft room where she beavered away on her knitting machine. I relished the warmth of her hospitality and admired her stoicism – her life had never been easy – and boundless positivity. For people she liked, she was a loyal, lifelong friend. She was also a shrewd judge of character, so it was both instructive and entertaining to hear her deliciously disparaging assessments of those who had disappointed her. I owed her a great deal, above all for her love and support when I was growing up – she was a kind of surrogate mum – but also during a difficult period when my own mother was hospitalised in Glasgow and dying. Over the years, Margaret and my mother, Evelyn, delighted in swapping patterns and magazines – *Stitchcraft* was one I remember – both devoted to knitting, sewing and *making* things. The lower the cost, the greater their joy.

It was during one of these conversations with my aunt that we joked about the prospect of me writing about her Pabay years.

Later she moved again, to Geary, high on the north-eastern edge of the Waternish headland, where she could look out over the Ascrib islands to Uig, and the Trotternish district of Skye. It was here, towards the end of her life, that I assured her that I'd write what we'd talked about earlier; her time on Pabay.

* * *

Pabay is a small, almost diamond-shaped island that lies just two and a half miles off the small, bustling village of Broadford, in the parish of Strath, south Skye. It is even closer to the coastal townships of Harrapool, Waterloo and Lower and Upper Breakish.

The island is only a mile across, and walking round its three-mile coastline of rough ground, bog, cliff, rocky outcrops, coves, sandy stretches and shingle used to take less than a couple of hours. The land area only amounts to 360 acres (145 hectares). Even so Pabay fills the edge of Broadford Bay, for which it acts as a kind of breakwater when the wind's coming from the north. But it is very low-lying – pancake-like, in some descriptions, when seen from the road to Heaste and the hills around Broadford.

From the old L-shaped jetty at Broadford from where most visitors to Pabay cross, Pabay looks welcoming. Easily picked out are a small whitewashed block of housing and the main farm buildings. Visible too, near the highest part of the island, are a couple of lines of straggling pine trees, originally planted as shelter belts.

Pabay's highest point is 89 feet, or 27 metres above sea level. Despite being windswept, from spring onwards Pabay is green and fecund-looking. It contrasts starkly with Beinn na Caillich, the conical, steep-sloping, glacier-scraped, stone-covered, cairn-topped,

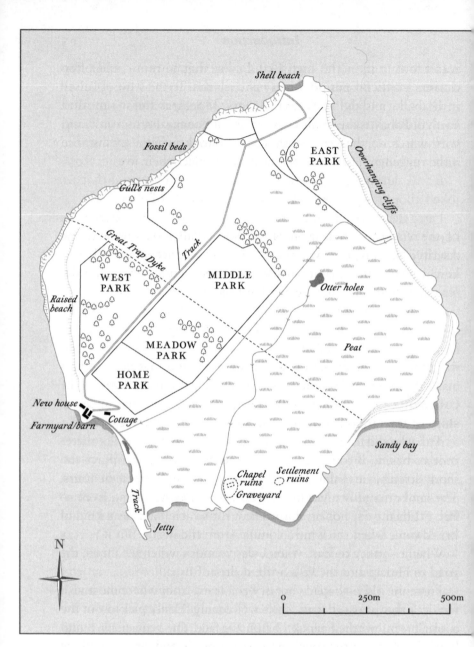

Pabay

2,400 foot (732 metre) high Red Cuillin that towers – and often glowers – over Broadford, its bay and islands. To the west of Pabay is the bulkier island of Scalpay. Lying off Scalpay's east side, and north of Pabay, is the small, rocky rump of Longay. Further east, and northwards, are the Crowlin islands. Beyond them in the far distance is the rugged mountainous peninsula of Applecross, in Wester Ross.

*   *   *

I don't remember the first time I set foot on Pabay. According to my deceased parents' time-worn, cracked-backed photograph albums, in which small, now fading black and white pictures were carefully placed, and then labelled by hand, it was in 1951. I was three.

For most of the years afterwards until the family left, I was on Pabay for at least part of what would soon become my school holidays – Easter and summer mainly, with the occasional Christmas trip. So keen was I to get to Pabay that I was barely into my teens when I began to make the occasional journey on my own. Bus from the outskirts of Glasgow to Queen Street railway station, where I'd catch the early morning train to Mallaig. From there I'd walk down to the pier for a ferry that would take me to Armadale, in the south of Skye. Thereafter another bus, to Broadford. There, bag in hand, I'd hasten down the short, sloping lane to the old jetty where I'd catch a whiff of the warm peat smoke from Rory McGregor's shoreside cottage. Paddington Bear-like, I'd then wait, hoping that someone on Pabay had seen me and would come over to pick me up. I was never let down.

Whether on my own or, when I was younger, with my parents, my sense of anticipation as we left the shelter of Broadford's squat jetty was intense. Usually, Len's boats were open, although some had a foredeck that provided some shelter. Suddenly I'd feel the blow of the cooler breeze off the open sea brush my face. The heavier swell and breaking waves of the rougher sea that I recall us crunching into as soon as we left the immediate confines of Broadford Bay beyond Rubh' an Eireannaich – Irishman's Point – did little to suppress my excitement, albeit mingled with just a stab of apprehension. The sharp showers of sea spray that soaked us were fun at first, but there were occasions when the waves were so high that there was nothing to see but the next one looming high ahead. Any unease I felt was short-lived. After a mile or so came the comforting sight of the tall red iron perch that marked the first of Pabay's treacherous rocks, which also made for calmer water, especially if the wind was blowing from a northwards direction. Once past the perch – which was always on the left or starboard side (to go to the other side of the perch was asking for trouble) – appearing to grow larger as we got closer were the family's small grey harled cottage and, nearby, the farm steading.

Harder to spot, but adding further elation when I managed it, was the smaller, rusting, black-painted perch that stood at the end of Pabay's long, sloping rubble-built jetty. We were nearly there. If I was lucky, I'd see one or more of my cousins scurrying down the shore-side track that led to the jetty to greet the incoming boat. Or the red Ferguson tractor moving in the same direction, its driver – sometimes Uncle Len – ready to offload stores from the boat and transport them to the house or barn. The crossing rarely took even thirty minutes.

From the jetty there is an open, rough, three-yard-wide, quarter-mile-long track that led to the cottage and farmstead. From here there's another track running north-east across the island to a small, shell-rich beach – for centuries a natural fertiliser for Pabay's farmers.

The larger, north-west portion of the island is considerably more cultivable than the south-eastern third, which is wetter and mainly peatland. Beyond the farm buildings the coastline on the west side of the island is flatter and low-lying beneath what is a grass-covered raised beach. Rockier, with higher cliffs indented by a series of coves, is the island's long eastern edge. Then, approaching the jetty again, the land levels out. With a burn running down to the shore, this is where there are the remains of an ancient chapel, a small burial ground and what's left of the stone walls of the houses belonging to what was a small settlement – marked 'Pabba' on ground described as arable on old Macdonald estate maps – that has been deserted since the mid-nineteenth century.

* * *

What I can remember more acutely are the leavings, the fond fare-wells. The sight of the beacon at the end of the jetty on Pabay getting smaller, along with anyone who'd come to wave us off, as the boat picked up speed. Leaving Pabay, even after a short stay, induced wrenching emotional pain that stretched beyond language, an intensity of feeling I'd later associate with unrequited love, or with missing someone I've loved dearly. The boat trip from the jetty on Pabay to Broadford's pier was bad enough, although the ache of departure was eased by the excitement of the sea crossing – especially if it was rough. Being allowed to steer was an even better salve. It was at the top of the steps of the old stone pier at Broadford that I'd begin to look backwards at what was gone.

True, my reaction was partly due to my mother's fascination with Skye as the romantic refuge after Culloden of the 'prince on the heather', and her insistence on singing the 'Skye Boat Song' as we crossed by the car ferry at Kyle. Born in Aston, like many English people of her generation who reached adulthood between the wars, her scant knowledge of Scotland's history was gleaned from the often insightful but also highly coloured travel writings of the Englishman H. V. Morton.[1]

Enormously popular and influential, Morton's journey through Scotland, reported in his frequently reprinted *In Search of Scotland*, was shaped by the nation's enduring myths: one of the sub-headings for his chapter on Skye, was 'I try to keep an appointment with Prince Charlie'. Imagining I was on the bonny boat and hearing the sailors' cry, the short sea journey on the car ferry at Kyle was for many years heart-wrenching, recent joys mingling with wisps of barely understood history; for one thing, I was taking my leave of Skye and not, like Charles Edward Stuart, on my way there. It was only later that I discovered the song had been composed by an Englishman, Harold Boulton, a century after 'Bonnie Prince Charlie' had died, a drunkard, in Rome.[2] And that Jacobitism was more than one man's tragedy but instead a movement of international consequence that had come close to toppling the British state.[3]

But even without my mother's sentimental overlay, I'd have felt gloomy. In the rear seat of my parents' car or, later, when I was able to travel alone and left Broadford by bus, I'd strain my neck looking leftwards as for ten minutes or so Pabay was not only visible but loomed larger as it was closer to the shore by Breakish. In the days of the ferry at Kyleakin, before the Skye bridge was opened in 1995, there was a point on the short passage across Loch Alsh where I could catch a fleeting glimpse of the island. And one more, from the brae on the old A87 near Balmacara. And then nothing. In front was a journey from exhilaration to the grey and dullness of everyday life at home in the suburbs of Glasgow.

I was a frequent but sporadic visitor. For my cousins, leaving was more or less a weekly occurrence during the school terms, after spending weekends, weather and tide permitting, on Pabay, in the company of their parents. During the week, they boarded with Margaret's parents in Broadford. For Stuart, it was a heartfelt trial. Many years afterwards he still associated cold, wet days 'with the necessary trip back to school'; the weather always seemed better when travelling the other way. Nor was there much sympathy for island children on the part of the teaching staff: for Anthea, standing around on the jetty at Pabay – incongruous in her well-polished Clark's school shoes – waiting for the tide, or for the boat's engine to start or a fouled propeller to be cleared, the worry about 'what Mrs MacSeen would say when we arrived late was terrible'. But it wasn't all bad. After Broadford primary school came Portree High. Living in a school hostel during the week had its drawbacks, but few pupils had the opportunity, as Stuart did, of catching the school bus to Portree on a Monday after having brought himself across to Broadford, sometimes with his younger sister Rachel, in an outboard motor-powered dinghy.

Although I knew nothing of this at the time, leaving, and loss, have on a more profound level been recurrent themes in Gaelic verse, partly as from the mid-nineteenth century onwards so many islands were abandoned.[4]

Other than the journeys back to Glasgow, my recollections of times on Pabay are brim-full with bliss of the kind captured by William Wordsworth; when 'to be young was very heaven!' For me it was as close as I'll ever get to paradise, which my cousins shared with me as we adventured through the days and into the evenings, and imagined ourselves as intrepid explorers, cowboy kings, marauding mariners and as water engineers when we tried, invariably unsuccessfully, to stop the tide flowing into or out of a particular rock channel on the seashore.

Rachel, Len and Margaret's third child and a younger cousin of mine, has 'only happy memories': 'paddling, returning home at night with wellingtons full of water, skimming stones, playing around on the rafts, avoiding jellyfish, pulling boats made out of wood and nails in the barn, the tool bench . . . a haven of nails and tools'. Beneath the house criss-crossing lines of rock had created what as the tide receded was a natural lagoon. Its sandy bottom and relatively shallow depth meant it was both a safe and delightful place for children (and, on occasion, adults as well) to swim and play in. Rachel recalls, too, a tranquil environment and the warmest family life imaginable, the tone set by her parents (and maternal grandparents), whose approach to their children's upbringing was to nurture and encourage rather than pick on the negatives, which they did their best to ignore. The others say much the same. But so do most of the children of the island's owners in the fifty years since we left, up to and including even the grandchildren of the current proprietor, David Harris.[5]

So many lives, particularly of the young, have been shaped by Pabay; there we were exposed to and experienced something both intense and unique, difficult to define, but impossible to shake off. Not that I've met anyone yet who wishes to shed the layers of Pabay memory that during their stays there they have unknowingly absorbed. Only for a very few has time on Pabay been overwhelming in a negative way – space, apartness, vulnerability and the logistics of island life are not for everyone.

Related to the positive memories are the many and varied jobs we were asked to do. If these weren't always fun, they were usually fulfilling and gave us all a sense of self-belief, a deep-seated confidence that if we tried hard enough, we could achieve anything. Ted Gerrard, who succeeded my uncle and aunt on Pabay, said something similar in an interview with the late Derek Cooper in 1976: when they arrived, his children were 'moving at half speed'; five years later they were 'quicker, more agile' and standing on their own two feet.[6]

Without realising it, we were being invited to take on just a bit of the responsibility that living on an island imposes: the fact that you're on your own, and in the end have to depend on your own abilities and resourcefulness. Islands, as Mairi Hedderwick has observed, are made up of communities 'carving out livelihoods with limited resources and supply chains' – what she calls the 'sea in-between', a recurrent theme of this book.[7] Pabay has made those of us who spent any time there, what we are: a bit more capable, stronger.

*   *   *

Len and Margaret lived on Pabay full-time for the best part of two decades, from 1950. But they hadn't been born there, or on Skye. They had come from the English Midlands. The Birmingham area. Flat. Over 100 miles from the nearest seashore, and many more from Scotland's lochs and mountains.

Yet, late in 1949, four years after the end of the Second World War, they upped sticks to relocate 500 miles north in a very different environment. To Pabay.

In so many respects they were venturing into the unknown. If it wasn't exactly an alien world, it was unlike the one they were leaving behind. Gaelic was still widely spoken on Skye. They knew not a word of it. Pabay was uninhabited and had been since before the end of the war. Not quite desolate, but deserted. There was no telephone, or electricity. The only habitation was a small, compact, stone-built, slate-roofed shepherd's cottage of the 'improved' kind that became standard in the Highlands from the later eighteenth century onwards.[8] Two rooms downstairs, one of which was a kitchen – a small dairy off, and two bedrooms fitted into the roof-space. It had no internal water supply or toilet facilities. To speak with any other adult human beings, they would have to make a sea crossing to mainland Skye in a small boat – after they had acquired one that is – and learned to handle it in sea conditions of which neither of them had any experience.

All this was in stark contrast to land-locked Birmingham. The city had been growing rapidly and was home to well over a million people. Hall Green, the district where my uncle had lived during much of the war, during which it was heavily bombed, was the most densely populated part of the sprawling conurbation.

The Whatleys were certainly not the first family from England to have moved to Skye. Those who came before, however, were more often than not affluent members of the upper middle class. Unlike Pabay's previous three owners, they were neither captains of industry or commerce, nor owners of an extensive estate. For the previous owners, island proprietorship was an add-on, somewhere to be enjoyed during the summer months or the autumnal shooting season, their every need catered for by estate employees who ranged from gamekeepers to domestic servants. Len's and Margaret's intention – they had no choice – was to live on Pabay permanently, on their own, and make it pay.

Nor did they have much in common with the people who had owned Pabay before it became a place of recreation. These were, respectively, the Macdonald and Mackinnon families, descendants of the clans of the same name who between them had for centuries owned virtually all of the land in south Skye.

But neither was Len a crofter. Crofters, holders of the ubiquitous, diminutive, usually rectangular-shaped lots of land in the townships that skirted the shore across the short sea channel that separated them from Pabay, struggled to eke out a living. Len was – or hoped to be – an island farmer. A smallholder, with much fewer than 100 acres of cultivable ground. For his and Margaret's first two children, who attended the primary school over the water in Broadford, the distinction was – at first – a cause of some friction. Perceptions of difference on the part of incomers, even if they have little foundation, can be exploited by those members of the host community who feel most strongly any threat to the world as they have known it.

This, then, is not another fondly told story of Western Isles crofting, although crofters appear from time to time. But not as they did in Aberdeen's *Press & Journal* in August 1963 – when Len Whatley was Pabay's resident proprietor. A minister from Dorset and his two sons on a rowing expedition out of Broadford had got into trouble. The trio's boat had been blown ashore on Pabay, where they were 'given shelter for the night by crofters'.[9] No they weren't.

In a very real sense, Len and Margaret were running against the grain, not by visiting Skye – tourists had become increasingly

numerous between the two world wars – but by staying.[10] For over
a century the island's indigenous people had been leaving, most of
them reluctantly, although some – their spirits drained by years of
unrelenting poverty and beckoned by the brighter lights of the city
or of a better life abroad – clamoured to go. The drift away would
carry on for some years yet.

By the 1970s the outward flow from Skye had been checked.
What had happened on one small island off Skye of course hadn't
changed history, but Len and Margaret played their part in stemming the tide.

There were occasions during their years on Pabay when the
number of people living there more or less permanently rose to over
a dozen, while with casual workers and visitors there could be well
over twenty. Nothing like this had been witnessed there for
well over a century – the early 1840s to be precise, before the devastation wreaked by the potato famine.

If they had come to Skye in the 1960s their move could have been
put down to fashion. As the narrator in William Wall's recent award-
winning novel, *The Islands*, observes, by the end of that decade, 'the
world had fallen in love simultaneously with two incompatible
mistresses – self-sufficiency and conspicuous consumption'.

The search for the former was part of the 'rural repopulation' of
the north-west of Scotland, as growing numbers of people turned
their back on urban life. Many of those who moved were English-
born, as Len was. However, at the end of the 1940s and during the
1950s this was a trickle compared to the much stronger in-rush of
migrants to Scotland that took place from the 1970s. The scale of
in-migration stoked fears about the 'Englishing of Scotland'.[11] So
called 'white settlers' were accused of taking the country's top jobs
or, as well-off retirees, buying property in Scotland's countryside
and villages, edging locals out of the housing market and, subsequently, from the communities in which they had been born and
bred.[12] This created such alarm that what had for centuries been a
largely dormant sentiment in Scottish society – anti-Englishness –
burst into the public arena in the 1980s and 1990s in the form of
ethnic nationalist organisations such as Siol nan Gaidheal (Seed of
the Gael), Settler Watch and Scottish Watch.

Len and Margaret were fortunate; they arrived before most of this. They were ahead of the curve, pioneers rather than disciples. And anyway, only one of them was English. Margaret had been born in Edinburgh. Her mother, Margaret Heggie, was a Fifer. Nor, as we've seen, did Len or Margaret have anything like the kind of financial resources conjured up by the connotations associated with 'white settler' colonialism. Altogether absent too were any traces of the social superiority commonly associated with middle- and upper-class English incomers. If their accents marked them off as different, or caused offence, it was that they sounded English rather than posh; theirs were not the 'clipped voice[s] of ... the English ruling class' that had reverberated around the dining rooms and bar areas in Skye's hunting lodges and hotels during the summer and autumn months in the 1920s and 1930s.[13]

In taking on Pabay, they were forcing nobody out – the island was uninhabited.

* * *

I didn't keep my promise to my aunt while she was alive. She died in 2005. Yet from time to time I would find myself wondering how – if at all – I could keep my word. What became apparent to me was that if I were to do justice to her, and her life with Len on Pabay, this would best be done within the context of the island's longer history. There would be risks associated with writing about just one family, even if, to quote one enthusiastic journalist from 1965, the Whatleys' story 'of how they have struggled with nature and misfortune in order to wrest a living from Pabay's rich soil would fill a book' and provide 'an inspiration to all who learn of their fortitude, determination and self-reliance'.[14] So true. But their achievements, of which there were many, are best revealed and celebrated – and tempered – by the knowledge of what had gone before (and what followed).

So Margaret's story has become a history of the island. And of its relationship with the adjacent parts of Skye, including the island of Scalpay. For several decades after 1894 Pabay was part of Scalpay estate.

But it is with some trepidation that I have written it. Roger Hutchinson, the prolific and respected Raasay-based author, commentator and historian, has remarked recently that the age of 'discovering' the Hebrides, 'even the smallest' or most remote of the islands thereof, has passed. 'Writers and broadcasters' who attempt to do so, he opined, 'are treading on worn footpaths.'[15] Writing as long ago as 1939, in the wake of the publication of books such as Neil Gunn's *Off in a Boat*, Louis MacNeice's *I Crossed the Minch* and John Lorne Campbell's *Book of Barra*, the Scottish nationalist – and island lover – Hugh MacDiarmid came to a similar conclusion.

The would-be island writer would be unwise to disregard MacDiarmid's critique of the quality of much island writing: 'the *olla podrida* [a Spanish stew] of old wives' tales, day trippers' ecstasies, trite moralisings, mawkish sentimentality, supernatural fantasies, factual spinach', and the 'outrageous banality which fills most books on this subject'. Publications of this 'thrilled to be on a Scottish island' kind, egotistical, patronising and cursory, continue to appear and, judging by their sales figures, have many admirers.

However, having heeded MacDiarmid's warnings and bought, or borrowed, and read much of the Hebridean island literature that is available currently, I decided to press ahead. For one thing, despite the fact so many island stories have been written, Pabay's hasn't.

In itself this need not be the most convincing reason for devoting the time I have over the past two and a half years to preparing this book.

What soon becomes evident when reading the more serious histories of the Hebridean islands is how much they have in common. In most cases they were first inhabited by Stone Age men and women – the Mesoliths. Then came early Christian settlements, and Norse conquest, until the Lords of the Isles supplanted the Vikings. Eventually, we come to the landlord-led expulsions of people in the nineteenth century and, all too often, ongoing decline thereafter.

Nevertheless, despite such similarities, as has so often been remarked, every island is different. And no wonder. Between them the Inner and Outer Hebrides comprise over 500 islands, large (and mainly inhabited) and small (increasingly, altogether deserted).

Generalisations – even the most poetic, such as a recent description of the Hebrides as a 'fractal scatter of rock and machair' – cease to have meaning when individual islands are looked at more closely. Pabay's rocks are not the rocks of the Outer Hebrides. The latter are formed of Lewisian gneiss, one of the oldest rock formations in Europe. Other than in Sleat, most of the Inner Hebridean island of Skye is underlain with younger sedimentary rocks of the Mesozoic era. There are only small patches of machair on Pabay. The elongated ellipse that is Pabay looks nothing like its nearest neighbours, Longay and Guillamon ('a small Ailsa Craig' is how it was once depicted), rocky protuberances mostly devoid of cultivable soil. And, therefore, more or less uninhabitable, other than for rabbits, birds or a few sheep in the summer.

Very different too is the larger, much more mountainous island of Scalpay, that lies a couple of miles to the north-west of Pabay. After landing there, on the jetty near Scalpay House a few months ago, within minutes I found myself walking along an avenue of established and still flourishing trees. The lower slopes of the hill behind the house are thickly wooded. There is even a walled garden.

It is nothing like Pabay, which is much less well protected from the elements. The quarter-mile track from the jetty to the house and farm buildings is open – as we've seen. Until the present century there were few trees there, at least none that were tall and straight; the most prominent was an old, low, bent-backed rowan tree in the patch of garden at the front of the former shepherd's cottage.

Pabay is small, but this seems not to have deterred its owners and inhabitants from turning it into a viable agricultural unit. Or trying to.

Highland landlords from the nineteenth century onwards have been condemned for prioritising the gains to be had from sheep rearing over the needs of the people for adequate parcels of cultivable land and, later, for converting sheep walks into deer forests. Pabay was not immune to these revolutions in land use – although its dimensions and terrain meant it could never carry deer. However, without the interest in and commitment to the improvement of Pabay by its owners over the course of the nineteenth century, and the first half of the twentieth century, the island that

Len Whatley took over would have presented an even more formidable challenge. His determination to succeed, and his tenacity in doing so in the face of innumerable obstacles, are something that as a child I was largely unaware of, and even later I only vaguely appreciated. But now, with a deeper understanding of the material facts of life – that making a living doesn't just happen but is something one does – my admiration and respect for what he and Margaret accomplished on Pabay is close to boundless.

The case therefore for a history became compelling.

But it also presented me with new challenges.

Professionally, I have steered away from any temptation to write Highland history. I have no Gaelic. I was aware therefore that anything I wrote would be even more incomplete than all history necessarily is. Island history without a knowledge of Gaelic may be even more prone to the risk of writing superficially, as an outsider looking in. This is because of the special place islands have – and have had – in Gaelic literature, whether prose, poetry or song. For Hugh MacDiarmid, poetry was the 'greatest product' of the Hebrides, and too little known or comprehended, except in the shape of 'a few vulgar misconceptions'. I am at risk of being a misconceiver.

My frustration about my linguistic inadequacy in relation to Gaelic is heightened by the knowledge that Pabay was tenanted at the turn of the eighteenth century by Lachlann mac Theàliach Òig (1665–1734), or Lachlan Mackinnon, a renowned Gaelic poet and song writer.[16] The little work of the 'Skye Bard' which has survived, I can read only in what by comparison with the original is flat-sounding English.

Frustrating too is the telling detail I might be missing. As Alexander Robert Forbes remarked in 1923 in his *Place-names of Skye and Adjacent Islands: With Lore, Mythical, Traditional and Historical*, 'Every knoll and hill almost had its name', as did so many other of Skye's features and places. These names, Forbes wrote, read as chapters of the history of places and ancient times, and 'tell the tales of life's varied experiences'.[17]

But there is no record of such nomenclature for Pabay, at least not published. What might have survived was partly lost in the 1870s. This was when surveyors from the Ordnance Survey decided that henceforth what had evidently been known locally as Eilean Pabba should become the anglicised Pabay – a fate suffered too by the nearby islands of Eilean Sgealpa (Scalpay) and Eilean Longa (Longay). We can infer from the surveyor's manuscript name books that this was on the recommendation of the local minister the Rev. Donald Mackinnon whose father (who had preceded him in this charge) had immersed himself in his parish's history. Also consulted but not necessarily heeded were James Maclean, and James Macpherson, a crofter from Harrapool, Broadford. The 'new' name reflected what was believed to have been the Norse derivation of Pabay – Pap-ey, the Priest's isle.[18] While the Gaelic names of burns were noted, they never appeared on the published maps. The only other traces of Pabay's Gaelic inheritance found on OS maps nowadays are the names An Gobhlach and Sgeir Gobhlach, both of which mark and capture the sharply forked nature of the rocks that lie off the island's southern edge. With Pabay described simply in the name book as being 'covered with good pasture land', the surveyors evidently concluded there was little else worth listing, other than the remains of an ancient chapel and graveyard, the former being attributed to the Culdees. We will return to this in Chapter 2.

Nor is there much first-hand evidence from earlier periods, but this applies to the West Highlands and Hebrides as a whole. Archaeological artefacts can help, but the stories they could tell are locked in, and wordless, intelligible only through inference and deduction – although done well, this can offer a believable kind of understanding.[19] Later, we have some charters and family histories, and travellers' accounts. By the time of the Restoration in 1660 the archives become much denser, and include government and administrative material, court and judicial minutes, church records, estate papers and a range of miscellaneous sources.[20]

But fewer of these than we would like relate to Skye. Strath in particular seems ill-served.

Even kirk session minutes are scarce, a real disappointment given the comprehensive knowledge parish ministers and elders had of those living within their bounds. Ministers such as the Rev. John Mackinnon (1786–1856) and his father and son (the Donald just mentioned) – also ministers of the same parish – were heavily involved in local affairs. They would have been familiar with Pabay's people, including no doubt, intimate details of their faults and follies, above all their sexual misdemeanours, the staple of parish elders' deliberations, punctiliously recorded in kirk session minute books. The one volume known to survive (for the period 1886–97), includes one such 'scandal' close to Pabay, but not on the island itself. An 'improper intimacy had taken place', it was alleged, between Ann Mackinnon, in Harrapool, and Christopher Macdonald of the same township. For 'the sake of clearing the character of Ann', Christopher Macdonald took the oath of expurgation before a meeting of the kirk session in Breakish school house (where Len and Margaret were to live for a time), and the matter was closed.[21]

Nevertheless, what there is, somewhat surprisingly given Pabay's compactness, is an abundance of evidence relating to the island for the eighteenth century onwards. For the interested reader this material is listed in the endnotes for each chapter.

And what I have also been able to retrieve are my own memories of Pabay. I've been able to talk with others who've lived there or who are familiar with the island, and weave their stories into the narrative, as well as carrying out more traditional library- and archive-based research. The result is a history written in what for me is a new genre, a variant of what is called life writing.

* * *

Pabay as a named entity rarely appears in anything that was written prior to the seventeenth century. One of the earliest references is to 'Pabay islet', in an account of how the Mackinnon clan acquired what the family's historian called 'the magnificent property of Strath, in Skye'.

Pabay's role in this was pivotal.

At the end of the fourteenth century, the Mackinnons' main stronghold was Mull. Clan legend has it that the heir to the clan chiefdom had been fostered to the Gillieses, who then owned Strath. On a hunting expedition on Pabay, Gillies's two sons fell out, fought, 'and in the contest were slain'. Heirless, 'old Gillies . . . became attached to young Mackinnon and [so it is reported] left him his patrimonial estates'.[22]

Strath remained in Mackinnon hands for more than three centuries, until the family was forced to surrender possession as punishment for the clan chief's involvement in the Jacobites' rebellion in support of James Francis Stuart, the so-called 'Old Pretender' in 1715; 150 Mackinnons may have fought against British forces at Sheriffmuir, just north of Stirling. Fervently anti-Hanoverian, Ian Dubh, by now in his mid-sixties, had no hesitation in leading 250 or more of his men into battle at Culloden in the cause of Charles Edward Stuart in April 1746. Whether anyone from Pabay was amongst these forces, and if so how they fared, is impossible to say.

On the first maps depicting Skye, which date back to the sixteenth and seventeenth centuries, Pabay is sometimes delineated but is nameless. It was in 1664 that 'Paba' appears for the first time, in Joan Blaeu's atlas, although the information for this was collected during previous decades. Thereafter, however, it disappears, even from John Cowley's 'New Map of North Britain with the islands thereunto belonging', published in 1734. A few years later though Pabay was back, on James Dorret's similarly named map of 1750, as it was, as 'Pabuy' on a French map of 'des Isles Britannique' in 1757.[23]

The sense this conveys, of an island that flickers in and out of history, is apposite. There are times when it approaches centre stage. On the other hand, there are long periods of silence. The following two chapters outline Pabay's place in history, not least its role as a sanctuary for some of Scotland's first Christians, possibly as early as the seventh century.

But for other reasons too, Pabay has attracted attention, and drawn people to it. Just why, how, and with what consequences, is what the rest of this book is about.

Chapter 1

Pabay: island revelations

Pabay had gripped the imaginations and pulled at the hearts of Len and Margaret Whatley almost from the time they first saw it. The moment was transformational. And profound in its impact. It changed their lives irrevocably. Ultimately it broke Len's health and contributed to his premature death.

But there was an attraction about Pabay that went beyond the circumstances of particular individuals or, in this case, a couple. We will see as our story unfolds that in part this was because Pabay is an island, and islands had in the past, and still have, a certain allure.

This is true of small islands especially. Although not always. Circumstances matter. Far from offering liberation, islands have been 'nightmarish places of incarceration', as for example Alcatraz in San Francisco Bay, a grim, federal prison until 1963, from which no one ever managed to escape over the course of its twenty-nine-year life.[1] Numerous of Italy's offshore islands have served the same purpose, jewels in the great Mediterranean Sea only for the free. Closer to home there is the tragic instance of Rachel Chiesley, Lady Grange. Lady Grange was the feisty wife of the Jacobite Lord Grange, who had her forcibly abducted from her lavish Edinburgh home and banished to be held captive on a series of islands. Heisgeir, St Kilda (where, in torment, she was unable to sleep), Uist and then Skye, where she died and was buried. This was at Trumpan (along the road from Stein), in 1745. Penury, privation and social isolation – on the basis of her class, language and sex – were her lot for the last thirteen years of her life.[2] Tranquil perhaps, but certainly no island idyll.

For those who seek out islands as refuges – from the world they have known, or in times of personal or national or global crisis

– they can be dangerously seductive. The absence of other people, and inaccessibility, were amongst the attractions that led Nigel Nicolson in 1937 to buy from Compton Mackenzie, for £1,750, the Shiant Islands, which lie off the east coast of Lewis. Nicolson's son Adam articulated his father's motivation as a yearning for 'that wonderful sea room, the surge of freedom which a moated island provides'.[3]

Island living – as opposed to short stays – can crush even the most ardent spirit. Heady imaginings clash with financial reality – the unseen price tag of 'simple' island life. Punctured, dreams dissolve, as the realisation dawns that the fetters of the mind are less easily left behind than the people or material clutter from which would-be island dwellers seek to get away. This is the lesson to be drawn from D.H. Lawrence's short story of 1928, 'The Man Who Loved Islands', in which the main character, Cathcart, sought solace on ever smaller islands. On the last, without any human company, he found only hallucinations, madness and a lonely death.[4]

On a less elevated level, and more specific to Pabay was what was said by one of Broadford's sages to the *Sunday Telegraph* journalist Helen Mason as she waited for the tide to allow her to cross to Pabay for an article she was writing about the Whatleys in the summer of 1967: 'islands always look bonny – from the mainland'.[5]

* * *

Pabay is only one of just under 800 islands that lie off Scotland's coastline. Yet not much less than a century ago, in 1927, the Edinburgh-based Free Church minister and Scottish Highlands and Islands enthusiast Thomas Ratcliffe Barnett singled it out as a special place – and shared his delight with weekend readers of *The Scotsman*.[6] A dedicated solo sailor who had been ashore on many of Scotland's islands, he treasured Pabay. It was, he wrote, a peaceful place, like 'a mystic island in the Aegean'. Its 'green waters', he declared, 'were buoyant and delirious to bathe in'. My younger cousins Rachel and Alison, and others who spent time on Pabay long after Ratcliffe Barnett's visit, would – and did – say much the same, recalling, as we saw in the Introduction, fond memories of days spent playing around in the natural, reef-protected sandy-bottomed lagoon that lay in front of the cottage. They describe day trips and picnics at favourite spots on the island, given names like Shell Beach and Sandy Bay, or amongst the other small coves that are found between the cliffs on the east side.

Pabay, though, was much more than a secluded bathing pool. For Ratcliffe Barnett, a profoundly spiritual man, Pabay was an 'Island of Revelations'. Early Christians who had once inhabited it, he delighted in telling his readers, had broadcast the 'news of Christ in an age of dark deeds and pagan superstitions'. Furthermore, Pabay abounded with fossils. Their discovery and the interpretation put on them by several of Britain's pre-eminent Victorian geologists had, for Ratcliffe Barnett, 'shed fresh wonder on the creation of the world'. We'll see what he meant in Chapter 10.

But in singling Pabay out, Ratcliffe Barnett was one of many people to have seen it, been enticed across, and spent time there. For centuries Pabay has intrigued, sheltered, fed and enchanted those who set foot on its shores of 'mostly shingle and tilted rocks'.

Reinforcing the theme of Pabay's extraordinary appeal over the centuries is the fact that it was only one of two islands to which Ratcliffe Barnett devoted separate chapters in his popular travelogue, *Autumns in Skye, Ross and Sutherland*, first published in 1930. The other was Handa, the bird sanctuary off Scourie in Sutherland – which he also visited more than once.

*　*　*

Today Pabay lies silent at the edge of Broadford Bay. Separate from mainland Skye.

It is no longer a farm where crops are grown and animals raised. Most of the time, it is now uninhabited, other than by wildlife. There are few visitors outside the holiday season. Or, even, during it, although the current owner and his family spend some days on the island every year.

To get to Pabay, you need a kayak, canoe, RIB or other small boat with a shallow draught. Or you could persuade a local fisherman to take you across, leave you for a few hours to explore, and then pick you up at the single jetty – provided the tide is reasonably high – before making the return journey.

It is only by landing there that the island's sounds are to be heard. Birdcalls mainly. Oyster catchers if you're there early in the summer, and many others throughout the seasons. An ornithologists' delight.

The ceaseless churning of the sea gurgling round rocks and through rocky channels, or swashing over occasional patches of sand, shells and shingle. Or, on wilder days, colliding with and spilling over reefs, fallen drops of spattered spray providing the encore. Audible too is the wind's faint hiss as it bends lightly the tall, thick clumps of rushes that abound now the cattle and sheep are no more, through the stands of mainly straggling trees that are the remnants of three shelter belts planted over a hundred years ago, and across the tops of some new, denser plantations.

This though is now. Pabay's off-shore isolation is deceptive, and in historical terms is a relatively recent way of seeing the island.

It is true that some of those who have ventured there imagined – or hoped – it was over the brink, out of this world, a Shangri-La, 'a few extra miles from civilisation' of the kind evoked by James Hilton in his immensely popular 1933 novel, *Lost Horizon*. Hilton's Shangri-La was a Tibetan lamasery, uncontaminated by 'dance bands, cinemas and sky signs', the antithesis of Western values, where the ageing process was slowed.

As we'll see shortly, eremites – that is recluses of one sort or another – were probably amongst those who found their way to Pabay as Christianity spread northwards many centuries ago.

In more modern times, like many smaller islands, it has attracted its fair share of dreamers and drop-outs. We will come across some of them in this book. Len and Margaret were, in their own way, idealists; he more so. But their search was not for seclusion, but a new centre. They, like most of Pabay's people, regardless of period, were of this world. Their aim was to make a living, raise their family and live full, enriching lives. Far from being a place of escape, Pabay demanded Len's and Margaret's total commitment to their new reality. The buck stopped right there: to duck it was to invite disaster.

We should be careful about the terms we use. 'Remote' or 'distant' imply being apart from somewhere more important. Yet what matters for most people is their immediate environment, the surrounding landscape and the factors that influence their daily lives. Pabay has been the here and now, home to and at the heart of the lives of men, women and children for several thousand years.

They were in the mainstream of the currents of continuity and change that have washed Skye and the Western Highlands and Islands over the centuries. Some folks have lived out their entire lives on Pabay. They were distant from events that took place elsewhere in Britain and further afield, but not disconnected, nor untouched by them. Climatic change, Christian missions, Viking invasion, clan conflict and the demise of clanship, potato famine, industrialisation, the fashion for hunting, globalisation, wars, absentee landlordism, government involvement in the Highlands, royal anniversaries and the like – even the General Strike in 1926 and the end of British rule in Africa; all have impinged in one way or other on Pabay's people over time.

It is not just that Pabay was connected. For a long time Pabay was close to the epicentre of developments that were key to the making of what would later become Scotland. Albeit indirectly, Pabay featured as Scottish kings, most notably James VI and I (of England from 1603), and the state, sought to gain control of – and inculcate 'civilitie, obedyence and religoun' into – the Hebrides.[7] This initiative had begun earlier, under James IV and James V. It was in 1493 that the Lordship of the Isles was annexed to the Crown, although it would be well over a century before the Western Isles could be described as settled.[8] It is since then that power in the British Isles has become concentrated in the south – London in England, Edinburgh in Scotland. It was only as this process advanced that monarchs, parliaments and state agencies rendered islands like Skye – and Pabay – peripheral.

But on the local, everyday level too, Pabay has been connected in ways that at least blur the idea of an island as a place apart.

In 1751, parts of the barony of Strath Suardal (or Strathwordel, also spelled Strathordell) were sold by John Mackinnon to Sir James Macdonald. These included 'the five double penny land of

Breckish and half of Pabay', along with land of the same value at Skulamus and 'the other half of Pabay'.[9] Not many years earlier, half of Pabay had been leased to Mary Mackinnon – along with three pennies of Breakish. The same terminology was still being used in 1925 when Pabay was disposed of as part of an island package to Sir Henry Bell, to whom we will return in a later chapter.

The terminology of leases and sasines (Scotland's record of land transfers) from the seventeenth and eighteenth centuries prompts us to appreciate that while Pabay was indeed an island, it was also an integral part of the rural economy and culture of the islands nearby – Scalpay in particular – and adjacent parts of the Skye mainland.

This invisible bridge over Broadford Bay is encapsulated by the example of Lachlan Mackinnon, the much admired 'Skye Bard' I mentioned in the Introduction. Born in Strath parish in 1665, Mackinnon was the son of a cadet member of the family of Mackinnon of Mackinnon. His funeral, in 1734, at Cill Chriosd in Strath was attended not only by a number of prominent clan chiefs and their retainers, but a 'numerous' band of Highland pipers preceded the bier, 'playing the usual melancholy coronach', while watching on was 'a vast assemblage of all ranks and classes'. The significance of this for our purposes is that on his marriage to his first wife, Flora, from Harris, Mackinnon leased the farm of Breakish – to which was adjoined 'the grazing Island of Pabbay'.[10]

Marriages too forged links across the water. In 1834 Charles McKinnon from Pabay married Flora Buchanan from Harrapool, a township adjoining Breakish. The following year, Neil McKinnon married Catherine Matheson. She belonged to Dunan, some few miles from Broadford, on the track to Sconser and Sligachan. Much later, in 1909, in Garngad, in Glasgow, Flora Mackinnon, who had earlier migrated from Pabay to Glasgow, where she worked as a domestic servant, married Farquhar MacPherson, who described himself as a 'Seaman (yacht)'. He was from Lower Breakish.[11]

The year following, Flora gave birth to their first daughter, also in Lower Breakish. In September 1911, the couple had a son, who was born in Breakish itself. The birth was reported to the local registrar by Angus Mackinnon, Flora's uncle – from Pabay.

The enduring interconnectedness of Pabay and the mainland of Skye is perhaps nowhere better to be seen than during the annual cycle of potato planting. In 1952 an old woman from Breakish – known only in the written record as 'The big man Willie Macleod's mother' – reflected on what she was convinced had been a deterioration of spring weather. 'March,' she recalled, 'was always a good month – warm and calm, and the bay would be just full of boats fetching seaweed from Pabbay.'[12]

As we will discover, taking seaware from Pabay for fertilising land set aside for potatoes elsewhere was not always so straightforward.

* * *

Pabay is located in Skye's Inner Sound, south-east of Scalpay, as mentioned in the Introduction. Scalpay sits to the south of the longer and hillier island of Raasay, the most distinctive feature of which is the nearly 1,500 foot (444 metre) high, conical but flat table-topped hill of Dun Caan. Raasay is best known as the birthplace of the twentieth-century Gaelic poet Sorley Maclean, author of 'Hallaig', the 'defiant, tragic . . . masterpiece of twentieth-century Gaelic literature'.[13] Or, more recently, as the place where the crofter Calum MacLeod overcame officialdom's neglect and worked tirelessly and alone, for a decade or more, constructing a two-mile road from Brochel Castle to his croft at Arnish.[14]

Pabay and the Inner Sound are part of what historians call the Atlantic Archipelago. This incorporates the several hundred islands that stretch from Shetland in the north, down along Britain's west coast to reach as far south as the Channel Islands. Within the Atlantic Archipelago was a fairly distinct Scottish Atlantic islandscape. It was a maritime world from which inland Scotland was largely excluded.[15]

Either in its entirety or in parts of it, this was territory that was fought over. Christians, Norsemen, Manx and other sea kings, then clan Macdonald, formally Lords of the Isles from 1336, all enjoyed periods of ascendancy between the fifth and the sixteenth centuries.

There are annals that tell of large-scale destruction resulting from Viking forays in the Hebrides in the late eighth and early ninth centuries. These included Skye and, more than once, the Christian monastery on Iona. Incursions were sudden, the raiders embarking from longships. Elegant, perhaps 120 feet in length, often with carved dragons in their raised prows, and capable of carrying eighty warriors whose painted shields were battened to the ships' sides, it is not hard to see why their victims and enemies labelled them dragon ships.[16] The sea-kings' formidable fleets of galleys inspired 'awe and terror in enemies and allies alike'.[17]

The Vikings' successors, the chiefs of the Campbells of Argyll, the MacLeans, the Macdonalds and the others further north on Scotland's western seaboard also recognised the importance of the sea as they pursued their territorial ambitions. The Mackinnons, who, as we know already, had secured their Skye lands, including Pabay, in the fourteenth century, also had their tussles. One of these was with the Mackenzies, whom they attacked at Eilean Donan castle in 1541.[18] Their preferred means of travel were the Norse-inspired, clinker-built, oar- and sail-powered galleys, and the smaller even more easily manoeuvrable birlinns of between twelve and eighteen oars.[19] In these vessels the clan chiefs and their warriors fought battles or, with their sizeable retinues, called upon neighbouring chieftains in search of hospitality and entertainment – drinking, carousing, listening to their bards' praise poetry, music-making and playing board games, including chess and throwing dice.

Some chiefs – including the Macdonalds and MacLeods of Skye – maintained facilities where they could build boats, as well as shelter and repair them. And little wonder: the first Lord of the Isles was said to have had sixty ships; some of the sea kings had even more.[20] One such service centre, belonging to the MacAskills, a sept of the MacLeod clan for whom they acted as coast watchers, galleymasters and bodyguards, has recently been discovered at Rubha an Dùnain on a promontory in the south-west of Skye.[21]

The sea was also the great connecter. Far from cutting people off, the sea is the umbilical cord that, albeit insecurely, sustains island life. Until relatively late on it was the mainland road to Skye that presented travellers with greater difficulty than coming by water. So neglected in 1799 was the 27-mile stretch from Glen Moriston in the west to Loch Shiel (from where it was best to get a boat to Skye), that it was said to be 'almost impassable even for a single horse'.[22]

It was by sea around 8,000 years ago that the first human beings on Pabay – stone-tool-using Mesoliths – got there. We'll see how, and why, in the next chapter. And it was by sea that the devout who appear to have been on the island from around the seventh century AD mainly travelled.

After that, the Sound was for centuries part of the main sea passageway between the Northern Isles (and Scandinavia) and the south. The channel through the Sound was particularly important during the five centuries of what have been termed the Viking and late Norse eras. These commenced around AD 780, but it is likely that for several centuries prior to this Northmen – a more accurate term for Scandinavians at the time – began to attack the Hebrides, or Sudreys (Southern Isles), as they saw them. There are historians who argue that the proliferation of brochs (circular stone towers) in Shetland, Orkney and the Hebrides – including Skye – points to the need for the inhabitants of these places to have robust refuges from invaders from the north.[23]

Once they had crossed the nearly 200 miles of open sea from the south-west of Norway to Shetland, and then made the 50-mile sail south-west to Orkney, they could soon follow what was in effect an extended coastline down the western side of Scotland until they reached Ireland and the Isle of Man. One way south was through the Minch, in the shelter of the long islands of Lewis and Harris. This, An Cuan Sgìth (The Tired Sea), was presumably preferable to the seaway to the west of the Outer Hebrides, exposed to the longer swells of the Atlantic and higher average wave heights.[24]

The other route was through Skye's Inner Sound, to the narrows of Kyleakin and Kylerhea and thereafter to the islands of Mull, Iona and Islay.[25]

The name Akin derives from Haakon – King of Norway in the mid-thirteenth century, who is said to have assembled his fleet of longships nearby what is now called Kyleakin (Kyle Akin), before sailing south to take part in what was called the Battle of Largs, at which he was defeated.

The importance at one time of this long watery thoroughfare is indicated nowadays by the standing remnants of a series of galley-castles sited at commanding locations, as at Duart on Mull, which overlooks the Sound of Mull, and Dunstaffnage in Lorne, which surveys the sea approach to Loch Etive. Tellingly for our purposes, the fragmentary broken tooth-like husk of one of these galley-castles – Castle Maol – stands at Kyleakin. Legend has it that it was once held by a Norwegian princess who demanded payment from mariners passing through the strait. Although the present structure has been dated to the fifteenth century, there was almost certainly some kind of fortification there beforehand.[26] Another advantage of this setting was the sheltered bay alongside, ideal for warships.

Pabay is positioned some seven sea miles beyond the north end of the narrows – a highly strategic position.[27] Today this is most evident when descending by car into the village of Kyle of Lochalsh on the A87 road from the east. Sitting centre-stage in the sweeping panorama of the Sound that opens up ahead is Pabay, framed, as it were, by the spectacular, crescent-shaped, single-span bridge that was opened to replace the car ferries in 1995.

Skye's Inner Sound has also long been an important waterway across the compass, connecting the west and north-west coast of Scotland's mainland with Skye and the Outer Hebrides. But it had a more immediate, local function too. One visitor in the early nineteenth century wrote of how the part of the Sound that separated Skye from the island of Raasay was 'enlivened by the frequent passage of coasting vessels, and by numerous boats, employed in fishing, or in keeping up the ordinary communication between the islands'.[28] At the hub was Portree, Skye's capital town. By this time Portree was also a frequent destination for boats sailing from Glasgow and Greenock, as well as for those bound to and from Ullapool on the mainland. It was also a point of departure for vessels crossing the Minch to Lochboisdale and Lochmaddy in the Uists, Tarbert in Harris and Stornoway in Lewis.

From around the middle of the nineteenth century and for a long time into the twentieth century, passenger steamers from Glasgow, Oban and elsewhere plied this self-same stretch of calmer sea, rounding Pabay. Most sailed under the flag of the company founded by Glasgow's David MacBrayne, and were easily distinguishable in their livery of black hulls and scarlet funnels topped by a black band. Locals in the 1900s and 1910s recalled the regularity of the *Claymore*, the *Clansman* and the *Chieftain* as they passed through the Sound, past Pabay, before stopping at Portree on their journeys from Glasgow to Stornoway.[29] There were shorter runs too, from Mallaig to Portree.[30] This daily service, provided for a long time by a paddle steamer, carried on into the 1960s. Another paddle steamer that plied the same route, stopping on the way at Kyle of Lochalsh and Broadford, was the *Fusilier*, which operated for around half a century, until 1938.

All changed two years afterwards, in 1940, when for the duration of the Second World War, passage through the Sound was suspended, with the two channels of Kyleakin and Kylerhea being closed other than for 'His Majesty's flotilla' of the Royal Navy. Before long the narrows at Kyleakin down to Loch Duich had become an important naval base.[31] Although wartime operations were scaled down after 1945, the Royal Navy and the Ministry of Defence continued to have a presence, with submarines in particular periodically coming to the surface – much to the excitement of the Pabay children. The sea area between the east of Raasay and Rona and the Applecross peninsula includes the deepest section of the UK's territorial waters – in which fishing is prohibited, and is a testing base for British submarine torpedoes and other weapons, and for sound emissions.

Now the only regular survivor from the era when MacBrayne vessels were an everyday sight is Cal-Mac's MV *Hallaig*, on the twenty-five-minute crossing between Sconser and Raasay.

MacBrayne's though did not have a complete monopoly of the Sound's shipping. Until the 1980s, Clyde puffers, immortalised by Neil Munro in his tales of the *Vital Spark* and its captain Para Handy, brought coal and heavy goods to Skye and the other islands of the Hebrides. This included Pabay, although not directly. Even with a shallow draft, landing a puffer on the island was difficult. One skipper tried to deliver supplies to the Whatleys early on, but gave up. Another, who had tried to avoid Pabay, ran aground. Consequently, Pabay's provisions from Glasgow were unloaded at Broadford.

In short, until the last decades of the twentieth century, the 'Road to the Isles' was a sea route, with Skye's Inner Sound being the mariner's equivalent of the British motorway system's spaghetti junction in Birmingham. The master of any vessel intent on sailing either north or south through the narrows of Loch Alsh and the Sound of Sleat had to avoid the treacherous reefs that stretched in most directions far out to sea from Pabay's shores. Chapter 12 details the dangers that lurk beneath the waters around Pabay when the tide is high and the sea apparently benign.

For some, it is. Over the centuries the deep, more sheltered stretches of water in the Sound have attracted generations of fishermen. Off Pabay itself there are notable fishing grounds – from which Lord Knutsford over a century ago was reputed to have caught around 400 fish of various species during a four-hour session.[32] This is just to the south of the area marked on Herman Moll's map of Scotland (1714), with the comment, 'Great quantities of Herrings cacht here'.[33]

Even during the 1960s it wasn't unusual for some of us, alone or in company, to go off in a dinghy in the evening and, with long weighted lines of feathered hooks, catch forty or fifty mackerel, along with a few saithe or lythe.

In so doing, we were tapping into an age-old tradition.[34] We had a sense of this in that Donald Fletcher, a Skye-born Gael whom Len employed as a general labourer, had advised us on the likeliest fishing spots, the best being off the north-west side of Pabay, on the way to Longay and with Dun Caan on Raasay dead ahead. It is only now, though, that the significance of that advice becomes clear to me, along with the reason for Fletcher's admiration for the saithe – otherwise known as coalfish or coley. This is because I've now read the early nineteenth-century geologist John MacCulloch's observation that this particular fish was 'a most important article for the people [of Skye]; as it forms the chief part of their diet, as far as fish is concerned; while it also furnishes oil for their lamps'.[35] But no longer. The Sound has been over-fished: Nick Broughton, who has been on Scalpay for more than forty years, has in recent years been out and caught nothing, his multi-hooked line splashing impotently in his boat's wake.

*   *   *

If in the early twenty-first century Broadford and the former crofting townships of Harrapool, Waterloo and Breakish to the west are now where tourists stay, the vantage points from which unpeopled Pabay is mainly viewed (but rarely visited), it was not always thus.

Sarah Murray, an intrepid beaver-hat-wearing female travel writer from Kensington who visited Skye along with other Hebridean islands in 1802, described Broadford as 'a single house at the head of a bay'. The 'house' was an inn. A 'very bad one', Mrs Murray remarked. She also warned those who might follow in her footsteps, that there was 'a wide disagreeable river to ford'.[36] Change was slow in coming, although by 1808 there was at least a 'very elegant bridge of three arches' by the inn. Wet feet were no longer a feature of travel through Broadford. Even so, John MacCulloch, the mineralogist, pioneer geologist, traveller, and somewhat sour observer of life in the Scottish Highlands and Western Islands at the time, commented somewhat brusquely, that 'Broadford has no attraction in itself'.

Rather, it was a convenient point of departure for the much more interesting islands that lay offshore, Pabay included.[37] And leaving Broadford by boat had as recently as 1807 been made a lot easier with another innovation: the construction of a simple L-shaped stone-built pier that still stands.

John MacCulloch's interest, however, was in Pabay's geology, which we will return to in a separate chapter.

What else had drawn people to the island? Answers are easier to provide for the last three or four hundred years. Before written records become available, it is largely mythical tales of former times, scraps of clan history and the investigations of archaeologists upon which we have to rely to make sense of what otherwise are vast interludes of silence. To fill these spaces, we can only speculate.

Even so, what at times can seem like grasping at straws does give us some sense of why people went there.

To begin, we have to go back several millennia.

Chapter 2

Papar: 'Priest's island'?

A round 11,500 years ago the last major glaciers that lay heavy over Scotland began to disappear. This happened remarkably quickly once the melting had begun. The process marked the end of the Ice Age, and the beginning of the so-called Holocene.

Prior to this, over the course of some 750,000 years, there had probably been eight occasions when the climate had become so cold that the whole of Scotland was covered by ice. Between these were what geologists term interglacials – periods of warmth which in their turn lasted many thousands of years.

Animals, including brown bears, reindeer, bears, lynxes, wolves and voles were able to survive during the last of the ice ages, when the country had the appearance of an arctic wasteland. But amongst the fossil bones that archaeologists have uncovered, there is no sign of human beings.[1]

Climatic conditions had to ease before people were able to migrate to and live in what we now know as Scotland. With the abrupt warming of the climate that precipitated the end of this last Scottish glaciation, herbs, shrubs and eventually trees appeared, their seeds carried north in the breeze and by birds. In the West Highlands, from Kintyre to Skye, tree species of the kind still seen today became established: birch, hazel and oak, in that order. Some pine too. Within a few thousand years, according to Richard Tipping, there were 'few parts of Scotland from which no trees could be seen'.[2]

Without doubt, Pabay was heavily wooded at this time – that is, approximately 6,000 years ago. It was the decayed trees, unable to survive the subsequent deterioration in climate that made for prolonged periods of wetter weather, cooler temperatures and more acidic growing conditions, that provided much of the organic material from which were formed the deep peat deposits that cover a large swathe of the island. Under this, as elsewhere on Skye where tree cover had been extensive, are to be found the stumps of the mainly birch and willow trees that once predominated.[3] By the time Christ was born, perhaps half of Scotland's trees had gone, replaced by blanket peat and bog.[4] Human beings had been active too, felling trees in order to make way for crops.

But this is to digress: what matters is the type of tree that had been there. It was after woodland had become established, many historians believe, that human beings began to migrate to the Inner Hebrides, perhaps in search of the hazel, with its important nut harvest.

The earliest such occupation by hunter-gatherers, around 9,500 years ago, was on Rum, not so far from the south of Skye.[5] A thousand or so years later these stone-using peoples were to be found on Skye, as evidenced by the numerous Mesolithic sites in the Inner Sound area. This includes the mainland peninsula of Applecross, An Corran near the north tip of Skye, and the offshore islands of Rona, Raasay, Scalpay. And also Pabay.

On Pabay there aren't many Mesolithic remains, partly due to the problem faced by all Mesolithic researchers in the Western Isles: organic materials such as bone, antler, skin and wood have mostly decayed.[6] Even so, a large, deep cave at the base of a cliff at the north end of the island containing limpet shells, some bones and other signs of human occupation has been identified. On the southern side there is a small lithic scatter (that is, a random collection of small stone tools), along with black soil and ash, directly on top of the post-glacial surface, suggesting the presence of some of the region's earliest human beings.[7] It is unlikely that they stayed long; Pabay's hunter-gatherers were most likely to have been seasonal visitors.[8]

Pabay's main attraction (as with other Mesolithic coastal sites) was the proximity of the sea and the seashore. Such locations offered a greater variety of foodstuffs all year round than did those further inland. In small boats – small, simple, hide-hulled *curachs* (or coracles), when the conditions were right, Pabay was blessed with suitable landing spots. The extended rocky outcrops that surround most of the island made for an ideal maritime environment for a variety of shellfish such as limpets and whelks, as well as crustaceans – barnacles, crabs, lobsters and shrimps. For a foraging people this was ideal. Shellfish – primarily winkles (small whelks), have continued on and off through the centuries to provide an important source of food, and income, for Pabay's inhabitants. Rarer, and more of a delicacy than anything else, were clams, forays for which were few and far between, being dependent on the lowest tides.

Until very recently, no one would have gone to Pabay in search of wood, and certainly not hazelnuts. In the Inner Hebrides the high speeds of salt-laden wind – 10 or 15 knots – are a powerful check on plant growth generally and for trees especially, even more so in an exposed location such as Pabay's.[9]

For Scotland as a whole, the great mass of woodland cover of prehistoric times had largely disappeared by around 1600. There are suggestions, however, that there may have been more tree cover on Pabay, and for longer, than elsewhere in the vicinity. Other perhaps than to the east of Kyleakin where in 1799 John Blackadder saw 'a considerable extent of natural wood thriving'.[10]

It is from the testimony of Donald Munro that we learn that Pabay continued to be wooded. Munro, from near Inverness, was in 1526 appointed vicar of Snizort, in the Trotternish district in the north of Skye. He also had the charge of Raasay, to the east. Munro was to become 'High Dean of the Isles'. Around the same time as this appointment (1549) he embarked on a tour of the Western Isles. However, it was Skye and its offshore islands that he knew particularly well. Pabay he described as being 'full of woods' – convenient cover for the thieves who he alleged lurked there. Joan Blaeu's *Atlas of Scotland*, published a century later, in 1654, provides confirmation. 'Paba' is depicted on Blaeu's *Atlas* as fully forested, unlike the other islands nearby.[11] These included Scalpay, which is marked by only a few clumps of trees, a visual depiction that coincides with Munro's reference on the same island to 'certane little woods with certane towns'.

Munro's remark about Pabay's thieves has often been quoted, but only in passing, an antiquarian footnote of little consequence.[12] However, the island's notoriety as a brigand's nest could well be something more significant. Pabay, it seems, was simply the worst-reputed of the islands in the Sound from which opportunist raiding of this kind happened. Rona, to the north, was similarly implicated, as was Longay, much closer to hand.[13] It is unlikely therefore that the Pabay men were rogue offenders, a handful of delinquents acting of their own volition. Rather, they may have been *buannachaan* – or redshanks – bare-legged fighting men of their chief's household, without other occupations, often deemed to be thieves and oppressors.[14] Support for this proposition comes from November 1586, when John Mackinnon from Loch Slapin was indicted for demanding payment from fishermen from the south, while the clan's chief (Mackinnon) was upbraided by the Privy Council for harbouring so many 'broken' men.[15]

Indeed, sea raiding of the sort described by Munro for Pabay was widespread in the Hebrides in the sixteenth century.[16]

Pabay, however, was particularly well located as a base from which to attack, seize or rob unwary mariners going about their lawful business. Despite being low-lying, from the island's highest point there is a clear 360-degree vista of the sea for almost as far as the eye can see. Testimony to the utility of this vantage point is that in 1962, a team from the Ordnance Survey arrived on Pabay to put in place one of their pre-cast concrete 'trig points'. This was one of several thousand mainly similar structures that were part of the Survey's re-triangulation exercise, begun almost three decades earlier, which created the grid reference system used on modern Ordnance Survey maps.

Not only could Pabay's marauders spot likely targets coming from all directions, it was relatively easy, too, to come out from Pabay in a small boat, attack one of the many fishing vessels or those carrying merchandise in the vicinity, and then beat a hasty retreat, the reefs and rocks around the island acting as a girdle through which it was almost impossible for the victim to give chase. Even if they got ashore, their attackers would have been concealed in Pabay's dense woodland.

A century and a half later, however, Pabay's trees had gone. In 1772, on a tour of the Hebrides, the Welshman Thomas Pennant described Pabay as 'verdant', but 'quite naked' as far as woods were concerned.[17] There is no sign of them on the plans of the island that were drawn up in the early nineteenth century by John Blackadder. Indeed, around this time – in 1806 – an English visitor to Scalpay looked over to Pabay and commented on what a 'beautiful effect' tree planting would have.[18] Its nakedness stood out.

In this Pabay was not alone. Dunvegan Castle in the north-west of Skye was described in 1798 as 'a paltry looking object, destitute of wood in the neighbourhood of heathy ill-looking hills'. More pertinent perhaps is that on Raasay, much nearer to Pabay, the same commentator noted on more than one occasion the 'considerable extent' of 'decaying' woodland.[19] We can only speculate about what may have been likely causes of the disappearance of Pabay's woods. Elsewhere in the north of Scotland, increasing numbers of black cattle (which were Pabay's mainstay) have been blamed for the gradual deterioration of woodland. In the warmer west cattle were wintered outside, finding shelter amongst the trees.[20] There they sought the shoots of new grass in the spring, but also sheared the heads of the seedlings and saplings that would have provided replacements for older trees. Peat, too, hindered tree growth. With demand for timber from the south increasing, we cannot rule out a reduction in woodland through human deforestation.[21]

Putting paid to any chance of significant natural recovery of the island's tree cover was the phenomenon known as the Little Ice Age. This was a long-drawn-out period that in Greenland and the Arctic may have begun as early as 1200.[22] But it was from the late seventeenth century onwards that climatic conditions worsened markedly; the coldest cycle affecting Britain ran from about 1680 until the 1730s. To abnormally low temperatures can be added prolonged periods of wet, and extraordinarily strong winds, with the deleterious effects just described. So severe were harvest conditions in Scotland from the mid-1690s that as much as 15 per cent of the country's population perished due to famine. In the north-west, including Skye, much land became unusable and lay waste.[23]

The same causes, probably, saw off the last vestiges of Pabay's woodland, unable in such hostile circumstances to regenerate naturally. There is nothing to suggest that on Pabay or indeed in the Western Highlands as a whole was there any of the landowner-led tree planting that was taking place on a massive scale elsewhere in Scotland during the eighteenth century.[24]

* * *

There is a yawning gulf in time between the Mesoliths and the nests of thief raiders alluded to by Dean Munro and Joan Blaeu. That part of Scotland stretching from the Ardnamurchan peninsula in Lochaber, to Shetland in the north, is for long periods a blank canvas as far as any kind of reliable history is concerned.[25]

There are some clues, in the form of a few silent stones, place-name research, local folklore and some scraps of circumstantial evidence, which allow us to fix upon the possibility that religious people – perhaps early Christians – may have been on Pabay from the seventh century, if not before. Even so, about those Christian men and women responsible for bringing their faith northwards, securing and presiding over their first native baptisms, one authoritative academic historian has recently written, 'we know little or nothing'.[26]

The name Pabay, though, gives us reason to suppose that the hypothesis is sound. *Papar*, from which Pabay stems, was a Norse term derived from the Irish word *pápa*, meaning father, or an ecclesiastic or anchorite – a cleric or hermit of some description who lived in isolation.[27] That 'Paba' was the attribution given for our Pabay strongly suggests therefore that it was a genuine signifier of the island's function.

Norse tradition has it that the *papar* of Orkney and Iceland wore white flowing robes and had books with them; monks and others associated with the insular Celtic churches often wore white habits. There appear to have been many such individuals (or communities) in the northern and western parts of Scotland. There are twenty-seven or more place-names based on *papar* in the region. In the Outer Hebrides, there are four islands named Pabay or Pabbay. Our Pabay is the only one in the vicinity of Skye, although there is a Papadil (possibly meaning 'valley of priests') on Rum.

At or near most of the *papar* sites there is evidence of a church building of some kind and, in the few instances where nothing survives, historians believe there may have been one in the past.[28] Indeed, it is possible that all or most of the churches associated with the *papar* were given up or even destroyed soon after Viking invaders arrived. On the other hand, that a Christian tradition pre-dating the Vikings has persisted in popular memory might suggest they tolerated the presence of Christian priests on an island such as Pabay.[29] Or, perhaps, they had been converted to Christianity and lived alongside the holy men.[30]

But this is guesswork. And there is also a powerful counter-argument. This is the compelling proposition that between the ninth and the eleventh centuries the Northern Isles, the north of Scotland and the north-west down to Ardnamurchan were subject to 'as clear-cut a case of ethnic cleansing [by the Scandinavians] as can be found in the entirety of British history'.[31] In the areas where the Norse settlers were most dominant – the Northern and Western Isles – the Vikings seem to have dismissed virtually all of the exist-ing nomenclature and instead drew 'on their own stock of place-names from their homeland'.[32]

This is what happened on the Inner Hebridean island of Islay for example.[33] Skye too is littered with Norse settlement names, such as Elli*shader* and Shuli*sta* in Trotter*nish*, and Col*bost* in Duirin*ish*.

Nonetheless, that the *papar* names stuck suggests that their priestly inhabitants – and their importance – had made a deep impression on the Viking intruders. Is it possible that the islands or places so named were invested with some kind of mystical or spir-itual aura?

The Rev. Ratcliffe Barnett was in no doubt. A 'flat circle of sheep grass' Pabay might have been in reality. But to 'gaze across the twilight seas to this little Island of the Priest when the clouds of evening, all golden rimmed, are floating like islands in the liquid sky', was to be 'conscious of a beauty that is almost pain'.[34]

Being on the island too, could – and can – evoke similarly intense responses. In December 1950, after a four-day gale during which it had been impossible to walk upright in the open air, came ten days' relief. 'Perhaps the longest period of absolute calm we have had,' Len Whatley reflected after less than eight months on Pabay. 'There is a quality of unreality.' Walking to the jetty that morning 'the sky was flaming above Kyle & as I held my breath life seemed in suspension – not the slightest sound anywhere – the sea like polished slate'. The distant islands, he continued, 'seemed to float above the surface – no movement anywhere until a heron rose leisurely from his favourite rock'.[35] Len would have endorsed William Wall's apt observation on the uniqueness of the light on small islands girdled by the sea: 'like living in a world where there is a mirror almost out of sight'.[36]

It is of course impossible to be sure whether this kind of numinous quality attracted the devout to Pabay centuries ago. But it seems likely.

From Victorian times, it has been understood that there are ecclesiastical vestiges on the island.[37] The foundations of what looks to have been a simple church or 'teampull', possibly from the thirteenth century, are still just about visible, near to a stream.[38] Alongside this there is a burying ground in which are what is left of the stone walls of a couple of buildings. In 1859 one of these was described as an altar – an irregularly made, semi-circular structure comprising large uncemented stones. Within this there was an even smaller circle of six stones. Is this a relic from the 'Age of the Saints' (the fifth to the seventh centuries), the period of conversion to Christianity, in the vanguard of which was St Columba?[39]

As with most of the *papar* sites, there are no carved stones on Pabay, not even with simple linear crosses cut into them. They may of course have been taken (a couple have survived on Raasay), long before the era of written records.

Attempts have been made since the first Victorian investigators, some professional, but mostly amateurish, to record the site and search for something that would help fix on a date, or purpose. As youngsters who knew no better (that archaeology is a disciplined pursuit that demands enormous patience, painstaking care and much training to recognise the significance of the otherwise insignificant) we would take along a spade and for a short time dig enthusiastically in the hope of uncovering a human bone or some other remnant of the people who once inhabited the site. With hindsight, it has become pretty clear that we had no idea of what might have been important. Such material has been found nearby, however, on Raasay and at the nearest point on Skye from Pabay, Cill Ashig, Breakish. But so far investigators on Pabay have drawn a blank.[40]

Nevertheless, and despite our naiveté, even at the ages of nine and ten and into our early teens my cousins and I felt there was something about the spot, an agelessness drawing us tight through time, that had us believe if we searched hard enough we could connect with these ancient peoples. We weren't alone; many visitors to Pabay with its 'sough of old-time history ... and a hint of lost things' have felt compelled to dig, as if by so doing they might strike lucky. Few historical sites can have been subject to so much inexpert investigation, with, unsurprisingly, such little return.

So, in the absence of any conclusive material evidence, it is to local historians and folk tradition we must necessarily turn, in order to piece together Pabay's religious history.

There are two names in the frame: St Columba, and St Maelrubha or Mael rubai, otherwise known as St Maree. Other versions of the name include Malrubius, Mulruy and Murie.[41]

But in narrowing down the founders' identities to two, we should be cautious: it is apostolic saints like these who have captured what can be described as the pseudo-historical imagination.[42] Squeezed out from the historical record are 'lesser' men and women whose roles in evangelising smaller places like Pabay may have been just as important. Early Celtic Christians generally were 'seasoned mariners' who in sailing coracles travelled from Ireland through the western seas as far north as Iceland and the Faroe Islands.[43]

Despite the variants on Maelrubha's name, they originate in assumptions about his appearance – that he was redheaded, with a bald forehead (which was shaven or tonsured, after the fashion of

Iona's monks). In truth, little is really known about either what he looked like or indeed what he actually did.[44] Nevertheless, there are sufficient grounds for supposing that he was a monk of some kind and endowed with a charismatic quality.

Born in 642, Maelrubha had royal blood, being descended on his father's side from the evocatively named Niall of the Nine Hostages, one-time king of Ireland. In 671, in Columba's wake, he sailed for Scotland. It is not certain, but the timing of his journey may have been due to the return to Skye from Ireland in *c.* 670 of Cenél nGarnait, a prominent Pictish kindred then striving for control of Skye. The island then stood 'at the edge of civilisation', and was therefore 'a sensible place to establish bases for exploiting the peoples beyond'.[45] Maelrubha may have sought the opportunity of leading the ecclesiastical element of this project. With his party of monks, he founded several churches, the most important being a monastery at Aporcrossan, now known as Applecross, established in 673.

It was over the next fifty-one years that Abbot Maelrubha's missionary endeavours spread into Easter Ross, but also in the other direction, towards Skye and the Outer Hebrides. Testimony to his assumed influence is the number of churches and locations that bear his name, including several in Skye.[46] For us, the most significant connection is Ashaig, close to the shore at Breakish. Ashaig is a contraction of the Gaelic *Aiseag Maol Ruibhe aite iomallach an domhain* – St Maelrubha's ferry, a place on the brink of the world; the spot, it is believed, where the saint landed after his voyages from Applecross.[47]

But what of Maelrubha and Pabay? The Rev. Donald M. Lamont was minister of Strath early in the twentieth century. He felt confident enough in the history of his parish he wrote in 1913 to speak for the saint, his favourite for the role of Pabay's Christian founding father: 'Looking across from Ashaig seaward, St Maree would naturally feel interested in that flat, well-wooded island lying not far off, and he enquired about its inhabitants. It reminded him of Iona and it was fixed upon to be the minister's residence ... On crossing over to the island the Ionian missionaries found groups of dwelling-huts lying on this side of the island next Skye.'[48]

Lamont's description of the huts was accurate enough: they were the remnants of a township that was marked on the Ordnance Survey Sheet XLI, published in 1882. But were they there in the seventh or eighth centuries? Probably not. What remains of their foundations and walls suggests they derive from the eighteenth century or first half of the nineteenth century.

But if we can imagine some sort of dwellings that were there many centuries earlier, who might have lived in them?

Lamont has the answer. His historical imagination fired, he boldly strides back over twelve centuries to report how the heathenish people on Pabay (and elsewhere in Strath) were converted to Christianity by St Maree, and how, 'instead of a Druidical grove, there was a little Christian chapel built'. It was 'a sight to see', he went on, as 'the hands that a short time ago clapped in honour of a heathen god', were now employed in raising the walls of a Christian church.

In the same inventive mould was our sailor clergyman, Ratcliffe Barnett. Imbibing the spiritual atmosphere sensed by so many of Pabay's visitors, Ratcliffe Barnett spent much of his time musing on the island's religious history. Like Lamont, his ruminations when committed to words on paper become (impossible) statements of fact. Wandering around and wondering about the 'rickle of grey stones' – possibly the remains of the former chapel – he reflected how 'on this very spot a succession of holy men preached Christ to the robbers'. Just in what way eighth-century Christians managed to preach to bands of sixteenth-century muggers is not explained. Even if the chapel remains are later, it seems unlikely that Pabay's outlaws would have had much interest in church sermons. Not clear either is how Ratcliffe Barnett can have known that from this spot on Pabay 'the lonely monk would often look across to Rhu Ardnish in Skye, where by a little creek stood Kil Ashik, or *cill-aiseag*, the Church of the Ferry'. This, though, was not the last of Ratcliffe Barnett's mental meanderings. How often, he continued, 'must Saint Maelrubha ... have been ferried across to Pabbay and to Kil Ashik from his own beloved Applecross!'[49] The answer is that we don't, and can't, know. It seems highly unlikely, but he may never even have set foot on Pabay.

Further thickening the mists of antiquity that surround St Maelrubha is an alternative account of the man or men who brought Christianity to Pabay, and when. Otta Swire was a folk-lorist who lived in Orbost House, near Dunvegan. This was from 1946 until her death in 1973. When she was younger, and a summer visitor to Skye, Otta had listened avidly as the island's legends were recounted during ceilidhs and at other social gatherings. Many of these tales she collected, wrote up whilst at Orbost and published in 1952. Early on, in what was a seminal work – *Skye: The Island and its Legends* – Swire describes the road from Kyleakin to Broadford. Here, looking out to sea, she reports that according to tradition, Pabay's small church was 'built by St Columba's monks'.[50]

Columba or, in Gaelic, *Colum Cille*, was well-connected politically (as a member of the north of Ireland's powerful Ui Néil dynasty), and also a charismatic Irish priest. In 563 he left Ireland for Scotland's west coast, 'in pilgrimage for the love of Christ'. Amongst the monasteries he founded was Iona, clerics from which spread out to convert and minister to the Scots in Dàl Riata, and Pictland.[51]

Subsequently he and his followers extended their influence north and westwards. Columba undoubtedly established a foothold on Skye, with several sites bearing his name, including the church and grounds at Skeabost bridge, formerly called Sanct Colm's Kirk.[52] The problem with attributing the church on Pabay to Columba, however, is the fairly substantial evidence that Columba's influence was greatest in the north-east of Skye – primarily the Trotternish peninsula, at the furthermost tip of which are the ruins of a small chapel dedicated to him.[53] St Maelrubha held greater sway in the south and west. On the other hand, there were Columban monks who yearned for greater isolation and hardship than on Iona, and sought island refuges in the Hebrides.[54] But further than that we cannot go. Let alone be sure about.

However, whoever took religion to Pabay, and whenever this happened, the oral tradition that Swire managed to capture is unambiguous about the presence of priests or clerics on the island who, most likely, were Christian.[55]

One of the legends she relates is of a Pabay priest, not long after Columba's appearance on Skye. On a visit to a household near Broadford to baptise a new-born baby, the priest was asked by a party of 'Daoine Sithe' to pray for them. The 'Daoine Sithe' in popular imagination were fairies, but, described by Swire as standing at three to four feet high, they may have been part of a surviving tribe of Picts seeking to accommodate themselves to Christianity. (The 'fallacious' notion that the Picts were small in stature however casts some doubt on this.[56]) Judging them evil, Pabay's priest refused to countenance them. Their souls unsaved, the 'Doaine Sithe' fell into a despairing wail 'which spread through the forest and up the slopes of Beinn na Calliach', but gradually turned to silence. Realising later that he had erred in failing to pray for the repentant 'little people', the priest returned to Pabay, 'and sought leave to dwell in the forest, where he preached continually, day and night, the forgiveness of God to all who would listen, birds, beasts, and trees'. Afterwards, Swire tells us, he lost his mind.

But for present purposes it is the unwitting testimony from this tale that is as important as the central narrative. Our priest from Pabay was not on the edge, but an integral link between God, the Catholic Church, centred in Rome, and mainland Skye and Ireland.

How long holy men like this remained on Pabay we can't tell. It may not have been many years. At the end of the eighth century and during the first years of the ninth, Viking raids on Britain became increasingly common. We've noted already that it was the Hebrides – Skye included – that bore the brunt of these initial attacks. They were characterised in the Irish annals as hit-and-run assaults, involving burning, pillaging and plundering. Perhaps it was at this time too that the Vikings – Norwegians, Danes and Swedes – removed anything precious that had been on Pabay. Reliquaries, shrines and mounts of book covers from Celtic monasteries elsewhere have been found in Norwegian graves, or were reused for secular purposes.[57]

On the other hand, if we are to place any trust in Donald Lamont's testimony, the church on Pabay was brought back into use by Norsemen who had converted to Christianity.[58]

Otta Swire is unconvincing about Columba. But at least in her narrative she cleared Pabay of its holy men – before peopling the place with its 'organised raiding community'. The chapel had 'fallen into disuse and the monks [had] left', she wrote, long before the arrival of the brigands of the post-medieval era. Appropriately, these 'broken men', the aforementioned scourge of law-abiding mariners, she reports, were themselves defeated in a battle with Satan.

Perhaps.

More likely they were removed from the island after their clan chief, Lauchlan MacKinnon of Strathswordale, had submitted in 1609 to the Statutes of Iona. Tiring of the 'irredeemable islanders', of which those on Pabay I mentioned earlier were one example, King James had determined by legislation to 'educate the fine [clan gentry, or elite] about their responsibilities as members of the Scottish landed classes'.[59] Mackinnon was one of eight clan chiefs to agree to adhere to the Statutes and improve the behaviour of their kinsmen, 'wild savages voide of Godis feare and our obedience'.[60]

The clan chiefs in question, to account for their progress in limiting the number of galleys they used (to one), disarming their clansmen, reducing the importation of wines and spirits to the Hebrides, educating their children in the south, taking action against beggars and vagabonds and 'rebels' and other measures, were required to make a yearly appearance in front of the Privy Council. The *buannachan* were shipped off to the British army, or as mercenaries in the Dutch and Swedish service, although in smaller numbers they found employment locally as clan chiefs and their tacksman turned their attention from feuding and fighting to farming.[61]

*　*　*

There may, however, be something else that helps explain Pabay's longstanding lure. This might even shed light on the nature of the island's religious community.

Invariably, Pabay has been described as a fertile island. Unusually so, in fact. The written historical record of course only takes us back so far. Even so, there is much in the earliest descriptions that would strike a chord with someone looking out to Pabay today, or landing there for the first time.

In 1703 Martin Martin, a native of Skye who at different times had been employed by both the Macdonalds of Sleat and the MacLeods of Dunvegan, published his *Description of the Western Islands of Scotland*. His extensive sojourns through the island probably took place in the second half of the 1690s, the particularly bleak decade in Scotland I mentioned earlier. Although Martin classified Pabay as one of the 'Inferior Isles' around Skye, he was impressed. The island, he wrote, 'excells in Pasturage, the Cows in it afford near double the Milk they yield in *Skie*'.[62] It may be no coincidence that it was around this time that Skye's cattle-droving trade gained the renown it was to maintain for at least the next century and a half.[63] At the time Martin was writing, Pabay was tenanted, and described as a 'grazing' island.[64] Nothing had changed by the 1790s, when Thomas Fraser of Inverness Academy described Pabay in his entry for the Old Statistical Account as 'only a wintering place for cattle', of which it could support seventy or eighty for six months. Initially the main markets were London and Edinburgh, but with Scotland's Lowland towns expanding at an unprecedented rate during the second half of the eighteenth century, demand for meat, leather and tallow intensified.

Around the same time – in 1800 – Alexander, second Lord Macdonald, embarked on an ambitious programme of improvement of his estates on Skye and in North Uist. By this time the Macdonalds had acquired Pabay along with other Mackinnon territory that had been sold in 1751 to pay off estate debts, as well as those incurred by John Mackinnon of Mishinish, who had succeeded to the estate after the Jacobite-supporting Ian Dubh's son John had died in 1737.[65] (John had been able to buy back his father's attainted estate from the Forfeited Estates commissioners in 1731.) As land 'in one of the remote Western Islands, was not an Object that could attract many Offerers', the opportunity had been taken by Lady Margaret Macdonald, mother of James Macdonald, sixteenth chief but then only ten years old, and his other tutors, to purchase 'Kinlochslapin, Broadford, and certain other lands in the isle of Skye'. This, it was claimed, was 'not on account of the Profit which might arise', but because of their situation, adjoining part of the Macdonalds' existing estate.[66]

By the end of the century, however, like other Highland landlords of the period, Eton-educated Alexander Macdonald, who spent little time on Skye, was keen – if not desperate – to exploit the commercial potential of his landholdings. Fundamental to this was estate reorganisation: the breaking-up of the former communal townships – the *baile* – and their replacement with single tenant farms, leased to the highest bidder; the first phase of the notorious clearances.[67] The many displaced tenants were relocated in settlements along the shorelines of Macdonald's lands, where virtually the sole source of paid employment was the burgeoning kelp – seaweed – burning industry, which for several years provided the bulk of clan Macdonald's income. Kelp was a form of alkali used by manufacturers of soap and glass in places like Glasgow, Newcastle and Liverpool. With Britain at war with France, the French had blocked the import of Spanish alkali, the usual source, thereby creating an unprecedented demand for the seaweed appropriated by Highland landlords such as Macdonald.

First, though, he had to invest – in roads, bridges, lime kilns, quays, public buildings including Kyleakin's first shop ('the grand supply to all the neighbouring Islands'), churches and even trees.[68]

The Macdonald lands in Skye as a whole had been deemed as eminently improvable. Much could be done in this regard, noted John Blackaddder, the Borders land surveyor Macdonald recruited in 1799 to advise him. As the memorandum that outlined Blackadder's commission stated: 'there is no Country whatever better adapted [for improvement] than Sky'. There were especially high hopes for the parish of Strath and its 'wonderful degree of fertility', despite the allegation that most land there was under 'indifferent' management, undrained, largely unenclosed, unmanured and over-cropped.[69]

Blackadder spent two months on his survey, which included Pabay. In fact, 'Pabba', Blackadder remarked, was the 'most improvable subject of any in Strath'. Already there were some 162 acres of arable ground, with a further 82 acres of 'improvable moss'. The lie of the land was such, he proposed, that simple, large, round-bottomed 'kettle' drains could readily be dug. This done, Pabay would become 'one of the best feeding pastures in Strath', with an estimated rental value of £70.[70] But, as he also pointed out, to be effective, the drains would require 'constant attention'. He was far from alone in offering this advice. In subsequent years it was too often overlooked, as Len Whatley was to discover exactly 150 years later.

Around the same time, James Macdonald wrote his *General View of the Agriculture of the Hebrides*. Macdonald too singled out Strath (as well as Sleat and Strathaird) for the quality of the soil and its suitability for growing grasses and green crops. He was pleased that a 'few gentlemen', including Lachlan Mackinnon at Corrychattachan, and Mr Macdonald on Scalpay had begun to exploit the potential that lay, literally, at their feet.[71] Mackinnon had evidently been swayed by Pabay's promise, and in 1807 secured from young Lord Macdonald a nineteen-year lease for the 'Island of Paba', along with Liveras farm, for an annual rental of £160.[72] An additional advantage of Pabay was the 'unlimited command' of shell, marl and seaware any lessee of Corry farm would have at their disposal.[73]

The impression that Pabay was especially lush was formed too by the geologist and Free Churchman Hugh Miller. In the summer of 1844 he embarked on a cruise of the Inner Hebrides with his former school friend, the Free Church minister the Rev. Mr John Swanson.[74]

During their July journey, Miller and Swanson spent much time sailing around Skye, and, in Miller's case, excitedly investigating the island's rocks. In Broadford Bay though, it was 'Pabba' that stood out. Anchored off Broadford after a miserable day spent on board in the rain, looking landward Miller saw 'a brown and cheerless prospect of dark bogs and debris-covered hills'. The seaward view, however, he found much more pleasing. A 'green level island', wrote Miller of Pabay, it differed in 'outline and colour, from every neighbouring hill'.[75] Indeed, it seemed 'a little bit of flat fertile England, laid down, as if for contrast's sake, amid the wild rough Hebrides'. As the rain and mist cleared after a night spent on board the *Betsey* off Broadford, Miller delighted to see a 'polished gem, all the more advantageously displayed from the roughness of its immediate surrounding'. He even fantasised about buying it.

The island's greenness was one of the things that had enticed Margaret and Len in the first place. There was the excitement too of what was new, including the spectacular surroundings. Subconsciously, however, there may have been a sense of recognition, of familiarity, in their minds' eye, with the flatter plains of Warwickshire.

* * *

The flatlands theme is worth exploring further.

As Barbara Crawford and other historians have observed, for the Norse invaders (and eventually settlers), Scotland's north-west coast and islands were a home from home.

The geological formation of the west coasts of Norway and Scotland is unique, and similar. Long sea lochs, like the Norwegian fjords, penetrate the steep mountains of the mainland. Many of the islands that lay off the Scottish coast were highly productive and, with the additional benefit of their rich fishing grounds, provided the Vikings with essential supply bases without compromising their access to the waterways they used for raiding expeditions. They may have served the same purpose for voyagers returning to Norway.

Furthermore, if, as is sometimes argued, it was population pressure and land shortages in Scandinavia that provide part of the explanation for the Vikings' takeover, the Northern and Western Isles had much to offer.

Intriguingly, what the *papar* places in Scotland's north-west appear to have in common is a relatively high level of soil fertility. This includes Pabay, which was graded 5/1 by the Soil Survey of Scotland, in 1982. In brief, what this means is that there is ample grassland all year round, and the potential for improved yields. This classification confirms what we have read in the comments of Donald Munro, John Blackadder and others – and will see more of in following chapters. Worth noting at this point though is that it was Pabay's 'rich black loam' that impressed Len Whatley when he first tested the ground there in the autumn of 1949.

In the slightly kinder climate that prevailed until around 1000 and a little beyond, that is, during the era of Viking domination, growing conditions would have been even more favourable than they appeared to be subsequently.

It would have made little sense if the Vikings had laid waste to everything in their forays to the south; this would have denied them the provisions they required if their supply bases in the north-west were to function effectively. With this in mind, historians have proposed – tentatively – that islands such as Pabay may have performed just this role.[76] As host to some kind of religious community that as part of its activities had exploited the island's agricultural potential, it is conceivable that Pabay's devout dwellers might well have supplied their conquerors with cereals, mutton, seabirds, fish and other staple items in the Norse diet.[77]

Supporting this possibility is suggestive evidence from other *papar* sites that intensive farming was carried out from an early date. What seems unlikely, however, is that cooperation between the invaders and the indigenous peoples lasted for long. When the Scandinavians began to settle in the north-west on a permanent basis, the clerical-farmer inhabitants of a small island like Pabay were liable to have been removed and replaced by Northmen, refugees from troubles in their own lands.

There is additional circumstantial evidence which adds appeal to this idea. To obtain the weapons, armour, table goods and exotic textiles Scandinavian chieftains purchased from abroad in the Danish *emporia* (where such business was conducted) they required something to sell. The Western Isles offered little of inanimate value.

They were, however, heavily populated. And could therefore be a source of a highly trade-able commodity: human beings. Able bodies would satisfy the demand there was for slave gangs in Scandinavia itself – as 'thralls', as well as in the Rhineland, Byzantium and the Caliphate.[78] Unprotected coastal island communities, including monastic settlements like Iona – but also, we can assume, Pabay and its neighbour Scalpay, where it is thought there are the foundation stones of a Viking 'village' – were defenceless.[79] Who knows if people from the islands that this book is about were amongst the thousands of men, women and children who were periodically swept up and shipped to Dublin, the holding centre for the Vikings' slave trade. If indeed some of Pabay's people went, at least the *papar* name remained, ensuring that Pabay's earlier function as a sacred place survived.[80]

* * *

What we can conclude at this point is that for several millennia Pabay has promised much. Its prospects excited and enticed. For some of those who saw and came, it delivered. For others, there was the elation of success, but as often as not, disappointment as hopes were dashed. The enduring Pabay story is one of extreme challenge. Small islands are for the brave, the resilient and the self-reliant. Pabay's geology and topography, location and natural environment, above all the weather, were – are – formidable obstacles. First impressions can be misleading.

Chapter 3

'Fair hunting games': Sir Donald Currie and Scalpay estate

Pabay was to all intents a desert island when an exhilarated Len and Margaret stepped ashore there in the autumn of 1949.

Not only had Pabay been uninhabited by human beings for six years, neither had any livestock been on the island. Arable farming too had been abandoned. Indeed, other than some potatoes and oats largely for their own use, the previous residents had grown little. They had been shepherds, not farmers.

In this respect, the island had been neglected (with troublesome consequences – as we shall see). But the stone-built jetty where the couple landed looked and felt well-constructed underneath, even if the surface layer of stones was breaking up and thickly overgrown with treacherously slippery seaweed. As far as they could judge, the land was cultivable. Even more promising on what was a brief exploratory foray was the presence on the south-western side of the island of a modern-looking integrated farm steading. As remarkable was its condition. There was no sign of the disrepair that might be expected with buildings that had endured six Skye winters unattended.

In good order were a large stone-built barn, stables, a pigsty, a cattle byre and a bothy. These were neatly enclosed and sheltered by a high, well-harled wall. All this was in marked contrast to the tumble-down buildings they would leave behind at Shawhurst Farm, Wythall, near Birmingham.

Initially, it was difficult to account for the presence of such an up-to-date farmstead on the remote island of Pabay, when *farmers* in the West Highlands – as noted by the ecologist and authority on the region's land use, Frank Fraser Darling – were few and far between. Directly across the water in the townships that fringed the sea to the east of Broadford, crofting was the norm. The narrow strips of land that comprised the typical crofter holding could never justify the construction of farm buildings on anything like the scale of those on Pabay. Crofting was largely communal; farming, on the other hand, implied individual ownership, usually a single tenancy, and hired hands, paid for their services.

The explanation for the apparent incongruity lay in the ambitions and interests of two of the most recent of the island's owners, Sir Donald Currie, and Sir Henry Bell. With Currie's acquisition of Pabay in 1894, a new chapter in the island's story was opened. This was to lay the foundations – literally as well as metaphorically – for Len and Margaret's venture half a century ahead. Sir Donald's period of proprietorship therefore was an important milestone in Pabay's development, and worth examining in some detail.

*　*　*

Sir Donald Currie was one of Britain's leading businessmen.[1] When he bought Pabay he was also a Liberal MP for Perthshire in the United Kingdom parliament.

In 1894 Pabay was un-let, and mainly used by the proprietor, Ronald Archibald Bosville, 21st baron, 14th baronet and 6th Lord of the Isles, Lord Macdonald, for grazing sheep. These, and a handful of cattle also maintained there, constituted a live larder, serving the needs of diners at Armadale Castle in Sleat, clan Macdonald's main residence on Skye, as required. Indeed, ten years earlier, in 1884, John Robertson of Corry, who kept an eye on Pabay on a day-to-day basis, was confident that if thirty or forty ewes were put on the island, with a tup, Pabay's plentiful grass would ensure that they 'would keep plenty of meat to our Lordship's family some years to come, if they would have lambs.'[2] Additionally, small but regular quantities of wool were sheared, and then sold.[3]

Pabay, however, was not the primary reason for Currie's interest in Skye. The centrepiece of his acquisition was the larger, adjacent island of Scalpay, which extended to something over 6,100 acres, or 12 square miles.⁴ Scalpay also boasted a hill 1,300 feet (396 metres) high, Mullach na Càrn – a striking contrast to Pabay, lying low in its lee to the south-east.

The name Scalpay may have Norse origins, meaning either ship (from *skalpr*) or scallop island. The second of these suggestions makes most sense. Writing in 1845 for the *New Statistical Account,* the Rev. John Mackinnon, minister of Strath parish, noted the presence of an 'extensive bed of oysters of a superior quality' in the Sound of Scalpay. These and other mollusks, he remarked, were 'much used as food by the lower orders during the summer months', and during periods of hardship.⁵

Pabay had been offered for sale at the same time as Scalpay was put on the market, and was purchased by Currie separately. The smaller islands of Longay and Guillamon – the last not much more than a diminutive steep-sided rocky protuberance inhabited by sea birds – came as part of the package with Scalpay, but were very much secondary considerations. It may have been Pabay's shootings – mainly of snipe and wildfowl – that persuaded Currie to buy it. It had been let for this purpose in 1892.⁶ Whatever his precise motivations for acquiring what collectively became Scalpay Estate, the quartet of islands clustered at the edge of Broadford Bay formed a compact Hebridean holding for Sir Donald.

*   *   *

Immediately prior to Currie's purchase of Scalpay, however, it was evident that the island had known better days.

On an inspection visit in 1893 commissioners from what was popularly known as the Deer Forest Commission, chaired by David Brand, sheriff of Argyll, 'saw comparatively little to engage their attention'.⁷ On Scalpay's landward side, across the sound from the poor and overcrowded crofting townships of Dunan, Luib and Strollamus, there was some 'old arable', and not much of that (50 acres). Otherwise the commissioners found mainly rough pasture that was then supporting some 1,400 sheep, although at the time of the island's sale the following year the number given was higher, between 1,600 and 1,700. This was at the upper end of what the island was considered capable of supporting.[8]

Scalpay House, the main building on the island, dated back to the eighteenth century. Along with its gardens and offices, it was proudly described in 1857 as 'one of the most Desirable Tenements on the West Coast'. Advertising copy by the 1890s was rather less effusive, with the house being downgraded in sale materials to 'commodious'.

By this time the boom in sheep farming that had been based on rising demand for wool in the 1850s and 1860s, was long over.[9] After a peak in 1872, prices began to slip inexorably downwards. Part of the problem was wool imported from South Africa and elsewhere, but above all Australia. Mutton imports too rose, after 1880 in the form of frozen meat brought in refrigerated ships from Australia. Consumers in the south developed a preference for lamb, which was increasingly satisfied by New Zealand farmers who took advantage of new cold-store facilities built in Britain from 1885.

At the same time, cost pressures at home rose. Those of wintering and smearing were the most obvious, along with shepherds' wages. These had more than doubled since mid-century.

Distinctions, nevertheless, have to be made between different sheep breeds. Those commonly farmed in Australia and the colonies relatively easily substituted with merino the finer wool of the Cheviots – the mainstay of the Macdonald estate's sheep stock. This included those on Scalpay. Blackface sheep on the other hand produced a coarser, longer fleece, which was well suited for carpets and rougher materials.[10]

Even this was no guarantee of survival, let alone success. In 1873 the New York stock market collapsed, ushering in a long period of economic gloom that spread far beyond America. This was the so-called 'Great Depression', which lasted until 1896. Prices fell, including that of imported wool to the UK. The effect was to reduce further the attractiveness of sheep farming.[11]

Consequently, by the early 1890s, demand for and rents paid for sheep walks were plummeting. Sheep numbers in Inverness-shire, which stood at around three quarters of a million in 1875, dropped every decade thereafter.[12] Even before this, however, those shrewd enough saw which way the wind was blowing and took evasive action.

Throughout the Highlands, sheep farms were hurriedly disposed of and flockmasters fled, thereby reversing the pattern set earlier in the century when sheep farming had been all the rage. Single-minded sheep ranchers had been lured to Highland Scotland from elsewhere in Scotland. One of the most notorious was Sutherland's Patrick Sellar, from the Moray burgh of Elgin, in the north-east.[13] Thus had been instigated the process of clearances of small tenants that denuded so many formerly populous straths in the Highlands, Skye and its offshore islands included. What was left were patches of rushes – bracken- and moss-pocked green that marked the plots of cultivated land which had once fed entire families. The remains of now roofless rubble-built houses stood as forlorn monuments to once-thriving communities, 'set adrift upon the world', with memories that were both poignant and bitter.[14]

The Macdonald estate, now in the hands of Sir Ronald Archibald Bosville, 21st baron, and 6th Lord of the Isles, was hard hit by the tumbling rentals for his sheep farms.[15]

This, however, was not the first time the family's domains had been subject to financial pressures. These had been exacerbated by extravagant spending – not least on the mock baronial-styled Armadale Castle (which was no such thing), that around 1815 had replaced – at the cost of some £20,000 – the more modest two-storey house that had so disappointed James Boswell when visiting with Dr Johnson in September 1773.[16] But Skye's economy at this time was thriving as never before.

*　　*　　*

After the end of the Napoleonic Wars in 1815, the financial affairs of clan chiefs such as the Macdonalds took a distinct downward turn. Government-sponsored public works schemes – building roads and bridges as well as cutting the Caledonian Canal – designed to create employment in the Highlands had come to an end. Estates descended into indebtedness as formerly buoyant activities like kelp-gathering and burning, fishing, distilling and quarrying experienced rapid decline.

The collapse of demand for kelp after the import duties on barilla and salt were removed in the 1820s, allowing cheaper sources of alkali to be imported, was particularly catastrophic.

For over fifty years, production had been rising, as, for much of that time, had prices. Suddenly, the many thousands of people formerly employed in the industry lost their main source of money income, and were now only able to pay their rents in kind.[17] And there were many more mouths to feed.

In congested Strath parish alone, the population had almost tripled (from 943 to 2,619) in the sixty-six years between 1755 and 1821 – although there were factors other than kelp-making which explain this. Indeed, such was the antipathy of Lord Macdonald's tenants to be forced to work at this most arduous and detested of occupations – the 'greatest slavery in the world for the common people'[18] is how it was described in seventeenth-century Orkney – that many of them preferred to emigrate, risking a voyage that could take between one and three months in sailing ships that normally carried timber, in hopes of a better life in North America.[19] In 1803, John Campbell, Macdonald's Skye chamberlain, calculated that as many as two-thirds of the people of Strath and Sleat had paid part of the passage money required to take them from Skye.[20]

Ironically, it was the demise of kelping, some observers were convinced, that had caused the population to continue to swell. Seaweed could now be used in abundance as a manure on the raised 'lazy beds' that are a ubiquitous feature – still visible, especially when the sun is low, and shadows deeper – of the mainly coastal landscape of Skye and the Outer Hebrides. This, according to Lachlan Mackinnon of Corry (the farm of which by this time Pabay was an appendage), 'tended indirectly to encourage early marriages and too great an increase of the population'.[21]

Whatever the reason, the unprecedented rise of a population that was increasingly impoverished brought in its wake unimaginable suffering as a series of crises hit the Highlands and Islands.

The first was in 1837, the second of two years of poor harvests – the worst in living memory according to John McInnes, a sixty-five-year-old crofter in Breakish. Over half of the population of Strath was destitute, dependent on what paltry quantities of oatmeal relief committees in Edinburgh and Glasgow could arrange to ship to Broadford.[22] This, though, was only the precursor to the severest of the great potato crop failures of the nineteenth century. The year 1846 proved to be the opening of a sequence of failed crops that lasted the best part of a decade.

The potato was the main item in the Skye household diet. Each adult consumed as many as eight or even ten pounds of potatoes a day, which provided as much as 75 per cent of their energy requirements.[23] In Strath the figure may have been even higher. Almost a century prior to the famine it was reported that the people there had become more dependent on potatoes and herring, and less on bread, than elsewhere.[24]

Although the fungus *Phytophthora infestans*, that caused potatoes to rot even before they were lifted from the grounds afflicted crops across Europe, in Ireland and in North America, in Scotland it was on Skye – along with the Outer Hebrides – that the resultant distress was greatest. And, as in 1837, Strath was one of the hardest hit districts. At the peak of the famine, late in 1847, over 2,000 of the parish's 3,150 inhabitants were classified as destitute.[25] In one fortnight in June 1848, 1,000 people had had to apply for assistance from the Highland Relief Board, which had been established the year previously – for which males, including boys, were forced to work, breaking stones and making roads. Others turned (usually reluctantly) to deep-sea fishing, with instruction provided by east-coast fishermen. Women were expected to knit woollen stockings, although at the fishing stations a few became fish curers.[26]

Reports abounded of lines of thin, starving, wretched people of all ages, weeping as they told of their suffering, desperate for their meagre allowances of oatmeal and its cheaper substitute, Indian corn meal (maize, usually fed to animals), fearing worse was to come in the shape of typhus.[27] So ragged had the clothes of some Broadford men become by September 1848 that the relief officer asked his superiors for lengths of material from which those in need could fashion kilts and blankets for the winter.[28]

Proprietors were hit hard too, but in their pockets rather than their stomachs. Despite the wretched conditions, Skye's population continued to rise through the 1840s – an unofficial estimate for 1850 was 27,000, just under 4,000 mouths more than in 1841.

By 1855, debts of over £209,000 had been accumulated by the Macdonald estate, partly as rents were not paid, and also due to the costs of famine relief – although Lord Macdonald's contribution was substantially less than that of Macleod of Dunvegan, whose generosity of spirit, and money expended, in the face of the crisis faced by his people was 'unique in the Highlands in the 1840s'.[29]

Nevertheless, large tracts of the Macdonalds' ancestral lands in North Uist and Kilmuir in the north of Skye were disposed of by trustees advised by one of the leading accountants of the day, Edinburgh-based James Brown. By clearing off the poorer tenants and reducing rent arrears, Brown greatly increased the attractiveness of the land concerned to potential purchasers.[30] Yet even after these disposals, the family still retained nearly 130,000 acres worth £11,614 annually (equivalent to around £967,000 in 2017).[31] The Lords Macdonald could count themselves fortunate; many of their hereditary landlord counterparts had been forced to sell their entire estates in the decades following the Napoleonic Wars.[32]

By 1886 however, with financial pressures showing no signs of easing, serious consideration was being given to selling Scalpay and letting out Pabay.

Scalpay was first advertised for sale early in 1894. Despite the drop in sheep prices, it was primarily as a sheep farm that Scalpay was promoted. So too was another of the Macdonald estate's holdings, Kingsburgh and its associated crofting townships. Kingsburgh had an advantage which the selling agents, Dundas and Wilson in Edinburgh, were keen to highlight: Kingsburgh House, the advertisement ran, is 'invested with particular interest on account of its historical connection with the Names of Flora Macdonald and Prince Charles Edward'. Unlike Raasay, the larger island to the north of them, neither Scalpay nor Pabay could boast such romantic associations – although, as we shall see, Sir Donald Currie soon created one.

Sheep husbandry, Scalpay's lifeblood hitherto, may now have been on life support, but it was evidently a challenge that Currie was prepared to take on. He also had hopes of putting onto the island long-horned, long-haired Highland cattle, which elsewhere in Britain had been arousing interest at agricultural shows. This was an enterprise close to Currie's heart; he had already raised a herd of the same type of cattle on his estate in Perthshire.[33]

There was another use to which Scalpay could be put. This was the hunting and shooting of various kinds of wildlife (otters were mentioned in the advertisement). Fresh water and sea fishing was the other side of the same coin.

And what could add a further dimension to Scalpay's attractions was to focus greater attention on red deer. Or, to use the term often applied to an activity that radically altered land use across much of Highland Scotland from the 1880s: deer afforestation. The conversion of agricultural land to sporting estates was the most prominent feature of a development that had been intensifying in the Highlands and Islands during the nineteenth century. This was to offer visiting gentlemen, in the form of gun and rod sports, opportunities for killing.[34]

Instead of providing the means of production of sheep for southern markets, land was now utilised in the service of conspicuous consumption *in situ*. The Highland estate was to become a 'machine for sport', the term Philip Gaskell used for Ardtornish and other former sheep farms in Morvern (on the mainland to the south of Skye).[35]

The transformation of land use in the north that occurred over the course of the nineteenth century can readily be demonstrated by using Scalpay as an example. In 1828 it was let as a farm, along with another 2,000 acres at nearby Strinidin and Strollamus. Scalpay's reputation apparently rested on the quality of its black cattle. Thus, in March 1828, the current tenant was leaving – but hoped to sell – the entire stock of cattle which, the advertisement in the *Edinburgh Evening Courant* ran (too late for the auction on the 18th), are 'so well known to dealers and rearers for the nicety of their stamp, and purity of their breeding'. To be sold too were a number of horses, the contents of the big house, farming utensils and boats.[36]

It was not long after this that, as in much of Highland Scotland, the island's population reached its peak. According to Malcolm Robertson, who conducted the island's first government census of 1841, Scalpay had ninety inhabitants. They formed sixteen families, or households. The farm, it appears, was tenanted by James Macdonald, aged forty, with most of the rest of the adults being male agricultural labourers and female farm servants. There were forty-five children aged fifteen or less (half the total) for whom no occupation was recorded, although there were in addition a couple of fifteen-year-olds, Hannah Macdonald and James Macintyre, who were farm employees.

The island also accommodated a carpenter, a handloom weaver and a gardener.[37] At the bottom of the social scale, living in utter destitution, were two cottar households, neither of which had any arable land to work, and only one cow each. Between them there were fifteen children to feed.[38] Household heads William McLeod and William Matheson – along with many others from every single settlement in Strath parish – were amongst those compelled to apply for relief during the potato famine.[39]

By the time of the 1861 census, carried out by the enumerator Charles MacRae, the island's population had dropped by a quarter, to sixty-nine. This was bad enough, but not so far away, on Raasay, there were entirely abandoned settlements, where twenty years before there had been forty and more people.[40] The drain of Scalpay's inhabitants – as from Raasay – was part of the tragic haemorrhaging of people from the Inner and Outer Hebrides that occurred in the wake of the potato famine. Well over 16,500 people fled, mainly to Australia and Canada. A handful were from Scalpay, all of whom sailed on the same vessel, the *Edward Johnstone*, which left Liverpool bound for Portland Bay on 17 June 1854. The Scalpay contingent comprised a married couple, Roderick and Catherine Munro, the Macinneses – a brother and sister – and, on her own, Catherine Macleod, aged twenty-eight.[41] They left under the auspices of the Highland and Islands Emigration Society, which had been formed not for those with sufficient means to fund their own passages, but to assist the very poorest members of what was described as the 'surplus population' – at the cost of £1 for each adult.[42]

As striking as the beginnings of what would soon become an exodus was the sweeping change that was taking place in the character of Scalpay's economy. In 1857, all of the cattle then on the island were auctioned off, along with farming equipment such as ploughs, harrows and fanners.[43] But unlike 1828, this time there was no re-stocking. Worth noting is that until at least 1853, Pabay too was still being used for grazing cattle – maintaining a tradition that had first been noticed by Martin Martin at the end of the seventeenth century.[44]

By 1861, however, the sheep revolution was well under way. Shepherds now headed two of Scalpay's fourteen households. Arable farming was becoming less important. The largest number of households (six), were headed either by fishermen or by fishermen's widows (a fact that speaks its own tragedy). The numbers employed at Scalpay House had risen too, with seven domestic servants listed, presumably under the direction of Catharine Macinnes, the sixty-year-old housekeeper.[45]

It was only six years earlier, in 1855, that Scalpay had been specifically advertised for letting as a sheep farm. As part of the package were grazings ('of the finest quality') at the recently cleared former crofter settlements of Borreraig and Suisnish, on Skye itself. Conveniently, the crofters and cottars from here had begun to be removed in 1851, with the remaining thirty-two families ruthlessly evicted on the orders of James Brown and under the direction of the aforementioned Robert Ballingall in 1853.[46] Ironically, some of those forced out found their way to the rocky slopes at Strollamus, Dunan and Luib, the first two directly opposite from Scalpay, where they scratched out a living.[47] Padlocks and chains stapled to the doors ensured their former cottages would not be occupied, apart from by vermin. In 1857, however, with less interest than had been anticipated in taking on Scalpay as a sheep walk, potential lessees were informed that if they wished, they could also lease the island's shootings. The wind of change was getting up.

By 1894, as we have seen already, Scalpay was still a sheep farm, but also well on the way to becoming a multi-faceted, all-year-round sporting property offering 'good winter sport along with fresh water trout and sea fishing'.[48] In this respect it was on the same trajectory as its larger companion island, Raasay, where by the 1870s under a succession of private landlords from the south, most recently Edward Herbert Wood, most of the arable land and grazings had been turned over to sheep – and game.[49]

Ultimately responsible for these changes in direction had been Godfrey, twentieth chief of clan Macdonald. In 1847, he had sold North Uist and, in Skye, Kilmuir. In 1855 he had let Sconser deer forest. This had been enlarged by his factor Robert Balingall, who drove several crofter and cottar families off from Aricharnach and Moll and other places.[50] By 1884 the forest extended over 10,000 acres of estate land that, as it happened, bordered the Sound of Scalpay, but which also pressed hard on the Sconser crofters whose crops were being damaged by the deer.[51] To complain was to risk eviction.

In 1861 the estate had further enhanced its sporting facilities, and let the 'shootings and fishings' between Torrin in the south of Strath parish, and Corry in the north, including the now-deserted crofting townships of Borreraig and Suisnish. With fewer human beings around to poach them, wild animal stocks could increase.[52] The lessee, from Middlesex, was to pay £150 for seven years, although at this stage, despite having the right to search for deer and woodcock and 'traverse and hunt over all the corries ... around Ben na Callich [sic]', he was restricted to eight deer per annum. He was also required to share the forest with Lord Macdonald and his friends.[53]

The direction of travel was unmistakable. Just before the First World War, not much under three million acres of the Scottish Highlands had been converted to deer forest and other hunting purposes.[54] In Ross and Cromarty and Inverness (the county of which Skye was part) at least two thirds of the land mass was devoted to deer stalking.[55]

*　*　*

Deer forests in the Highlands and the Hebrides dated back to medieval times when the term 'forest' was less the misnomer it became later. Initially kings, abbots and nobles hunted deer on land that might also contain large tracts of natural woodland; this mattered not a jot as far as the main aim of the hunt was concerned – which was to drive the deer into a great circle (the *tainchell*) or other enclosed area, and then slaughter the terrified creatures en masse.

Skye too had its deer chases in former times, Archdeacon of the Isles Donald Munro commenting in 1549 on the 'mony woods, mony forrests, [maney deir], [and] fair hunting games' on the island.[56] In the summer of 1772 Thomas Pennant, on a trek near Loch Slapin (in the south of Skye), was shown 'a stone dyke or deer fence called Paraicnam Fiadh'; in English, the enclosure of the deer. Partly this was hillside but there was also a hollow which, noted Pennant, 'in the days of Ossian, [was] a pitfall covered with boughs for the destruction of the animals chased into it'.[57]

Scalpay, 'a fair hunting forest', was very much part of this picture.

In the nineteenth century interest in the sport intensified.[58] Queen Victoria's and Prince Albert's avowed enthusiasm for field sports, and the excitement that was generated when the latter shot two stags near Drummond Castle in 1842, deepened Britain's elite's zeal for the hunt. Rentals rose above those that sheep farmers could bear, so that they were unable to make the kinds of living they were used to.[59]

Initially, most large sporting estates were in the hands of English aristocrats and others with money to spare.[60] Increasingly however, newly rich or second- and third-generation manufacturers, merchants and bankers joined them, either by purchasing land or renting it. These were the beneficiaries of the unevenly distributed rewards of Victorian Britain's industrial revolution, and the commercial hegemony that accompanied it. Exploiting the crippling financial problems being faced by western Highlands' landowners, they were able to satisfy their lust for land at affordable prices when such opportunities elsewhere in Britain were rare.[61]

Improved transport helped. In the mid-eighteenth century, the journey from London even to the Lowland towns of Edinburgh and Glasgow could take ten days. It wasn't long, however, before access to Scotland's north-west coast and the islands of the Hebrides became both easier and more affordable.

First came horse-drawn carriages, then sea-going paddle steamers. Screw-propelled steamboats followed the inauguration of a passenger service from Glasgow to the Outer Isles in the 1820s. From 1863 there was an overnight rail link from London to Inverness. By this means, in the 'Season' (early August onwards with slightly different end dates for grouse and deer respectively), coachloads of well-heeled 'southrons' were transported at their ease to the north of Scotland. Across the narrow sea channel from Skye, Kyle of Lochalsh welcomed a rail connection in 1897. With the completion of the West Highland line in Mallaig in 1901 another visitor route to Skye was opened, with travellers making the short ferry crossing to Armadale.

Some – the very richest – came, literally, under their own steam. This was in lavishly furnished yachts which their owners used in the summer months to reach and then cruise, explore, picnic and play in the Hebrides.[62]

Socially ambitious, men of this stamp not only had surplus funds at their disposal, but with their businesses established, they had time to indulge themselves in leisure pursuits in a part of the United Kingdom that was accessible but still sufficiently remote to enable them to escape from the pressures and less salubrious environment of the industrial south.[63]

They found pleasure in being in and associated with the wild Scottish landscape of heather, craggy mountains and the roaring and regal antler-crowned stag, portrayed and popularised by the foremost painter of Scotland's deer in the early Victorian era, Sir Edwin Landseer. Deer hunting was practised in a vast arena – nature inviolate – from which the indigenous population were being driven, and their memory consciously erased, although not obliterated.[64]

There was a Spartan, ascetic element too in a sport that involved no little discomfort and considerable physical effort from participants on long marches and during lengthy waits in search of their prey. If part of the gratification of blood sport was masochistic, running through it was a streak of homoeroticism: the fitter males of the gentlemanly classes versus the power, athleticism and virility of the stag.[65] The carnal ritual of bleeding, disembowelling and decapitation marked the triumph of man over noble beast.

Such was Sir Donald Currie's admiration for the monarch of Scotland's glens that he arranged for a Highland stag (aptly named Donald) to be shipped to Cape Town to act as regimental mascot for the Cape Town Highlanders (founded in 1885). The regiment's tartan-clad volunteers, redolent of the Scottish martial tradition, had evidently greatly impressed him.[66]

He was well aware too that the prestige that resulted from being able to display a stag's head replete with a formidable set of antlers was a primary driver for Scotland's late summer sportsmen.[67] The more antler points, the greater the esteem. The grandiose appellation 'imperial' was ascribed to the very rare prize crop of fourteen points. By the middle of the nineteenth century no Highland country house or hunting lodge or cottage was complete without an array of antlers to adorn the walls of virtually any room. Appropriately, greeting visitors in the entrance hall to Currie's sumptuously furnished Scalpay House was a stag's head in all of its antlered glory. This, however, pales into insignificance when set against the duke of Fife's ballroom at the rebuilt (after a fire in 1895) Mar Lodge in Aberdeenshire, the ceiling of which was decked out with 2,435 antlered stag skulls.[68]

It is this context that provides us with at least part of the answer to the question of why Sir Donald Currie took the decision to purchase his Skye islands.

Self-contained, islands had a special attraction as sporting estates. With steam yachts at their owners' disposal, getting there was not an issue. Skye itself by this time had become a magnet for southern visitors and their money. This had followed from the popularisation of the island by Sir Walter Scott and his friend and correspondent the pioneering geologist John MacCulloch in the first years of the nineteenth century. One of the recommended highlights was the Spar Cave, described by Scott in his 1815 poem, 'The Lord of the Isles' as, 'the mermaid's alabaster grot ... Strathaird's enchanted cell'. By 1849 the track to the cave, 'one of the greatest wonders in the Highlands', was 'continually walked for six months of the year by the Publick and all Strangers from England and all parts of Europe'.[69]

Serving much the same end – after a voyage in 1858 that included Skye – a correspondent for the *Manchester Weekly Times* urged 'those of our countrymen who seek change of scene and air, and who do not wish to have the annoyance of passports, to make a tour of the Hebrides ... [with their] more beautiful and interesting scenery than in any part of the world frequented by tourists.'[70] Enthusiastic accounts of this kind, including Alexander Smith's *Summer in Skye*, published in 1865, portrayed an island that awaited exploration by the bolder visitor who was prepared to put up with some minor discomforts.

But there was also history, or a version of it in which the Highlands were the heartland of the Scottish nation.[71] Some of those so tempted, including Sir Donald Currie, were not content simply to rent a property or stay in a hotel, but yearned to have a firmer foothold on the island of mountain and mist, resonant in its associations with Charles Edward Stuart ('Bonnie Prince Charlie') and Flora Macdonald.[72]

Although neither Scalpay nor Pabay could boast an obvious Jacobite connection, Currie did his best to inaugurate one. This he accomplished by buying a drawing room sideboard that was believed to have belonged to Flora Macdonald at Kingsburgh. If the authenticity of this was questionable, what could be reliably established was that the piece had at one time belonged to descendants of the Macdonalds of Kingsburgh (Flora's family) – who for a long time had lived on Scalpay. At some point in the nineteenth century they had sold the sideboard, which had ended up in the Kyleakin Hotel. It was from here it was purchased for Currie by his factor James Mackintosh.[73] Currie was overjoyed. His pleasure is felt still. The piece sits today in the drawing room of Scalpay House, much to the obvious delight of Scalpay's current owners, Michael and Veronica Walford.

Confirmation of Currie's interest in Scotland's past and his identification with the Jacobite strand in the nation's history is that before long he had hung in the dining room a portrait, in oils, of the Prince and the heroine Flora.

Chapter 4

'What a place to retire to': fashioning an island empire

According to *The Scotsman*, when Sir Donald Currie bought the Scalpay Estate he was 'one of the most influential men in the commercial life of the Empire' – and near the pinnacle of his commercial career. At the time of Sir Donald's death in 1909 his net wealth was estimated to be £2.4 million (over £296.5 million at 2017 prices).[1]

He would have had no difficulty finding the £6,500 (over £640,000 now) he paid for the four-island group.

Currie was born in Greenock on the Clyde coast in 1825, the third son of a barber and his wife Barbara. Between them they produced ten children. The family soon moved to Belfast however, where he spent most of his boyhood. From start to finish, Currie's working life was in shipping, with the sea his lasting passion from childhood, when he amassed an enviable collection of toy boats. That the sale particulars about Scalpay included the claim that it offered a suitable anchorage for a yacht is likely to have caught his eye; indeed, it was on his steam yacht *Iolanthe* that in October 1894 he made one of his first visits to Broadford and his newly purchased island empire.[2]

After leaving school at the age of fourteen, Currie crossed the Irish Sea to the buoyant port city of Liverpool where he joined, and then rose through the ranks of, the Cunard Company. Liverpool was the destination for many Scots keen to improve their lot, and Currie appears to have been at the top end of the range of individuals single-mindedly intent on money-making as a pathway to personal and family security, wealth and status.[3] He also found his wife-to-be there, Margaret, the daughter of John

Miller, a Scots-born merchant who also had a large mansion at Ardencraig, on the island of Bute on the Clyde.

At Cunard, Currie's particular responsibility was the transatlantic cargo arm of the business. He resigned, apparently owing to ill health but at the same time, in 1862, he branched out by setting up his own company, with some half-dozen sailing ships travelling from Liverpool and London to Calcutta (modern-day Kolkata). However, the opening of the Suez Canal in 1869 persuaded him to change direction, and during the 1870s he established himself in the African Cape trade – first by using steam vessels belonging to the Leith, Hull and Hamburg Steam Packet Company, his brother James' undertaking, in which he had an interest. A feature of Currie's business career was his keenness to work with and employ family members whenever this was practicable.

His adoption of steam, however, was reluctant; his preference was for sail.[4] Indeed, for many years Currie was Commodore of the Royal Forth Yacht Club. But astute operator that he was, Currie adopted as his first external shareholder John Nixon, a Welsh colliery owner whose coal could be shipped to Calcutta but also, in due course, supply Currie's steamships.[5]

Currie established the Castle Mail Packets Company, the reputation of which was based in part on the regularity and reliability of its service. Early on, Currie recognised how lucrative government contracts and state support could be, and he spent much time lobbying key figures in Whitehall, notably in the Colonial Office, the Foreign Office and the Admiralty. But the relationship was by no means one-sided. Castle Line's fast ships brought intelligence back from South Africa during periods of conflict – before the telegraph cable was laid – and transported British troops to the region during the South African War of 1899–1902.

Although he could be abrasive in his business dealings, Currie, chameleon-like, was also able to charm politicians at home and abroad – nowhere more so than in South Africa – to serve his commercial interests. The Cape contract owed much to Currie's cultivation from as early as 1871 of John Charles Molteno, first Prime Minister of Cape Colony from 1872 (until 1878), one of whose sons married Currie's younger daughter Bessie in 1889. So widely known was Currie's proclivity for influential networking that, in 1884, following his elevation to a knighthood, he was caricatured in one society magazine as 'Knight of the Cruise of Mr Gladstone'.[6] The sniping reference was to a voyage Currie had taken William Gladstone on in 1883 on the *Pembroke Castle* – the first for what was then the largest ship in the Castle Line fleet. This was not the only sea jaunt on which Currie had been accompanied by Gladstone, the Liberal leader and the country's pre-eminent politician. There had been earlier cruises, in 1877 and 1880.

The itinerary in 1883 included Kirkwall and, after that, the somewhat grander haven of Copenhagen. There Currie delighted not only in playing host to Gladstone, Prime Minister at the time – amongst the party too was Lord Tennyson, the Poet Laureate, as well as Prince Edward, later King Edward VII of Great Britain. Also there were the kings and queens of Denmark and Greece, and the Russian czar and czarina. The page those present signed in Currie's autograph book, his obituary recorded, 'was amongst his proudest possessions'.[7]

By the time of his death in 1909 at the age of eighty-four, what in 1899 had become the Union Castle Line (after a merger between the Castle Line and their former rival the Union Steamship Co.) boasted a fleet of no fewer than forty-eight steamers. Many of the firm's ships were named after Scottish castles, including those of Armadale and Dunvegan on Skye, with the expanding fleet being assembled in the 1880s and 1890s with eye-catching frequency from the shipyards of Barclay, Curle & Co. Ltd and the Fairfield Company on the Clyde, and Harland & Wolff in Belfast.

Restless in his search for new business opportunities, Currie was an early investor in the South African copper- and gold-mining industries. Even more impressive were his cleverly timed forays into diamonds, and the way he extended his interest in the vast Kimberley mines. In 1888 he became chairman of the London board of De Beers Consolidated Mines, but also, with family members and close associates, ran a highly lucrative gold-mining company of his own.[8]

Like many prosperous Scottish entrepreneurs of the period, Currie amassed a large art collection (including many by J.M.W. Turner). In London he owned a town house in Hyde Park Place.

But of greater relevance for the Pabay story is Currie's interest in land pursuits and landowning. This last-named ambition was accomplished through the purchase, in three stages, of the Perthshire estates of Garth, Glen Lyon and Chesthill.

Although by the time of the first of these acquisitions, in 1880, the golden age of what has been termed 'High Farming' was nearing its end, there was still money to be made from Scottish agriculture, with its focus on mixed farming as opposed to England's concentration on wheat, which suffered in the free-trade environment of the later Victorian era.[9] In the first years of the twentieth century Currie's Perthshire estates, which supported twenty-six farms and a number of smaller pendicles, were producing a healthy annual rental of around £10,000.[10]

*   *   *

But as we have seen already, it was to the Western Highlands and Islands that many prosperous merchants, rich industrialists and well-to-do lawyers turned to acquire land. Many of the great hereditary estates – like those of the Macdonalds in Skye, the Mackenzies of Seaforth in the Outer Hebrides and the McNeils of Barra, and others – were broken up and sold off for reasons outlined earlier. It was a buyer's market.

So canny was Currie that he only made his bid for Scalpay and Pabay after the islands had failed initially to find either a lessee or a buyer, and had been put on the market again in August 1894 at a reduced asking price.[11] For Lord Macdonald this was a grave disappointment; less than ten years earlier he had hoped a potential buyer would pay £10,000 for Scalpay – a sum that would have reduced the debts of a household now bordering – relatively speaking of course – on poverty. Pabay was to be let to anyone who would take it on.

*   *   *

There was however another, more specific appeal for a newcomer to this part of the crofting county of Invernessshire who wished to increase the value of his asset and enjoy conflict-free proprietorship: there were no crofts on either Scalpay or Pabay.

In fact, this was explicitly stated in the notice advertising the islands for sale. It was an important consideration.

Living close to the margins of subsistence, the decline in sheep prices had been heavy blows for crofter households after two decades of steadier – albeit low – incomes. The lingering resentment felt by many crofters about the clearances of the 1840s and 1850s began to break through what had been the thin skin of relative prosperity. More articulate crofter voices were to be heard. There was a newfound confidence about their (Gaelic) culture. This, and a deeper sense of indignation about the attitudes and actions of landlords and their factors had been instilled by radical, anti-landlord newspaper editors such as John Murdoch. In 1877 in Inverness he had founded *The Highlander*. The paper's clarion call was for land reform.[12]

Currie was a Member of Parliament belonging to the governing Liberal Party during the period of the Land War that on Skye and elsewhere in the Highlands had raged on and off between 1881 and 1886. He would have been acutely aware of the crofters' grievances, and the dangers for the authorities, including landlords, of their taking direct action. Indeed, in a speech he gave in May 1885 to the tenants of his newly acquired estate of Glen Lyon Currie alluded, with some regret, to the fact that relations between landlord and tenant had been such 'as to call for the intervention of Parliament'.[13]

From the start of the protests in Skye that culminated in mass gatherings and violent resistance, the island's crofters posed a particularly difficult challenge for the forces of law and order. The Government was rightly fearful of an equivalent of the near-revolutionary Irish Land League getting a foothold in Scotland's crofting districts, although widely read pamphlets from the London-based Land League Reform Association emphasised how important it was that collective action should remain 'within the bounds of the law'.[14]

Overcrowding and growing pressure on land resources – for peat, and cattle and sheep grazing – on the Glendale estate in the north-west of Skye played its part in Pabay's story. Around 1879, as conditions worsened and relations between the estate's factor and the crofting people in the area broke out into open hostility, one couple from the settlement of Ramasaig departed with their daughter and two young sons. There are no more details, other than that their destination was Pabay. Kenneth Mackinnon (and his wife Catherine) abandoned a life of semi-independence (and penury) within the crofting community in which they had been raised; instead Kenneth became an island shepherd.[15]

The Mackinnons, however, had not seen the last of the factor whom many would have accused of making it impossible for them to remain in Ramasaig without his approval.

In May 1883, members of the Napier Commission set up by the government to 'inquire into the condition of the Crofters and Cottars in the Highlands and Islands of Scotland' had sat in Broadford to hear the testimonies of local people. The seven-strong panel – a mix of landed aristocrats and members of the Highlands' professional class who had some sympathy with and knowledge of the crofters' grievances, learned that Pabay was currently tenanted by one of Skye's most notorious factors and single-minded (as well as knowledgeable) sheep farmers, Donald Macdonald of Tormore in Sleat.

Macdonald was better known throughout the island simply as 'Tormore'.[16] A relative of Lord Macdonald, and a firm believer that land was an asset to be exploited as a means of enhancing his employer's and his own fortunes, he had been factor for the Macdonald estate and held leases of several other farms on Skye and the mainland. For the alleged harshness of his treatment of the crofters on the lands for which he was responsible, which included Glendale, Tormore was a target for protesters during the subsequent conflict, the first rumblings of which were felt on Skye – on part of Lord Macdonald's estates – in 1881.[17] It was these disturbances that had led William Harcourt, the Home Secretary, to establish, as a matter of urgency, the Commission under its chair, Francis, 9th Lord Napier and 1st Baron Ettrick, formerly a colonial administrator who had for a short spell been viceroy of India.[18]

Tormore's hardheartedness (some would rather say his hard-headed commercial acumen) was apparent even in his management of Pabay.

William Fraser, a sixty-two-year-old crofter in Lower Breakish, around a mile distant and the nearest township to Pabay on Skye itself, reported to the Commission that despite his need for seaware as a fertiliser for his potatoes Tormore had denied him access to Pabay's shores, the best local source. Many decades before, the lotters (so called as they bid for 'lots', from which they could be removed on the factor's whim) of Lower Breakish had offered to pay Lord Macdonald £45 a year for the seaware at Ardnish, the rock-fringed promontory that lay in front of their portions, but by the 1880s this had been over-harvested.[19]

Finlay M'Innes, on the other hand, a fisherman and crofter in the adjoining township of Waterloo (the even more densely crowded population of which a *Scotsman* reporter described as 'literally swarming over crofts'), admitted that he and others could obtain Pabay seaweed, but that they had to pay five shillings a year for the privilege. They had little choice. Continual cropping had exhausted the soil in which the seed potatoes were planted; seaware contained the essential nutrients that had been lost. Even on peaty and rock and stone-strewn soil, seaweed would force what Osgood MacKenzie of Inverewe in his *A Hundred Years in the Highlands* called a 'bumper crop'.[20] It was for this reason that even the right to a weed-carrying rock on the shore near Harrapool (the township which lay between Breakish and Broadford) was in 1881 the subject of a dispute between Neil Ross and Samuel Campbell, which Macdonald was asked to resolve.[21]

Given the demand there was for it, Tormore's contention that there had been over-cutting of Pabay's seaweed rings true, more so than his assertion that for the right of his tenants to harvest seaware, 'one shilling I never received'.[22] Uncontestable was the physical difficulty lotters and crofters from Breakish and the adjoining townships had in obtaining Pabay's seaweed. The best and densest of this was sub-littoral, as opposed to the more accessible rock-weeds.[23] Most profuse at a depth of two and usually more fathoms, it could only be cut and ferried during the six days of spring tides. Not unusually the weather was unfavourable for at least some of the time. And while several crofters did own boats, for those without there was the cost of hiring one for as much as seven shillings a day, as well as the provision of food and drink for the four or so men required to cut and transport the unwieldy cargo back to the Breakish shore.[24]

Tormore's association with Pabay, however, was short-lived. In 1879, he gave up his position as factor for Lord Macdonald's estate, although he held onto Pabay for a few years more. His replacement as Macdonald's factor was his near namesake Colonel Alexander Macdonald. Macdonald managed five of Skye's estates, and until 1886 he had under his management some 85 per cent of the island's population.[25]

His territory included Pabay. The uncrowned 'King of Skye', Colonel Macdonald was no benign ruler. He had little sympathy with the crofters' complaints, convinced that the agitation of the 1880s was fomented by outside agents. Like Tormore, he had earned a reputation as an unflinching instrument of his proprietor employers and as an oppressive tacksman, notwithstanding the respectability of his position as a bank agent, Skye's sole lawyer, based in Portree, and as holder of several public offices such as memberships of school boards.[26] The public face of their landlord employers, who preferred to remain in the background, factors across the region induced feelings that ranged from affection, through respect and awe, to unforgiving hatred.

Recognition of the power Macdonald wielded, and the fear of its consequences, is hinted at in a letter written to him by one of Pabay's residents, Angus McEwan, in 1885. This was over an accusation that McEwan's dog had been killing rabbits. These had recently been introduced to the island, sales of their fur offering a new revenue stream. 'Mr McDonald,' wrote McEwan somewhat obsequiously, 'I am not such a disobedient servant as that I will not send the Dog away out of the Island if you insist on doing so or if you think the Dog is the least injury to any Stock that might be on the Island – or to anything belonging to you at Pabay.' With some hesitation he pointed the finger at a Mr Gibson, a rabbit trapper who, rather than catching the agreed number of pairs of rabbits, had blamed the dog, or poachers, for the short supply. He would say no more, McEwan concluded, before once more acknowledging his subservient position and loyalty: 'He [Gibson] was allowed to depart in peace since we knew that he was here on our Master's Business.'[27]

More disturbances had followed the infamous Battle of the Braes in 1882. Indeed, so concerned had Tormore been about his personal safety that he had armed himself with a revolver.[28] Constables brought from Glasgow and Inverness supplemented the island's police force of eleven men. By the end of 1884 two gunboats and a troopship, HMS *Assistance*, had arrived, carrying 350 red-coated marines and 100 naval seamen. In the short term at least the marines' presence was effective, with not a single bullet being fired in anger for their seven-month stay.[29] The truce, however, was short-lived.

Late in 1886, according to Macleod of Dunvegan's son, Skye was 'in a state of anarchy'. Macleod had reason to be fearful. Two years earlier, his father, Norman Macleod, had done his best to charm a delegation of six aggrieved crofters from Harlosh who had demanded an audience with him at Dunvegan Castle. He had personally served them with wine and whisky, and shown them round the castle and grounds. Demonstrating 'no sign of any ill feeling towards the Proprietor', the delegation was reported to have left quietly.[30] But paternalist gestures of this kind were no longer sufficient to cap the rising well of social discontent.

In fact, so uncomfortable had life become for Lord Macdonald earlier in the year that, following threats on his life, he and his wife ('sad and indignant' at her husband's treatment by 'people who have known him so long') decided to abandon Skye and spend the summer at Cowes, on the south coast of England. They would then winter in London, but 'living in a smaller way' than they had been used to, owing to mounting financial pressures which caused them to cut their expenditure and pay off some of their Skye servants.[31]

Of great interest to Currie then, as he pondered whether to buy in Skye, would have been his assessment of the measures taken by William Gladstone's Government to pacify the protesters. Fortunately, as we know, Currie knew the Prime Minister well.

Like Gladstone, he was sympathetic to the tenant class. Shortly after his election as MP for Perthshire in 1880, at an event organised on behalf of the tenantry of his Garth estate, Currie had referred to 'the inherent right [of tenant farmers]' to be 'protected from the unjust actions of unreasonable landlords'.[32]

If the pressing issue in 1880 was the Hares and Rabbits Bill, and the rights of tenants to kill this class of game, as far as Currie's Skye interests were concerned the critical piece of legislation was the Crofters Holdings (Scotland) Act of 1886. This statute, according to the leading historian of the Highlands, Jim Hunter, was 'so radical as to be little short of revolutionary'. Applicable to virtually every crofter in north-west Scotland, the legislation dealt with four main issues. These were: security of tenure to the crofters in the seven crofting counties; the right of crofters on relinquishing a holding to claim compensation for unexhausted improvements they had made; and the right of the crofter to bequeath his croft to a family member. It established too the Crofters Commission that would henceforth fix fair rents for crofters' holdings and adjudicate on arrears. Greeted with howls of outrage by many landowners and their friends in sections of the press, the Crofters Act was condemned as an attack on the rights of property owners, and perhaps even as the herald of communism.[33] Certainly for a time the Act put a stop to eviction and may have held back the exploitation of crofters' land for sporting pursuits.[34]

But with Scalpay and Pabay excluded from the terms of the Act, Currie was free to proceed to exploit his Hebridean assets without hindrance.

*   *   *

To be fair, Currie's vision for his Skye islands was bolder than simply game hunting. For one thing, he was able to – and did – shoot stags on his estate in Highland Perthshire, which he had turned into deer forest. Yet even this was insufficient to satisfy his appetite for stag shooting. He frequently rented from his near neighbour in Perthshire, Lord Breadalbane, Drummond Hill, a five-mile-long park and deer forest at the eastern end of Loch Tay.[35]

It seems he wanted something more – but less tangible – from his ownership of land, parcels of which he was continually adding to his portfolio.[36]

Even though by the later nineteenth century landownership was no longer a guarantee of the deference of the people below – for many observers a conspicuous aspect of Scotland's rural society only decades earlier – old attitudes died hard. On his purchase of Garth, Currie had declared that, 'It was not to be a mere laird or owner of land that he had purchased the estate', although his comment seconds later that he hoped 'to die amongst them [his tenants] as his laird and friend' rather confirms the contemporary perception that Currie greatly relished the role of paternalist landlord, master of all he surveyed.

In November 1880, in his mansion house at Garth, Currie assured his assembled tenants of his commitment to 'the material advancement of the people in Highland Perthshire, to the improvement of stock rearing . . . [and] the increased productiveness of the soil'. His words could have been equally appropriate when he acquired his islands in Skye's Inner Sound.[37]

Like some but not all 'capitalists from the south' whose purchase of Highland estates had been noted by the Napier Commission, Currie was amongst that group of active investors who paid for new buildings, agricultural improvements, plantations and 'embellishments of every kind'. As with many of the new Highland landowners, Currie was keen to emulate and even surpass the efforts of the older landed gentry by adding to the amenity of the estate generally, and around the big house through tree planting. There was a utilitarian motive to this too: woodland provided shelter for game and deer.[38]

Currie the landlord was as much an innovator and moderniser as he was in business. He masterminded a series of building projects in his Perthshire village of Fortingall, with designs by some of the country's most innovative architects, including William MacLaren, a pioneer in the Arts and Crafts style.[39] With MacLaren's death in 1890 however, it had been left to two of his former employees – William Dunn and Robert Watson – to complete the work.[40]

And within a year of his taking over his Inner Hebridean archipelago, Currie had begun to transform Scalpay (and improve
Pabay), now assisted by Dunn and Watson. Old Scalpay House
was, according to one newspaper report, 'entirely obliterated' and
replaced by a new mansion that echoed the architectural style he
had adopted in Perthshire. Currie's rebuilding project was much
needed. Obliteration, though, was an exaggeration; renovation,
enlargement and reconfiguration provide a more accurate description of Dunn's and Watson's commission – fitting in Watson's case
given his dislike of originality for its own sake, preferring instead
to refresh the best of what was there already. The thick walls and
the two wings of the former house were retained, although the
addition of harling, crow-stepped gables and blue slates for the
roof – features at Fortingall – were very much hallmarks of the
Dunn and Watson partnership. Extensions were added to each
wing, along with a new projecting porch bearing Currie's initials
– DMC – and the date – 1895. Great attention was paid to the
amenity of the interior, with wood panelling lining the main public
rooms, which were now better proportioned.[41] The 'marine feel' of
the place reflects Currie's enthusiasm for things nautical, and the
fact that Dunn and Watson had designed the saloons of some of
the Castle Line ships.

On completion, the house was a powerful statement of the new
owner's status that had numerous counterparts in impressive
contemporaneous shooting-lodge construction projects elsewhere
in Highland Scotland. Boasting six bedrooms (as well as three for
servants, with others to be accommodated in cottages nearby),
large dining and drawing rooms, both sumptuously furnished, and
a butler's cabinet stocked with the finest wines, Currie and his
guests wanted for nothing.[42] Having said that, Currie's wife – no
shrinking violet – evidently rarely stayed in the house, preferring
instead the greater opulence of her husband's sumptuously
equipped yacht, the *Iolaire*, lying offshore from the semi-circular
quay that Dunn and Watson are thought to have laid out.[43]

By March 1897 *The Scotsman* was able to report on the 'very
large sums' that Currie had laid out, 'making it [Scalpay] a comfortable residential Highland resort'. Trees – one and a half million of

them, mainly Scotch fir, larch, spruce and birch – had been planted out. Roads were driven into the moor and laid – mainly to open up the island for low-level shooting. Trout from Norway had been shipped over to stock a couple of the island's four freshwater lochs. Modern farm buildings in keeping with the needs of the new agricultural regime were erected. Currie was keen to demonstrate that there was greater potential for more ambitious farming on Skye than was generally believed by generations of crofters and cotters, who concentrated their agricultural efforts on rearing a few cattle or sheep and planting potatoes, oats and kail.[44]

Visitors were impressed. In January 1901, *The Scotsman* published an article, the writer of which had followed by sea the journey in the Western Isles taken by James Boswell and Samuel Johnson in 1773. Even viewing Scalpay from afar, standing out amongst a 'mass of foliage', the *Scotsman* journalist could see the 'white walls of the mansion-house' which Sir Donald had built. Clearly visible too were the roadways he had constructed 'all round the island'. Riding 'gracefully at anchor' was his steam yacht *Iolaire*.

The writer – unfortunately anonymous – then reflected on what Currie might consider his greatest achievement. It was not, he speculated, Sir Donald's great Castle Line, his period as a Perthshire MP, or the knighthood from Queen Victoria (which Currie would almost certainly have prioritised). Rather, it was that he had 'wakened Scalpay out of its long sleep of death with a thrill of new-born life', and 'caused the cheering sound of human activity to replace on its shores the cry of the sea birds'.

If this impression was complacently mistaken in its assumption that the somewhat unkempt island Currie had purchased in 1894 had perhaps for centuries been an empty wilderness, the tribute it paid to the special places islands are is as valid now as it was in 1901. Currie had created nothing less than an island kingdom, all of his own – 'What a place to retire to from the fruitless chattering at St James'.[45]

But there were fewer of the cries and less laughter of innocent children than were heard forty years earlier. In 1901 only five youngsters were left, four of whom were listed as scholars. All the fisherfolk had gone. Reflecting the island's current focus, the key individuals were Alexander Macrae, the sheep manager, his son Duncan, the gamekeeper, and the housekeeper Harriet Davidson. There was a ploughman, presumably for the home farm, but most of the rest of the adult inhabitants (sixteen in all) were employed to maintain Scalpay House and its gardens.[46]

* * *

What, though, of Pabay? As on Scalpay, the number of people on the island had fallen. In 1841 Pabay's permanent population was probably at an all-time high: twenty-one. Each of the four households was headed by a man listed as an agricultural labourer – John Mackinnon, James Grant, an older John Mackinnon and Charles Mackinnon. No other occupations were given. All seem to have been employed by Lower Sculamus Farm, of which Pabay was an appendage. As with Scalpay, it was a strikingly young island community; almost half of the inhabitants were aged ten or less, the youngest being Alexander Mackinnon, at six months.

There was then a sharp decline – to two families in 1851. Ten years later there was one. Almost certainly it was the potato famine that led to the population loss. The outward flow was staunched temporarily at the end of the 1870s with the arrival from Glendale of Kenneth and Catherine Mackinnon and their children.

Before they came, the only people left had been an odd couple, Charles Mackinnon (eighty – or thereabouts – in 1881), a shepherd who had been on Pabay from at least as early as 1841, and his second wife – also Catherine – who was half his age. Charles's six children had all left. Catherine is most likely to have been the feisty woman Angus McSwan complained to Alexander Macdonald about in 1885. McSwan wanted to put some hay in the loft above the stables where she resided. But, he reported, 'she won't allow nothing [except her potatoes] to go there ... whether it belonged to myself or to the Factor or to Lord Macdonald'. To change her mind would require, McSwan advised, 'a few lines' from Mr Macdonald, which he would then read to her 'in Robson the Ground Officer's presence'.[47]

Not long after the arrival of the younger Mackinnon couple, they produced another son – Donald – and had also been joined by a nine-year-old niece, Catherine Nicolson, described as a scholar. Another son, Alexander, born in March 1883, was, as far as I can tell, the last child to be born on Pabay. (The four children of Len and Margaret Whatley who were conceived on Pabay were born in Broadford hospital.) Also part of the household was Catherine's widower father, an annuant, or pensioner.

Ten years later there was no trace of Charles Mackinnon and his wife. Kenneth Mackinnon too was dead. Catherine's father had taken over as the island's shepherd, the last of Pabay's inhabitants whose first (and only) language was Gaelic; the others claimed to be competent in English as well as Gaelic – increasingly the case for Strath parishioners according to the local schoolmaster Donald Logan. Kenneth's unmarried son Norman, a mason, was there, along with Catherine's three sons, all of school age. Catherine Nicolson, now seventeen, was a dressmaker. No one was married (or had a surviving partner).

The pattern – including that of single lives – continued.[48] By 1911 only five people remained on Pabay: Catherine Mackinnon (now aged sixty-four) and her two sons, Donald (who was head of the household) and Angus; Catherine Nicolson, who was approaching middle age and listed as a cook; and Norman MacSwan, the mason. Soon, as we will see, there were just two.

Detailed records of work done on the island during the period of Currie's improvement drive appear not to have survived. What we can gather, however, is that there was much to be done. Not so many years before Currie took it over, Pabay was only of marginal value to the Macdonald estate, and in need of attention. The barn was described as being 'almost a wreck' – hence Angus McSwan's efforts to store hay in the stable loft.

In 1883 though, Pabay was identified as a possible solution to a particular, locally troublesome problem.

This was when Tormore had offered to lease it to some Lower Breakish crofters. No doubt to persuade members of the Napier Commission of his generosity, he described Pabay as a 'valuable' asset. However, the intended beneficiaries had declined Tormore's proposal, on the grounds that they had too little capital to turn the island into a viable proposition.[49]

There was a cruel irony in their situation. In 1883, along with many others on Skye, the lotters of Lower Breakish, a 'hamlet skirting the shore', had threatened to refuse to pay their rents. Around forty-four families inhabited the township, each with a full share of land comprising some four acres with which to cultivate potatoes and oats and graze two cows. Others had half of this. They were not allowed to keep sheep – although some did. According to Donald Mackinnon, of Kilbride, who took the trouble to write to Tormore in their support, 'they have less for their money than any tenants of the estate'.[50] With no horses of their own, they dug and tilled the soil – on lazy-beds – with the simple, home-made *chas-chrom*, or foot plough.[51] Six years earlier their hill pasture had been taken – without compensation of any kind – and transferred to the township of Upper Breakish, where crofters were able to keep more cattle, sheep and horses for ploughing. With the fishing in the vicinity in 1883 having been a 'complete failure', and this on top of a recent retreat of fish shoals from the immediate vicinity, the inhabitants of Lower Breakish were deep in debt, and struggling to subsist. Consequently, great numbers of households were said to be in 'distressed circumstances'.[52]

Across the narrow stretch of water they could see Pabay, where in former times Breakish livestock had been grazed. Directly in their line of sight were the island's south-eastern cliffs and rockiest shores, the most productive of Pabay's seaware-growing locations. In different circumstances, Pabay might have promised salvation, a means of relieving their current woes. So near, yet out of their reach.

Instead, they began to encroach on the croft lands of Ashaig, to the east of Breakish, appealing in 1889 to the newly established Crofters Commission to support their claim for enlarged holdings.[53]

It wasn't long after this that Currie began his work. As on Scalpay, a rubble-built jetty was constructed. For the first time, Pabay now had a half-decent landing place, although not at low tide, when the sea barely licked the end of it. Crucially too, a water supply had been identified and a means of storing it – in tanks – provided. In March 1899, the *Inverness Courier* reported that fencing was under way and trees were being planted. By 1905 there was 'a farm with a handsome little farm steading and a dwelling house' that replaced existing but dilapidated buildings in more or less the same locations.[54] The new constructions mirrored the 'model farm steading and dairy' that Dunn and Watson had had constructed on Scalpay.[55] By and large this was what Len Whatley inherited when he took over Pabay in January 1950.

We can't tell how often Currie visited Pabay. As was usual with the Highlands' new class of landlords, most years he was only on his island estate for a few weeks, invariably in the summer or autumn. Yet what is clear is that for the relatively short time he owned Scalpay estate, he was a looming presence, especially in and around Broadford Bay, in which lay his island demesne.

* * *

Even though Currie spent most of his time away from Skye, he demonstrated a keen and active interest in the island's life. He was astute enough to recognise the kudos that resulted from identifying with Skye in general and Broadford in particular. Invited to open the Reading Room in Broadford in September 1897, he was cheered after declaring his pleasure in being able to 'promote the welfare of the district' and to 'encourage anything that tended to help a spirit of enterprise and to assist the young men in their endeavours to be a credit to Skye and Broadford'. A similar institution, he recounted, in which he had been involved in his younger years, had been the making of every one of its members, the books they read having enabled them through the study of historical events to 'shape their lives in accordance with the lessons of the past'.[56]

But while his participation in island life was necessarily sporadic, Currie lost few opportunities to make his mark. The occasion of Queen Victoria's diamond jubilee in June 1897 provided one of these. To celebrate the event Currie ordered sixty of his men to build a 30-foot-high bonfire on top of Glashbhein. His wife, Lady

Currie, sent every one of the island's residents a jubilee mug, while Harriet Davidson, the housekeeper, pinned commemorative medals on the children's chests. In the evening, a piper led a party of seventy of the estate's employees and family members to the hilltop to light the fire. If the descent of a thick mist reduced its visibility (and that of the several rockets which were fired off), on Pabay and in the surrounding townships the spectacular display could certainly be seen, so concluding what in some quarters was judged to be the most spectacular jubilee celebration in the Highlands.[57]

By far the most obvious sign that Sir Donald was in the area was the presence of the *Iolaire*. This was one of many grand yachts that would anchor near Kyleakin at the turn of the twentieth century, their owners, masters and crew breaking their voyages to the north or the south in order to take on supplies and catch up with their counterparts amongst the yachting fraternity.

Mary MacPherson, in her teens at the time, recalled 'the lovely sight it was to see those floating palaces lit up on a summer night'.[58] Members of Scotland's mercantile and manufacturing elite owned most of them. The Coats textile family from Paisley had three yachts, although this was unusual. Most of the others, such as Sir William Mackinnon of Strathaird on Skye, who like Currie had made his fortune in Africa, as well as in the Far East, had one – vying with each other over who could boast the biggest and the finest yacht in the informally assembled fleet. As with Currie, several of the entrepreneur-owners who traversed the waters around Skye had become proprietors of Hebridean islands – like George Bullough of Rum, inheritor of a textile machinery manufacturing firm who was responsible for the construction of the incongruous, eye-watering, intriguing monstrosity that is Kinloch Castle.[59]

But it was with the *Iolaire* that local people on Skye most strongly identified. 'DSS', a newspaper correspondent from the east coast, noted that people around Broadford spoke of it as 'the yacht', thereby distinguishing her 'from the many which now sail these popular waters'.[60]

Locals also closely scrutinised the seamanship of their crews. Deliberately, Currie recruited west-coast Highlanders, including men from Strath itself.[61] It was a shrewd move, the employment created further endearing him to the surrounding community.

Sir Donald actually owned two *Iolaire*s. The first was launched from Ramage and Fergusson's yard in Leith in January 1896. Significantly, this was two years after Currie had become a Skye landowner, which probably explains his adoption for the vessel of a Gaelic name, *Iolaire*, meaning eagle. Creag an Iolaire is eagle rock, the lowest spur of the Cuillins, and the likely inspiration for Currie.[62]

Nevertheless, grand as this 700-ton, 203-foot-long, 27.5-foot-wide boat was, it evidently had its limitations. A voyage to the Mediterranean in 1897 had necessitated a complete refit. The capability to get to the Great Sea and return in comfort, in ships that were fitted out with sufficient opulence to impress guests invited aboard, was crucial for their socially ambitious owners. 'What a highway and byway of fashion just now is the Mediterranean,' wrote the society magazine the *Bystander* in April 1906. 'Royal yachts, ducal yachts, ships of the Squadron, and home-coming, Royalty-bearing steamers cross and re-cross each other in its waters.' Amongst them, it was noted, was Sir Donald Currie's *Iolaire*, heading for the Adriatic where, it was thought, King Edward VII and his Queen Consort Alexandra were also bound.[63]

This, however, was *Ioliare* number two. Launched from William Beardmore's Clyde yard in 1902, the second *Iolaire* was longer, broader and of a greater tonnage – 862 compared to 700. Costing £350,000 (some £40 million today) and built to Currie's specifications, she had three decks and was powered by a triple expansion engine. With a single funnel, clipper bow and a long, overhanging stern, the new *Iolaire* was graceful and elegant. She was also palatial, with staterooms and separate smoking, dining and ladies' rooms equipped with silver fireplaces (as well as rooms at the rear for stewards and maids). In pride of place at the front of the upper deck was the 'owner's room'. This was fitted out with a bookcase, a bureau and writing table, and furnished with leather-upholstered chairs.[64] The *Iolaire* was, wrote one admiring local, 'like a small liner, gleaming white'; impressive too was the 'large crew of sailors, stokers and stewards', and the 'attendant steam launch and sailing pinnacle'.[65]

During the winter months, the new *Iolaire* was to be found tracking between Mediterranean ports such as Marseilles, Venice and Naples, as its predecessor had done. During the summer, her base was the anchorage off Scalpay.[66]

Currie, however, was not satisfied with spending time in the Inner Hebrides alone, or with his wife Lady Currie and family. A sociable man, as we have gathered, Sir Donald also liked to impress people in high places. Consequently, during the period of his proprietorship many distinguished visitors were conveyed to Scalpay and the other islands in his possession.

Not to be overlooked, however, were local worthies. Currie was well aware of the utility of befriending them. In the summer of 1907 Currie's cruising guests included Skye's leading lawyer Ronald Macdonald – successor to his notorious father Alexander Macdonald – and his wife Elizabeth. Currie himself planned daily excursions around Scalpay and across into the sea lochs of Ross, which the party explored in the smaller steam launch or red-sailed dinghy that accompanied the *Iolaire*. Thoughtfully, on the Macdonalds' departure, Currie presented them with a caged canary for their children.[67]

Currie's standing as a national figure, and a demonstration of his assumption of pre-eminence in the seas around Scalpay, were manifested in August 1906. The background was the growing fear of war with an increasingly militarised Germany, and the consequent restructuring and modernising of the British navy. This had commenced under the First Sea Lord, Admiral Lord Fisher, in 1904. The deep waters of Skye's Inner Sound provided ideal conditions for Royal Navy exercises; they are still used for this purpose today.

It was during one of these manoeuvres, involving a destroyer and a number of torpedo boats belonging to the First Flotilla, that Currie intervened. At his invitation, the ships' officers and crew spent time on Scalpay walking and playing football on the level parkland in front of the house, before being provided with tea on the shore by Lady Currie. The following day Sir Donald took the captains and officers with him to Portree, for a hotel luncheon and then to the

View of Pabay from the summit of Beinn na Caillich. Clearly seen is Pabay's prominent position in the Inner Sound that lies between Skye and mainland Scotland. (Whatley Collection)

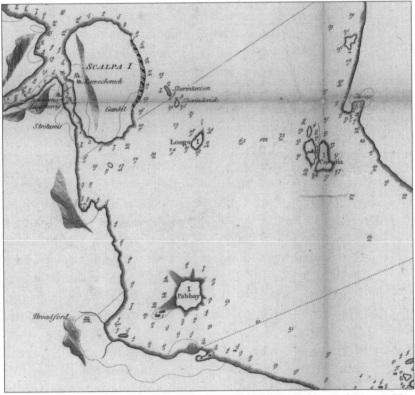

Map, showing part of Skye's Inner Sound, 1776. Pabay is near the centre of the map. The four islands that would later comprise Scalpay estate are shown as Scalpa, Longa and Pabbay (Guillamon, to the south of Scalpay, is un-named). Note the shallow-water depths marked around Pabay, and the long dark tongues of rock exposed at low water, so doubling the island's size. (Murdoch Mackenzie (1712–1797), 'The south part of Sky island and the adjacent main of Scotland' (1776). Reproduced by permission of the Trustees of the National Library of Scotland)

Pabay, from the old graveyard at Ashaig, Breakish. It has been claimed that this is the site of St Maelrubha's ferry; the spot, it is believed, where the saint landed after his voyages from Applecross, and from where he would depart for Pabay. (© Christopher A. Whatley)

Image of a West Highland galley, or birlinn, carved on the 1528 tomb of Alasdair Crotach MacLeod of Harris. Such vessels, clinker built, and shown here with oar-ports and sternpost rudder, were ubiquitous and would have been a familiar sight in the waters around Pabay until as late as the 17th century. (© David H Caldwell)

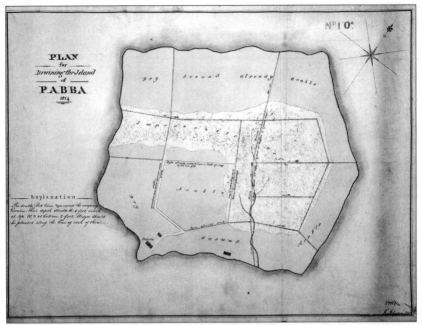

Map of Pabba. Proposed improvements to drainage on Pabay by John Johnston (1814), following John Blackadder's survey of the Macdonald estate in 1799. The main ditch runs roughly north to south. This was to be 6 feet deep, 10 feet wide at the top and 3 at the bottom – essential if the island was to fulfil its promise, both for arable farming and grazing stock. (Macdonald Papers, Museum of the Isles, Armadale, Isle of Skye)

Sir Donald Currie (1825–1909), of the Castle Line, Member of Parliament and associate of William Gladstone, and proprietor of estates in Perthshire and Skye – which included Pabay. Later 19th century.

Scalpay House, 2018. The house today is much like it was following Sir Donald Currie's renovation between 1894 and 1897, although it was then gleaming white. Currie, with his architects William Dunn and Robert Watson, added the crow-stepped gables and the front porch, upon which are carved his initials, DMC, and the date, 1895. (© Christopher A. Whatley)

Group outside Scalpay House, *c.*1900. At the rear are Sir Donald and Lady Currie. Seated, in the middle on the right, is Harriet Davidson, the housekeeper. At the front is either the captain or a senior crew member of the *Iolaire*. (© with permission of Allen and Merle Linning on behalf of the Davidson family)

Sir Donald Currie's steam yacht the *Iolaire*. 236 feet long, 30 feet wide and 16 feet deep, the *Iolaire* was built on the Clyde at William Beardmore & Co's yard in Govan, and launched in 1902. She was the most impressive of the vessels owned by Pabay's proprietors and a stunning sight when cruising in the Inner Sound. (© University of Glasgow Archives & Special Collections, William Beardmore & Co. Ltd Collection)

Skye capital's Highland Games. But it was in the *Iolaire* that they were transported to Portree and back, and it was the *Iolaire* a short time later that led the flotilla, now supplemented with another six destroyers, as it sailed from Broadford Bay to Kyleakin.[68]

Currie's time on Scalpay and amongst his other three islands was brief, cut short by his death in April 1909. Feeling ill, he had abandoned his annual cruise in the *Iolaire* in favour of the gentility and gentler climate of Devon's renowned watering place, Sidmouth, under medical supervision.

Condolences flowed in from all quarters. Senders included King Edward VII, the Prince of Wales, several lord provosts and mayors, shipping magnates, South Africa's leading politicians and a series of colonial governors. Literally hundreds of wreaths were sent for his funeral, in Fortingall, to which flocked streams of mourners. Amongst the first to arrive were Captain Stanley of the *Iolaire* and a detachment of her crew, who also carried his coffin from the parish church to the graveside. Memorial services were held in Dunkeld Cathedral, St Paul's in London, Holyrood Church, Southampton and, appropriately, in the Seamen's Institute, Cape Town.[69]

Within five years of Currie's death, the tragedy of what would be termed the Great War had commenced. As hostilities intensified, the *Iolaire* was requisitioned by the Royal Navy and used for training officers. It was only with the return to peace in Europe following the signing by the major powers of the Treaty of Versailles in June 1919 that the yacht reverted to the family. (Contrary to what is sometimes thought, Currie's *Iolaire* was not the vessel that so tragically foundered off Stornoway harbour on 31 December 1918, with the loss of 205 returning soldiers' lives.) A refit was needed to restore the vessel to something of its former splendour. Lady Currie and close family members continued to visit Skye, and use the yacht, but the end was in sight.

This was little sign of this at the end of 1919 however, as the family once more enjoyed the pleasure of being reunited with the *Iolaire*. The Molteno family newsletter captured something of the atmosphere: 'During September [1919] Aunt Bessie, Jervis and Islay had a delightful trip on the "Iolaire", Lady Currie's beautiful yacht ... As the first few days were rather stormy, they lay off Scalpay and spent the time enjoying the beauty of Skye from the yacht and fishing for lythe off the island and trout in the loch on it. Then came an absolute "dream day" – blue skies, warm sun, glorious green blue sea, and most wonderful views of mountains in the distance and towering rocky cliffs near at hand; so off they went, between Raasay and Rhona, with the glorious hills and mountains of Rosshire on the other.'[70]

The party then sailed for the Outer Hebrides, past the Shiant islands and into Stornoway, before turning east for Gairloch on the Scottish mainland.

This was probably the last happy voyage for the Currie family amongst their Skye dominions. Lady Currie died the following spring.[71] Sir Donald's children (and grandchildren) to whom Scalpay, Pabay, Guillamon and Longay now belonged, had less interest in their late father's Skye islands than in the Perthshire estates. These, after Lady Currie's death, were to go to his three grandsons, F.D. Mirrielees, Donald (Jervis) Molteno and Leslie Wisely.[72] Accordingly, in 1922 the four islands were offered for sale. So too was the 'handsome' yacht *Iolaire*, which in January was auctioned at London's Baltic Mercantile & Shipping Exchange.

During the Second World War, as in the First, the yacht was used for naval purposes, as an Admiralty headquarters operating in Scottish waters. This time however, there was no peacetime return to her former role. In August 1948, *The Scotsman* carried the doleful news that the *Iolaire* had been bought for the knock-down price of £4,500 by the British Iron and Steel Corporation and was to be taken from Southampton to Blyth in Northumberland and broken up for scrap.[73]

Sir Donald Currie was the first and last of the owners of Scalpay and Pabay who had a vessel as grand as the *Iolaire*. From 1925 onwards, much smaller boats served the two islands. Although, as we shall see, there was still some ostentation as far as the Scalpay launch was concerned, both islands came to depend on much more precarious craft, sometimes with near-fatal consequences.

Chapter 5

'Pappay will never pay': Sir Henry Bell and the *boidach*

On 1 July 1925, Scalpay estate's direct association with the Currie family had all but come to an end.

The new owner was Sir Henry Bell. Like his predecessor, he was an anglicised Scot. Both men were in shipping. Britain's shipping magnates appear to have had something of a penchant for island proprietorship.[1] As with Currie, Bell was a staunch Liberal. Although he never became an MP, he did stand as the Liberal candidate for the Inverness Burghs seat in 1895 – around the same time as his brother James became Lord Provost of Glasgow.[2] Even so, he was less prominent in politics than Currie and, greatly to his disappointment, had fewer connections amongst the nation's great and good. Perhaps this partly reflected the fact that while he had become wealthy, the gross value of his estate at the time of his death was £344,212, around one-seventh of that left by Currie.

As with Sir Donald, Bell was aware of some of the issues that dominated Highland politics and society. He was also astute. Like other prospective land purchasers in the Highlands, he was nervous about the implications of the pre-war crofting counties' legislation.[3]

Neither the Crofters Act nor the Crofters Commission, nor the Congested Districts Board set up in 1897, had been sufficient to silence the further demands there were for land reform.[4] By this was meant additional land. Such was the extent of land hunger that even during the First World War protests continued. Indeed, in 1917, land raiders occupied parts of the Macdonald estates near to Scalpay and Pabay – at Kyleakin and Sconser, where they planted potatoes and grazed cattle.[5] Promises made during the years of conflict that army recruits would be rewarded with land when they returned from the war heightened expectations, as did the legislation designed to implement this pledge, the Land Settlement (Scotland) Act of 1919.[6]

Progress, however, was slow. Hebridean protesters had no hesitation about demonstrating their dissatisfaction. On Skye alone there were another seven land raids between 1919 and 1922, including on Raasay, Rona and even Broadford, where the three male land raiders were all ex-soldiers.

News travelled fast and far: the Highland land question commanded UK-wide attention, and at the highest political levels.[7]

Consequently, before making his purchase not only did Sir Henry Bell send his sons to inspect Scalpay and the other three islands that comprised the estate, he wanted too to know more about what he had heard recently – 'that there is some trouble with the Crofters about Scalpay'.[8] His concern was misplaced. The Board of Agriculture for Scotland had moved slowly, but by 1924 an additional 51,000 acres on Skye had been purchased and added to the land already taken over by the Congested Districts Board.[9] Sir Henry could rest easy. Just about. It was only in 1932, when Scalpay was once more on the market, that it was revealed that there was 'an old woman' cottar living in a small thatched cottage 'of little or no value' who had occupancy rights under the terms of the Small Landholders (Scotland) Act of 1911. Upon her death, however, the land would revert to the proprietor.[10]

Excluding moveable items (including the stock and horses), Sir Henry paid £6,600 for his Skye property. The moveables cost a further £2,771. All in all, at today's values, just over half a million pounds. That he now owned an island – four in fact – fulfilled a long-held ambition.[11]

The estate, of course, included Pabay, which since 1909 had been let to a Colonel Lachlan Kenneth Macdonald DSO, of Tote, near Skeabost on Skye, for £50 a year. The island's benefits included up to 100 acres of ground deemed fit for cultivation, and the tree plantations put in by Sir Donald Currie, which afforded 'good shelter for stock'.

For Bell and his two sons (his wife had died before he came to Skye) what seems to have been of greater importance was the abundance of snipe and wild fowl on the island, and its reputation as a good place to shoot.[12] Sir Henry was a keen sportsman. He had long been in the habit of renting shooting lodges in Scotland for the season and had a special affection for Loch Kennard in Perthshire, where he and his invited guests had shot for several years prior to the First World War.

This, however, was not his sole motive for acquiring the Scalpay estate. Sir Henry was in his mid-seventies in 1925. As early as April 1928 he confessed that at his age he was unable to travel to Skye as often as he would have wished.[13] Additionally, the son who had most interest in shooting was in poor health. As a result, neither Scalpay nor Pabay was regularly shot.[14] For reasons that will become clearer in a moment, Bell had other plans for his islands in the north.

Even so, he did what he could to improve the deer stock on Scalpay, to the extent of introducing a stag – from England.

* * *

About Henry Bell's origins – he was born in 1848 – there is some ambiguity. Bell's version had it that his father had been a private country banker, living at Summerhill, Shandon, on Gare Loch in Argyll, until he became bankrupt in 1863. Census records suggest something more prosaic: that he was born into a fairly crowded household in Oswald Street, in Glasgow. His father, John Bell, seems to have been a fairly successful flesher, or butcher. Into this trade followed Henry Bell, who by 1871 was living in Cadder, near Bishopbriggs, just outside Glasgow, and employing ten men and four boys.[15] He remained here until 1878, when he moved to London.

There were two main phases in his business life. Possibly through his father, or other family members in the butcher trade, by the 1860s he was importing meat from Canada. It was by this means that he eventually became senior partner in the firm of Bell Brothers and M'Lelland of Glasgow and London, a shipping company which expanded to develop the trade in meat with Australia, New York and South America.

Indeed, in developing this global meat transportation business Henry Bell was something of a pioneer, although not always in the way he wanted some of his auditors to believe. He much preferred the designation of merchant or ship-owner and played down his background in the unfashionable trade of butchering.

Importing chilled meat from America was considerably cheaper than transporting live cattle. Ice-refrigerated ships were bringing increasingly substantial cargoes of beef across the Atlantic from the American Midwest from the early 1870s. Bell's involvement was largely through Timothy C. Eastman, of Chicago and New York, the city's leading cattle dealer and shipper, whom Henry Bell had sailed across to visit in July 1873. It was from New York that Eastman's meat, packed after being brought by refrigerated rail-cars from American ranches, was sent, ice-chilled, on Bell and M'Lelland ships, or, more likely at this stage, vessels they had leased, to Britain. The connection between the two families was strengthened in 1883 when Henry married Eastman's daughter Lizzie.[16]

Shipping meat by sea, however, depended on large quantities of ice. An on-board ice-making facility was what was wanted. A Frenchman, Charles Tellier, seems to have had some success in this direction in 1876 and 1877, using ammonia vapour. However, it is Bell who has been credited, with a John Bell (possibly a cousin), and Joseph James Coleman, a Fellow of the Royal Society of Edinburgh, assisted by the Belfast-born, Glasgow-based engineer Lord Kelvin, with the invention and patenting of an on-board coal-fired compression refrigeration machine. Exactly what part Henry Bell played in the invention of the dense-air machine that bears his name is not clear; it may be that he funded the necessary research and experimentation. Regardless, in 1880, Bell-Coleman refrigeration equipment was used for the first time to transport successfully a meat cargo from Australia and, after that, New Zealand.[17]

Before long the Bell-Coleman Mechanical Refrigeration Co. was supplying many of the leading shipping companies with their cooling equipment. The Bell brothers, in alliance with Eastman, subsequently sold much of the meat they imported to the urban working classes, through a national chain of 330 butcher's shops.

The second and even more lucrative phase of Sir Henry's business career had taken him to South America. His particular focus was Argentina.[18] Over the course of the second half of the nineteenth century and up until the First World War this former isolated outpost of the Spanish empire – now part of Britain's 'informal empire' – was transformed into one of the world's richest countries, the most prosperous in Latin America.[19]

With the state's blessing and support in the form of free land and tax concessions, Sir Henry played a substantial part in the country's infrastructural development, largely by pushing forward railway projects that connected Argentina's vast 'flat, featureless but hugely fertile' pampas lands, ripe for wheat growing, cattle ranching and sheep farming, with the port of Buenos Aires and, subsequently, markets in Europe.[20] Around 1900, some 5.3 million hectares were under commercial cultivation; by the time Bell purchased Scalpay estate, this had grown to well over 21 million hectares, and was still rising.

In 1899, following the death of the pioneering George Drabble, Bell became chairman of the River Plate Fresh Meat Company (founded by Drabble in 1882), which slaughtered, froze, shipped and then marketed Argentinian beef in Britain.[21]

In 1909, when he was made a baronet, Bell's local newspaper, the *Surrey Mirror*, took pleasure in reporting that 'Many millions of British capital' were invested in railway companies with which Bell was connected, 'and every penny of it is earning dividends'.[22] By this time over 10,000 miles of rail track were spread over Argentina, with many more to come – the so-called 'English octopus'. Bell himself acquired semi-heroic status for the part he played; around 1912 he embarked on a journey from Buenos Aires that took him over the Andes to Chile, during which he was fêted by the mayor and crowds of locals at each of the stations en route.[23] He even had a town named after him.

Bell's purchase of Scalpay estate was not his first land acquisition in the British Isles. As the nineteenth century drew to a close, he had bought a 400-acre estate at Mynthurst, Leigh, in Surrey. Despite his ongoing business interests in South America, including his own ranch, Estancia La Primavera, he took seriously his farm and gardens at Mynthurst. Drawing on his long-standing interest in the meat business, and perhaps upon what he had learned from his Argentinian experiences with cattle rearing (the Aberdeen Angus breed in which he specialised was introduced there in 1879), he became a 'stock-breeder of some distinction'.[24] Repeatedly, cattle from his herd won awards at stock shows at Smithfield, Redhill, Tunbridge Wells and elsewhere. He earned accolades too for his cattle feed – as for instance at a local agricultural show in 1929, when he won first prize for his mangolds and his swedes.[25]

*   *   *

When he acquired his Skye islands in July 1925, Sir Henry was beginning to wind down his overseas business commitments – although he never quite abandoned them. It was clear from the start, however, that he was prepared to devote some of his time, effort and money into improving his Skye estate.

No one had paid much attention to the upkeep of Scalpay since Currie's death some sixteen years earlier, when his trustees had taken over. Within weeks of purchasing the estate, Bell employed a firm of architects from Inverness, and tasked them with upgrading Scalpay House. This included adding to the number of bathrooms, improving the accommodation for visitors' 'manservants', installing a hot-water boiler and constructing a plant to generate electric light. Internally, he instigated the buying of new blinds to replace those already in the house, which were 'practically all down'. Bookcases too were fitted into some of the rooms. For the farm workers, he ordered that a water closet be provided in the farm steading, to replace the foul-smelling dry closet that they had used hitherto.[26]

Sir Henry had little time for delays and excuses, notwithstanding one of his Inverness architect's claims that it was hard to persuade contractors to tender for work 'in a place like Scalpay'. By this he meant an island. And, when workers did come they were not easily managed, as 'they are not under my eye'.[27] Without supervision *in situ*, island employees were not always the most diligent, while collectively they could even become dysfunctional. It was a lesson learned by Sir Henry Bell the hard way.

In spite of his intention of being in Buenos Aires for the first part of 1926, early in December 1925 he sent word to George Mackay Fraser, the Portree solicitor who managed the estate for him, that on his return to Southampton the following June, he hoped 'to hear from you that the work is completed at the house'.

He could not have predicted that the General Strike would bring the country to a halt for ten days in May 1926. Its impact was felt even on Scalpay. The various components required for the electrical work, Mr Ballantyne the architect reported on 11 May (two days before the strike ended), were 'somewhere on the railways', rather than waiting at Kyle, as planned. Sir Henry's personal secretary in London, Edward Tappenden, sympathised, remarking that 'It only remains for the Miners to become more reasonable', and industrial peace would break out. Yet a few days later, on 28 May, he wrote to Fraser expressing his hope that 'all the alterations are nearing completion'.[28] Tappenden no doubt was feeling the pressure of his employer's impending return from Argentina.

On Scalpay, mild panic was setting in. Christina MacPhee, in Scalpay House, wrote anxiously to Fraser that she feared 'the house will never be ready' for Sir Henry's July visit as the painters were unable to finish a single room owing to a shortage of materials. To her credit Mrs MacPhee kept at it, and only days before her master's arrival was in Inverness purchasing furniture and materials in accordance with his instructions: for her diligence, according to Ballantyne, 'she deserves well of her employer on all counts'. Delays also beset the new dog kennels, the railings required being held up by short-time working in the foundries, while the railway companies were 'only handling such goods to suit their convenience so that the prospect of a quick delivery is rather gloomy'.[29]

Sir Henry's visit, however, went well. In eighteen months, he had spent just over £4,732 (more than £200,000 today) on upgrading the house and farm buildings, and adding extensions.[30] This expenditure, it was observed later, 'was largely on the luxury scale and for his own personal convenience'. Scalpay House had not only been refreshed; it now met the demanding expectations of its twentieth-century owner.

However, with less in the way of surplus funds to dispose of, Bell made no attempt to match his predecessor in the boating stakes. Not for him anything as ostentatious as the *Iolaire*, but instead a smaller private launch. Indeed, the relative modesty of his seafaring ambitions is to be seen in 1927, after one of Bell's sons had pronounced the present launch to be less than seaworthy. 'Captain Shaw' had found a replacement but, wrote Bell, 'what he has got is more of a boat for spending a night or two at sea than for the short trips we want'.[31]

Nevertheless, Sir Henry clearly had a taste for the good life. A locked butler's cupboard discovered after his death contained a generous quantity of wines, port, beers and spirits. The most numerous bottles (seventy-four) were of champagne, including eighteen from the principal French producer, Champagne Pol Roger, founded in 1849. The beneficiary was not Scalpay's new proprietor, who was altogether more frugal in his tastes, but John Campbell of the Broadford Hotel who was able to acquire the entire cellar for £23.

*   *   *

Having begun to make significant progress on Scalpay, Bell turned his attention to Pabay. His priority was the buildings. Scalpay's, he was pleased to note in September 1926, were already 'first-rate'. When the electric light was put in the dairy, gunroom, stable and byre, he was confident they would be 'as perfect as they could be made'.

Although he had more modest ambitions for Pabay, Bell did want to improve things. Having been out there during the summer of 1926 and examined the small dwelling house as well as the farm steading and indeed the ground itself, he was clear about what was required.[32] Despite being assured when he had bought Pabay that the cottage and steading were 'in good order', Sir Henry was not impressed with what he saw. His particular concern was rotten wood on the slatted barn doors and elsewhere, concealed under the paint. The Pabay buildings were to be put in the 'same good shape as those on Scalpay now are'.[33] The cathedral-like barn doors he ordered to be repaired over the winter of 1926–7, by Alexander Robertson, a carpenter from Broadford who lived on Scalpay during the week.

This was the last time work of this nature was done prior to Len and Margaret Whatley's arrival in 1949. (In fact, the 'great barn doors' had been one of the features that Margaret remembered from her first trip to the island.) Following a plea from Donald Mackinnon, one of Sir Henry's two employees on Pabay, about the dangers of using a more or less vertical step ladder to reach the upper rooms of the sole house on the island (and having seen a similar replacement in the keeper's cottage on Scalpay), Robertson fitted a permanent narrow staircase – the one that the Whatleys would use when they arrived in 1950. Pine linings were added, the norm for the homes of the relatively humble. Scalpay House was extensively panelled in oak.

Refurbishing the buildings on Pabay was fairly straightforward. Very different was the challenge of making the island pay. At first this seemed not to be a problem. We know that when Sir Henry Bell bought his Skye estate, Pabay was leased to a Colonel Macdonald, who had become something of a local hero during the Boer War, and had raised a Skye squadron for the Lovat Scouts. In fact, Macdonald had shown some interest in buying the island, as did a friend of his, Frank Caldwell, who was 'experimenting in agricultural matters at Morar', and 'desirous of getting an Island'.[34] Bell, however, was not interested in selling.

Even so, Macdonald stayed on. He was someone else who was optimistic about Pabay's prospects. He was convinced that Pabay was 'a superb place for prize cattle and horses'. But as regards the last-named, not, as might have been expected, the garrons or smaller hardy horses bred for the agricultural conditions of the Scottish Highlands and Islands. In fact, Macdonald was to have considerable success in the later 1920s as a breeder of Highland ponies, winning several championships.[35] Macdonald's intention, however, was nothing less than to breed racehorses. Whether he

would take a longer lease than the yearly arrangement he had
currently (Bell wanted him to sign up for five years), was dependent on the performances of a small number of horses he may
already have reared on Pabay, and then shipped out to take part in
fashionable race meetings in India – in the 1920s still part of the
British Empire, the Raj.

Hardly surprisingly, the venture failed. Macdonald informed
Fraser in April 1927 that while his horses were 'strong, fast and
splendid jumpers', they were poor racers.[36] After the long journey
by sea and through the Suez Canal they wouldn't eat. Having 'not
yet sufficiently proved themselves', Macdonald informed Fraser
that he was surrendering his lease.

Macdonald's dream over, responsibility for managing Pabay
reverted to the estate, and the farm manager on Scalpay, Donald
Robertson. He had recently succeded Alexander Macrae, a father
of four young children, who had accidentally shot himself on
Guillamon in February 1926 while out setting an otter trap.[37] On
Pabay itself, what work required to be done would be carried out
by Angus Mackinnon – a farm worker and shepherd who, following his parents' arrival from Ramasaig around 1879, had been on
Pabay virtually all of his life, along with his brother, Donald. Under
the terms of Macdonald's lease from Sir Donald Currie's trustees,
they could only be removed with their written consent.

And it was as a sheep farm that all those concerned with the
island believed that it could prosper. Keen to balance his islands'
accounts, in 1928 Sir Henry urged Robertson to increase the
numbers of sheep on both 'Pappay' and Scalpay.[38] He was not to
know that the price of mutton and wool would fall so catastrophi-
cally three years later. In 1930 best quality animals could command
over 91 shillings per head; by 1932 this had fallen by two-thirds, to
less than 30 shillings. Turning Pabay into a viable agricultural enterprise was proving harder than anyone had anticipated.

Why? For one thing, despite its lush appearance as seen from
the Breakish or Broadford shore, or even from Scalpay, much of
Pabay's land was waterlogged.

For sheep, with small hooves that easily sank into muddy
ground, this was bad news. Ewes were unable to lie down, and the

flock was at risk of contracting liver fluke. Nor was such an environment conducive to good grass growing – rushes were what flourished – thereby limiting the number of animals that could be kept.

Drains had been cut – over a century earlier, in accordance with the advice given to Lord Macdonald by John Blackadder.[39] But for the main drains to have any utility, they had to be deep, wide – and well maintained, as Blackadder had instructed. Alex Macinnes from Drumfearn in Sleat spent a fortnight working on them in the autumn of 1882.[40] Some clearance work was also carried out during Sir Donald Currie's time, but not enough.

Deep drains, however – cleaned out or otherwise – were also death traps for sheep (and cattle), if they were unfenced. And while some fencing had been put in alongside some of Pabay's smaller drains, the main drain was open – and sheep were being drowned in it. If fenced, Col Macdonald had been confident the island could then support 150 or even 200 ewes, and at least break even financially.

Fenced or not, for Pabay to thrive as a sheep farm, 'the island would require complete new drainage', Fraser wrote to Sir Henry Bell's London secretary. Donald Robertson was of a similar mind. Until it was 'drained proper', he opined, 'Pappay will never pay' or be 'right for sheep especially in the winter'.[41] Many of the current ditches were too level: 'to get a fall on them to let the water run would be a very big matter and mean very considerable outlay'. The main ditch was even more challenging, being so broad, and 'full of long grass'. In its flat central portion, it was simply gathering water.

Sir Henry listened. What he proposed was to leave the main drain unfenced and concentrate instead on improving the island's grassland by making more effective those drains that were already in place. To carry out this work he identified two men on Pabay he was already paying: the Mackinnon brothers, at £78 per annum each, plus National Insurance payments. Bell felt he had a right to ask for more from the pair, having kept them on the payroll partly as an act of kindness, 'as the one stated he could not launch and draw up a boat alone'.[42]

Sending instructions from London or Scalpay House was easy enough. George Fraser, usually the intermediary who passed on Sir Henry's orders to Donald Robertson, had a more difficult task. Getting the Mackinnons on Pabay to spend more time on the ditches was even harder.

It was around this time that Sir Henry had become more concerned than formerly about the cost of running the estate, and the fact that it was actually losing money. The shortfall in income over expenditure in 1927 was bad enough – over £653. But on seeing the accounts for 1928 Sir Henry demanded that Fraser provide an explanation: the loss this time was £1,288.[43] Bell couldn't see 'why Scalpay and Pabbay should not at least pay for their own upkeep'.[44] His suspicion was that Donald Robertson, the farm manager for his two main islands, was failing in his duties. He had a point.

It was one of Sir Henry Bell's sons who first drew attention to Robertson's darker side – or what was alleged to have been such. The son in question, Major Henry James Bell, wrote to George Fraser in September 1928 saying that 'I don't much like the atmosphere at Scalpay at the moment'; he had noticed that Robertson 'has changed much in looks since last year'. He was now 'purple in the face' and smelled of drink.[45]

In fact, he wrote, other Scalpay employees thought Robertson was a 'habitual drunkard'.

Robertson was accused too of being away from the island when the Bells were gone, of having a high-handed attitude to the use of the estate launch, and of purloining wood from Scalpay as well as taking 'boatloads' of corn to Breakish, either for his own use or that of friends. He was known too to have made a couple of appearances in Portree's police court, albeit on minor charges. Indeed, two years earlier, Robertson had been accused of fighting with the foreman of the building contractors working on Scalpay House.[46] On the other hand, he evidently enjoyed the company of the painters employed at the time. Three of them had accompanied Robertson on a late-night fishing expedition in the estate launch, with a splash net, the use of which for such a purpose was queried by the new gamekeeper, Angus McLeod. Robertson's actions, in

McLeod's opinion, showed a 'want of tact and principle on the part of Sir Henry's representative here'. Once off Scalpay he went on, the painters would spread the word about having been out poaching, and sooner or later 'give the place a bad name'.[47]

Bell's stance was unambiguous: if Robertson was guilty as charged, Fraser should dismiss him. Fraser, however, urged caution. There may have been something in the complaints against the manager, he conceded. But in response to the accusation of his heavy drinking, Robertson had admitted only to taking an occasional 'refreshment'. And in this, Robertson was far from alone. As recently as November 1925, John MacPhee, a workman on Scalpay, 'appeared peculiar', according to Ballantyne, the Inverness architect, and had failed to appear in Broadford on one occasion, to take him across to Scalpay. Again, drink was suspected as the reason.

More pertinent, Fraser wrote to Major Bell, in his experience, in 'a small place like Scalpay, which is cut off from the rest of the world more or less … local prejudice and differences do arise'. Along with a generally positive testimonial he provided for Angus McLeod a few years later, Fraser reiterated his view about the internecine struggles that could mar working relations on an island, although he remarked too that gamekeepers could be particularly difficult. Perhaps, he speculated, this was because they were 'in more personal contact with the Proprietor than farm servants'. In McLeod's case, he had 'presumed upon this a little'.[48]

But there many worse offenders than McLeod. Amongst the several bundles of papers relating to Scalpay estate held in Portree's archive centre there is one labelled 'Personal Papers, October 1928 – April 1930'. It comprises entirely letters and notes containing accusations and denials of and explanations for untoward behaviour, hand-written by Sir Henry's Scalpay employees. Little surprise then that Sir Henry, who read a great deal of this kind of correspondence, confided in a letter to Fraser that, 'It seems we have got a queer crowd at Scalpay.' It was virtually impossible to judge the rights and wrongs of the various disputes: those concerned, he observed 'just tell whatever story suits themselves best, and many of these stories I think are made up'. It is hard to disagree.

Perhaps, then, Bell's readiness to dispense with Robertson's services may have been the wrong call.

There were benefits in keeping on a man like Robertson. For Fraser – who spent most of his time in Portree, and who was directly answerable to the owners of the estates he factored – the continued employment of a man with local knowledge and familiarity with the people in the townships around could be invaluable. Thus, for example, as the shooting season for 1932 approached, word went out that a ghillie was wanted. Robertson's assessments of the applicants were to the point. Matheson of Breakish, he advised Fraser, he would not approve as he was a bad timekeeper, so much so that his previous employer wouldn't have him back. Another man, from Luib, had apparently 'run away sailing'. But his strongest objection was to Donald Macinnes of Strollamus. Robertson advised Fraser that he was 'be very much against giving him [Macinnes] the job he is one of the poachers there and it would give a chance to know the lay of the Deer'. What truth there was in this or any of the other allegations we cannot know, or how far Robertson's views were based on personal animus. What we can be sure about however is that none of the men Robertson had reservations about got the job. And scrawled in large blue letters in Fraser's hand on Macinnes's application were the words 'No chance'.[49]

This instance alerts us to another problem for island proprietors: security. The main concern here was sheep stealing. In March 1929, for example, Scalpay's gamekeeper, Angus McLeod, was asked to keep his eyes peeled when doing his rounds on the island. He was to look for 'any suspicious boats'. Fraser had reason to believe that sheep farms facing the mainland were especially vulnerable to the depredations of sheep stealers whose boats came 'more or less in the dark or the gloaming'.[50]

Intrusions of this kind were not new.

In the 1880s Angus McSwan on Pabay had complained to the factor, Alexander Macdonald, that Hugh and John Ross, from Waterloo – across from Pabay – had been over-cutting rushes and damaging the grass. Despite his entreaties, they refused to stop.[51]

Soon after taking up his post as gamekeeper, Angus McLeod's attention was drawn to a boat apparently making its way to

Longay but detouring around Pabay. In Broadford by the time the boat returned, he identified the two men concerned, namely the barman and a cattleman from Broadford Hotel. In the boat they had three sheep and some rabbits, which had evidently been shot. McLeod couldn't be sure but had reason to believe the rabbits had been killed illicitly on Longay, their landing justified as the offenders had been keeping some sheep there. This, McLeod thought, was not a good policy, as it would encourage further poaching.[52]

In fact, little escaped McLeod's notice. In March 1931 he had watched through his telescope as Murdo MacLeod from Black Park in Broadford, along with another two men he was only able to identify later, landed on the south side of Guillamon Island. They then proceeded to set fire to the heather. By the time the gamekeeper in Scalpay launch could be got there, all that were left were charred, smoking remains.[53] Malicious damage, the reason for which couldn't be established.

* * *

Farming on Scalpay and Pabay – as on small islands generally – presented unique challenges, mainly to do with their location and consequent running expenses.

Scalpay was not easy to access and required its owner or tenant to maintain a motorboat, thereby adding to the cost of transportation of virtually anything to and from the island. There was the expense of boarding employees, and the difficulty of finding and then paying for additional labour when required. Recruiting suitable workpeople who were prepared to live on the island – even during the week, separated from family, friends and community – was far from easy or straightforward.

Neither was what looked like the obvious solution: the employment of married men – but not if they also had school-age children. Under the terms of the Education (Scotland) Act of 1872, educational provision had to be made if the children concerned were more than three miles from the nearest school – as they would be on Scalpay.

Such a case arose in 1928 when Fraser had had to employ Lachlan Macinnes from Breakish, the father of four children, aged five, seven, nine and eleven respectively. Although most of the costs of running what were called Side Schools on an island such as Scalpay were borne by the education authority, the complications associated with this requirement inclined George Fraser – who was expected to initiate the call for such special provision – to employ those unencumbered by young families. Indeed, he had tried unsuccessfully to hire a childless shepherd. This strategy was the preference too of Inverness's Director of Education, Murdo Morrison, who if he were to re-establish a Side School on Scalpay (which would be under the superintendence of nearby Dunan Primary School), would have to apply for permission from the Scottish Education Department in Whitehall. Lachlan Macinnes, however, held firm, insisting that it was 'quite out of the question' for his children to attend Dunan school on mainland Skye.

Morrison therefore had no choice but to accept Macinnes's case, but even so thanked Fraser for his efforts in trying to find an unmarried man 'for such an outlandish [and costly] post like this'. With attitudes of this nature held by those in positions of influence, it is little wonder that island dwellers were vanishing – along with the Gaelic tongue that the schools system in the Highlands and Islands was actively discouraging in favour of English.[54]

But there were other hidden costs for those who were unfamiliar with island economics. For instance, when embarking on a 14-acre tree-planting project in 1929, Sir Henry expressed surprise that the estimated expenditure would be so high. The island 'premium' was in the region of 30 per cent, according to Major Frank Scott of the Forestry Commission in Inverness, who was advising Bell on what trees to plant.[55]

When the charges associated with maintaining Scalpay House and gardens were included, it was simply impossible to run Scalpay estate at anything else than a loss. The point was driven home when the property first came on the market after Sir Henry's death in 1931. There was little immediate interest. This, in the opinion of the assessor, was due first to the initial effects of the Great Depression that had followed the Wall Street collapse of October

1929, but more to the 'simple fact ... that Scalpay is a pure luxury ... and can scarcely be made economic'. George Fraser concurred: it was an economic proposition that 'could only be dealt with by a wealthy man who might take a fancy to the place'.[56]

Scalpay farm accounts for the year ending December 1931 showed a massive loss: £1,532 from a turnover of £3,632.

And Pabay was not helping. By the late summer of 1929, both Sir Henry and Fraser had reached a new level of exasperation about the slow pace of progress there. Not even a quarter of the small drains had been finished. In July Fraser was summoned by Sir Henry to Scalpay to meet with him to discuss the matter, and then directed to cross to Pabay to find out what was happening.

Under pressure to get things moving, in August Fraser wrote an unusually sharply worded letter to Robertson. There was no reason whatsoever that the Mackinnons should not 'at once clear all the small drains and ditches in the Island'. He went on to express his disappointment that 'they have not done more of this already'. There was 'no work on the Island as regards sheep etc to take up the whole time of one of them, much less two ... you must immediately see that they go on with these small drains'.[57] Unusually, Fraser followed this up by writing directly to the Mackinnons along similar lines.

They had their excuses though. Lambing was one of them, along with what they called their 'spring work'. Bad weather had been a further cause for delay, or so they said.

But becoming apparent even to the Mackinnons (who were now losing sheep too) was that something had to be done about the main drain, including putting up fences along its length. Consequently, in 1930, work was begun on a planned 4,000 yards of fencing. To bridge the main drain and the other larger ditches, it was proposed that second-hand railway sleepers were used.

Not unusually, nothing happened fast. Some fencing was put in place, but the ditch-clearing efforts more or less came to a halt. The Mackinnons' efforts would have to be supplemented by contract labour – but as Fraser reported to Sir Henry in September, the two men he had approached 'were both very shy to tackle it'.

By this time, however, Sir Henry, now over eighty years old, was tired and losing interest. He was within the last six months of his life (which ended when he collapsed and died, owing to heart fail-ure, on a train journey from Redhill to London in March 1931). He asked his son, Major Bell, to liaise with Fraser about what should be done. Having investigated first-hand, and perhaps with an eye on his inheritance, Bell thought that any sizeable capital expenditure would be likely to generate only a 'slightly greater revenue'. Indeed, he was against any further drainage operations on Pabay's east side, as this 'might ruin the only thing . . . the island can be really good for and that is snipe shooting'. Even though sheep numbers had increased – there were over ninety in October 1931 – the financial situation showed no sign of improvement. By the end of the year prices had collapsed to 40 per cent below their previous level. The next year was even worse.[58] In short, as far as Pabay was concerned, 'it was better to do nothing'.

In the sale particulars issued in 1931 reference was made to cultivation on Pabay in the past, but it was conceded that 'now no part of the island is under the plough'. Mossy grazing and marsh-land were the island's predominant features. Pabay's chief value, 'was as a sporting proposition', owing to the numerous snipe to be found there.[59] As regards land utilisation, not much was to change up until the time Len Whatley took over.

George Fraser had had no argument with Major Bell's decision to sell up, pointing out that it 'had cost your father round about £2,000 a year, sometimes more sometimes less'.[60] Small wonder then that when the novelist and Scottish nationalist Compton Mackenzie was approached with a view to buying Scalpay estate his response was firmly negative: 'I fear,' he replied, 'they [Scalpay and Pabay] will be beyond my means'. Prudence in this instance outweighed Mackenzie's long-standing love of islands, especially those of the Hebrides.[61]

* * *

Yet there were others who were interested, even if a few enquirers quickly took cold feet on discovering – apparently with genuine surprise – that an island estate entailed the very practical matter of making a sea crossing to get there.[62]

Meanwhile, Major Bell set himself the task of stemming the outflow of cash. On Scalpay, staff numbers were cut, with only Robertson, Alex Grant the shepherd, two gardeners and Mrs Robertson as caretaker of Scalpay House being retained.

He was ruthless too about reducing his own expenditure. Scalpay was still in the process of being sold in the late summer of 1932, so there was the opportunity for a last visit. This, he announced to Fraser would be 'the cheapest holiday I am likely to get anywhere'. Just why soon became clear. To staff Scalpay House, he would bring his own servants. Fraser was to engage only a temporary gamekeeper and a ghillie.

It may have been Major Bell's final shooting season on Skye, but at least he had some success, bagging plentiful grouse and stags on Scalpay, as well as some snipe on Pabay.[63]

Still living on Pabay were the Mackinnon brothers, known locally as *boidach*, the old – or small – men, a reference to their short stature. Understandably, they were fearful about their future. Although the older brother, Angus, had been born at Glendale, the two men had never lived anywhere else. But as part of Bell's cost-cutting measures, they had been served with notice that their employment would cease at Martinmas 1931.

Their apprehensions are understandable. Economic conditions in the Highlands in general and Skye in particular during the 1920s and 1930s were bleak. Many of those who had left to find work in the industries of the Lowlands were now redundant and had been driven back to their homelands, swelling the numbers of the unemployed and putting further pressure on what were barely sustainable crofter household economies.[64] Desperate, as they had 'no other place to go to', the Mackinnons appealed to both Fraser and Sir Henry Bell's London-based secretary.

Their preference was for a yearly tenancy agreement, for which they could raise £30 or £40 (the island's valuation at the time was £50 per annum). Failing this, however, they asked, could they stay in the house on Pabay for the winter of 1931–2, until 'they had used up the crops which they had planted for their stock including potatoes and also the peats they had cut'.[65]

For his part, Fraser had to ensure that any tenancy agreement with the Mackinnons was short, so as not to deter any prospective purchaser. He was conscious that the brothers could have appealed to the Scottish Land Court under the terms of the 1911 Small Landholders Act – which, if successful, would have given them lifelong tenancy. Mercifully (as far as Major Bell and Fraser were concerned) they showed no sign of taking up this option and, much relieved, Fraser granted them a three-month stay of execution, with the possibility of an extension depending on a new owner's wishes. As part of the arrangement they also bought the sheep that they had formerly been employed by Sir Henry Bell to husband, at market value.

Potentially this was a good deal for the brothers. With sheep prices at rock bottom levels, they could look forward to the prospect of substantial gain if the market recovered.

Notwithstanding the losses that the estate had incurred, and the problems the two main islands had presented, the valuer appointed by Sir Henry's solicitors – Mr John S. Paterson from Inverness – was favourably impressed. This was in spite of visiting both Scalpay and Pabay in rough, windy, wet weather early in July 1932. Scalpay, he wrote to Fraser, was 'a better place than I expected to see'. The sheep he thought 'thriving well', and the sport good (even if in recent seasons little had been shot). The brown trout in the island's lochs were a decent size and in addition there was sea fishing. Seldom had he seen such a well-furnished mansion house, which was 'in excellent order'. In prime condition too was the walled garden with roses, flowers and fruit growing in abundance. Nearby was a vegetable garden. A purchaser, Paterson was convinced, could take over without any additional expense. Yes, there was the 'impossibility of direct approach by motor car', but compensating for this was 'the undoubted advantages of Yacht Anchorage', for which nearby Guillamon offered shelter.

Pabay too was 'a better proposition' than he had anticipated, certainly for grazing, but also, 'if necessary, or expedient, from a tillage point of view'. Fraser was not best pleased with what he considered to have been an ill-informed verdict and, partly as a counter, scribbled on Paterson's report, 'Very difficult of access'.[66]

Paterson's valuation of the estate in its entirety was in the region of £5,000.

Paterson's positive assessments were something of a disappointment, as Fraser had appointed him in part because in his former employment with the Department of Agriculture he had 'always valued pretty low'.[67] However, there was little argument as, much to the chagrin of Fraser and others involved in the sale of the estate, James Mackenzie, the district valuer, also rated the property highly – at £7,500. 'Absurdly high' was Major Bell's reaction to this valuation, aware that the higher the price the greater would be the burden of death duties, if indeed a purchaser could be found. Consequently, steps were taken to sell the estate at auction, in Glasgow in August 1932, with an attractively low up-set price of £3,000.

Given the economic circumstances of the time, and the political uncertainties of the national government under the premiership of Labour's Ramsay Macdonald, after a slow start the volume of interest in the Scalpay estate comes as something of a surprise.

Yet, as we saw in an earlier chapter, islands had by this time acquired a certain lure that for those who could afford one transcended considerations of market value.

Advertisements for the sale were published in the most likely Scottish newspapers, as well as *The Times* and *Country Life*.

At least one enquirer was from Wales, although most gave English addresses. There was even one from Lt-Colonel Campbell of the 5th Battalion, the 2nd Punjab Regiment – at first sight incongruous, but actually there were many precedents for what might have become another India–Skye connection. Many Skye men had and still served in the British army in India. Furthermore, in the past several Skye families who had made fortunes in India had returned to and purchased property on the island.[68] Correspondents with Fraser, who dealt with enquiries by letter and in person, ranged from the very well-heeled to those more moderately well off, such as L.H. Smith, from Wellington in Surrey, who asked if the smaller islands might be sold separately; failing that, he would 'be glad to hear of a single, small, reasonably accessible island for sale or long lease'.[69]

In the end, the offer accepted was that from a Captain Gerald D.E. Muntz, of Umberslade Hall in Tamworth-in-Arden, near Solihull, Warwickshire. The Hall was a seventeenth-century mansion at the heart of a sizeable estate that had been in the family's hands from the middle of the nineteenth century. Muntz, whose father had been a Birmingham ironmaster, had served in the Royal Naval Brigade during the First World War, and in 1928 had been Warwickshire's high sheriff. The price he paid was £5,500 – less than the estate had cost Sir Henry Bell, but a little more than Paterson's estimate. Muntz, who had been 'looking for a small place up on the West Coast', had made various enquiries about what was on offer – Scalpay in particular. But all he had seen before making his bid were tracings and photographs. On 26 August, he arrived by train at Mallaig, was met in Broadford by George Fraser and then taken across to Scalpay by launch to set foot for the first time on his new acquisition. He liked what he saw, having been escorted by Major Bell who was able to show him what it had to offer in terms of shooting and fishing.[70]

Bell's going wasn't without regrets. 'It is tragic,' he wrote in one of his last letters to George Fraser, 'that I have to let Scalpay go.' But, he continued, 'it would have been madness for me to attempt otherwise'. Helping to salve any pain he felt about his impending loss was that he had got what he considered to have been an 'excellent' price.[71]

Muntz too was happy. So much so that almost immediately after his purchase he turned down an offer of up to £10,000 from Colonel Gerard F.T. Leather, the owner of Middleton Hall in Northumberland, who had been unaware the auction was taking place. His purchase, Muntz declared, had not been for speculative purposes; it was for 'personal occupation'.

Unfortunately there is little information about Captain Muntz's Skye venture.

What can be said is that his farming interests were largely confined to Warwickshire. Unlike the larger island of Eigg, one of the Small Isles to the south of Skye, neither Scalpay nor Pabay during the 1930s would benefit from the kind of investment – and commitment to farming and estate improvement – that Lord

Walter and Lady Runciman devoted to that island. He did, however, continue to cultivate the gardens. Within a year of his arrival, using the same gardeners – William and Donald Gunn – he had won first prize for cut flowers from Scalpay at Inverness's Highland Horticultural Show. This was in the summer of 1933.

But it was evident that his main interest was in hunting. Not content with what Scalpay and Pabay had to offer, he was also known to take Strollamus shootings for the season.[72] He carried on in this vein right up to and after the outbreak of war with Germany in 1939. Indeed, two excellently preserved mounted stag heads in the lobby of Scalpay House today – along with dates – offer vivid testimony that he carried on shooting well into the war.[73] For at least part of the duration of the conflict other members of his family were resident there too. In October 1941 Mrs Muntz advertised the post of governess on Scalpay, for her two children, aged six and seven.[74]

* * *

The 1930s represent a fallow period in Pabay's history. Angus and Donald Mackinnon continued as tenants. Their income came mainly from sheep – the numbers of which grew (presumably in response to the rise in sheep prices that had happened since 1931), so that in the early 1940s they had some 130 black-faced ewes and 36 ewe hogs. They also had three milk cows, two stirks and a black bull. Arable farming they kept to a minimum, by growing some 'corn' (possibly oats) and potatoes for their own consumption.

In the spring of 1943 things took a dramatic turn. An opportunity arose for Angus Mackinnon to take over from Donald Robertson, who had intimated his intention of leaving Scalpay. Angus was keen to make the change, for even though he was sixty-four years old, he knew Scalpay well.

The interpersonal dynamics on Pabay had also altered somewhat: relatively late in life, at the age of sixty-one, Angus had married Mary MacInnes from Sandbank, in Broadford.[75] Two brothers might have been good company for each other, but with Angus now having a wife, things may have become difficult.

The post on Scalpay would be something of a test for him, as he had neither experience of operating electric plant, nor of silos. On the other hand, he could manage a launch and he was also knowledgeable about sheep and, to a lesser extent, cattle, and had a certain competence at bookkeeping. His new wife was an additional asset, as she was capable of doing dairy work, housekeeping and even catering for a man or men to be boarded on Scalpay.

There was a major hitch though, if Angus were to leave Pabay. His unmarried brother Donald wouldn't stay on the island alone. And if Donald left, the sheep would have to go too – otherwise 'a man would require to be resident on the Island on account of the ditches and drains'. Pabay's age-old problem.

With the war raging, and most young men (below the age of forty) being away on active service, labour on Skye was in short supply. Such were Pabay's economic circumstances that to pay someone to assist Donald Mackinnon would be unaffordable. The best solution, George Fraser reluctantly informed Captain Muntz, who had now returned to Warwickshire, was to appoint Angus Mackinnon as farm manager on Scalpay and allow him to take a couple of his milk cows, employ Donald Mackinnon as a farm hand on Scalpay, and move the sheep across too.[76]

Fraser was acutely aware of the consequences. Not only, under the terms of the Mackinnons' lease, would Muntz would have to buy Pabay's sheep, but in addition, it was highly unlikely that anyone else would be persuaded to go to Pabay. The result, Fraser feared, would be dereliction. The departure of Pabay-born Donald Mackinnon severed the island's final link on anything like a permanent basis with Skye's indigenous population.

And with the death of Captain Muntz in 1947, the future was at best uncertain.

Chapter 6

'There are no communists in our midst': revolution and the road to Skye

In 1951 the Rev. Murdo Macleod MacSween completed what was a short description of his Strath parish for the Inverness volume of *The Third Statistical Account of Scotland*. As the name implies, there had been two previous 'statistical' accounts of Strath. These were written in 1795 and 1845 respectively.

The statistical accounts are compendiums of mainly factual information on matters such as population, the local economy, agriculture, employment, and flora and fauna. Their originator, Sir John Sinclair of Ulbster, a product of Scotland's Enlightenment – with its emphasis on rational enquiry – envisaged them as objective records. However, written in the main by individual clergymen, on some matters they necessarily reflect their writers' own interests – and prejudices.

Although Murdo MacSween had only been the Church of Scotland's minister of Strath since 1944 – when he had been translated from the island of Lewis – he was content with the moral condition of the people he felt he was responsible for. The Sabbath continued to be observed as a day of rest, not 'because of any hard and fast puritanical bigotry' but rather as 'an elixir to soul and body'. Weddings and funerals too, he was convinced, were less drunken affairs than in the past.

There was, though, a falling-away from the Church. This he attributed to the 'general materialist outlook', and 'a few incomers to the parish who show little interest'.

But, he was keen to emphasise, 'As far as is known, there are no communists in our midst'.[1]

Little did MacSween know that the full name of the new owner of Pabay – whom he refers to in his text simply as 'Mr Whatley' – was Arthur *Lenin* Whatley. MacSween's mention was brief. 'Mr Whatley' was listed as one of thirteen 'landowners' in Strath, compared to the two who had held the entire parish a century earlier.

Len, as he was commonly known, had been born in September 1919. His first name, Arthur, was uncontroversial, and was taken from his father's brother, who had been killed at the Battle of Ypres in October 1914. However, like many on the political left in Britain in the heady aftermath of the Russian Revolution two years earlier, Len's parents, convinced that the new dawn of social equality had arrived, had named their second son after the Bolshevik leader Vladimir Ilyich Ulyanov, otherwise known as Lenin.

Len, however, was no communist, although throughout his adult life he was left-leaning, a consistent Labour voter. If anything, it was Margaret who was the more politically minded of the two. Her favourite reading included the autobiographies and biographies of earlier generations of Labour politicians. Nor was she afraid to speak her mind. Much later, during the General Election of 1966, she seized the opportunity of a chance meeting in Breakish with the Tory candidate David Wathen to take him to task over his party's position on the Common Market, and the Government's record on Highland development.[2] Len's preference was for *The Farmer's Weekly* and *The Artist*. Slightly shy, and with a gentle disposition, he was also less forthright, in public at least. But he was observant and had a wry and understated sense of humour that could mask what otherwise would have been telling rebuke.

Nevertheless, not long after Len's and Margaret's arrival on Pabay, other members of what the Rev. MacSween might have thought of as a dangerously different kind of family were tempted to settle in Skye.

*   *   *

Looming large was Margaret's father, Len's father-in-law, Henry Hilditch. Hilditch shunned the Communist Party, but he was an enthusiastic reader of the democratic socialist publication *Tribune*, and the *New Statesman*, the origins of which lay in the Fabian

Society. Tall, on the stout side but robust and energetic, he had no qualms about flying his political colours.

There was much about 'Grandpa' Hilditch, as most family members knew him, that MacSween would have admired. Born in April 1881 in Sandbach, Cheshire, he had been a volunteer service-man at the start of the First World War, when he joined the machine-gun corps of the Argyll and Sutherland Highlanders. Rising to the rank of captain but badly injured in action, he saw out the last two years of the conflict at home.

Henry Hilditch's experiences on the battlefield were gruesome, the stuff of a future lifetime's nightmares, and personally transfor-mational. He had lost a close friend – Bobby. He had witnessed appalling human suffering, both of men who had stood by, fought and slept at his side, and the many more of those whom he knew only as fellow soldiers. He had been appalled at the slaughter of hundreds of South African soldiers at Delville Wood during the interminable Battle of the Somme in the summer and autumn of 1916. For the gallantry he had demonstrated during the carnage, he was awarded the Military Cross.

Yet whilst he was relieved when the guns were eventually silenced, he despaired at the terms of the Versailles peace treaty. 'There was,' he reflected in his typescript autobiography, 'no real good that we fought to defend that was now more precarious, or no evil that we set out to destroy that was no more entrenched.'[3] Long before the rise to power of Adolf Hitler, he saw the dangers in squeezing Germany's economy until the pips squeaked. The demand for reparations he recognised – following J.M. Keynes' *Economic Consequences of the Peace*, which he had read – would be counterproductive. And how. One of the direct outcomes was that the chemical engineering firm for which he worked soon closed its doors. In 1921 he was laid off. And with the job gone, so too did his company house.

Brought up as a Methodist, during the 1930s he became a lay preacher and anti-war campaigner who believed that only by loving God would mankind be at peace, putting aside what he called 'smaller loyalties'.[4] By these he meant kings, rulers, nations, states, empires, races and political systems – and capitalism. 'The

Gospel of God above is absolute', he wrote in the notes he prepared for a sermon he delivered as what he called the 'chaos' of war loomed once again.

By this time Margaret, my aunt, had been born in October 1928. This had followed Henry's marriage to Margaret Heggie, from Tayport in Fife. His first wife, Margaret Munn, had died three years earlier, although in 1916 she had given birth to Henry's son, Harry. If anything, having a young family intensified his opposition to conflict – of any kind.

Influenced by the example of the Indian lawyer Mahatma Gandhi's use of non-violent civil disobedience in South Africa, Hilditch was one of the first members of the Peace Pledge Union (PPU). The PPU had been founded in 1936 by the Rev. Richard, or 'Dick', Sheppard who, like Henry Hilditch, had been seared by the experience of battle and become a convert to pacificism.[5] From 1938 – with the approach of war – Birmingham's Bull Ring frequently resonated with the sound of Hilditch's powerful oratory at well-attended open-air meetings made livelier by his ability to turn, usually wittily, on hecklers. To make clear to those present he was no lily-livered coward (an accusation frequently directed against pacifists), he was sure to wear his military medals.[6]

He was also prepared, quite literally, to pay the price for his pacifist convictions. Within weeks of the outbreak of hostilities in 1939 he gave up and sold the Birmingham-based non-ferrous scrap metal business that he had built up from scratch during the early 1930s. To have carried on as managing director of a firm that made gunmetal would have meant he was hand-in-glove with the armaments industry and fuelling the war effort.

So, at the cost of surrendering most of the previous year's profits, he cancelled all advance orders. To do this he paid out some £2,000 (just over £91,000 today) in little more than a week.[7] His son Harry, who was also a partner in the company, and a pacifist, followed him out.[8] Instead, the family's efforts were devoted to assisting the war's opponents and its victims. Central to this was Henry's purchase of the Grange, a six-bedroomed farmhouse in Wythall in Worcestershire. Very much in keeping with other PPU-inspired experiments in communal living, the Grange became a refuge and advice centre for pacifists as they made their cases against conscription.[9] It also offered accommodation for elderly people from the bomb-ravaged Birmingham area. Instead of making metal, Henry found himself working long hours in the Grange's gardens, planting potatoes and milking cows.[10]

He had been a member of the Labour Party from 1921, having converted to socialism in the immediate aftermath of the Great War.

In 1944, he stood as a Christian Socialist in the Kirkcaldy by-election. Pitted against an aggressively pro-war Labour candidate and the Scottish Nationalist Douglas Young, he had proposed a 'revolutionary alternative to the capitalist system'. This included the nationalisation of the banks and key industries in Britain, and negotiations for peace with socialist representatives from the warring nations.[11] In the wartime circumstances in which he fought the election it was no surprise that he attracted not much more than 7 per cent of the votes cast, and lost his £150 deposit.

He was more successful during the General Election of 1951. Aged sixty, he was the Labour Party's candidate in Stratford-on-Avon. His rival was the Conservative John Profumo, whose political career ended in disgrace in 1963 following revelations that he had had an affair with the notorious Christine Keeler. This, though, lay some years ahead. Despite Henry Hilditch's vigorous defence of the Labour Government's record since 1945, in 1951 Profumo won the seat.

But as we will see, it was Henry's business acumen and entrepreneurial flair that would prove crucial for the success of the Pabay venture. These he had demonstrated as a boy and honed thereafter in his search for reusable higher-grade metals at the lowest prices possible in the testing economic environment of inter-war Britain – the era of the Great Depression. He readily admitted the part that 'low commercial cunning' played in his success as a businessman.[12]

There were times when this made the difference between his daughter and son-in-law staying on Pabay or retreating to mainland Skye.

* * *

Nevertheless, it was shared ideals and political values rather than business brains that set the stage for Margaret Hilditch and Len Whatley to become a couple. For not nine miles away from Wythall – in Birmingham's Bordesley Green – was another family of left-wing pacifists. This was Herbert William Whatley and his wife Florence Mary Davis (known as Mary), and their two sons, Allan and Len.

It was in this environment that Len grew up. It was this that played a large part in shaping his approach to life, and contributed much to the unique character of the Whatleys' Pabay years.

Born in 1884, Len's father, Herbert, had begun his working life at the age of eleven, as a farm servant in the Wiltshire village of Heytesbury. Early on – in his unpublished autobiographical notes written many years later he says he was twelve – he had become aware of the gulf in life chances between someone born into a farm labourer's family and someone born into that of the squire. The disadvantages Herbert observed were both educational and economic. Consequently, he had felt a growing sense of resentment 'as experience revealed the gross injustice to our family and those other families who made up the majority of our village'.[13]

Struggling with the physical demands of looking after horses, he soon gave up agricultural work, became a telegraph messenger and then an assistant to a draper's packman, who sold his wares from a horse and trap. Thereafter he became a live-in shop assistant. This was less onerous, but no idyll either. The rulebook of one drapery firm in Bristol he was employed by included forty-seven fineable offences. With employers at the time acting as virtual dictators, it was easy to cross the line and commit an offence, written or not. Instant dismissal could follow. More than once in his career in commerce Herbert found himself out of work. But in his later teens and early twenties he had begun to read and learn – largely untutored – and develop the ideas and views that would in due course, and indirectly, become one of the stepping stones to Pabay.

Reinforcement of his developing ideas followed his meeting with his wife-to-be, while working in the silks section at Cavendish House department store, Cheltenham. Florence Mary Davis had risen to the position of secretary to the managing director. With her, Herbert shared a growing interest in some of the more unorthodox thinking of the time about an impressively broad range of moral, social and political issues, above all the unequal distribution of wealth. William Morris, Sidney and Beatrice Webb, H.G. Wells and George Bernard Shaw were amongst the most influential thinkers and writers they read and talked about. In their approach to politics they favoured the Fabians' emphasis on argument and persuasion rather than violent revolution (though as we have seen, they were to support the Russian Revolution of 1917). However, perhaps like Clement Attlee, the future Labour leader, they may not have been entirely at one with the 'ponderous, pontifical and self-important' (and often bearded) Fabian intellectuals.[14] As political activists they were drawn to the Independent Labour Party (ILP).

Even so, the ideals that had given birth to the Fabian Society, articulated by the short-lived Fellowship of the New Life, founded in 1883 and disbanded in 1898, remained with them throughout their lives. It was almost certainly from this source that their views about women's suffrage and sexual equality were derived. They were disciples of Annie Besant (1847–1933), a socialist and theosophist, and Marie Stopes (1880–1958), and her pioneering commitment to birth control rather than abortion as a means of containing the size of already overcrowded working-class households. They were against vaccination and lukewarm on alcohol ('my drink is water bright' was a catchphrase of Herbert's) but not total abstainers. About ethical vegetarianism they were passionate advocates, based in part on their commitment to animal rights. In this their greatest influences were the well-known anti-vivisectionist (and fellow pacifist and socialist) Henry Stephens Salt (1851–1939), and Shaw.

In 1912, Herbert and Mary married. Determined no longer to be wage 'slaves', and despite having precious little capital, they opened a small wholefoods shop in Boscombe, a suburb of Bournemouth on England's south coast. While Herbert concentrated on weighing, cutting and bagging, his wife cooked and sold – to the delight of customers – a variety of vegetarian dishes, including nut rissoles and nut roasts. More than a century later, these are still Whatley family favourites. Every few weeks I make one, to the exact same recipe.

The business was sufficiently successful for them to purchase 'The Myrtles', which they opened as a vegetarian guesthouse. Having been joined by their son Allan, born in April 1913, all seemed well, even though the First World War had broken out in August 1914. As confirmed pacifists, and fervently anti-imperialist, they had opposed the conflict and campaigned against it. Visitors who were welcomed to their Boscombe home included prominent radicals – the poet and philosopher Edward Carpenter (1844–1929), for instance (who had been active in the Fellowship of the New Life), and even the Russian anarchist, Peter Kropotkin (1842–1921). Exiled for more than forty years, Kropotkin returned to Russia after the Revolution. But otherwise life had gone on, more or less as usual.

By 1916, however, the British army was running short of soldiers. The initial flush of volunteers who had signed up for front-line action in a war that was to be over by Christmas 1914 had slowed. In January 1916, a Military Service Bill that introduced conscription for single men aged between 18 and 41 was brought before Parliament. A few months later married men were included in the legislation. The finger of fate was moving towards Boscombe.

By 1916 official policy towards conscientious objectors (COs) was hardening, and the couple became members of the No-Conscription Fellowship (NCF), which had been set up by Fenner Brockway and Clifford Allen late in 1914. Herbert's self-assigned role was to write letters to pacifist conscripts who had been imprisoned, provide them with writing paper and to send them when requested left-wing reading matter, such as the *Labour Leader*.[15]

It was not until January 1917 that Herbert was called up and drafted into the 4th (Reserve) Hampshire Regiment. After refusing to cooperate he was court-martialled. In March, he was sentenced to 112 days' hard labour – 'the severest [punishment] inflicted by English law', according to one contemporary writer on the subject of conscientious objection.

This source, a pamphlet written by Arthur S. Peake, *Prisoners of Hope*, was amongst Herbert Whatley's modest personal library. Yellowing, fragile and torn, Peake's publication was kept close to hand – literally – by his son Allan (my father) right up until the day he died, in September 2017.[16] The copy was marked and underlined by his father in various places – as for example the sentence: 'They [COs] suffer cruelly from cold in their cells, frequently very insufficiently heated.' This was simply one of the many torments he endured (at Wakefield prison where he had been first incarcerated and, afterwards, in Wormwood Scrubs), as of course did the hundreds of other men who had dared to stand up for the right not to fight, and to choose – as they saw it – mankind and brotherhood over king and country. Those resisting on 'socialistic principles' (as Herbert did), found that theirs was a particularly 'rough journey'. Solitary confinement, enforced silence, lack of exercise and isolation from the outside world (no letters into or out of prison were allowed until two months had passed) added to the inmates' miseries. The punishing regime, which for Herbert meant sewing mail bags and cook-room duties, stretched the endurance of most COs to their limits, and in some cases beyond, breaking some men's physical health and in a few cases leading to psychological collapse.[17] 'Herbert!' wrote one of his correspondent comrades from an army barracks at Tonbridge in May 1916, 'the mental agony is torturing.'[18]

Herbert's own experience of what he called 'the hateful military machine', was harrowing enough. But his wife Mary suffered too, not only because she missed the husband with whom she was passionately in love. Exhausted by having now to run the shop and the boarding house on her own, and care for her young son Allan, she lost a baby girl – Grace – in May 1918. Her crusading spirit survived, though, and she continued to attend meetings of the Anti-Vivisection Society and the No Conscription Federation. Her husband by this time was no longer in prison. He had left the previous May, after only a few months inside – and made home visits between working, using only manual labour, on land clearance projects that he had undertaken as a condition of his release. As the more extreme pacifists – including, it seems, Mary – viewed this as a breach of the principle that COs should do nothing to aid the war effort, even indirectly, Herbert worried that he had let the side, and her, down. But he could take no more. Uncannily, land work was what his son Len – as yet unborn – would be doing, during the Second World War. A precedent had been set.

So along with pacifism, another seed was sown in the period around the First World War that would lead to Pabay. This was a love of the land, instilled in both of his sons by Herbert, who had grown vegetables in Boscombe and later became a keen allotment holder. This had followed the family's move to Birmingham in 1919, after they had disposed of their Boscombe businesses. Herbert had taken up the offer of a manager's post at Pitman's Health Store.

The family found accommodation in what was England's first 'Ideal Village', in inner-city Birmingham's Bordesley Green. Aimed at artisans, work on this had begun in 1908, to the plans of Barry Parker and Raymond Unwin, who went on to design Welwyn Garden City in Hertfordshire. Although not quite finished when the Whatleys arrived, the small semi-detached house they now had – 603 Bordesley Green – was comfortable enough. Other than having a cold, unlit, outside lavatory.

The household was political, although not overbearingly so. Herbert and Mary were keen players at cards and board games. Jigsaws became a pursuit for all of the family. Although no one played a musical instrument, there was a gramophone player, which provided aural entertainment. As before the war, the couple continued to be avid readers, of books, political literature and newspapers: their favourite was the Trades Union Congress-sponsored *Daily Herald*. As he grew up during the 1920s and 1930s, Len absorbed many of the values held by his parents, including from his father a generosity of spirit and an open-mindedness about opposing or different points of view, or at least a preparedness to listen. On the other hand, their more cautious approach to life, especially on the part of his mother, failed to rub off on him.

Even so, his parents were uncompromising in their principles. They did more than talk politics. Herbert was as committed as ever to the ILP, and in the course of time took his wife and sons along to Sunday evening meetings at Alum Rock Road school that were addressed by leading figures such as the party's firebrand MP, James or 'Jimmy' Maxton, George Lansbury, Emmanuel 'Manny' Shinwell and others. Many had been conscientious objectors. Gatherings of the faithful concluded with rousing renditions of socialist songs – 'The Red Flag', 'Jerusalem' and 'The Internationale'. When the visiting speaker had been invited to stay with the Whatleys overnight, the singing was merely an interlude prior to further politics-dominated discussion.[19] Others who came to '603' were the philosopher and anti-war campaigner Bertrand Russell's wife Dora, as well as – more than once – Katherine Glazier, the widow of John Bruce Glazier the Scottish socialist, one-time ILP leader and another opponent of the Great War.

And, presumably so that he should appreciate with pride the name his parents had given him, around 1930 Len was gifted a copy of Lenin's wife Nadezhda Krupskaya's *Memories of Lenin*.

Mary Whatley's preference was for the co-operative movement. After a period of unemployment in the early 1930s Herbert had managed to gain a foothold in the same organisation, and by 1939 had become an inspector of coal measures. Coal delivery men were not averse to giving short-weight to their customers, by slipping an additional empty coal sack into the pile of unloaded sacks that cost-conscious housewives would carefully count to make sure they had had their money's worth.

Weekend walks were a fixture in the family's leisure calendar. This was something Len enjoyed from an early age. However, as he grew into his teens he hankered for more ambitious outings than Sunday strolls with his parents. Trips organised by his school, Saltley Secondary, took him to the Lake District. After leaving he joined the ex-pupils' 'Wanderbruder' rambling club.[20] His elder brother Allan was a leading light in another informal walking group – 'The Gang', which originated in 1933. This comprised mainly Birmingham city council personnel of one kind or another, who would spend part of their days off on what were usually convivial expeditions into the countryside around Birmingham. The twenty or so friends would gather at prearranged locations

– travelling by car, motorbikes, pedal cycles and sometimes the train. By the summer of 1938 Len had become a member, and in June led for the first time – with his girlfriend Daphne Blackmore – a party of fifteen walkers on a 17-mile hike.[21]

By this date – after leaving school – Len had become a clerk in the council's accounts department. His mother was keen that her sons should not have to deal with the financial anxieties she had been subject to when her husband had been in prison. He had been unemployed for part of the duration of the Depression. More than once the family had teetered on the edge of homelessness, unable to pay the mortgage on their Bordesley Green home. Lodgers were taken in, to tide them over the bad patches.

Mary's more genteel background and high social aspirations meant that for her there was an additional dimension to the ache of scarcity. (Despite her politics and the anger she felt about society's injustices, she tended to be somewhat aloof from those working-class neighbours she considered to be 'rough'.) Consequently, using her local political networks, she made enquiries that led to an opening for her eldest son Allan in the city's Libraries Department in 1930. Later she secured for Len his clerical position. In his search for work his second name hadn't been helpful: at least one potential employer, he told me, had frowned darkly over his gold-rimmed glasses – and turned his application down – on learning that Len was short for Lenin rather than Leonard. But a secure job that was deadly dull wasn't for him. He was miserable in the confined environment of an office, and determined then to be outside, and to work and live, rather than live to work.

He had a penchant too for the arts, including amateur drama and music. He demonstrated an aptitude for drawing and painting, handicraft and design, and in his tiny Bordesley Green bedroom had fashioned for himself a divan bed, along with a set of low shelves.

*   *   *

Despite the coincidence of the Hilditch and Whatley families' interest in and commitment to left-wing politics, as well as

pacifism, there is nothing to suggest any kind of personal acquaint-
anceship until the second half of the 1930s. As the likelihood of
military conflict with Hitler's Germany intensified, Herbert and
Mary Whatley began once again to agitate on behalf of the anti-
war movement. By 1937 they had become energetic members of
the PPU. Looking on with interest and admiration were their two
sons, Allan and Len. Neither, however, was as deeply involved as
their parents. Allan was focused on his career as a librarian, and
the brothers shared an enthusiasm for sports of various kinds
(Len's love was for rugby and cricket, Allan's for tennis), countryside breaks and, as we have just seen, long walks. Girls too were
high on their list of priorities.

Change, though, was on its way. On 1 September 1939 Nazi
Germany launched a three-pronged invasion of Poland. Two days
later, on 3 September, Britain's Prime Minister Neville Chamberlain
declared war on Germany.

Not many months afterwards, in January 1940, Len – now aged
twenty – was called up for military service. Birmingham was one
of many town councils that had begun to suspend the 140 members
of staff suspected of being pacifists; libraries had already ordered
the removal from public display of left-wing material. Supported
by his father, who was drawing on his own experiences from 1916
and 1917 to aid a new generation of pacifists, he made his case for
exemption. The tribunal accepted that he was a genuine CO and
ordered him to undertake agricultural duties.

In effect and without knowing it, this was Len's apprenticeship
for Pabay. Wartime employment took many forms, from assisting
a nurseryman who grew exotic vegetables to tree and brush clearance and tearing up golf courses – thereby adding to the nation's
acreage of cultivable soil.[22] What he enjoyed most was tractor
work, and the range of operations involved in making newly
ploughed land cultivable. With machinery frequently breaking
down at a time when spare parts were in short supply, he also
learned to make running repairs, and how to adapt and make do
in all weathers. His resourcefulness would prove invaluable later.
He got used to long hours, often being required to work seven days
a week.

Initially, Len lived with his parents. As the conflict intensified, London and Britain's industrial regions became targets for the German Luftwaffe's bombing raids: the *Blitzkrieg*, better known as the Blitz. From the late summer of 1940 through to May 1941 Birmingham, a major arms, aircraft and motorcycle manufacturing hub – and bombing target – was subjected to seventy-seven air raids. Over 1,800 tons of bombs were estimated to have dropped, along with almost 5,000 incendiaries. Over 300 factories were damaged or destroyed, along with city-centre shops and public buildings.[23] Thousands of civilians were injured and 2,241 were killed. As many as 12,000 homes were completely destroyed by the rain of explosives, with another 100,000 suffering damage of one sort or another. Like many others in wartime Britain who lived in the shadow of industrial premises or near strategically important railway lines, the Whatleys became all too familiar with the warning wail of the air-raid sirens, the staccato bursts of anti-aircraft guns, the thundering roar of low-flying planes overhead and the thuds and explosions as bombs landed. Terrified, they sheltered, crammed tight together, sometimes for hours on end, under the stairs.[24] Although Bordesley Green wasn't directly in the Luftwaffe's sights, it was close to their target areas and in April 1943 suffered direct hits – the last bombs that fell on Birmingham.

Fortunately, though, the Whatleys had a way out. Through their PPU involvement, Herbert and Mary had met Henry Hilditch. Aware of their situation, early in 1941 – at the height of Birmingam's bombing ordeal – Henry offered them a room at the Grange. Gratefully, they accepted and stayed there, returning to their own home during periods of calm, for the rest of the war.

In instigating the family's temporary removal from Bordesley Green therefore, Adolf Hitler and Hermann Göring, commander-in-chief of the Luftwaffe, who had ordered the commencement of the air assault on Britain's cities, provided another of the elements that would lead Len Whatley to Pabay.

The friendship forged by Henry and Herbert was to last the rest of their lifetimes. After the war they kept in close touch, writing to each other at least once a month. They were devotees of Wilfred

Wellock (1879–1972), the First World War CO and Labour MP, PPU activist, Christian socialist, ascetic and vegetarian. Hostile to the materialism of the machine age, by the 1940s, Wellock – an idealist for whom socialism was a spiritual movement rather than a fight for higher living standards – had, following William Morris, begun to advocate a return to a pre-industrial world of self-sufficiency and mutual aid. Co-operation.[25] Both Henry and Herbert continued to correspond with Wellock into the 1960s and read and disseminated his pamphlets. Never obtrusively, values they shared with Wellock – quality of life over material acquisition, and the importance of learning and meaningful self-improvement – filtered down into the Whatleys' Pabay household.

Robust in their views, and openly disdainful of the Tories, Henry's and Herbert's continual refrain – even in old age – was for more socialism, not less. Len's mother was of a similar mind, and during the war was giving public lectures on the merits of the Soviet system. Although wary of Communists (and in Henry's case also of Roman Catholics, whom he condemned as the products of an equally undemocratic system), they extolled the virtues of the USSR well into the 1960s. It was just as well that neither man lived long enough to see the Russian leader Mikhail Gorbachev's launch in the mid-1980s of *perestroika*, in effect an admission on the part of the Communist Party that the socialist experiment in economic planning had failed.[26]

When the Whatleys arrived in Wythall, the Hilditches' daughter Margaret was only thirteen, and still at school. Although Len only stayed at the Grange occasionally – he later moved to Baldwin's Lane, Hall Green – he quickly became aware of how attractive this slim, shapely, raven-haired and fun-loving girl was. Having very recently broken up after a three-year, on-off relationship with Daphne, whom he felt to be overly possessive and domineering (but also so captivating that according to my mother he bought her a present once a month), he was besotted. Classically handsome, more experienced and with a healthy lust for life and loving – and with ideals that matched those of her parents – Len, twenty-one by this time, was hard for Margaret to resist. By the autumn of 1941 they were going out together.[27]

Their relationship, however, wasn't entirely smooth. For a few months in 1942 Len was involved with a mysterious 'Vi'. Increasingly however, he was to be found at Wythall. When they were married in June 1945, sixteen-year-old Margaret was already pregnant. Their first daughter, Anthea, was born on 28 September. For a while inter-family relations were frosty, Len's mother having been outraged that the Hilditches had failed to prevent what she had called the 'moment's excitement' that in her eyes had been her son's downfall. But Margaret seemed able to brush off rebukes of this kind, and on Pabay, and later Skye, her attitude towards pre-marital sex would prove to be at odds with that of her mother-in-law. She revelled in the role of match-maker and was inclined to turn a blind eye to such goings-on. I am not alone in recalling that one of the joys of staying under her roof was her open-mindedness about sleeping arrangements, on the very rare occasions when, in my later teens, I turned up with a girlfriend. Although Mary Whatley never quite forgot – nor was inclined to forgive – she had joined the small wedding party in June, and afterwards relieved Margaret on occasion by looking after baby Anthea. And she was soon able to suppress her domestic disappointment by committing to yet another cause, this time as an uncompromising member of the West Midlands Rent Tribunal, battling for fair rents for working people.

For newlywed Len and Margaret, housing was also one of their priorities. With the war with Germany over in May 1945, Henry Hilditch had no further use for the Grange. The young couple therefore had little choice but to find somewhere else to live. And, in Len's case, to secure work and earn enough to support his wife and daughter. His wartime experience of agricultural employment had not only whetted his appetite, it was now what he intended to do. In April 1945, he advertised for a cottage or house 'with or without land' within 20 miles of south Birmingham.[28] Recognising the burden for small farmers of transporting grain to a mill that might be many miles distant, he set up a one-man mobile threshing business for farms in the Birmingham area. On his trailer was a hammer mill which he connected to the tractor's take-off with a leather belt. He would need to come up with many more ingenious solutions of this kind in the coming years.

Late in 1947, however, Len's farming ambitions looked like being realised. The last of the Richards family who had worked Shawhurst Farm – in Wythall, and therefore familiar to Len – died.[29] Grasping the opportunity, he took over the tenancy, leaving behind the cramped house the couple had rented in Hall Green. Len was well-prepared, and keen to innovate. Margaret's older brother Harry was a lecturer at Croft College near Bromsgrove. One of the Educational Settlements Association's colleges for adults (of which Ruskin in Oxford was one), Croft College's purpose was to provide education for agricultural and rural workers.[30]

Through Harry, Len was introduced to the principles of organic vegetable growing, inspired in part by Wilfred Wellock. Wellock was fiercely opposed to the use of chemicals and pesticides and promoted instead, through the Soil Association, organic cultivation.[31] It was an approach that Len maintained on Pabay through the Henry Doubleday Research Association, established in the early 1950s, its name a tribute to Doubleday, who had pioneered the use of Russian comfrey as an instant compost for organic crops.[32] The importance of soil preparation was something Len had witnessed at first hand with his father's scrupulous management of his compost heap on his Bordesley Green allotment. Impressed by Len's determination to stick to his principles and apply them on Pabay, Wellock (then aged eighty), and his wife visited the island and spent a night there in September 1959, during a journey to Skye and the Outer Hebrides.[33]

Shawhurst's buildings, however, had seen better days. The brickwork was crumbling. Timbers were rotten. In places the roof had fallen in. In addition, not only had Wythall's population been growing steadily since the 1920s, but house-building was beginning to encroach onto Shawhurst Farm itself. The writing was on the wall. Rural Wythall, which bordered the increasingly populous city of Birmingham, stealthily spreading ever outwards, was on the way to becoming semi-rural or worse, semi-urban. Over the following decades a series of housing estates was built. Shawhurst eventually became a riding stables. The farm disappeared from view.

So too did Len and Margaret. But now with a second child, Stuart Richard Whatley, born in October 1947. By Christmas Day in 1949 the family was over 500 miles north of Wythall, staying at Kinloch Lodge on the island of Skye. There, Len was making arrangements to get across to and live on the compact, uninhabited island of Pabay.

At the time, even the road journey up through the spine of the British Isles was a formidable test of endurance. Motorcars were less reliable than they are nowadays, and slower, while the roads – especially those in the Highlands and on Skye – were poor. An assessment in 1948 revealed that around 40 per cent of the roads in the county of Inverness (of which Skye is part) had a gravel surface – the lowest grade. (The best was asphalt.) The equivalent figure for the UK was 8 per cent.[34] Road travel anywhere in the Highlands during the winter months was treacherous, owing to snow and ice. Glencoe, Invermoriston, Invergarry and Glen Shiel were renowned as stretches of road that either slowed journeys to a crawl or forced drivers to give up. But this is how Len made his way to Skye, after a twenty-eight-hour drive from Birmingham with a trailer in tow. Even less burdened, and without the deep snow he was met with at Glencoe, and that was packed hard as ice near Cluanie, the trip by car was reckoned to take twenty-four hours.[35] Margaret and Anthea and Stuart came by rail. Unable to book a sleeper, they had spent the entire journey from London to Mallaig stuffed upright into a standard coach. Once in Mallaig they transferred to a steamer to take them to Kyle. With a stiff wind blowing, the sea getting up and dark falling, Margaret's anxiety levels rose. The narrows at Kylerhea, two miles or so long and only a few hundred yards wide between towering mountain masses on either side, can be a test of endurance for even the most experienced seafarer. Other than between the tides, there is a fast current that the wind can rapidly funnel into precipitous seas.[36]

Despite being hungry, neither Margaret nor the children were inclined to eat. The Gaelic chatter around them added to what was a vague sense of alienation: 'speaking English', Margaret later recalled, 'seemed out of place'.[37] No wonder. Gaelic was still commonly spoken on Skye at the time. Only in the Western Isles

– Barra, Harris, Lewis and the Uists – did a higher proportion of the population speak in the region's native tongue.

However, being the festive season, and despite their boisterousness, their fellow travellers seemed friendly.

Between them Len and Margaret had many of their worldly possessions. Such furniture as they owned was to be brought by rail. By the time it had been unloaded at Kyle and then, a few weeks later, ferried to Pabay, it was sodden. The smell of damp permeated the entire load, fungus had begun to take hold, while some items fell apart, the glue no longer able to do its job.

* * *

What led Len, with Margaret, to take their leap in the dark – over the sea to Skye? They had next to no savings. Nor much else, in the way of material assets. Len had no acquaintance with the sea, its tides, currents and dangers. His aquatic experience was limited to poling a punt on the River Avon. But anyway, they didn't have a boat. We've seen already that neither he nor Margaret spoke any Gaelic, nor did they have any previous knowledge of Skye's people or its culture.

We know that Len was becoming disenchanted with what farming he would be able to do, with his limited financial resources, in the English Midlands.

Clear too is that Len and Margaret had enjoyed a short visit to Skye three months earlier. This was entirely serendipitous. The couple – with Anthea and Stuart – had come for a holiday on Skye in October, joining one of Len's old school friends, Jack Surridge, and his wife Joyce. Their base had been Kinloch Lodge, a country house hotel in Sleat, to the south of Broadford.

They had come at just the right time of year. The gales associated with the autumnal equinox are in the past. Instead the air is crisp and there are often more prolonged periods of blue sky than during the summer months. This was unlike the often-leaden skies above southern England's larger towns, which in the winter months were often fog- or, worse, smog-filled. The contrast with Birmingham was particularly stark. Its grand Victorian architectural inheritance was now jaded. The city's industrial heart was still recovering from the battering, constant demands and consequent exhaustion of five years of war.

Hardly surprisingly therefore, Margaret enthused about Skye's scenery, while Len relished walks on the heather-clad hills and what for him were the new pursuits of deer-stalking and fly-fishing.

But they also saw Pabay. Bathed in sunshine. They were hooked. Within days they had decided this was where they wanted to be. Their future. The long slog home by car to Birmingham was not one spent simply sharing memories of a glorious autumn break, but instead, working out how they could come back.

By the end of December, they had done just this. They were on the cusp of an altogether new way of living.

Because another coincidence had worked in their favour.

The Muntz family's Umberslade estate was less than eight miles from Wythall, not much longer than a ten-minute drive along what is now the M42. With Gerald Muntz now dead, the future of the Scalpay estate was in the hands of his son and his fellow trustees. The details are hazy, but it seems that Len approached Mrs Muntz – who as we saw earlier had lived for a time on Scalpay – to enquire about the possibility of acquiring Pabay. She agreed to sell. It was a momentous decision for Len and Margaret, but also for the island. For the first time for centuries, it was to be sold in its own right, rather than as part of the barony of Strathwordell, or along with lands in Breakish and elsewhere on the adjacent mainland of Skye, or as an appendage of the Scalpay estate.

The Muntzes' preparedness to dispose of the island on its own was in its way a sign of the times. Frank Fraser Darling, the ecologist who even as young man had yearned to own an island in the Western Isles, spent many years living on them. Small islands, he observed, belong to big estates, 'the owners of which are not generally disposed to part with one small portion for what is to them an inconsiderable sum'.[38] What may have been true in the 1930s however, was no longer so. Captain Muntz had left an estate worth £75,264, much less than the previous owners. His successors had little interest in Highland sport, and had no intention of propping up a loss-making island property. Not altogether happily, the trustees concluded that the estate had to go, in separate lots if need be.

On one level, Len's and Margaret's resolution can be interpreted as little more than a whim. To even contemplate taking on and farming Pabay might seem to the casual observer to be rash at best, and at worst foolhardy. Len's mother was horrified. Later, when it was suggested that she and Herbert should move to Skye, she resisted firmly, having 'no desire to live with dark hills and mountains surrounding me all day and every day'. Not for her the picturesque sublimity of a landscape that since its 'discovery' by the Romantics in the later eighteenth century had lured poets, painters and literary tourists from the south.[39] Len's father, who came to Pabay on his own a few months after Len and Margaret had settled there, to see for himself what his son had taken on, was concerned, and far from optimistic. He'd much have preferred Len – as he would later his grandchildren – to have taken a 'safe' job. Margaret's mother also feared the worst, and throughout her life carried a grudge – which mainly she suppressed – against what she saw as the Whatleys' rashness and their takeover of her daughter.

Locals shook their heads. A family from England. Without much money. On an island. No one expected them to be there for long.

And with good reason.

*   *   *

The couple's decision, however, was based on more than the intoxicating illusions of a better life that a perfect holiday a long way from home can induce.

During the war, Len had not only been amassing the skills and experience he would need to work a farm, he had also been reading. And dreaming, as young men do. But not of the impossible.

In 1944 *The Farming Ladder*, a book by a George Henderson, had been published. On the basis of his own and his brother's experiences in taking over a smallholding in Enstone, Oxford, in the early 1920s, Henderson had offered a blueprint for young men at the end of the Second World War who wanted to become farmers. Henderson's aim, set out in his Preface, was to 'demonstrate how a happy, secure, and useful life may be spent, on ... a few barren acres, without the toil and drudgery associated with small-holding'. Key to his model was organic farming. He also held out the prospect of 'a financial return ... comparable with that in any other business'. And this with little initial capital – precisely the kind of advice Len needed. Which he had acted upon, by taking on Shawhurst.

There may have been another straw in the wind. As an intelligent, well-informed young man growing up in Midlands England in the 1930s, it is entirely likely that Len would have been at least faintly aware of the growing attraction of 'the North'. This, observes the journalist and writer Madeleine Bunting in her *Hebridean Journey* (2016), 'took a particular hold on the British imagination' in the mid-twentieth century. According to John Buchan, author of *The Thirty-Nine Steps*, 'The North was where a man can make his soul or where the man who knows too many secrets can make his escape.' This, according to Bunting, was, 'An apt assessment of a generation, burdened by the trauma of their fathers' war.'[40] Bunting's sculptor father made such a journey after the Second World War, to a remote single-acre-sized plot in North Yorkshire, where he built a chapel. But when Yorkshire became crowded, she reveals, 'he dreamed of escaping to the Hebrides'.[41]

We know that islands have long held a special appeal. Learning of the sale of the Scalpay estate to Captain Muntz in 1932, the *Dundee Courier* had been prompted to comment in a feature article, that 'one more idealist has succumbed to the craze of owning a habitation far remote from the madding crowd'.[42] Those who had managed to find a private Garden of Eden were to be envied. There followed a list of the fortunate few. The article concluded that an island home was perfection on earth, 'provided it is small enough and there is always a motor boat handy'.

The magnetic force of small Hebridean islands remained just as strong in subsequent decades, enticing a steady stream of settlers. Some have been well prepared for the trials ahead. Others have either been hopelessly unrealistic, or altogether lacking the capacities, including immense personal courage, to survive for long.[43]

Sir Henry Bell (on the right), with his son Major Henry James Bell, on Scalpay, mid-1920s. (© Mary Jeffrey-Jones)

Sir Henry Bell's launch, at Scalpay, mid-1920s. Although still grand, it was much smaller than Sir Donald Currie's *Iolaire*. Bell would have preferred something even more modest. He enjoyed going out in the sailing dinghy moored to the rear of the launch. (© Mary Jeffrey-Jones)

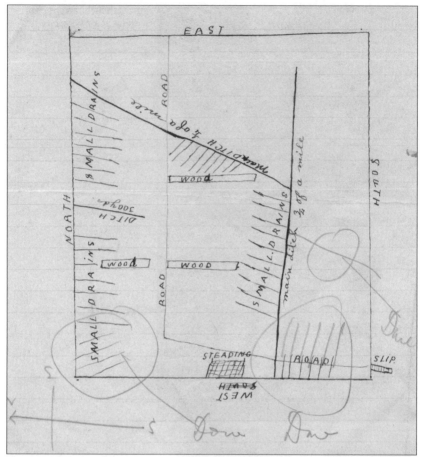

Above. Sketch plan of Pabay's ditches and drains, *c.*1928. Keeping these clear was critically important if Pabay was to succeed either for livestock or arable farming. Sir Henry Bell was one of many owners who tried to drain Pabay in order to increase sheep numbers, but with little success. (© Macdonald and Fraser Solicitors' Records, Skye and Lochalsh Archive Centre, High Life Highland)

Right. Henry Hilditch, 1951, as Labour Party Parliamentary candidate in the Stratford-upon-Avon constituency. His Conservative opponent was John Profumo. (© Michael and Carole Whatley)

Cookhouse prisoners, Wakefield Gaol, June 1917. Herbert Whatley, Len's father, a conscientious objector on socialist grounds, was incarcerated here, and at Wormwood Scrubs, where he was sentenced to carry out hard labour. He is in the second row from the front, second from the left. (Whatley Collection)

Political education session, The Grange, Wythall, *c.*1941. Bought by Henry Hilditch with the proceeds of the sale of his scrap metal business which he sold on the outbreak of the Second World War, The Grange was used to advise conscientious objectors on making their case for exemption from military service, and to house older people at risk from German bombing raids. It is where Len Whatley met Margaret Hilditch. (Whatley Collection)

Len Whatley, aged two, on the beach at Bournemouth, with his brother Allan and mother. (Whatley Collection)

Above. Birmingham's Bordseley Green, a long road as well as being the post First World War 'ideal village' in which Len Whatley was brought up, at number 603, in the 1920s and 1930s. (Whatley Collection)

Left. Shawhurst Farm, Wythall, Birmingham. Despite being blurred, this picture, of the barn roof, hints at the run-down condition of the farm which Len tenanted before taking the decision in 1949 to move to Pabay. (Whatley Collection)

How conscious was Len of all of this? We can't be sure, and even if he was, it is doubtful if it had any direct influence on the couple's decision. He and Margaret had contemplated leaving Shawhurst. But never, Margaret recalled much later, had they talked about an island, and certainly not one in the north-west of Scotland.

However, in accounting for Len's eagerness to take on Pabay there is something else – possibly unspoken – that may have been at the back of his mind.

One of the few letters he wrote that has survived provides our clue.

During the 1930s and even as the war raged, another lover of the natural world – as an ornithologist – Cardiff-born Ronald M. Lockley (1903–2000), had written several partly autobiographical books. Their subject was Lockley's discovery of, and life on, an island.

As a boy, Lockley had daydreamed. He had envied in turn, 'the Swiss Family Robinson, the Coral Islanders, and Robinson Crusoe'. He wrote later of how he 'wished intensely to become a Crusoe'.[44] And after scouring many islands, including the Hebrides, but as far afield as Arctic Spitsbergen in the north of Norway and Tristan da Cunha in the south Atlantic, he found what he was looking for. Skokholm, an island of some 250 acres, which sits two and a half miles off the west Pembrokeshire coast in Wales. There, in 1927, Lockley settled. His plan initially was to go alone, like Daniel Defoe's hero, but when Doris – formerly a friend – expressed her wish to come too, they married and he gave up his vow of celibacy.

Significantly, in the letter Len wrote to my father and mother in December 1950, he reported that he was *re*-reading Lockley's *Inland Farm*, which had been published in 1943.[45] Chapter 1 was entitled 'Dream Island' – the title Lockley had given to his first book in 1930. In the same letter Len also commented on how 'quite remarkable' the similarities were between Skokholm and Pabay.[46] He was right. Both islands were low-lying, and a similar distance from the nearest point on the mainland.

It is impossible to be sure how much and in what ways *Inland Farm* influenced Len's decision to go to Pabay. It may be entirely coincidental of course, but the resemblances between the two

young couples' experiences of their respective island farms are
little short of uncanny.

This was so from the outset. Lockley describes his initial visit to
Skokholm, which he had learned about by chance whilst exploring
other islands in the Bristol Channel. On this occasion, he was on
Skomer. His companion was a Cardiff dentist and (as indeed Len
was) an amateur artist. Both men 'felt obliged to get out into the
open from time to time, and live for a while in sight of a wider
horizon'. They wanted 'to retreat to some island, preferably uninhabited, where they could be alone'. Skokholm lay before them,
the more 'desirable and enchanting' as owing to adverse weather
conditions they were at first unable to reach it.

Lockley wrote: 'It was from the fishermen who ferried us over
from Marloes, the nearest mainland haven, that we learned about
Skokholm . . . They told us . . . that the farm and the house were in
ruins, had been unoccupied for nearly twenty years and that,
beyond casual fishermen, nobody cared to visit the place.
Apparently it was too lonely and inaccessible; the landing place
was very bad; there was no safe harbour; tides swept strongly on
all sides, and to get there at all occupied an hour's steady sailing,
or two or three hours of rowing. In bad weather it was impossible
to get near the island.'[47]

Pabay's buildings were in better order than those on Skokholm,
but in virtually every other respect, the description could have
applied to Pabay.

And as with Len, who made up his mind to acquire Pabay after
a single trip, once Ronald Lockley had finished his initial foray, he
'would never be content until I lived permanently there'. (Nigel
Nicolson evidently felt the same after he had spent just a day
during 1937 on the three steep-sided basaltic rock plugs that form
the Shiant Islands, four miles to the east of Lewis. Although, unlike
Len and Margaret, Nicolson had the family's newly restored home
and gardens at Sissinghurst Castle in Kent to fall back on, should
he have tired of his 'shepherd's bothy, a stream and a large population of seabirds'.[48])

This was just one of many parallels in the two couples' island
lives. Both strove to make a living from the produce of their island

domains, not infrequently being reminded by their bank managers how precariously balanced their finances were. In their different latitudes, they confronted similar natural hazards, from winter gales that blew for days 'without cessation', to infestations of thousands of rabbits whose proclivity to breed had been unchecked for years.[49]

What is clear from the way he tracked down Lockley's other books is that, from the Welshman, Len drew both succour and inspiration, and possibly some practical advice. His indebtedness is revealed in his decision to name one of his first boats *Shearwater* – a favourite bird of Lockley's, about which he had written an important book, *Shearwaters*, in 1942.

Len's and Margaret's decision to live on Pabay may of necessity have been taken in haste. But they were not naïve.

Len was acutely aware that the challenges he faced required some local knowledge if he was to rise to them. To that end, even in the hotel at Kinloch, he began to make arrangements to have Inverness County Library provide him with the reading material he thought would be useful. Books on boats, seamanship, navigation, tides, weather and farming in the area were at the top of his list.

But if he was to apply his learning, Len's first priority was to find a suitable boat, just as Lockley had had to do in Wales.

Chapter 7

'Initiated into the mysteries of being soaked five times a day': Pabay, 1950

New year 1950 was not the most propitious moment to embark on a search for a second-hand boat on Skye. A gale just before Christmas had not only uprooted countless trees and damaged much property, it was reportedly the fiercest storm on Skye for decades, perhaps since 1921, when a destructive hurricane had swept the Outer Hebrides and Skye.[1]

This time, 100 mph winds had ripped from their moorings and washed out to sea, or smashed to smithereens, boats that Len might otherwise have been able to buy. Necessarily, therefore, he embarked on a mission that was now even more pressing, and fraught, than would have been the case earlier. One possibility had been to hire the Kylerhea ferry to get the family's possessions across to Pabay, 'but the storm had carried it so far inshore that it would be impossible to get it off before Spring tide'. Another blow was that the scarcity of small boats had induced a sharp rise in the price of those that were still available. ('My usual luck to try buying on a rising market', Len reflected ruefully.) And even this number was reduced by the need for a craft with a relatively shallow draught in order to be able to get alongside the jetty on Pabay at anything other than high tide.

But as an introduction to Skye life, some of its people, their attitudes and culture, Len's boat hunt was an eye-opener.[2]

His search took him not only to Kylerhea but also to Mallaig and Kyleakin. A Major Ellice had a fine boat at Glenelg, but the £350 he wanted was too much. Even further out of his reach was a 'beautiful launch' at Portree. This was owned by the uncle of the Broadford garage proprietor Alastair Sutherland. But he wanted

£400. As with other sellers, there was no negotiation. 'The crofters, fishermen etc, poor as some of them may be,' Len observed wryly, 'are all sufficiently independent to be able to refuse to lower the price they fix for an article.' But no deal didn't mean the end of the discussion. Often meetings of this kind had been preceded by what Len called a 'drop of the crathur'.

Although not a teetotaller, neither was Len a regular drinker, and he was certainly unaccustomed to what to the uninitiated can appear to be the industrial measures of whisky that are typically offered in the Western Isles; he quickly had to develop a technique for 'avoiding these "drops"', so as not to offend his host. (I've had to do something similar myself when spending new year on Skye: it must have come as a shock to more than one generous soul in the days following my departure, that their pot plants had a distinct whiff of whisky about them – if indeed they'd survived the sudden deluge of alcohol that I'd surreptitiously poured onto them.) But what struck him most was the pace at which business was conducted. After explaining that he was unable to afford Sutherland's launch, he was invited back to the house for refreshments, accompanied by talk of 'Pabay, Kinloch sport, Skye politics, [and] boats in general'. This, Len noted, was 'a far cry from a Wythall business contact of a similar nature'. Yet, pleasant as such conversation was, it had one drawback: the time taken to conclude (or not) even a single transaction.

The protracted nature of proceedings may well have been due to the time of year: the festive season. A couple of years later, in a search for piglets, Len stopped at a number of croft houses where they were known to be for sale. His companion, his first full-time employee, Stan Robinson – from the south – was disappointed that rather than being offered a dram, they were asked, 'Will ye have a wee strupach?', in other words a cup of what they discovered was usually strong, stewed tea.

The drawn-out trip to Portree, however, was not entirely time wasted. One of the garages there had in their workshop the electrical parts of a boat engine that was being overhauled as it had been under water. Learning of this, Len made enquiries and discovered that the boat in question was owned by Colonel Swire of Orbost

House, near Dunvegan – the husband of Otta Swire, the folklorist. A telephone call revealed that Swire was prepared to sell.

The following day Len drove the 50-mile journey from Broadford to Orbost and met Swire, a 'pukka gentleman (a real story-book colonel) in a house full of curios from the far east'. Having devoted himself to market gardening (then in its infancy on Skye) Swire had neglected what was a converted lifeboat, the *Sea Otter*, which, unfortunately, was now waterlogged. The bilge water hadn't been pumped out after the recent storm. Although the 21-foot boat had cost Swire £200, he had no inclination to make her seaworthy again, and was prepared to sell to Len for £75. 'A real bargain', was Len's delighted verdict. The price of a boat that had a cabin that would allow Margaret and the children to travel 'in comfort' and could even sleep two people, was to include tools, cabin upholstery, crockery, anchors, chains and mooring. For a further £10 Len was confident he could restore the craft and return her value to the £200 Swire had paid. The only drawback was that it was unsuitable for carrying heavy or awkwardly sized cargo. Before long the significance of this shortcoming would become only too obvious.

But they were now ready to go, although Len's initial runs across to prepare for Margaret and the children's arrival were made in an open dinghy, the Lockley-inspired *Shearwater*. Yet as a family making their maiden crossing to Pabay – in April – they were confronted by something that would have an immeasurable influence on them in the coming years: inclement weather that was predictable only in its unpredictability. Drenching rain and sharp showers of sea spray kicked up as they entered the rougher sea beyond the immediate confines of Broadford Bay. It is one of Anthea's first memories: her mother – no lover of sea travel – shielding two-year-old Stuart in the stern of the small dinghy that was powered by a Seagull outboard with its distinctive harsh growl, as oil-blotched sea water swilled around the bottom of the boat. And neither then, nor ever during the family's time on Pabay, was there a mention of life-jackets or other safety equipment.

But the bedraggled huddle of island pioneers was joining a long list of first-timers to Skye to experience the capricious Misty Isle's wet welcome. John Blackadder's enthusiasm about Pabay in 1799 was certainly not based on his initial impression: on 7 June he'd come by boat from Loch Shiel, 'with mist and driving rain which deprived us from seeing any part of the Country'; Broadford as he landed, was 'very wet', while the country around 'looked ill'.[3] In the early summer of 1836 James D. Forbes – later to become Principal of the University of St Andrews – embarked on a geological expedition in the Scottish Highlands. It was from Broadford on 1 July, after a day of 'hopeless drizzle' that he wrote confessing that 'I have not yet reconciled to be continuously wet & to sit wet as the denizens of this happy country are'; but, he added, 'I am gradually being initiated into the mysteries of being soaked five times a day'.[4] At least he could console himself as he sheltered in Broadford's inn by reading – as only an aspiring physicist would – J.R. Young's recently published *Theory of Equations*. It was just as well: the rain continued to fall for some days yet.[5] Almost a century later, in the summer of 1930, James Cameron, later to become a distinguished journalist, was a teenage reporter cutting his teeth with Dundee's DC Thomson press. He had been sent to Skye. With his companions, he spent the first evening and night in Broadford. The weather was fine, and the scenery splendid. Across the bay was the smooth green island of Pabay.

Then came the rain. The irony of Cameron's apprentice-style journalism is contrived – but even so his comments would have rung true – and still do – for many newcomers to the island: 'It does not always rain on Skye. It would be rather foolish to suggest it does. But it must be admitted that it generally is raining. Or, if it is not actually raining, it is just about to, or has newly stopped . . . The rain, when it falls, is a phenomenon in itself.'[6]

For Len and Margaret, the priority was to get the family's furniture and other bulkier possessions in place. Weather conditions had deteriorated as the ferry they had hired to transport their belongings from Kyle was making its way to Pabay. With nowhere to take shelter off Pabay, there was no alternative therefore but to quickly offload at the jetty and head back to Kyle. Without a tractor, the couple had to carry everything by hand along the rough, quarter-mile-long track to the cottage. Some lighter items were lost, carried away in the near gale conditions.

As they reassembled the furniture that had fallen apart in transit, helped by a spell of clear weather that enabled them to put outside and dry some of it, and settled into the former shepherd's cottage, Len and Margaret were able to take stock. The realisation dawned that their first impression of the island and its prospects less than six months earlier had perhaps been overly favourable. Or, let us say, there were more hurdles to overcome than they had anticipated. But typical of the character they would demonstrate so often in the coming years, their response was not to become despondent, but rather to dig deeper into their reserves of optimism. The couple's resilience was matched by their self-reliance and resourcefulness, and their ability to make and mend and adapt to the circumstances in which they found themselves. These were qualities they passed onto their children, who as soon as they were capable – they were always willing – began to assist inside and outside the house. Len especially was a generous, patient and encouraging teacher whose influence is felt still by those fortunate enough to have been his pupils.

With impressively thick walls and internal wood panelling, the cottage was both wind-proof and warm, except for a small dairy room off the kitchen. There were limitations though. Water was piped from a tank that filled from an underground spring near the top of the island to a tap at the back of the house. Cold water. Heating water for a clothes-washing was a major chore. Rinsing was done in a stream that ran near to the house. There was no bathroom. Toilet facilities were crude, in the shape of a lean-to shed that enclosed a chemical 'Elsan' commode.

But this was no worse than Len had been used to in his boyhood home, and with which Margaret had been familiar as a guest there. Inside, the two upstairs rooms, reached by the narrow twisting wooden staircase that had been fitted by Alexander Robertson in the mid-1920s, were long, narrow and short on headroom. Downstairs the décor was dull, until after scraping away layers of green, grey and even dark brown paint Len brightened the kitchen and sitting room with a coat of cream distemper.

Drawing upon and applying her handicraft skills, Margaret made good the absence of particular items of furniture. Disused orange boxes for instance became bedside cabinets – which she covered with chintz material, with small curtains run along the open side on spring wire. Material from flour sacks she bleached, then decorated and turned into candlewick bedspreads.

Initially anyway, heat for comfort came from turfs and peat (taken from a store in which it had been left years beforehand by the Mackinnon brothers), driftwood from the shore and a paraffin heater. Margaret cooked on an old stove – until a Rayburn cooker was fitted. It was with this that her culinary and baking skills came into their own: family, friends, employees and visitors all marvelled at the variety, simplicity yet also the sheer excellence of the savouries (including a very English curry), bread, cakes, scones, meringues, puddings and other delicious delights that she managed to produce not only on Pabay, but afterwards when she ran the Edinbane Lodge hotel. The Rayburn too, now connected to the water supply, provided hot water. Stream-washing became a thing of the past. The Rayburn was also used to warm the flat irons that sat in the holders which Margaret had hand-knitted.

Light came from Tilley lamps and candles until Len and a young local electrician, Ewan Mackinnon, managed to construct a small wind-powered generator that fed glass batteries (and later a car battery), which at least gave the family something in the way of electric light – and powered a radio.

Outside, too, it was clear that Len's initial assessment of the island's condition had been misleading. Swathes of the cultivable land that had promised so much when seen from afar on closer inspection proved to be waterlogged. And while the pebbled areas around the cottage and farm steading were miraculously free of weeds (something that had surprised the couple on their exploratory visit), the island's drains were choked with 'years of vegetation'.[7] In places the sides of the deep ditches had collapsed, preventing the water from running off. Not only that, but several of the basic stone bridges that crossed the ditches had fallen in. Those made of wooden railway sleepers had rotted, so much so that when Len managed to get a tractor to Pabay – a second-hand wartime Fordson – he was unable to get it far.

Sir Henry Bell's and George Fraser's fears about the consequences of neglect had been well founded. From the time of John

Blackadder's survey of Pabay at the turn of the nineteenth century, no one with any interest in farming there was in any doubt about the importance of good drainage if the low-lying island were to fulfil its potential as a viable farming unit. Failure on this score revealed starkly Pabay's Achilles heel.

Compounding the problematic drainage system was the condition of the fencing – where it existed at all.

There was little point in bringing cattle to Pabay (even if they could be fed) without fencing off the ditches. Otherwise, some of the animals would simply slip and stumble in. And, in the deeper drains, panic, sink further, choke and slowly drown. Which is what happened. Just how much anguish such a tumble could be for both man and beast is illustrated by what happened in May 1953. Len was spotted crossing to Broadford in a dinghy, urgently seeking the vet. A heifer had been stuck in a ditch for a week, and would require four men to pull it clear – with a rope around its neck. The vet, however, first offered the animal a concoction of bran and stout, enough to encourage it to try to scramble out.[8] Fortunately, on this occasion the vet's intervention was sufficient to restore the young cow to full health.[9]

Nevertheless, and in spite of an ambitious fencing programme, cattle continued periodically to find their way into the island's deep ditches. Putting in fencing that was robust enough to keep cattle from searching out the spring grass that grew along the edges of the open drains was not straightforward. Stan Robinson, who worked for Len on Pabay during the early 1950s, recalls how difficult it was to embed the fencing posts securely in what was deep peat.[10] On the other hand, it was almost impossible to drill holes into the hard, basaltic rock dykes that criss-crossed the island, with the result that there were stretches of fencing that were vulnerable to any pressure from animals intent on pushing through.

One of the most tragic instances occurred just a year later, when, unusually, Pabay was covered in snow following a blizzard. With the ditches now invisible, the island's milk cow – 'Jezebel' – had plunged into one. Despite frantic searching, neither Len nor Stan could find her – until too late, when her snow shroud had melted, exposing what was now a carcass.[11]

But even had the drainage system been better maintained, Len would have faced another difficulty, although in this respect Pabay was little different from anywhere else in the Western Highlands and Islands. Traditional arable farming systems depend for their success on key nutrients, the most important being nitrogen and phosphorous. Prolonged periods of heavy rain, however, reduce the pH value of the soil and leach from it its essential minerals, so inhibiting the growth of useful crops.[12] Obtaining, and above all retaining, these in the soils of north-west Scotland are major challenges.[13] Typically what has been termed 'inherent poor fertility' was associated with waterlogged, boggy land just like that which cloaked large parts of Pabay's eastern side. Actually, the deterioration process had probably been taking place over centuries, following the reduction of woodland cover. A compensating factor for Pabay was that on the island's northern side there was a sizeable colony of gulls. Frank Fraser Darling – author of another of the guides to island life consulted by Len – observed that islands so blessed are usually greener, or swathes of them are, the soil in the vicinity of the gulls having a higher content of lime and phosphates.[14] But on Pabay this applied to one corner only – the 15 acres of West Park, and some of North Park; it was not enough.

For Len, whose farming experience had been acquired in a more benign environment, these were travails of a different order. Typically, rainfall in England's Midlands is just over half that of the Western Isles.[15] And the 60 inches that typically fell on Pabay annually was more than on other Hebridean islands further to the west, such as Tiree and Lewis.

Untended for several years, Pabay's cultivable land had not been planted extensively since the early nineteenth century, when the island was turned over to sheep. Where sheep have grazed heavily, unpalatable grasses, sedges and rushes tend to flourish.[16] It was some time too since cattle had been maintained in sufficient numbers to have made a difference through the use of their dung, a long-practised means of raising nitrogen levels. Fortunately, there was on the north shore a much-prized shell beach, the calcium carbonate from which would reduce acidity levels if ploughed in – which over time Len did.

But first it had to be treated. Large grains of shell sand can take twenty years to disintegrate in the soil. Yet ground down, the lime content of the Pabay shells was a very satisfactory 84 per cent. As pleasing was Len's discovery that the sandy beach that lay in front of the house was 'practically pure shell sand', with identically high lime content.[17] Finer, the need for grinding was obviated. There was ample seaweed too. With this, Len followed the Breakish crofters' example. He gathered tons of driftweed that had been swept onto the shore after the winter storms, and then spread this onto the ground he had allocated for potatoes. Although he could use the tractor for some of this work that on a smaller scale was usually done by hand, it was still a wet and laborious business. In the spring of 1952 alone some 50 tons of seaweed were shifted.

The hand of history was on his shoulder: it was the volume of the 'cast ware' and the availability of coral sand 'on its own shores' that a century and a half beforehand had persuaded John Blackadder of Pabay's potential for improvement.

As we shall see, however, despite Len's commitment to organic farming, in practice this proved to be difficult. Additionally, he had to import powdered lime, hundreds of tons of it, year after year, to restore – after decades of leaching – the soil's fertility, lighten it and improve its texture.[18] It was fortuitous, therefore, that in early in 1952 some 'local gentlemen in Kyleakin' formed a company to open a lime quarry at Torrin, the initial aim of which would be to produce 2,500 tons of powdered lime annually, enough to supply all of Skye's requirements.[19]

But even with these supplements, the land in Skye, as in the rest of the Western Isles, is less productive than locations with less rain and more sunshine. Skye is cooler. Mean daily temperatures at sea level are similar to those on Snowdonia, the Welsh mountain region, at around 1,000 feet (305 metres).[20]

The growing season with which Len was familiar lasted seven or eight months. On Skye, it begins later and ends sooner. Telling, was the observation in 1772 by the naturalist, traveller and antiquarian Thomas Pennant – who in 1763 inherited and subsequently improved his family's estate at Downing, Flintshire in North Wales – that the difficulties of the Hebridean farmer 'are unknown on the south: there he sows his seed, and sees it flourish beneath a benign sun and secured from every invasion'. Here (in the north) 'a wet sky brings a reluctant crop'. Making things worse, the winds grow 'stronger and stronger till the autumnal equinox, when they rage with incredible fury'.[21] The husbandman could only look on as his crops were laid prostrate, 'ripe corn shed by the elements', despairing with the dawning realisation that a hungry winter lay ahead.

Within two years of being on Pabay Len had confronted just this reality. Overnight, thirty acres of good-looking oats had been wind- and rain-battered and flattened, leaving only six acres to harvest. He confessed later to feeling, for the first time in his adult life, close to tears.[22] Nor were animals spared the debilitating discomfort caused by constantly blowing wind and driving rain.[23]

Exposed to the Atlantic and the deep depressions of the winter months, both the Inner and Outer Hebrides are pummelled by particularly high winds from September to March. Those driving in from the east – from Russian Siberia and the steppes, Scandinavia and the North Sea – bring bone-chilling cold. Gales are commonplace. Before his first year on Pabay was out, Len was in no doubt that the worst feature of the weather was the wind. In their closely observed portrait of Skye at the end of the twentieth century, Jim Hunter and Cailean Maclean astutely reported the words of one islander on the subject: 'It's easy to hate the wind in Skye.'[24]

Although Len never quite said this, he was acutely aware of its force. During prolonged periods of gales, he wrote, 'one gets numbed & work is confined to the buildings as the effort of walking about outside is too great'. But so too, as he found to his cost, was any attempt to shout above it. The first of the physical impacts upon Len of living and working on Pabay became apparent even at this early stage. Having exacerbated damage to his vocal chords by competing with a roaring Seagull engine, henceforth and despite several visits to ear, nose and throat specialists Len's voice had become and remained huskier, even hoarse-sounding, for the rest of his life. Smoking – the proffered cigarette packet being the common bond between most Pabay males – didn't help.

Finally, there was another major – and unexpected – problem: rabbits (so much so that they merit a chapter on their own). It was only at the end of his first growing season that Len realised how serious Pabay's rabbit infestation was.

* * *

Early in 1950, however, and regardless of these obstacles, some of which took time to become apparent, Len had had to get some planting done if the family were to survive on Pabay.

Already he had met with sceptics, having been accosted in Broadford with jesting enquiries about 'the Groundnut Scheme on Pabay', a reference to a grandiose project then in train to cultivate large swathes of the then British 'Cinderella' colony of Tanganyika (now Tanzania) by growing groundnuts – better known as peanuts, a source of cooking oil, of which there was a global shortage in the post-war years. Backed by the Labour Government under Prime Minister Clement Attlee, with implementation beginning in 1947, vast sums of money (some £36 million in total) were poured into what has been described as a 'sump of official incompetence'.[25] Abandoned in 1951, the scheme, emblematic of the 'fallacies (and fantasies) of late colonial developmentalism', was a disaster.[26] But it was also a very public fiasco, which on Skye drew resentment about the money spent, a fraction of which, if devoted closer to home, it was protested, would not be similarly wasted.

Those familiar with Highland history and agriculture would have been sceptical too of Len's intention of establishing arable farming on Pabay, as opposed simply to grazing cattle or sheep. Dr Isobel F. Grant, the historian and ethnologist founder in 1935 of Am Fasgadh, a small Highland Folk Museum on Iona, and later its successor at Kingussie, had accumulated a lifetime's knowledge of the nature and challenges of Highland husbandry. In 1961, she wryly observed that: 'The nature of the physical conditions of the Highlands of Scotland make them, and have always made them, more suitable for the raising of livestock than for the cultivation of crops, or perhaps one should say ... the Highlands are less unsuitable for the raising of animals than for the growing of grain.'[27]

If these were hardly promising omens, there were other mainly younger locals in and around Broadford who were more support-ive. They welcomed the fresh blood the Whatleys represented and liked what they managed to glean about Len's 'progressive' propos-als for Pabay. Jobs in the area were scarce, and the likelihood was that the newcomers would need paid assistance.

And despite the immediate havoc that had been wreaked by the December storm, it was not a bad time to be trying something new on Skye. True, too many people were leaving. Depopulation, according to Alexander William Nicolson ('Ally Willie'), from Struan in the west of Skye, founder-editor in 1951 of the *Clarion of Skye*, was a 'dread disease, thinning our ranks year by year'.[28]

Skye was, however, beginning to recover from the war, when all road-building and other works, including planned improvements at Broadford pier, had been halted. Farming and commercial life had been hit hard by the cancellation of steamer services, and the requirement for passports. Skye had become so important strategi-cally for the Admiralty that a passport was required in order to use the ferry at Kylerhea.[29]

Len was much taken with Skye Week, which was to be inaugu-rated as part of an effort by leading figures on the island, along with the Skye Council of Social Service, to promote Skye as a place to return to (in the cases of those who had left), live on and visit. Backed by the newly created Scottish Tourist Board, Skye Week was the Misty Isle's equivalent of the Edinburgh Festival of Music and Drama (launched in 1947). Although it would be another fifteen years before it happened, coinciding with the appearance of Len and Margaret on the scene was the start of a campaign for a Sunday ferry service to Skye. This was in the teeth of strong – and often shrill – opposition from the Lord's Day Observance societies in the region.[30]

It was within this more optimistic scenario that Len began to work Pabay. In April 1950, he put in seed potatoes. Three acres in all. Vegetables too were sown – in cold frames – the aim being self-sufficiency in this regard. Near the house he set out blackcurrant bushes, which grow well on Skye.

*   *   *

With little in the way of produce to sell in their first year, the family's finances looked distinctly shaky. And there were four mouths to feed.

Entirely by chance, there had been a short period when they ate very well indeed. In the summer, a puffer from Irvine, on the Clyde coast, had accidentally run aground on Pabay. The puffer belonged to a John Campbell. Grateful for the assistance Len had given the stricken vessel and her small crew, some weeks later another of Campbell's puffers delivered – at Broadford, for the Whatleys – a large box of greengrocery and fruit, a sack of potatoes and two hundredweight of 'first quality' anthracite. The skipper was also under orders to inspect the jetty and shore on Pabay to assess whether in future it would be 'suitable for a shallow-draught puffer'. It wasn't. However, the connection with John Campbell, who was favourably impressed by Len's ambitions for Pabay, was to be of crucial importance later, as we shall see.

By the autumn of 1950, the windfall had been consumed. Len had harvested some potatoes and vegetables. There were fish, including cod and mackerel, to be caught in the sea that surrounded the island – although not for eating by Len, who stuck to his parents' vegetarian diet. Margaret discovered that seagulls' eggs were not only edible but added something to the quality of sponge cakes. There was a market, too, for rabbit meat, which could be exploited if a trapper could be employed.

But what they needed urgently was some cash – for those foodstuffs they were unable to produce for themselves, as well as for other essentials.

Fortunately, the rocks that proliferated around Pabay's coastline were thickly clustered with various kinds of shellfish. We have seen already their attractiveness for Pabay's earliest inhabitants. It is highly likely that over the centuries they continued to be collected: shellfish have been defined as a 'famine food', resorted to by ordinary people living on north-western coasts at times of scarcity.[31]

Of the several varieties of shellfish that were to be found, it was winkles – or 'wilkes' – that were of greatest interest. These were one of the smaller species of whelks that flourished just below the half-tide line. In Martin Martin's time these were called '*gil-fiunt*'.

They would be beaten into pieces (including the shell), boiled, strained and consumed, and were said to be a remedy for kidney stones.[32]

While there was no local demand in 1950 for what were in fact small sea snails, winkles were popular in London, being sold hot from stalls operated by street vendors and sprinkled with vinegar. In fact, it had become a regular trade before the Second World War. The travel writer H.V. Morton – aboard the *Glencoe* in the later 1920s, when it regularly stopped at Broadford's larger, wooden pier – had been astonished when told that from 'this little backwater' millions of whelks in their 'bulging sacks which scrunch strangely as they are lowered gently on deck', were dispatched for the Cockneys of Bethnal Green and Shoreditch to consume.[33]

From the railhead at Kyle, they went to Billingsgate in London, in hundredweight (around 50-kilogram) hessian sacks. In return, if they had found a buyer, came cheques for amounts that rose towards the end of the year as demand increased. On average, they made £4 a week. For Len and Margaret, that within easy reach of the cottage and farmstead there existed this hitherto untouched marine harvest was an unexpected and welcome blessing. So thickly clustered were they on some rocks that if they were lucky they could go down at the bottom of the tide and sweep up the winkles with a brush and dustpan.[34]

This, though, was in the early days, and anyway was exceptional. Best collected in the winter months, winkle-picking was unpleasant work. The unknowing onlooker might point to the compensation of being in territory normally submerged beneath the sea. And to the birdlife.

But there was little time to look and listen, and no waiting for the weather to improve. Picking had to be done as the tide receded, and before it was in full flow: roughly a four-hour window of opportunity.[35] This was time necessarily spent bent down and stooping, with only the briefest of breaks, as, for Len and Margaret, unaccustomed to the job, the full shift was needed to pick enough winkles to fill a sack. Prising them from their hold on the rock or from crevices and gullies was best done with bare hands, which were soon scratched and lacerated as they scraped along the rock or against the barnacles or limpets that inhabited the same spaces as the whelks. Salt water and sand particles added to the discomfort – and, by the end of the session, acute pain. In the wet and cold and perhaps with a bitter wind blowing, winkle picking was not for the faint-hearted.

Yet it had to be done. Even if this meant leaving young Anthea and even younger Stuart on their own for long periods. Anthea was unable yet to tell the time, and remembers her mother explaining that it would be lunchtime when the hands on the mantelpiece clock matched those she had set on Anthea's toy clock.

However, one way and another the family not only got through 1950 but were able to enjoy a festive Christmas. At the heart of the household were the children. Len and Margaret were devoted parents, as they would be for the four more siblings that would follow. Any shortfall in Anthea's and Stuart's presents from their mother and father was made good by what was contained in parcels sent by relatives. These included very welcome 'tit bits' that were either unaffordable or unavailable in Broadford. There was even time to reflect upon and appreciate their new situation. As we saw in Chapter 2, Len was impressed by the tranquillity that could follow a storm, and which 'more than compensate[d] for the rigours of the gales'. The stars visible from Pabay – different from those down south – also caught his attention and sparked sufficient interest for him to want to learn more about the cosmos.

Len was sufficiently encouraged too to plan for the next year's farming operations. This he could now do with some confidence. Len's old school friend Jack Surridge had not only come for a look around but enthused about what they might do together. In fact, it was Surridge who had found the money to secure the island from the previous owners the Muntzes.[36]

Meanwhile, gaps in his knowledge Len addressed by reading exhaustively on a range of topics. On local agricultural conditions he devoured Raymond O'Malley's *One-horse Farm: Crofting in the West Highlands*, published as recently as 1948. He was taken immediately by O'Malley's opening description of Achbeg, the farm near Loch Carron (on the Scottish mainland near Kyle of Lochalsh, so not many miles from Pabay), to which O'Malley and his wife had moved from Devon in 1943: 'With its irregular, scattered patches of run-down soil, its hill of bracken, peat and rock, remote from shops and markets ... washed out by the West Highland downpour, Achbeg was a farm economist's nightmare.'[37]

As a hill farm in a more elevated location than Pabay, and comprising mainly rough grazing, not everything at Achbeg was identical. Even so, much that O'Malley described and explained was instructive: his book was a compendium of invaluable practical information on *how* to farm in the north-west, upon which Len could draw. The reasons for his successes are carefully documented, but so too were the experiments that had failed, including composting (one of Len's enthusiasms), a topic which, 'like folk-art', seemed to attract 'all kinds of querulous and bigoted people'. Having experimented with a variety of compost mixes, O'Malley and his wife decided to revert to the 'rough composting that is traditional along the western shore, the layering of seaweed and muck on the midden', along with modest applications of artificial fertilisers. This became Len's preferred method too.

Although O'Malley was ten years older than Len, that he had been a pacifist during the war further endeared him. So too did the fact that O'Malley's conversion from schoolmaster to small farmer had been instigated by the tribunal that heard his case for exemption from military service. Like Len and Margaret, O'Malley neither spoke nor understood Gaelic, nor had he any advance knowledge of Highland Scotland or of its traditions and customs.

And although O'Malley was an idealist, committed to small-scale 'intensive' and, as far as possible, self-sufficient farming as opposed to industrial-scale, mechanised agriculture, he was brutally realistic about the nature and trials of farming in the environment of north-west Scotland.

There was nothing romantic about the 'aching vastness of weedy potato-drills ... the worry of March and April ... and still no sprout of new green ... the trickle down the spine and the squelch of feet in leaky boots; the endless drizzle ... there was maggot, the living death; the weeks of painful waiting for the dentist ... and the midges, the petty, crawling, stabbing, insignificant, insufferable multitudes of midges'. He was at pains to stress the enormous

responsibilities that lay on the shoulders of the self-employed
farmer – from judging the day's weather, deciding when and what
to sow, what kinds of poultry to bring in, and how to deal with
and overcome the inevitable and all too frequent adversities.

But there were joys too, minor in isolation perhaps but cumula-
tively a treasure trove, stored, 'ready for the slightest beck of
memory'.[38] Over time Len would experience all of this and so
much more, but at the time he read O'Malley, it was heartening for
him to know that fairly close to hand, kindred spirits had trodden
the path upon which he and Margaret were now embarked. But
while O'Malley and his wife left Achbeg after four years for a
more comfortable life, eventually, in O'Malley's case, to become a
university lecturer, Len stayed and was still on Pabay nearly twenty
years later.

Even at this early stage though, he recognised the pertinence of
some of O'Malley's assessments. Farming Pabay on his own was
proving to be difficult – perhaps even impossible. 'We have already
found,' Len reflected after only a few months, that 'one family is
rather too small a unit for an island', even one the size of Pabay.
There was not only the myriad of routine farm tasks. Before he
could really get going there was the reclamation work. To keep the
rabbits at bay he would have to erect hundreds of yards of net
fences, sunk deep into the ground. And if, as he planned, he was to
bring cattle across and overwinter them, he would have to grow
more and better grass.

On an island with no telephone, business with all manner of
suppliers and prospective customers was necessarily conducted by
letter, which ate up his time. Additionally, there was the matter of
attending to the boat – its upkeep, repairs and mooring, and trips
to and from Broadford and Kyle and sometimes the nearby islands
of Scalpay and Raasay in order to obtain materials of one kind and
another, which had barely been factored into Len's planning.

Writing of Achbeg, O'Malley had stressed the 'intrinsic value of
neighbourliness' in working a croft. Achbeg, though, was an inland
farm. Pabay was an island farm, and Len had no crofting neighbours. He needed help, but as we saw earlier, in relation to Scalpay
as well as Pabay, getting reliable labour onto an island was neither

straightforward nor cheap. We can understand his elation that Surridge was to join him.

O'Malley's was just one of the many books Len pored over as part of his self-devised introductory course on life in the north-west. Less practical in nature than the essential reading he had done even before he got to Pabay on tides, navigation and seaman-ship, he began to explore Highland history. O'Malley – a graduate of Trinity College, Cambridge – may have whetted his appetite, his commentary on the social aspects of Strath Ascaig enriched by his ability to layer the observed present onto the recorded past.

Len was conscious that he had crossed a cultural threshold. Keen, therefore, to comprehend better the background to the land issue he heard raised periodically and passionately even in casual conversation on Skye, he ordered from Inverness County Council's library the seminal *History of the Highland Clearances* by the son of a Gairloch crofter, Alexander Mackenzie, published in 1883. In order to familiarise himself with Skye's history, he delved into Alexander Nicolson's classic *History of Skye*.[39] Even though Pabay was a long way from the Highland capital of Inverness, Len availed himself of his entitlement (based on that of a lighthouse keeper) of a generous cargo of eighty or so books, which he and those around him delighted in rummaging through when it arrived every couple of months.

In their own fragmentary way, Len and Margaret were starting to play their part in turning back the tide of Skye's recent past.

The timing is crucial. They were doing so in the 1950s and 1960s, just when, in the words of one recent historian of the Highlands, the 'tension between old and new reached the moment of its final conflict'.[40]

For Pabay, the 'old' had been represented by the Mackinnon brothers. Len and Margaret's appearance heralded something new. Yet as we will see, much that was old impinged on the new. It was easier to chart a new direction than follow it.

Chapter 8

'Sweating about money': Pabay problems, 1951–56

The year 1951 began well. Indeed, for the next two years Len's excitement about the Pabay project permeates the few letters he had time to write. His boundless energy and determination that it should succeed is recalled by those who knew him at the time.

At first it looked like Jack Surridge would provide the additional assistance he needed to make progress in turning Pabay into a thriving farm. Surridge and his wife Joyce decided not to live on Pabay but in Broadford. To set up a home base on a small island in the Inner Sound on a full-time basis was evidently a step too far, but anyway, as things stood Pabay could only accommodate one family. On the other hand, the frequency of rough weather and high seas ruled out anything like a daily commute to work.

In the end, Surridge's arrival achieved little, although the two men did manage to get a tractor brought over on a small ferry borrowed for the occasion, and some ploughing and planting done. With money borrowed from his mother (who was to be disappointed that the £200 loan was never repaid), Len had bought a new Ferguson tractor to replace a pre-war Fordson. With its all-metal wheels and spade lugs the Fordson was good on soil, but it was cumbersome to handle and tore up the loosely packed stones that formed most of the island's tracks. The Ferguson, fitted with rubber tyres, was altogether superior, a multi-purpose machine. Developed in the 1930s, the now affordable 'Fergie' had become the 'must-have' piece of equipment for farmers and crofters throughout Scotland, although for those working closer to the margins of subsistence it remained beyond their means.[1]

Progress, however, was sluggish. With poor spring weather, it was not until June that Len was able to put in fodder beet, and this by means of a manually pushed Anzani drilling machine – a physically exhausting method. This was on ground ploughed and rotavated into a fine tilth by his brother, Allan, who had become a skilled tractor driver during the war. As a CO he too had been ordered to perform agricultural work in the Birmingham area, and did so from July 1940 until he was discharged five years later, in June 1946.

This, Allan's first visit to Pabay, was timely even if, as he was in full-time employment in a Glasgow college, it only provided a short-term solution. Len and Jack Surridge's partnership arrangement had soured to the extent that by the end of the summer Len was taking steps to buy Surridge out.

As a consequence, Len was on his own again. Somehow, he had to raise the capital to satisfy his erstwhile partner but also to find the wherewithal to purchase essential farming and associated equipment. In order to ascertain the market value of the island, which would determine how much Len would pay Surridge, Pabay was put up for sale for £5,000. No one came close to offering the asking price (and anyway Len would have been reluctant to sell), and Len was unable to raise the £1,000 or thereabouts he required to pay off Surridge, a heavy and nagging burden that was only finally lifted five years later.

Even with his brother's assistance, the results of Len's second harvest were at best mixed. The root crops were poor. The mangolds had failed entirely. Fodder beet was 'hopeless'.[2] The silage was judged to be inadequate. Better was the oat crop, which was 'good for the area'. Potatoes too were reasonably successful, at seven tons to the acre, although by mid-October much was still in the ground and in danger of getting overly wet, and rotting. The first two acres of potatoes had been lifted by lads brought over from local schools, but there were still another ten acres to go.

As winter approached there was still no livestock on the island – at this stage there was insufficient means of feeding them. Yet cattle, sheep, pigs and poultry would make it more likely that Pabay would provide Len and the family with a livelihood. If George Henderson's model of sustainable small-scale farming were to be followed, incorporating livestock into the production cycle was of critical importance, both to maximise the productiveness of the arable, and as a means of keeping costs low by not having to buy in artificial fertilisers.

Furthermore, it was primarily livestock husbandry that the Department of Agriculture, under the terms of the Agriculture (Scotland) Act of 1948, would support. This was the Scottish variant of the Labour Government's Agricultural Act of 1947, which 'perpetuated the principles of state help for farming' that had begun in the 1930s.[3]

For marginal farms like Pabay, this and other forms of government assistance made the difference between borderline sustainability and failure. To this end, and recognising the government's keenness to encourage meat production, Len assured a technical officer from the Department of Agriculture in Portree that his intention was 'to buy a few head of Ayrshire cows and some beef calves to rear on the pail feeding system'. He also intended to rear some pigs. On this basis the officer recommended that 'a further period of time be given to Mr Whatley to make good his promise to stock the island'.[4] It was touch and go.

He said as much to his father at the time; things were 'pretty tight'. As far as extending his farming operation was concerned, his hands were tied. Indeed, in order to make ends meet, he was seriously considering selling the *Sea Otter*, and to depend entirely on the dinghy. Meantime, however, he would need an overdraft of up to £175 from the Westminster Bank, for which he appealed to his father to act as guarantor. Without this, Len explained, he would have to sell something else at a loss; he was, and felt, 'stuck'. The situation, he pleaded reluctantly, was now 'urgent'.[5]

It was as well that the potato crop had been secured, as it was potato sales alone in the first months of 1952 that kept the family afloat financially. On this occasion Len was on the ball when it came to judging the right time to sell: by March 'All sorts of people were crying out for potatoes'. He had plenty in store, ready to bag and take by boat to Kyleakin or Broadford and supply to grateful buyers.[6]

* * *

Not much more than nine months later, however, the situation had been transformed, or appeared to have been.

In July 1952, persuaded by Margaret to sit down and assess the progress made, Len noted with evident pleasure that, 'The place now looks & smells like a farm.' He even had a collie dog, Forsa, acquired from a Skye crofter keen to rid himself of a dog that chased sheep and was unable or unwilling to take part in the orderly in-gathering of the flock.

On the island were sixty pigs, which Len anticipated would increase to a hundred the following year. By then too he would have learned from this year's mistake of sending pigs to Carlisle for grading without realising how much weight they would shed on the way down: for the best prices they would have to be fatter when they left Pabay.[7] He had also acquired eighty Sussex hens, 'for winter production'. By October they were laying, with their eggs selling at six shillings and sixpence (about 32 pence) a dozen. Not much to modern eyes, but with production rising to several dozens in a week, eggs – for a time – became Pabay's main revenue stream.

Len's hopes were highest for his thirty Aberdeen Angus heifers – a breeding herd to be run with a bull, with the calves being reared and wintered out on Pabay, and sold as one- and two-year-old store beasts. Although the results of this strategy would take time to come through, he expected that cattle sales would be 'the main export because they are convertors of our best crop – grass'. Indeed, what gave Len a particularly warm glow of satisfaction was that most of the animal fodder he used was Pabay-grown – mainly re-seeded grass, another step towards his goal of being more or less self-sufficient. The animal feed included fodder beet (sown in June 1951) on which the pigs were fed in folds sheltered from the wind. The wilted tops the cattle then ate, in the process leaving behind them quantities of welcome manure. In this instance, and unusually, local climatic conditions were a boon, the folding system made possible only 'because of the absence of snow & frost'.[8]

So well were things developing on the stock front that in October Len purchased from Sutherland a pedigree Aberdeen Angus bull calf – 'quite a big beast' although only seven months old – for £50: 'Lord Ivac of Cape Wrath'. Not many months later – the winter of 1952–53 over – a Department of Agriculture official highlighted the condition of his heifers as one of Len's most impressive achievements.[9] Less pleasing was his discovery that Lord Ivac had only one testicle. He was immediately castrated, thereby initiating a search for a fully equipped successor. Although older, and de-horned, 'Balnakeil Barnabus' proved not only to be popular amongst the cows, but with Len and others too. Stan Robinson (see below) recalled later that 'he had the nicest temperament of any bovine I have met'.[10]

Other crops too were flourishing. Probably at no point in the past had Pabay been as bounteous as it was at this time – even when it had been supporting four sizeable households in the 1830s and early 1840s. A range of vegetables including potatoes, cabbage, carrots, leeks and celery were doing well, with a good sale anticipated. An inspector from the Department of Agriculture confessed to being 'amazed' by the difference a year had made: 'There wasn't grass anywhere like it on Skye', he pronounced.[11] Grains – oats (with beans), barley and wheat – promised much too. Before the end of August, the oats, standing almost five feet high, looked like they would produce a 'marvellous' crop. Even better was Len's experiment with wheat, which by mid-August was almost ready for harvesting. We have 'certainly exploded the myth that wheat cannot be grown in the NW', he declared, as he looked forward to home-grown, home-baked bread. Nurtured on them by his parents, throughout his life he held firm to his belief in the importance of natural, whole foods.

He was not alone in his positive assessment of what had been achieved so soon. 'We have had praise from all & sundry', he wrote. Cutting hay in May had 'made local jaws drop', as the usual time for haymaking on Skye was July and August. By sowing oats in August he hoped to exploit the longer days of summer the next year, a benefit of Pabay's northern latitude, and harvest them earlier. But so prolific was the harvest of 1952 that it was becoming apparent that additional barn space was needed at the far end of the island, to be closer to where the grain was growing.

One of the rock shelters on Pabay in which have been found limpet shells, bones and other indications of human habitation during the Mesolithic era. (© Christopher A. Whatley)

Broadford pier, or jetty, *c*.1958. This was the normal point of departure for Pabay. In the middle of the picture is Len's brown varnished launch, and Stuart and me. (Whatley Collection)

The jetty on Pabay, around low tide. In the foreground is George Jolly's boat, the *Curlew*. Familiarity with the tides was essential unless hours were to be wasted waiting for it to flow and make access to the jetty possible. (Whatley Collection)

End of the jetty, Pabay, *c.*1958. From the left are Margaret, Alison, Rachel, Stuart, and Neil MacRae, long-time Pabay employee and, at the time, the island's boatman. (Whatley Collection)

Stuart and I collecting eggs from some of the arks that were distributed around the island, *c.*1958. To the rear are some remaining trees from one of the shelter belts planted out by Sir Donald Currie in the 1890s. (Whatley Collection)

Len Whatley packaging day-old chicks for onwards distribution around Skye, the Outer Isles and parts of north-west Scotland. From the mid-1950s, this was his biggest success financially. Indeed, amongst older inhabitants on Skye and elsewhere, poultry from Pabay's attested breeding station is still remembered. (Whatley Collection)

The Lias rock strata of the Ob Lusa–Ardnish area, on the eastern edge of the bay, looking over to Pabay. The 'Broadford Beds' were exposed 'in [an] unbroken series along the beach'. Consisting of marine limestones, sandstones, shales, mudstones and clays, the Lias dates back to the early Jurassic era – the secrets of which in the early-mid 19th century were just beginning to be uncovered in Scotland. (© Christopher A. Whatley)

Great trap dyke on the north side of Pabay. The figures in the centre, walking near to the dyke, emphasise the great height of this natural feature that so impressed the early geologists. (© Christopher A. Whatley)

The *Coruisk*, bought mainly for her engines. She broke free from her mooring off Pabay and grounded in front of the pre-fabricated bungalow that Len had built. She was a valuable storehouse of materials both for Pabay and to sell on – and, for children, a great place to play. Later, the bow section, upturned, was used as a henhouse. (Whatley Collection)

Selection of Pabay stamps, from 1964 and 1965. Launched by Len in 1962, stamp sales, along with the role he assumed as Pabay's postmaster, provided a surprisingly useful additional source of much-needed revenue. (Whatley Collection)

Len, with his children Alison and Michael watching, preparing to go off in the *Klepper* sailing canoe, with outriggers. This was the boat in which Donald and Judith MacLachlan arrived on Pabay in 1965. Len greatly enjoyed the new experience of sailing, although like so many of his boats the *Klepper* was lost in a gale. (Whatley Collection)

Len and Stuart Whatley inspecting the results of an early firing of pots, early 1960s. The small kiln was situated under a lean-to shelter in the yard of the farm steading. It was around this time that Len began to believe that pottery might be an income earner, a double delight as making things gave him enormous satisfaction. (Whatley Collection)

Len, fashioning pots, Edinbane, 1973. By this time he was becoming an accomplished potter and, with Stuart, had established Edinbane Pottery. (© Christopher A. Whatley)

Above. Edinbane Pottery, 2007, and still growing strong. A direct and lasting legacy from Pabay, following Len's early discovery of and inquisitiveness about clay, and his decision, with his son Stuart to establish a pottery at Edinbane once Pabay had been sold. (© Stuart Whatley Collection)

Right. Stuart Whatley, throwing a large jug, Edinbane Pottery, 2008. (© Stuart Whatley Collection)

Gotland rams and Shetland ewes herded into the farmyard on Pabay. The seaweed-eating Gotland breed – from Sweden – was successfully introduced to the island by Anne and Ted Gerrard in the 1970s. They continued to be bred and their fleeces and meat sold from the island until the 1990s, when David Harris moved them across to Corry Farm.
(© Nick Broughton Collection)

Storm harbour, Pabay, mid-1980s. Blasted out of the rock at the jetty by Ted Gerrard in the early 1970s, this facility added enormously to the security of boats lying at Pabay. Previously there was no protection from wind and gales from the south and east. Had it been there beforehand, Len Whatley would have lost fewer boats than he did.
(© Nick Broughton)

Margaret (Whatley) Mackinnon, late 1990s, hand finishing a pullover in her knitting workshop and showroom, Dunhallin Crafts. For several years after leaving Pabay and then Edinbane Lodge, her one-woman knitting business flourished. She produced bespoke knitwear for customers from around the world and relished conversations with visitors. (© Anthea Beszant)

Stuart and his son Richard on the track on Pabay from the jetty to the main buildings, June 2018. Without livestock or rabbits, there is much more greenery than there was in 1950. The former cottage and extension have been extended upwards and outwards. In the background, behind the now neat, whitewashed farmstead, the current owner's large house can be seen, while on the cliff are two powerful wind turbines. (© Christopher A. Whatley)

Not everything fulfilled this early promise. The oats yielded less grain than anticipated; in fact, they were decimated, as we saw in the last chapter. The main crop – potatoes – disappointed too, even though Len's gave a better return than elsewhere on Skye, in what was a poor year. All in all, though, the outcome was heartening.

What had made the difference?

Firstly, Henry Hilditch and his wife Margaret had taken the decision to leave the Midlands and move, lock, stock and barrel, to Skye. At just over sixty years of age Henry was, in his own words, 'too young to settle down'. And while he would not be seeking re-adoption as the Labour candidate in Stratford, he had no intention of giving up politics. During subsequent years he fired off letters to the *New Statesman*, the *Glasgow Herald*, *The Scotsman* and other papers on what he considered to be the failings of the Conservative Government's agricultural policy and other issues that roused his ire. (In an early example of 'fake news' the same newspaper that reported Henry Hilditch's send-off by the Birmingham and Hall Green Labour Parties insisted that Len Whatley 'wears the kilt, not without right, for he speaks Gaelic'. Of course, neither claim was true.[12]) The big plus for the Hilditch couple was that by moving to Skye they would be much closer to their daughter Margaret (whose mother had not been happy with her departure to Pabay), and their two grandchildren, Anthea and Stuart. And a third was on the way: Rachel was born in March 1952.

So swiftly did Henry and his wife make the transition from Birmingham to Skye that by the time of Rachel's birth they had been on the island upon which they had never set foot previously for more than a month. More than that, Henry's son Harry thought he would leave Cornwall, where he was then working for the proprietor of a combined farming and hotel business, and join his parents on Skye, at least on an experimental basis over the summer. His intention initially was to assist Len, with whom, as we have seen, he had worked after the war, and perhaps look out for a smallholding of his own.

For the Whatleys on Pabay, the Hilditches' arrival and presence in Broadford, where after renting for a while they bought a house

– 'Seaside' – that looked directly over to Pabay, was of monumental importance.

For one thing, it resolved the issue of the children's schooling. As had happened on Scalpay during the 1920s, the local education authority was obliged to provide a teacher for Pabay. Although this was what Stuart would have preferred, on this occasion his older sister's wishes prevailed: she wanted to go to the primary school in Broadford. With their grandparents being so close to hand, the two children could now lodge with them. The arrangement wasn't ideal, not least as weather conditions sometimes made it impossible for Anthea and Stuart (and later, Rachel) to return home to Pabay for the weekend, or get back again to Broadford on the Monday morning. Not that this had any effect on their performance, with both regularly being at or close to the top of their respective classes.

In the short time they had been on Pabay, Len and Margaret had not really contemplated the consequences of being on their own on an island. When asked if they had thought in advance of what would happen in the event of an accident, Margaret replied that if she and Len had allowed themselves to dwell on such things they would never have gone.

But to some extent the unexpected could now be dealt with, by the crude signalling system they devised, using torchlight flashes, which would be seen by the ever-alert Hilditches at 'Seaside'. Although not during daylight. Then, if an emergency occurred, a sheet was to be hung out in a pre-agreed spot.

Any faint awareness Len and Margaret had of local hostility or cultural alienation had been more than compensated for by the launch on 1 January 1951 of what would be the long-running six-day-a-week BBC radio serial *The Archers*. This 'everyday story of country folk' brought into the cottage kitchen on Pabay the rustic Midlands and 'Brummie' accents of their previous life. Broadcast via a radio powered with a short-life battery, the programme for Len and Margaret was essential listening, second only to the Met Office's shipping forecast. This they prioritised after Len realised that the BBC's national or even regional weather forecasts were wholly inadequate.

Mrs Dale's Diary, and Saturday evening plays too, were enjoyed when the battery held out, as was some music. In effect, the 'wireless' became their neighbours.[13] For Margaret, the radio also eased the social isolation that troubled her during these early days. She was immensely sociable, and loved company. During the lengthening nights as winter set in in 1951 her sense of aloneness had been intensified; the village of Broadford and the other settlements along the coast to the east at the time lay mainly in the dark, and remained so until the newly completed hydroelectric plant near the island's capital of Portree was able to supply power and light.

But the close proximity of Margaret's parents added to the couple's sense of security, as both mother and daughter got into the habit of scouring the sea beyond them, looking out for boats bound for Broadford and Pabay respectively.

Within a couple of years, communications were improved with the acquisition of an ex-army shortwave transmitter and receiver set, powered by a hand-cranked generator – a walkie-talkie. Condemned at first as illegal by the GPO, who sent three men across to interview Len about how he'd acquired it and whether he was up to no good, permission to use the device was eventually – after five years – secured. Len and Margaret could now talk with Henry Hilditch on a daily basis, albeit at prearranged times.

Also on a practical level, almost immediately Len was relieved by Henry of one of the more onerous and time-consuming of tasks: writing business letters and sending and responding to telegrams – which necessitated a return boat trip to the post office in Broadford. He could now devote more of his energies to the farm – by making pig troughs and hen houses for instance, cultivating more of the neglected land, and 'umpteen other things and all wanting to be done at the same time'.[14]

Henry too was able to assist his son Harry after he decided to stay and establish himself with his wife Olive as guest house proprietors and then hoteliers in Broadford. The Dunollie Hotel as it stands today – overlooking Broadford's old pier and out onto the bay and Pabay – is testimony to Harry's grit and practical skills in electrical work, plumbing and joinery, allied to the entrepreneurial abilities of his father. Once Skye's most highly regarded hotel, Dunollie now boasts eighty-four en-suite bedrooms, although in the quality stakes it has fallen behind.[15]

This, however, is to digress, although we will have occasion to return to Dunollie in later chapters.

Unsurprisingly for a man who loved work 'so much I could lie down beside it', within days of his arrival on Skye Henry had thrown himself into his new role as Pabay's unofficial operations manager, accountant and head of marketing and distribution. His capacity for problem-solving, wheeling and dealing, cajoling (local and national government officials especially), and even bullying where need be, were a necessary combination if Pabay were to be a viable proposition financially. Allied to this, and a product of his acute political antennae, was his knowledge and understanding of government policy, above all in relation to the Highland and Islands, and his willingness to find ways both above and below board of tapping into any financial assistance available.

His first impression about Len's chances of making Pabay pay was only cautiously optimistic. He was surer that even in the short time Len had been on Pabay he had gone some way towards turning it into a 'saleable proposition'. At the same time, however, he recognised how close to bankruptcy the project was. Jestingly, in a letter to Len's father, he drew the prospect of himself 'standing at the Bgham P.O. selling Old Moore almanacs', with Herbert Whatley holding out the hat.[16] Over the summer and into the autumn Henry busied himself on all manner of tasks, from arranging the transport of pigs to Carlisle and the distribution and sale of eggs on Skye, through gathering up corrugated iron for Len to hammer into pig troughs, to identifying a source of Nissen huts to be used as barns for storage, shelters for the cattle and to house workers who were on the island for any length of time.

It was in risky dealings of this kind that he came into his own. The huts he found, of which there were a dozen that were usable, were *in situ* near Oban. After discussion with Len, who was less certain about taking the gamble of buying twice as many as he needed, Henry bought the lot for £130. Six were to be re-erected on Pabay at around £35 each, including the cost of rail transport and then ferrying them, plus the cement for the foundations

– although in the event only five went up. The rest he sold for £65 each. If all went well (as it did, eventually, but for a short time only), Len's outlay would be zero, while at the same time he would benefit by having the facilities the huts would provide. Henry was as proud as Punch, teasing Herbert with the taunt that 'if you had been offered the choice of a dozen or more when you were thinking of three ... you'd have been so scared stiff that you'd have taken none'.[17]

By the end of 1951 Len had also managed to make inroads into what his father-in-law called the 'labour problem' by recruiting additional workers.

He had had some help during his first year from local school children who, as elsewhere in Scotland, were able to leave the classroom for the autumn 'tattie holiday'. The practice carried on for some years, with 'big boys' from the Broadford area 'invading' the island for a few days as the crop was lifted. Although she was discomfited by the presence of the boys, Anthea too assisted, grading the potatoes as they arrived in the yard, and sewing closed the hessian sacks in which they were sent off. This was but one of the tasks which Anthea and Stuart – and later on, Rachel and Alison when they were able – could help with, thereby making time for Len and Margaret and the other adults to concentrate on what they did best.

Tasks deemed suitable for the younger members of the family included finding, herding and milking the cow, sterilising the dairy utensils, collecting eggs and feeding hens, candling eggs (that is, checking they were fertile), cleaning out the incubators where chickens were hatched, and then caponising (neutering) them, boxing chickens, laying out newly cut peats for drying and bagging them when dry, haymaking and assisting in gathering the sheep, and then with the dipping and shearing.

Doing 'jobs' was never an issue; it was what everyone did on Pabay, regardless of age or relationship to the family. Non-participants were rare, and easily spotted – and found their time on the island cut short. Nor was age a barrier to assuming real-life responsibilities: I was just twelve when, with Anthea, we overhauled a dinghy; by this time too Stuart was used to handling an air gun, and shooting rabbits and starlings that were feared to be carrying disease that passed to the poultry.[18] There was only one chore that chafed: dish-washing for the large numbers of people who would often be on Pabay for what otherwise were usually lively, convivial lunches. Amongst my late mother's papers was a card I sent her: was I complaining, I wonder, with my closing sentence: 'Was washing dishes 12 times in a row.'

The first of the permanent workers was the aforementioned Stan Robinson, from Sussex, formerly a BBC employee at the Droitwich transmitter. After National Service and, influenced by the ideas of Clive Bell (a pacifist and, amongst other things, an ardent countryman) he decided to change tack and take up farm work. To prepare himself, he enrolled on a course in agriculture at a farming institute in Sussex. He advertised his availability in the *New Statesman* – which of course was read by Henry Hilditch. Stan and he met, followed by a meeting with Len, and a deal was done, made easier as Stan was looking for a different lifestyle rather than a hefty wage.[19] Henry Hilditch was enthusiastic too about another possible hand, 'a young fellow ... [from] a Rugby pacifist family' who was currently studying full-time at Moreton Morrell Agricultural College in Warwickshire. Others too were tempted by the prospect of island life, but rarely lasted long.

Robinson, however, stayed. Having experience of mixed farming, he was adaptable and as at home working with the tractor as milking cows or on the boats, and played an important part in Pabay's unfolding story. To have another pair of hands was for Len invaluable, and allowed him – for example – to pursue his aim of obtaining from the island feedstuffs for his stock. It was with Stan that in March 1952 he was able to cast a fishing net and catch dogfish that provided his pigs with a source of cheap protein – animal feedstuffs then still being rationed.[20]

For a couple of years this arrangement worked reasonably well, although netting operations were frequently brought to a halt by the weather. Even in a moderate sea hauling the nets proved impossible. An alternative protein source was gulls' eggs, although gathering – stealing – these, required a stiff nerve as angered adult gulls swooped and dived around the heads of those interfering with their nests.[21] None of this was enough, however, to supply the pigs' requirements, and they were sold off.

In these early years, as Len battled on a number of fronts to improve the island's infrastructure – at the same time as coping with the multiple demands of the annual farming cycle – more assistance was essential. Contractors could be hired to supplement Len's and Stan Robertson's input for certain jobs, such as threshing. There was fencing too, which the two men could not do alone. In fact, this – like dealing with the island's choking drainage system – was now urgent.

Cattle losses were becoming a serious issue; five cows fell off the cliff edge at the eastern side of the island before this was fenced off in the summer of 1953. A similar number died after they had broken into a field of rich spring grass. Gorging on this bovine equivalent of chocolate cake, they became bloated, and died. Others became ill when grazing near a particular stretch of shoreline.

As a matter of urgency, the vet in Broadford was sought out and brought across. Arsenic poisoning was the diagnosis, the result perhaps of consuming too much seaweed, which contains high concentrations of the toxin. Although not known at the time, subsequent scientific research on Orkney has identified a link between kelp burning in former times and elevated arsenic levels in surrounding soils.[22] It is possible that on Pabay too, with its plentiful endowment of seaweed (including the most desirable sub-littoral *Laminaria* tangles, with their free-branching blades), kelp-burning had taken place during the trade's boom years. To the bitterness the subsequent suffering the industry's collapse created in the crofter communities, we can now add its hidden toxic legacy for livestock.

And the rabbits continued to take their toll.

Local men were taken on, on a casual basis, to tackle jobs as they arose. Alex McLeod was one of the first, an adept threshing machine operator. This raised the issue of what appeared to be a weakly developed work ethic on the part of some of those Len employed. This had for over a century been an accusation levelled mainly by Lowlanders against lazy 'Caledonian Celts' who 'preferred their habitual mode of life – their few days of desultory labour intermingled with weeks of lounging gossip', in preference to 'regular well repaid toil'.[23]

In truth, the men concerned were products of a long-established Highland culture that valued leisure and social interaction over income maximisation – not least because, for most, such a prospect hardly existed. The concept of working regularly at a single job for one employer was foreign to men accustomed to constructing a living opportunistically from a variety of sources. And this in a weather environment that was unpredictable and variable in the extreme.

Useful too were visitors to the island who, usually serendipitously, turned up and were either persuaded to return and work, or who, once on Pabay, found themselves unable to free themselves from the island's spell. Casting it were Len and Margaret, for whom friends, once made, were friends for life.[24] Young at heart, tolerant and, in Margaret's case, open about her own anxieties and interested in those of others, unwittingly they offered a kind of sanctuary entirely fitting for an island that centuries beforehand had probably served just this purpose.

In the summer of 1954, for instance, Len brought back from Broadford a trio of youth-hostelling friends who had been on their way to Wester Ross but, wandering around Caisteal Maol at Kyle, had met Alan Browne, an artist and photographer who had recently returned from a spell mountain guiding in New Zealand. He persuaded them to detour on to Skye. Browne knew the Hilditches, in whose garage they slept the night. The following day they met Len and Margaret and the children, who had come across for supplies. The three young travellers joined Len and Margaret on their return, for what was supposed to be an overnight stay.

Their impressions were immediately favourable. In fact, they were entranced, at least two of them were. Peter Bromilow, a young Cheshire-born actor who had recently returned from India working on tour with the post-Raj Shakespeareana Company run by Geoffrey Kendal, the actress Felicity Kendal's father, went on to feature in films such as *The Railway Children*.

His two companions, however, in different ways, became part of the Pabay firmament. Dorothy Harrop was a librarian in Manchester who was so enchanted by Pabay and the Whatleys that she seriously considered moving to the island to live, perhaps by taking over the poultry side of the farm – even though her least favourite job was plucking and dressing hens for sale, an aversion that was widely shared. Bound to repay her course fees however if she resigned her post, she became instead a regular visitor, and a willing, multi-tasking worker. Her companion was Rosemary Horn – Rosa – a medical student at London's Middlesex Hospital. Rosa's stay was briefer, but no less life-changing. Despite a less than warm initial meeting with Stan, who asked 'Who the hell are you?' when she handed him down a box from Broadford pier just prior to her maiden trip to Pabay, they fell in love, and married a couple of years later. But to live in Devon, not on Pabay, which Stan left later in 1955 to be replaced, eventually, by Allen Wood, who was recognisable mainly by his thick beard and his heavy smoking habit.

Back on Pabay, Rosa's influence was longer-lasting. On her second visit, she had been accompanied by a friend, Liz Taylor, who met and married Wood. The newly married couple stayed on Pabay. The close proximity engendered by island living, along with the freedom from normal constraints, can spark the most intense longings – and love. But the same environment – as we've seen in the case of Scalpay – can also turn minor irritations into smouldering antagonisms. And, occasionally, into raging interpersonal furies. The details now are lost, but this, it seems, was partly what eventually brought the Woods' time on Pabay to a premature end.

There were local men upon who Len came to rely: Neil MacRae from Broadford was one of these, introduced to Len by Harry Hilditch, who had employed him on building work at Dunollie. Married to Chrissie and father of three chidren, Neil had a personable manner and a roguish twinkle in his eye capable of melting even the hardest heart. Donald Fletcher, mentioned earlier, was another, from Breakish. On first acquaintance surly, but actually painfully shy, he was small in stature but strong as an ox, hardy, hardworking and hard-drinking (not on Pabay but over long weekends at home, which sometimes took him till Tuesday to recover from). Formerly in the RAF, he was also highly intelligent, exceptionally well-read and polite – always removing his trademark black cap at mealtimes. Unobtrusive (when sober), Donald had what Rachel called a 'magnetism' for each of the children when they were young – they would follow him around as he carried out his various duties. This Donald had been preceded by 'Black Donald', a Skye man who had been in the army (he employed his army rifle to shoot – very accurately – rabbits). Strong, resourceful and useful, his time on Pabay was brief, simply announcing one day, 'I must be going now, to be building myself a house.'[25]

Len's preference at this stage was for full-time, resident workers, who were multi-skilled. Or just willing to learn how to do new things. Finding the right people, however, was far from straightforward. In the circumstances, above all Pabay's financial situation, a straightforward employer–employee relationship, with each party serving their own interest in the manner described by the eighteenth-century philosopher and economist Adam Smith, would not do. There had to be an emotional commitment to the project from whomever Len took on; as Henry Hilditch remarked sagely, 'We just can't afford passengers.'[26] Thus it was in the *Farmers Weekly* and the *New Statesman* that advertisements for additional hands were placed, on the assumption that these journals would be more likely to be read by people with an appreciation of what farm work entailed, and perhaps with a sense of commitment to the collective good.

Even this measure was no guarantee of successful recruitment. Early in 1953, for instance, an experienced stockman who had his own farm in Cornwall – which was being let to a tenant – was taken on for a year. Six feet tall and with a black beard, he looked the part. His wife, a keen gardener, came too. Almost immediately though, seeds of doubt were sown. Within days Henry Hilditch had noted that he was 'not a tremendously energetic fellow' when it came to physical work. Even Stuart, Len and Margaret's five-year-old son, observed the same failing and, with the innocence of youth, told him, 'My daddy would do that in half the time.'[27] The couple's stay was soon curtailed.

Even with individuals who did fit the bill, owing to the variability of the weather and the necessity of a sea crossing, progress on important operations was intermittent and frustratingly slow. What Len had to quickly adapt to was the immense impact of the state of the wind (and tides) on virtually every aspect of life on Pabay.

A problem that would rear its head consistently over the coming years was what could be lengthy delays – lasting several days or even weeks – in landing materials and equipment. This was in spite of Len's deepening ability to read the sky and the breeze and judge whether he would be able to make the sea crossing to Broadford and back safely – on the same day, or even over the next couple of hours.

Often, visits from the vet or departmental officials had to be cancelled. It was intensely disappointing if an inspector from the Department of Agriculture travelled from Inverness only to find Pabay inaccessible. Unless the inspection was carried out, and found satisfactory, no payment could be made.

Few officials, however, were as doughty as the 'wifey', 'Ms' Luke, who turned up at the end of April 1956 to blood-test the poultry. Len took her over in what was already a heavy sea, which looked likely to worsen. He planned to put her up on Pabay overnight. However, she insisted she had to return to Inverness that day, so Len took her back. When he turned in to Broadford pier, 'She was in the bottom of the boat – blue with cold (North wind), and scared stiff.' Evidently conscious that Len had taken something of a risk in bringing her across, she had the good grace the next day to telephone to ask Henry Hilditch if he had arrived back on Pabay safely.[28] It was not the last time that Ms Luke would suffer on the Pabay crossing: it was something of a family joke that her visits seemed to coincide with rough seas. In October 1959, the then boatman, Neil MacRae, turned around before even attempting to land her on the island. This time her appearance on her return at the pier at Broadford was described as 'green'; she declined Henry Hilditch's offer of lunch and hurried back to Inverness.[29]

The concepts of regularity and predictability ceased to have any significance. That is, for six days of the week. On Skye, the Sabbath was still a day of rest, threatened only during the summer months by visitors and their motor cars.[30] To maintain it as such had up to this point been, and continued to be, the Church of Scotland's Skye Presbytery's most pressing concern. Ordinary parishioners could be of a similar mind.

Early on, whilst shopping in the Co-op in Broadford, Margaret was gently upbraided as – from across the water – she had been seen hanging out her washing on the previous Sabbath. Even more subtle had been the response to a lazy summer afternoon's fishing trip that Len and Stan had embarked on. Finding a spot off the rocks where, in Stan's words, 'the fish beg to get into the boat', they caught too many and went over to Broadford and invited the locals who were standing around to share with them some of nature's bounty. They were met with a row of silent refusals. It was Sunday.[31]

But it was not only Margaret's washday practices that earned the rebuke of locals.

Len and Margaret could never be categorised as 'wealthy half-wits', one of several mildly demeaning terms applied to English incomers to Scotland in the 1950s and 1960s. Perception was what mattered, however, as Anthea and Stuart found to their cost as they tried to integrate with their new schoolmates. In public, the resentment about incomers from England was not as noticeable as it would be later,[32] but children are often willing to voice in the playground what their parents are much more guarded about. Adding to the Whatley children's burden, they were from a farming family, not crofters. Perceived therefore as being well-off *and* possibly fancying themselves as superior, they had to be put in their place – a duty undertaken with alacrity according to Anthea, by the school's headmistress, a Mrs MacSween.

Unlike many of their classmates, however, they were not subject to the tawse – the leather strap punishment inflicted on local children for daring to speak in school the Gaelic language that was the norm at home. Being spared this ordeal and being so obviously 'different' had its downside: being ostracised – and, in Stuart's case, bullied.

*   *   *

Notwithstanding the positive advances made on the farming side, financially 1952 had not 'turned out as well as one hoped or expected'. In fact, it was a 'rotten year', wrote Henry Hilditch to Herbert; we are 'sweating about money'. He was to get used to the sensation. The pressure to increase stock levels and the need to improve the house by putting in new windows to replace the existing and inadequate ones, and to build up the farm's infrastructure, including additional accommodation for workpeople and animals and to store oats, potatoes and the like, more than consumed what the cash from sales of produce generated. Len's overdraft facility with the Westminster Bank was stretched to breaking point. In a quip laced with just a smidgeon of forced optimism after spending a year on Skye, sixty-two-year-old Henry thought things would improve, 'before I'm seventy'.[33]

There is nothing to suggest that when Len and Margaret determined to settle on Pabay they had in mind any kind of specific state support. Len was vaguely aware of the terms of the Agriculture Acts referred to earlier.[34] These offered subsidies for certain kinds of farming activities, but Len was not sufficiently knowledgeable of what was available in Scotland to have been able to factor this into his thoughts about how he would make the island pay. In fact, his silent mentor, George Henderson, had been against government involvement in farming, including subsidies which were 'always at the expense of the community at large'.[35] Skye's Inner Sound, however, was not the Cotswolds.

It was only after he had absorbed the contents of books like O'Malley's *One-horse Farm*, and acquainted himself with local Department of Agriculture officials, vets and other Skye farmers, that Len became fully aware of the government's agricultural policies in Scotland, and their implications for Pabay. Even so, he had been sufficiently savvy to invite officials across in 1950 to seek advice on how the island could be improved, and how the Department might assist – although it seems incredible that it took four years for an engineer who had been asked to advise Len on the ditches to get over to the island.[36]

In his ability to master what Jim Hunter has called a 'bewildering array of financial aids', Henry Hilditch had few peers.[37] And in his preparedness to battle to secure them he was in a league of his own. But Len was no slouch when it came to challenging official-dom. An early dispute was over his cultivable acreage. In order to obtain support for arable farming, the fenced area had to be a minimum of 50 acres. This Len managed to do on a surface that comprised large areas of peat and, on the northerly section of the island, rough, stony grassland, before embarking on the difficult job of persuading departmental inspectors that his measurements were correct.[38]

Even so, it is largely coincidental that at the time of the Whatleys' arrival on Skye the post-1945 Labour Government had embarked on an ambitious programme designed to check and then reverse what had been a long tide of depopulation from the Highlands and Islands.[39] Not only were push factors at work; there was also the lure of city life elsewhere in Scotland or the United Kingdom, or the prospect of a fresh start overseas made possible with an assisted passage to get there.

Agents from countries like America, Canada, Australia and New Zealand had from the later nineteenth century been employed to persuade potential emigrants of the opportunities abroad. The Highlands and Hebrides were a much-favoured recruiting ground. Indeed, as recently as the 1920s one Canadian recruiting agent had given lectures to impressively large and enthusiastic audiences throughout Skye, from Staffin and Uig in the north, through Dunvegan and Edinbane, to Breakish in the south.[40] Ironically, it was those most desperate who were unable to leave, owing to the cost. However, National Service, compul-sory from 1948 for most males over the age of eighteen, offered young men a way out, by opening new horizons, thereby exacer-bating the outward flow.

Any solution, or solutions, would necessarily be radical.

Arthur Woodburn, Secretary of State for Scotland between 1947 and 1950, had thought long and hard about the problem, which he judged to be second only to the task of re-industrialising the Scottish Lowlands.[41] The alternatives were stark. One option was to allow the process of depopulation to carry on unabated, leaving the Highlands to 'go back to the wild', and inhabited mainly by those interested in hunting and fishing, and who were prepared to endure a low standard of living. The other choice was that 'the nation ... take steps to providing such amenities as are necessary to make a relatively contended habitation possible'. It was this approach – understated as articulated here by Woodburn in his *Autobiography*, but in its way game-changing – that Woodburn decided to adopt.

Government policy for the Highlands prior to 1939 had mainly been concerned with landlessness and overcrowding, and to preserve what existed already. Even during the 1930s, however, fresh thinking was in the air, and proposals were made, for example, for a Highland Development Commission with wide-reaching powers to initiate schemes that would bring investment in agriculture, hydroelectricity, forestry, transport and marketing.[42] The potential of employment from tourism was noticed too – notably by Thomas Johnston, the long-serving Labour MP, who in 1906 had founded the socialist weekly *Forward*.

More pertinent for present purposes is Johnston's 1909 book, *Our Scots Noble Families*. This has been described as a 'savage assault on Scotland's landed gentry', an assessment based on Johnston's allegations that the lands they possessed had been 'stolen either by force or fraud ... rapine, murder, massacre, cheating, or Court harlotry'; these are charges that land reformers of the present time such as Andy Wightman are convinced still stand.[43]

Having identified those he believed bore the guilt of the region's decline, Johnston's 'cherished dream' was to revive the Scottish Highlands.[44] As Scotland's charismatic and energetic Secretary of State from 1941 until 1945, he had the opportunity to put some of his ideas into practice, which he did in part through the creation of the Hydro-Electric Board in 1943, the remit of which was not only to generate and distribute electricity in the Highlands but also to promote and encourage economic and social welfare. Wartime Treasury constraints on spending, however, frustrated Johnston and other advocates of change. Vested landed interests too – notably Johnston's nemesis, Highland landowners – fought tooth and nail to block anything that might blight their idealised view of what the Highlands and Islands should look like.[45]

Johnston's aim after 1945 therefore was to create a new kind of economy. In the driving seat as Scottish Secretary from October 1947 was the man who had been his parliamentary private secretary, the aforementioned Arthur Woodburn. Woodburn, however, was removed from office in February 1950.[46] Still, behind the scenes, officials at the Scottish Home Department had been preparing a White Paper that presented proposals outlining the means by which Johnston's and Woodburn's ambitions might be realised.

A Programme of Highland Development was published in the summer of 1950.[47] It was a product of the ambitious 'Marshall Plan' for the Highlands that Woodburn had announced in 1948 (a reference to the United States-led scheme to boost the economies of Europe's war-battered nations that had recently been approved by the US Congress).[48]

Usefully, the *Programme* summarised what financial support was already available from central government and the local authorities. It also set out priorities for the future and provided strong indications of the kinds of projects that might attract assistance in the form of grant aid.[49] Although its publication was little-noticed and in fact it was not until the following April that the paper was debated in Parliament, Henry Hilditch's political antenna was twitching; he had a nose for anything that might help Len and Margaret on Pabay.[50]

Despite the length of time he had spent in England, Henry was not unaware of Scotland's economic travails, and had followed with some interest the very public debates there were about how to overcome these. So he lost no time in obtaining a copy of the *Highland Development* paper. He familiarised himself too with the intricate details of existing aid schemes, having urged Len's father, Herbert, to visit the Stationary Office in Birmingham and buy 'anything' they had on the Highlands.[51] Primary legislation such as the Hill Farming Act of 1946 had been followed by a series of regulations and orders. With post-war governments of both main parties dedicated to increasing farm output, a new marginal land programme was launched in 1952, offering grant aid for improvements such as fencing, drainage and liming, as well as for buildings, the provision of electricity, farm roads, shelter belts and so on.[52]

While Len had no doubts about the potential value of these subsidies, he was less sure about how to secure them, or for what he was eligible. Writing applications and form-filling too took time, of which he had little to spare. Henry Hilditch had the necessary aptitude, time and no qualms. He wasted not a moment in exploiting every avenue there was to tap the funding sources on offer.

Within weeks of arriving on Skye, he was in deep discussion with his son-in-law as they calculated how much stock the island could carry on the assumption that the animals would feed on Pabay's own resources. Cattle looked the best bet, but in the meantime Henry's advice was to get 'sufficient pigs, hens etc to keep things ticking over'.[53]

And this they did. From 1952 onwards it was increasingly the poultry side of the business that generated the cash flow that was critical for keeping the Pabay venture afloat financially. Before long, production had risen to around eighty dozen and after that a hundred dozen eggs a week.

Henry's hard-driving selling techniques and his preparedness to take the boxes of eggs to customers on Skye, in Kyle and Mallaig, or ship them to Lochboisdale in South Uist and even London (by rail), were indispensable. Invariably he managed to secure sufficiently high prices that avoided him having to sell to the government (Ministry of Food) packing station. Here, as the Government had targeted a 90 per cent increase in UK egg production, they were guaranteed a return, but a low one.[54] Whilst benefiting from premium prices most of the time, Henry was acutely aware of how far the market could fall; during January 1954 demand slumped and the price he could obtain for a dozen eggs had fallen from six shillings to four shillings, but of course on Pabay the hens continued to lay. The surplus – 500 dozen – he sold at three shillings and sixpence for pickling, while at the same time buying those from a rival, Jack Copson, 'primarily to insure he doesn't cut our price in Kyleakin!!!' he wrote. Later, Len bought out Copson's business, for much the same reason – but also to acquire his equipment, including hen houses, which were floated on rafts across to Pabay.

There, Len was attempting to tackle a related issue, the rising cost of animal feed. He was intent too on keeping egg production going through the winter – when demand was usually high, as were prices.

Accordingly, he took the bold step of adopting the deep litter system. This is a type of indoor free-range poultry-keeping arrangement where the henhouse floor is covered in layers of litter. It differs from the more regimented battery system which was being developed at the time. To do as Len did was something of a gamble. The deep litter system was widely used in the USA, and was well known in England, but had few adherents in Scotland.[55] For Len, an important advantage was that the system involved less in the way of start-up capital, other than the cost of an ex-army Nissen hut. Also, having hens ranging freely in and around arks situated at various places on the island accorded better with his farming philosophy. Against this was that the deep litter method was less hygienic and more labour intensive.

The future, however, lay in poultry sales. Poultry-feed rationing – a wartime measure – had ended in 1953. Poultrymen were being exhorted not only to increase their output of eggs more efficiently, but also to improve the quality of their stock that ideally would be dual purpose: providing eggs and meat.[56] Cutting-edge research – of which Len was aware through his ardent reading of the *Farmers Weekly* – had shown how new lighting regimes could encourage early laying. Fourteen hours of light meant that hens would continue to lay through the more lucrative winter months. With Stan, Len connected by means of a Heath Robinson-esque system the batteries from the wind generator to the Nissen hut in which the laying hens were to be housed. Even cruder, but effective, was Stan's light switch system, which was connected by a piece of string to an alarm clock – to wake the hens during the night.[57] In December, Len had put a paraffin-fuelled incubator in a loft in the barn. This was to hatch chickens and produce eight-week-old cockerels in February, and pullets for laying in June and July. Eggs at this time of year tended to be scarcer.

First though, he needed some quality layers. These he acquired – in the form of five dozen hatching eggs – from his farming guru,

George Henderson, in Oxfordshire. The two trays of eggs, tied together by string, were brought the several hundred miles to Pabay by Stan, who made the journey by hitch-hiking.

In Len's sights too was the prospect of rearing chickens for the Christmas market in cities such as Aberdeen and Glasgow. For the rest of the year his brother-in-law Harry at Dunollie was a steady customer, while the chef at the Lochalsh Hotel nearby agreed to take around £25-worth of table birds each week.

Plucking chickens took an ever-increasing amount of Len's and Margaret's time, as well as Henry's, who used his garage for this purpose. Visitors to Pabay who stayed for more than a day or two soon discovered that the price of their board was a shift of de-feathering hens (or another of the many jobs that needed to be done and were quickly learned, like clearing the foul-smelling, soiled litter from the hen houses). Plans too were made to supply day-old chicks to the Outer Isles, where a Crofters' Co-operative was in the market for young birds.[58]

It was on Christmas Day 1954 that the first chickens broke out of their shell cocoons; the three children were mesmerised; the adults raised a glass and wished the new venture a success. For the youngsters, it heralded the start of a daily chore they would do whenever they were at home: taking feed to the hens, providing them with fresh water and collecting eggs. Anthea relished the job of candling the newly laid eggs before they went to the incubator: this involved inspecting each one individually against the light, to ensure that the shell was even, and that the egg was fertile and contained a good air bubble for the chick developing inside.

A leaflet Len produced in January 1955 for distribution around Skye to advertise his wares illustrates just how far and fast things had come. Apart from hens' eggs he could offer Aylesbury duck eggs and eggs of a flock of Chinese geese – the flight of which over the lagoon in front of the cottage captivated family, workers and visitors alike. These, Len had been planning to sell at Christmas – but he baulked. He 'couldn't do that', he admitted, as they 'gave such an air to the place'.[59] Pride of place went to the day-old chick-ens, but he also sold cockerels, chickens at six weeks, point-of-lay pullets and, at £1 each, broody hens. Ducks and goslings were on the list too. Perhaps uniquely, on one occasion they had become inebriated, having eaten oats from sheaves that instead of drying had fermented.[60] The expression 'drunk as a tufted duck' might well have been coined had there been further occurrences.

The reputation of Pabay's poultry spread rapidly. Particularly successful was Len's pitch, 'Non-laying hens – cull them now – exchange for 8-week-old pullets.' He sold the old birds to Dunollie. Within months of setting up, the business was flourishing. Henry was sure there was more to come: 'we have so far only touched the fringe of the market', he reported, even though between 160 and 180 chicks were being hatched every week. By June demand was far outstripping what could be supplied.[61]

Len's dream was to have a productive, thriving farm and the personal fulfilment that came from this; Henry wanted the same, as long as it was profitable. In August came news that served both men's purpose. Provisional approval had been given for Pabay to become an accredited poultry-breeding station, under a scheme that had only fairly recently been launched, in 1947.[62] Before long station number 1654 was up and running, and offering high-quality closed stock throughout the Western Isles.

Apart from the urgent requirement for cash, the other priority was a mortgage, to pay off Jack Surridge, but also for investment purposes. Henry's first approach, to Scottish Agricultural Securities (SAS) was turned down. Undaunted, he immediately composed and sent off letters to his political allies in higher places, condemning the Tory Government's credit squeeze. He even asked Hugh Dalton, a Chancellor of the Exchequer under Attlee, to approach Rab Butler, the current incumbent at the Treasury who had in March raised the bank rate to 4 per cent. It made no difference, but Henry relished the scrap.[63]

What did pay off was his perseverance. The SAS, established in 1933 to provide long-term finance for farmers in Scotland, especially those holding marginal land concentrating on milk production and livestock, finally agreed to a loan of £650.[64] This was not sufficient to clear things with Surridge entirely. It went some of the way, however, and allowed Len and Henry to concentrate their efforts on support schemes and subsidies that would turn Pabay into the fully functioning farm that Len aspired to run.

In fact, before even the first of the mortgage applications was made, Henry had begun to master the intricacies – and possibilities – of the new Marginal Land scheme. In August 1952, he and Len had managed to come up with proposals that would have cost £8,700 – although in the application they submitted this was scaled back to a more realistic figure.

The first priority, though, was to extend the fencing, as well as increase and improve Pabay's cultivable acreage, which would largely be achieved by scouring out the existing ditches and drains and cutting some new main drains. This was a major undertaking – the deep ditches requiring heavy specialist equipment. In all, there were as many as 14 miles to be dealt with, although on the plus side it was thought that once the job was done, Pabay's value might double.[65] The challenge was get the seven-and-a-half-ton machine – in effect a giant plough – they would use across to the island.

There was a need too for additional buildings, shelterbelts and upgrading of the island's tracks and jetty.[66] At the same time, now that cattle had been brought to the island, Henry looked forward to benefiting to the tune of some £750 from subsidies for winter-feeding, cows in calf and calves at six months old, and for cultivat-ing marginal land.[67]

Len didn't hide his excitement about the help that appeared to be on the horizon. In the summer of 1953 he wrote enthusiastically to his brother about the proposal he, with Henry, had just submit-ted under the new Marginal Land scheme. 'Really something to get our teeth into', he concluded, as, if successful, it would cover a period of ten years, and pay for 'miles of ditches, tons of lime, hundreds of trees etc etc'. Henry's faith in the virtues of Stalinist socialist planning was not lost in what he pencilled in for Pabay.

The first indications from the Inverness officials whose approval was being sought were positive. In June Henry was informed that the two five-year plans had been well received. Even if one of the assessors expressed slight disappointment about the number of cattle and calves Len had forecast Pabay could carry, he was in no doubt that 'the rehabilitation of this small island would be a remarkable achievement'.[68] In this respect Len was more fortunate than the many Skye crofters who were unable to meet Department of Agriculture demands that their holdings should be capable of carrying at least 300 sheep, and after 'rehabilitation', stand on their own feet economically.[69]

Even without formal approval, Len pushed on. By midsummer 1953 over a mile and a half of fencing had been put in. When it was finished it would cost around £800, Henry calculated. But for Pabay the net outlay would only be £60 – significantly less than a 50 per cent contribution. How was this achieved? When approved, the Marginal Land scheme would pay £400. In addition, Len's and Stan's time would be chargeable. Henry, on behalf of Len, would also be able to invoice for a high proportion of the cost of fencing posts that Len had cut and shaped himself from trees from the shelterbelts planted in Sir Donald Currie's time that had rotted in the wet ground or been blown down.[70]

This was only one instance of Henry's ingenuity. He managed to concoct a means by which lime – hundreds of tons of it – could be bought from the Glasgow paint manufacturer William Forsyth's recently opened lime quarry at Torrin, by Loch Slapin, to Pabay (for which there was also a generous transport subsidy), 'for less than nothing'. He didn't always do as well as this, but rarely paid more than a fraction of the true cost.

By the end of the year, Henry reckoned that over £2,500 had been spent on Pabay, mostly on fencing, but also on Nissen huts, ditching and electricity. It looked like it had been a better year all round, as in addition to egg sales (£800 for the year) and poultry (£300), the oat and barley crops had been good. On finalising the year's accounts Henry was pleased that 'for 'the first time on record, they have just about broken even'. Looking forward to the later 1950s, and assuming Len had managed to pay off Surridge, he reckoned Pabay would clear £1,000 annually.[71]

Yet Len's and Henry's high hopes, whilst not entirely dashed, dissipated somewhat as negotiations over the Marginal Land proposals with officials dragged on, and on. It was not until early in 1954 that a draft of what would be an acceptable bid was finally agreed.[72] With much of the work already paid for – the bought-in fencing posts, wire and netting, for example – and with limits on what cash could be generated from egg and poultry sales (which were roughly the same as the previous year), the viability of the Pabay enterprise depended on the bank's preparedness to continue Len's overdraft facility.

Making matters worse was that the barley crop had been nothing like the previous year's. So prolonged was a spell of wet weather in September that Len had had to resort to hand scything. There had been 'heartbreaking' cattle losses, while calf sales too had been 'beyond talking about'.[73] Consequently they had had another break-even year in 1954, but barely. Again, Henry reported being in 'an awful sweat'. Despite assurances they would be paid, departmental processes were labyrinthine, with payments having to be approved locally, in Edinburgh and then at the Treasury in London. Such was his frustration with the snail's-pace progress of the payments system that at one point Henry announced that if he had still been politically active, 'I would be shouting H[ome] Rule for S[cotland]!' He wasn't serious.

Welcome, vital indeed, as the agricultural subsidies were, there was a downside. As we saw in the previous chapter, Len had hoped to improve Pabay's soil by using organic materials found and produced on the island. By March 1953 he and Stan had built stacks of seaweed mixed with pig and poultry manure that were so high they could be seen from Broadford. All that had to be imported were some phosphates – as seaware was deficient in this regard and was only partially compensated for by shell sand. It was a shock to discover that neither the 100 and more tons of seaweed mix, nor Pabay's ample supplies of shell sand (and the man-hours of effort required to collect and spread these) attracted the level of subsidies that were payable for artificial fertilisers. As Henry Hilditch commented, 'You would think it was the ICI who were paying . . . Any poor fellow who believed in organic fertilisers only' is 'just right out of the picture'.[74] Only half of the cost of spreading shell sand could be claimed.

*   *   *

As 1955 drew to a close, Len's and Margaret's financial situation took a decided turn for the better, or seemed to. John Campbell, the Irvine shipping agent one of whose puffers had run aground on Pabay in 1950, had retained a keen interest in Len's progress. In June 1953, he had returned to Skye, keen to see Len, Margaret and the children. Whilst waiting to cross to Pabay, he spent time in lively conversation with the Hilditches and Len, who had come over to collect him.

This proved to be a fortune-changing evening. Visiting Pabay the next day Campbell had been impressed by 'the alteration' he had seen compared to 1950. Already he had mentioned the possibility of investing, but nothing had transpired. However, on this occasion it emerged that Campbell, Len and Henry Hilditch had more in common than Western Isles farming and boats. This was their pacificism. Like Len's father, Campbell had been a CO during the First World War.[75] As a member of the Christian Brethren Church he believed that war was a sin and abhorred any kind of violence. Consequently, from 1916 he had spent the war either in labour camps or Wormwood Scrubs – where Len's father had also been incarcerated for a time. There, it seems, the two men had met, albeit briefly. It was not until December 1918, after the war had ended, that Campbell was released.[76]

The deepening relationship between the three families in the early 1950s had made it easier to discuss in detail Len's financial constraints. Of these the most pressing was what he still owed to Jack Surridge. By November 1955 the balance of what was due to Surridge was ready to be transferred to him once the deeds for Pabay that were currently held by the solicitors of the Muntz family's trustees had been handed over. These, however, went not to Len but to Sarah Campbell, John Campbell's wife since their marriage in 1920.[77] Her security – in return for a mortgage of £1,000 – was the island. Len and Margaret were mightily relieved. For the time being the Campbells had saved the day.

It was as well that they had. For notwithstanding Henry's hopes that 1956 would see Pabay in surplus, it was not to be. The poultry business had disappointed and produced a gross profit of only £50 against a forecast of £400. A lesson had been learned though: hens laid well for one year but not two. On the other hand, the harvest had been good – the best yet – so while no cattle had been sold during the year (as losses from previous years were being made up), there would in future be sufficient feed to increase the number of breeding cows to fifty.

But it was the unexpected expenditure that had thrown Henry's accounts awry: a replacement boat that cost £75 for example, as well as a new mower for the hay. Losses for the year may have been as much as £2,500, the equivalent today of a hefty £43,631.

Not helping either was the fact that for the past few months Len had been working more or less alone.[78] Stan had gone and Neil could only help out occasionally.

Replacement workers, whilst promising on paper, proved not to be cut out for island farming. One young man, Nick Henson, who had spent time bird-watching on Bardsey Island, which was even smaller than Pabay and lay some two miles off the coast of North Wales, seemed a likely prospect. From Birmingham, he had been interviewed initially by Len's parents, who thought he would fit the bill. After hitch-hiking from the south of England, he arrived on Skye in the middle of February 1956. He was biddable enough, but lacking initiative, and with less interest in farming than bird life; a month later Len had seen enough and bade him farewell.[79] On this occasion it was Henry's wife Margaret who had sensed a problem even as he waited at 'Seaside' to be taken across for the first time, pointedly remarking to him as he excitedly regaled her with accounts of sightings of birds he had seen on his journey to Skye, 'there's a lot more things to be done than bird watch on Pabay'. But he was not easily diverted. Even though he was a late riser (another reason for dismissing him), and the daylight hours were few, during his brief Pabay interlude he managed to identify fifty-nine species of winter birds, about which he subsequently published a paper in the *Glasgow Bird Bulletin*.[80]

As 1956 drew towards its close, another concern grew. This was about the crisis in the Middle East that had broken out into the second Arab–Israeli War. Britain became involved through its interest in the Suez Canal. By the start of 1957, Skye's hoteliers were aware that advance bookings for the summer were dropping, due to fears over petrol supplies. With fewer visitors, demand for Pabay's eggs and poultry too looked like falling off.

Accordingly, Henry slashed the figure he reckoned Pabay could clear annually to £500. But, if the worst came to the worst, and Len was forced to sell the island, such was the value of the live-stock that he was fairly certain all the outstanding debts could be paid. But neither he – nor Len and Margaret – were for giving up yet.

Chapter 9

'There isn't a thing growing': old challenges, new departures

Notwithstanding the ongoing challenges, in many ways Len and Margaret at the end of the 1950s could be satisfied with the progress they had made since their arrival at the start of the decade. Most of the two miles of fencing had been put in, the drains and ditches had been cleared and some new drainage channels cut. The Nissen huts were up again (where they had been blown away during an earlier gale) and teeming with poultry. A sheep fank near the jetty – for containing the animals for dipping, smearing and shearing – would be finished soon. Len had eventually acquired a boat fit for Pabay's purposes and found a man capable of managing it.

The poultry side of the operation was an enormous success; the main source of regular income, in fact. From November 1957 Len had been able to advertise Pabay as 'The only accredited [poultry] station in the Western Isles' and boast that his carefully bred chicks were productive layers and entirely free from salmonella. He focused on three breeds only – Brown Leghorn, Light Sussex and Rhode Island Reds: 'A West Highland Bird for a West Highland Climate' was his claim. Demand was such from the 500 or so customers Len now had that it became an endless slog to keep up, producing literally thousands of birds each year. Especially intense were the weeks leading up to Christmas, when for several years Pabay cockerels and hens were to be found for sale not only on Skye and in its vicinity but also the Outer Isles and as far south as Glasgow.

But sitting back and resting on their laurels was not an option; they still had a sizeable bank overdraft, and other debts. Even during their first years on Pabay, Len and Margaret had thought and talked about how else they could turn their respective skills and ingenuity to good use.

As we saw earlier, from the outset Margaret had made furnishings for the house. But she also fashioned clothes for the children, often dexterously reusing those Anthea had grown out of for Rachel. Before long she had begun to knit, at first by hand and then by a machine she mastered over the winter of 1955–56.[1] Selling direct from Pabay and locally at Dunollie, as well as in shops in Portree and Kyle, her reputation had grown to the extent that less than a year later she was receiving advance orders for her jumpers.

In keeping with Len's desire for self-sufficiency, and to exploit to the full the island's resources, in the summer of 1959 Margaret found a spinning wheel and loom and brought them over. The aim was to use the wool from Pabay's sheep that would then be hand-spun and woven – or knitted – into garments that included not only jumpers, but also socks, ties and scarves. It wasn't long before Len was able to report that Margaret was 'gnashing away on the K [Knitmaster] machine', with scarves and stoles 'pouring off'. He even managed to make a dozen scarves himself during one long evening. With no time for finishing, fringing was put out to Neil MacRae's wife.[2] Although nothing much came of it, Len and his brother Allan came up with a design for a Pabay or 'MacWhatley' tartan, inspired by colours found on the island – ragwort, thistles, cattle and even the red of the tractor.

If knitting was just about a joint endeavour, painting and pottery were very much Len's domain. A reasonably gifted amateur water-colourist, he was keen to paint in oils. And, on his doorstep, was someone who could teach him: Alan Browne.[3]

In the longer run however, the much more significant development was his adoption of pottery.

The first step in this direction was taken early on, by accident, when during ditch-clearing operations Len had come across some dark red boulder clay. Ever the patient parent-teacher, he wanted to show Anthea and Stuart what the raw material he had collected in a bucket could become. Using a disc made of board, driven by a hand drill clamped into a vice, with Stan Robinson's help he made a very basic throwing wheel. And tried to make a pot.[4] Keen to learn more, he ordered some fairly elementary books on the subject (the only ones available) from Inverness. Over subsequent years he continued to experiment, but early on arranged for a trial firing in Edinburgh of the first pots he made from Pabay clay.

This was with the assistance of Alexander Sharp, who at the time was working at Highland Home Industries (HHI) pottery at Morar. Born in Barrhead, just outside Glasgow, in 1918, Sharp had impressed Bernard Leach (1887–1979), the St Ives-based doyen of British studio potters, with a kick wheel (for throwing) he had engineered. Using a heavy cast concrete flywheel, at the time Sharp's innovation was deemed to be a major advance – revolutionary, according to one source.[5] Leach consequently took him under his wing, as well as introducing him to the legendary Japanese potter Shōji Hamada. On returning to Scotland – and the Morar pottery – Sharp had also taken on the role of advisor on the craft, which is why Len had contacted him. With Sharp's help, Len acquired a small cube-like kiln that was located in one of the Nissen huts near the steading.[6] In this he managed to make some small earthenware items – ashtrays decorated with caricatures of Harry and Olive Hilditch – for the tables at Dunollie.

Around the same time excavation work for the foundations for an extension to the original cottage and a new four-bedroom bungalow to the north of the farm steading had begun. Both were second-hand Seco prefabricated structures, an advertisement for them, at cut-down prices, having been spotted by Len's father in Birmingham. The 'prefab' had been identified during the war as an answer to Britain's housing shortage, worsened by wartime bombing raids. Between 1946 and 1949 over 156,000 were built, often on bomb sites and in public parkland. Reckoned to be a short-term measure, with a life of between ten and fifteen years, in London they began to be dismantled in the mid-1950s.[7]

These additions had been envisaged in the original plan for the island, developed in 1952 and 1953. Although at one stage it looked unlikely, virtually the entire costs of £1,690 (including the sheep fank) were met by the Department of Agriculture. Just.

As the Department wouldn't fund prefabs – which were rightly judged too flimsy – Len had constructed concrete walls around the shells that were strong enough to stand up to the strongest winds, and got the subsidy. Much to the amazement of wary officials both from the county council and the Department of Agriculture, most of the work, from the initial drawings to the completed buildings, was deemed to be of first-class quality. From start to finish – as architect, draughtsman, mason, plumber, electrician and roofer – Len had been responsible, although Margaret too had had a hand in the design and implementation.

Her particular delight was the new Rayburn Royal stove and oven. Transformational too as far as comfortable living was concerned was the successful construction of a diesel-powered generator, which produced enough electricity – reliably and independent of the wind – to light all of the island's buildings and provide a power source. And hot water, from an immersion heater, on demand rather than being entirely dependent on the Rayburn. And all at a lower cost than the Hydro-Electric Board supplied its customers in Broadford.

Prior to this, cash, as ever, had been in short supply, but had to be raised somehow. Not only did money for the materials have to be found (months in advance of departmental reimbursement), but any time Len or anyone else spent on building work meant that additional labour had to be hired to do essential farming tasks. A larger overdraft from the bank helped – obtained without Len being entirely open about the precariousness of Pabay's financial situation.

But so too did the appearance of George Jolly and his wife Sally, with their young daughter Fiona. In some ways they were not so dissimilar from Len and Margaret; they were recently married (in 1954) and had honeymooned on Scotland's west coast, been captivated and determined to return.

Although Jolly was a research scientist, the pair were much taken with Pabay (although how they'd heard about it isn't clear) and, similarly to Len and Margaret a few years earlier, quickly decided they would like to stay, and establish a market garden. The two men, Len and George – they were around the same age – shared interests in best agricultural practices, and went as far as discussing and agreeing the terms of a partnership. As a start, Jolly offered – in return for land and accommodation – to advance Len £500, which Len could then use to construct the bungalow that Jolly and his wife hoped eventually to inhabit.

On occasion, he helped Len out on his building jobs and farming operations, although reports reached Henry Hilditch that Sally might have been less willing to contribute to the common good – a bottom-line requirement for harmonious living on a small island.[8] Quiet and reserved is how her daughter Fiona describes her late mother. These were characteristics which meant that Margaret – socially gregarious – found it hard to relate to the island's other resident adult female and mother. The two couples had less in common in other respects too: George had served in the Royal Electrical and Mechanical Engineers during the Second World War, was traditional in his views, and inclined towards the Tories politically.[9]

The Jollys' objectives for Pabay, however, were bold. They had what seemed the right background. George had spent time at East Malling (Fruit) Research Station in Essex (where he met Sally); she was a botanist, a good sign. All seemed well in May 1958 when Ted Comber – from the south Skye island of Soay, and who had a large enough boat – brought the couple's furniture over to Pabay.

On board too was their piano – probably the first ever to have been played on the island, although not on Skye, with pianos and other stringed musical instruments having in the earlier part of the eighteenth century become integral elements of the entertainment provided by females in gentry households such as those of the Macdonalds and MacLeods.[10] The golden age of the clan pipers – vital members of a clan chief's numerous retinue – was coming to an end.[11] Another indication that the Jollys were in for the long haul was that they commissioned Comber's son Geoffrey to build them a boat, the *Curlew*.

*   *   *

However, the island was still not paying its way. Financially, 1958 was as bad as any year previously. In January 1957, a short-lived storm had been the worst any local could remember.[12] The winter of 1957–58 too had been harsher than usual. Even at the end of March 'everything' was 'burnt up with this cold E wind ... there isn't a thing growing when there is normally an inch or two of new grass'; as a result, cattle feed had to be bought and brought over.[13] It was only a partial fix: not all of the cattle survived. Len reckoned that each dead cow cost them around £100, taking into account the subsidies that were lost on unborn calves. The sheep had suffered too, although not to the same extent as the rest of Skye, where 'literally hundreds' not only of ewes but also lambs had perished due to the prolonged spell of cold weather. Pabay's had done better than most because, entirely by chance, the ewes were later in lambing – due to fencing work being done in the previous autumn there had been a delay in putting the rams out.

It would be 'at least another year's delay before Pabay really gets going', reflected Henry Hilditch, in a refrain that was now uncomfortably familiar.[14] So too was his new forecast for profitability – moved yet another five years ahead.

After what had been the wettest, windiest winter in the Whatleys' time on Pabay it was apparent that yet more shelter-belts would have to be planted if cattle were to be kept outside, and alive.[15] But this was no short-term solution. Fortunately, the following spring was much better, with sixteen calves born (more than had been expected), along with fifty lambs, a number bolstered by Len's purchase late in 1958 of thirty-one ewes and a ram from Scalpay.[16] He was now halfway to his target flock size of 150. With an estimated income of only £3 per sheep (including £1 for the fleece and allowing for the inevitable losses), this made sense.

The formerly lucrative egg sales business though was tottering. An already overcrowded market pushed prices even lower in the spring as crofters' eggs came onto the market. Furthermore, there were concerns that William Forsyth was going out of business (he had already sold his farm at Kyleakin), and that his lime quarry at Torrin – from which, as we have seen, Pabay was supplied at a marginal cost – would be closed down owing to the dangerous working conditions there.[17] Exacerbating Len's worries was that Forsyth's K6, which had been bought mainly to ship lime to Pabay, was now a wreck.

Compounding the gloom affecting all concerned was an unexplained fire in August that entirely consumed the Nissen hut that contained most of the equipment, tools and machinery that were used on an everyday basis. Even the potter's wheel and kiln had gone.

Immediately, Len and Margaret left the island in a frantic expedition to replace the most essential items that had been lost, leaving the children on Skye with their grandparents.

Yet there was a silver lining. The tractor – arguably the most important piece of apparatus Len had – had also been engulfed in the fiery inferno. It had been on its last legs, and costly to run, and Len had been actively considering a replacement. What had stymied him though was finding the £600 and more it would cost. With the first tranche of insurance money – paid out remarkably swiftly – he was able to buy a brand-new vehicle, the running costs of which were around a quarter of the older machine. And, resilient and positive as ever, Len – with the help of his brother, Anthea and others – not only had the debris on the site cleared, but threw himself into planning for a better, custom-built workshop. Nevertheless, what no amount of optimism could entirely conceal was that even excluding depreciation, the total losses for the year amounted to over £1,550.

The Jollys' experiment too was running into difficulties. But it had begun well. George identified and fenced off two plots for cultivation – one at each side of the island. Sally had applied her botanical skills to create a small flower garden. To his credit George did manage to master Pabay's growing conditions to the extent that – mainly under polythene – he produced a variety of salad crops and vegetables: lettuce, potatoes, turnips, cabbages, broad beans, peas and cauliflower, for instance.

Unfortunately, despite ambitious sowings, the quantities harvested were often small and not always of the best quality, which disappointed Harry Hilditch in Dunollie who liked to use local – Pabay – produce where possible. George's glass frames and fragile polythene tunnels were no match for the wind – which tore off both kinds of covers from their frames, while the rabbits managed to undermine – literally – his fencing. His main plot was close to one of the island's shelter belts, from where hoodie crows took note of what was being planted – and then swept down fearlessly to take off seed potatoes.[18] Something of a dreamer – or, perhaps, with more of an academic approach to life than conditions on Pabay demanded, to Len and Margaret and others watching on, he seemed not to recognise the effort and time needed to make a success of such an undertaking. A boat trip to Broadford with a box of six lettuces, Henry Hilditch observed bluntly, was no way to make a living.

Little wonder then that sales barely covered the cost of George's seeds and fertilisers.[19] With money short, before long George began to apply his mathematical talents to a system that would improve the odds of winning the football pools. However, judging by the response rate to his advertisements, few of the nation's mainly small-time gamblers were convinced his advice was worth paying for.

Nor in other respects was Lady Luck on his side. High hopes of supplying Skye with premium-priced early potatoes (George's big idea for 1959) were dashed when Ayrshires appeared much earlier than usual.[20] Mishaps abounded. On more than one occasion he was seen drifting out at sea, unable to start his outboard motor. Once he spent all morning getting the engine going, determined to stick with his intention of having a picnic on the nearby island of Longay – a birthday treat for young Fiona – even though the wind was getting up. He and his heavily pregnant wife, and his daughter, were stranded for a night, without shelter.[21] If wiser heads shook, for Fiona it was simply a glorious adventure – making beds with the heather and using the life jackets as pillows (in this respect the Jollys were unusually prudent – no one else on Pabay took such a precaution), and sleeping under the stars.

By the spring of 1960 the Jollys' relations with Len and Henry Hilditch had become severely strained, in part as the Jollys had drawn heavily for everyday living expenses on the sum George had advanced for the house. There were other costs too, to which

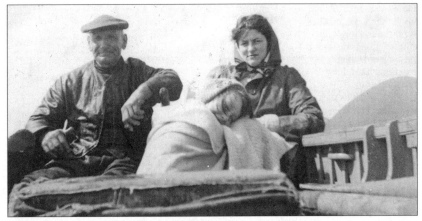

Margaret Whatley, with Anthea, on the family's first, spray-drenched, crossing to Pabay in April 1950. (Whatley Collection)

Above. The somewhat bleak exposed track from the jetty to the cottage and farm buildings, Pabay, *c*.1951. Largely tree-less, there was no shelter from the south-westerly winds. Anthea, Stuart and myself are the children in the picture. (Whatley Collection)

Right. Len – already looking weather beaten and island-hardened, Margaret and Anthea, Stuart and baby Rachel, outside the cottage on Pabay, 1952. (Whatley Collection)

Ploughing, 1951. Allan, my father, Len's brother, is on the tractor, with Anthea alongside. Len is pushing a drilling machine; hard, lung-bursting graft. This was the first time this part of the island had been cultivated for a century. (Whatley Collection)

Collecting seaweed, 1952. Tons of seaware were blown onto the shore in front of the cottage during the winter gales. This was then used, mixed with manure, as a fertiliser. Stan Robinson, in the centre of the picture, built great mounds of this compound, which could be seen from Broadford. (© Stuart Whatley Collection)

First threshing, harvest 1952. In the picture are Margaret (who was no slouch when it came to manual labour), Alex McLeod, owner of the threshing machine, Stan Robinson, Len and Stuart. (© Stan Robinson Collection)

'Lord Ivac of Cape Wrath'. Len's first bull, an Aberdeen Angus bull calf purchased at seven months in 1952. Here he is with Stan Robinson. Sadly, he was found to have only one testicle, and was subsequently castrated, sold off, and replaced by 'Balnakiel Barnabus'. (© Stuart Whatley Collection)

Nissen huts being erected, with Stan Robinson in the picture, c.1952. The huts, bought cheaply by Henry Hilditch, were critical for storing equipment and machinery, as workshops and for chicken and egg production. Sadly, some were soon lost, blown away in a severe gale. (© Stuart Whatley Collection)

Nissen hut, after the fire, 1958. (Whatley Collection)

Len, in thoughtful mode, at the knitting machine, *c.*1961. In the early days of this venture – which became Pabay Knitwear – he and Margaret worked closely together on designs for all kinds of woollen goods, including jumpers, scarves, ties and socks. (Whatley Collection)

George appeared oblivious: not least the use of and fuel for Len's tractor. Far from moving into the new bungalow, for which they would now have to raise another £500, it looked as if the Jollys would have to leave, or else pay Len £1 a week for their present accommodation and the land they were using. 'Or, buy me out', said Len, partly in jest, but perhaps with an inkling of what lay ahead.

The following year brought the Jollys' island adventure to a close. With their daughters Fiona (who had been home-schooled up till this point, but would soon have to board at Portree) and her younger sister Heather, they had decided to leave in the autumn. George was to pay what he was alleged to have owed to Len by working for him, spreading lime and leaving the netting fencing he had put up.[22] At least, that was what was supposed to have happened. Angered at what he felt was the injustice of his situation, George went out one night and pulled it all up. By this time he had secured a post at the Agricultural Research Council in Aberdeen and went on applying his skills in statistics to develop an innovative 'mark-recapture' technique (the Jolly-Seber model) for estimating the size of animal and fish populations.[23]

The Jollys' last months on Pabay might have been difficult, but for George his 'story of an away-from-it-all life' was well worth telling, and was, in published form, in the former pupils' magazine where he had been schooled, Mackie Academy in Stonehaven.[24] And in his later work as an ecologist of some distinction – in the UK but also East Africa and elsewhere overseas, it was in part his Pabay experiences that taught him of the flaws in statistical models used to predict wildlife movements that failed to take account of the effects of wild and remote locations.[25]

The difficulty in finding reliable and hard-grafting workers continued to plague Len. Allen Wood was at one time a real asset but, married to Liz, no longer as enthusiastic. Now noticeably taciturn, together and in other company, the couple's proposed departure in August 1958 to embark on a market gardening project in Wales was sad, the end of an era. But it was something of a relief too, not only because relations with Len and Margaret had soured, but also as the figures showed they were no longer paying their way.

But how to replace them? The two local men, Neil MacRae and Donald Fletcher, were important, but the former was part-time and focused on the boat. There was more to be done than Fletcher was able to cope with. As before, friends of friends turned up periodically, paying for their keep through casual work. But their capabilities varied. As, for example, in August 1958, when three lads appeared, two of whom were fine, but the third, 'a communist and a Aldermaston marcher . . . just vanished when any work was on'.[26] Another young man, Tony, who began work early the following year, was 'very good', but lasted only a few months. Despite being extremely well read, with 'most wonderful and weird ideas', he was a 'born rover' and unable to deal with the isolation he felt whilst on Pabay.[27] He was there long enough, however, to recognise that the Pabay children had from an early age taken seriously their roles in the family's island venture.[28] Anthea, not even into her teens, on a weekend home from school in Portree had decreed she and Tony would not only work as a team, but that she would provide the brains and him the hard work.

Without the assistance of people he could rely on, Len was stuck, unable even to take a short break. Tony's successor, Bill, simply could not be left on his own – one of the 'stupid thoughtless things' that led to this conclusion was his attempt to chase a straying sheep on the tractor, which became stuck solidly in a ditch. More than a day was spent (or lost) getting it out.[29]

And this was just the sort of chore that Len no longer needed, or wanted. After almost ten years of relentless endeavour, his body had begun to suffer. He had had minor accidents in the past – as when, attempting to get a boat's engine to fire, the starting handle had flown off and smashed and loosened some of his front teeth. In the summer of 1958, however, he slipped off the back of a trailer when unloading some hay and damaged his back. Within weeks he had wrenched his back again, this time whilst moving a heavy section of a hen house. The following July, he again strained his back, but was unable to take time out to recover: felt had to be laid for the bungalow roof and a great load of fertiliser required to be spread – after he'd recovered the tractor, which had become embedded in a ditch.

While not apparent at the time, Len's injury was to mark the beginning of the end of his attempt to turn Pabay into a viable farm. It presaged a stream of visits to specialists in Glasgow, Birmingham and London, initially in hope, later in desperation, but invariably with the same outcome: disappointment.

Chapter 10

'Every rock is a tablet of hieroglyphics': geology and the geologists

In January 1956, my father received a letter from Henry Hilditch. It was a request for him to 'find a list of Technical Colleges that have courses in Geology, and if possible names of Heads of Dept'. He had by this time taken up a post in a Glasgow commercial institute, where he taught cataloguing systems to librarianship students, and might therefore be expected to have been familiar with the country's college sector. Henry explained that already his son Harry, in an attempt to extend the season at Dunollie Hotel (which, like Pabay, was barely breaking even), had been in touch with some universities and that he had three sets of student bookings for March and April of the current year.[1] It was an inspired move: within just over twelve months parties of geology students had arrived from St Andrews, Queen's in Belfast, Sheffield, Oxford and elsewhere.

The benefits to Dunollie of additional guests in the quiet season were obvious. For Len and Margaret also, there were advantages. The students needed to be ferried to Pabay and, while there, they might be tempted to spend some money on island produce, including Margaret's baking, and her widening range of knitted garments.

It was a move very much in keeping with the couple's diversification strategy. But what was it that had led Len, Harry and Henry to believe that young geologists and their tutors from prestigious educational institutions around Britain might be attracted to Skye, Broadford – and Pabay?

As far as Pabay was concerned we were provided with a clue in Chapter 1, with the Rev. Ratcliffe Barnett's eagerness to designate Pabay as an island of geological revelation.

As children, we were vaguely aware that there was something extraordinary about Pabay's rocks. Stuart, for instance, was fascinated by what seemed to be stone bullets, which could be found mainly on the eastern side of the island. I know now that these small, one- and two-inch-long fossils are probably belemnites. These were marine animals that looked something like modern squid or cuttlefish. What we categorised as bullets was the belemnites' guard, tail, or 'rostrum'. Comprised of fibrous calcite crystals, these, unlike the softer, longer body and tentacles, have survived in fossilised form.[2]

Rostra, however, were but one of many fossil types to be found on Pabay. In the *New Statistical Account* of 1845 the Rev. John Mackinnon, Minister of Strath, described the abundance of 'petrified fish, principally eels, from six to eighteen inches long', while also to be found 'in the same state', were 'oysters, mussels, whelks, and limpets'.[3] Most of these we came across too, along with gryphites and well-preserved ammonites (squid-like creatures with elaborate coiled shells) of various sizes. These we prised from the thin, easily split seams of soft shale, and then stuffed into our bulging trouser pockets. After a few hours, we would then take them home to admire and display on window ledges. We knew the objects we had were very old, so that in our imaginations we could just about envisage a primeval world long gone. But beyond that we were in the dark.

*   *   *

'The most complete sequence of Jurassic sedimentary rocks in north-west Scotland is preserved on Skye.' So wrote the authors of an *Excursion Guide* to Skye's geological features in 1986.[4] They were in good company in claiming so much for the island. Archibald Geikie (1835–1924), one of Scotland's – and Britain's – most eminent and influential geologists (the only geologist to become President of the Royal Society of London, and knighted in 1891), was even more impressed. Skye, he wrote after a visit to the island in 1853, afforded the student of geology with 'as rich a field for investigation as is to be met with in any spot of equal compass in

Britain'.[5] But what he also acknowledged was that notwithstanding the potential of Skye and the Western Isles for the geologist, little as yet was known about the islands' prehistory.

Indeed, little was known about geology *per se*. It had become a separate science less than fifty years beforehand. The discipline had emerged following the pioneering work of Scotland's James Hutton (1726–97) and England's William Smith (1769–1839). Famously, on the basis of his observations of sediments, erosion, uplift and igneous activity, Hutton had in 1785 advanced the then radical proposition that in studying the earth, 'we find no vestige of a beginning – no prospect of an end'.[6] These few words not only challenged the biblical account of the nature of creation (six days of labour and one of rest), but also the age of the Earth, in which countless Christians were firm believers.[7] In the seventeenth century, James Ussher, Archbishop of Armagh, had fixed on Sunday, 23 October 4004 BC as the date of the Creation. The foundations of Christian faith were further shaken by Smith's revelations. The 'Father of English Geology' had been able, by studying fossil types, to order England's rocks chronologically.[8] Not everything had happened at once.

Others too contributed to the emerging discipline. Swiss-born Louis Albert Necker had worked on geological maps of Scotland in the early years of the nineteenth century. However, it was not until 1832, perhaps 1834, that the first detailed geological survey of Scotland was completed.[9]

This had partly come about by accident. Its author, John MacCulloch (1773–1835), who had been an army surgeon before becoming an ordnance chemist, had begun his work with a much narrower aim in mind. His mission was to search for suitable grindstones for the Board of Ordnance's two gunpowder mills. Those currently in use were worn and disintegrating and had to be replaced. Stone chips entering the powder and causing sparks was a recipe for disaster.[10] With the war with the French emperor and military leader Napoleon Bonaparte raging, new stones were a national military priority. However, the former source of non-siliceous durable limestone, Namur in France, was cut off.

MacCulloch's nationwide quest, begun in 1809, had taken him to Skye in the late summer of 1812, where he thought he had found what he wanted, in Strath. This was the 'vast strata of fine white marble' that Thomas Pennant had seen on his visit to Skye in 1772, which he believed had been used for the altar in Iona Abbey.[11] Nevertheless, for a variety of reasons, including the failure of the Board's contractor, Richard Elliott, to find blocks of sufficiently flaw-free limestone large enough for the seven-foot-wide grind-stones required for the gunpowder mills, and the end of hostilities with France, the quarries on Lord Macdonald's estate were, for a while at least, abandoned.[12]

By this time, however, MacCulloch had conceived a plan for a geological and mineralogical map of Scotland. Between 1811 and 1821 he often devoted some five months a year to the project, funded for a good part of this time by the Board of Ordnance. With his prior knowledge of the country, this was sufficient to allow him to complete his seminal *Description of the Western Islands of Scotland*, published in 1819.[13]

It was in this publication that Pabay made its first appearance as a place worthy of the attention of geologists.

True, on a mineralogical tour of Scotland's west coast at the end of the eighteenth century – in late July and early August 1798 – the Scottish geologist and natural historian Professor Robert Jameson had spent three weeks on Skye. For several days he and his companion Charles Bell stayed with Lachlan Mackinnon and his wife at Coire-chat-achan near Broadford. He had even climbed, with some difficulty on its steep, stone-strewn surface, Beinn na Caillich, which loomed above the Mackinnons' house at the bottom. From the summit, where the 'dark, lurid . . . Cuillin mountains resting in awful majesty' induced thoughts in the two men's minds of the 'power and omnipresence of the framer of this wonderful globe', Jameson noticed 'Pabby' and the other islands off Skye's east coast.[14] But he didn't ever visit Pabay. He and Bell did stay for several days exploring Raasay, and also visited Rona, Fladda and Scalpay, but that was as close as they got. *Ammonites Jamesoni* was the name later given to the most prolific of Pabay's ammo-nites, and the ammonite-bearing strata became known as the

Jamesoni-beds.[15] Yet it seems that the professor had collected these fossils on Raasay, where he ordered a 'proper' box to pack them in; a few days later he arranged at the inn in Broadford to have them shipped to Leith in a vessel that was 'going that way with Kelp'.

What for MacCulloch on Pabay were 'particularly conspicuous as well as numerous', were the 'trap veins' that had broken through the soft shale beds that were to be seen around much of the island's shoreline. By protecting the sedimentary strata from being eroded by the sea, these hard rock seams accounted for its existence.

Pabay was part of a low-lying floodplain which by the start of the Jurassic period around 205 million years ago was being covered by the sea. The climate was tropical, and the water warmer and shallower than it is today, enabling a range of living organisms such as corals, bivalves and ammonites to flourish. Close by, on land, dinosaurs roamed.[16]

Limestones, shales and sandstones were deposited on the sea beds. It is in these rock formations that are to be found the fossils that have drawn geologists to Skye – and Pabay – for more than two centuries.

It was much more recently – in geological time – that the igneous rocks that had so struck MacCulloch had appeared. Dating back some sixty-five million years, what MacCulloch was describing were the basaltic remains of great masses of magna that forced their way through a series of cracks or fissures in the earth's crust during what may have been north-western Europe's most extensive volcanic episode.[17] This was when Greenland and North America broke away from Europe, and the North Atlantic Ocean was being formed. It was this epic process that gave rise to what is Skye's most distinctive feature: the immense jagged gabbro of the Cuillin ridge.

On a smaller scale, Pabay was intersected by more than one of these igneous intrusions (MacCulloch's 'trap veins'), mainly trending NNE–SSW across the island.[18]

It is the autodidact, ardent Christian and founding father of the Free Church (but no literalist interpreter of the Bible) and amateur geologist, Hugh Miller from Cromarty (1802–56), who has left the best description of Pabay's trap dykes (along with a hint as to why they would be of interest to aspiring geologists).[19] They were, he wrote, 'beyond comparison finer than those of the water of Leith, which first suggested to Hutton his theory', and 'stand up like fences over the sedimentary strata, or run like moles far into the sea'.[20]

The largest of these dolerite and basalt incursions, which look as if they could be man-made, stands some 13 feet (4 metres) tall at its highest point – as youngsters it seemed to soar above us. It is still impressive. It was where Miller disembarked on Pabay, the dyke having served as a make-do pier for his dinghy.

The former Scots-born soldier and gentleman-scientist Roderick Impey Murchison (1792–1871), another geologist who would achieve national fame (and a knighthood, in 1863), and who also visited Pabay, would have shared our boyish amazement. The 'Dykes raise to a great height', he scribbled in his otherwise illegible hand in his notebook in 1827 when, in the company of another geologist, Adam Sedgwick, he had spent time exploring Pabay. One of the dykes, was 'at least 8 or 10 yards in breadth & standing quite above the Cliff has the appearance of a ruin'.[21] Archibald Geikie thought the the rocks in question bore 'a strong resemblance to some works of art', but otherwise was of the opinion there was 'little in their occurrence worthy of special remark'.

Rather it was the island's fossils that were putting Pabay on the geologists' itineraries. Notwithstanding Jameson's, MacCulloch's, Murchison's and Sedgwick's awareness of them, it was plaid-wearing Hugh Miller who was the most eloquent and enthusiastic promoter of the 'fossil-mottled' island as a geologist's paradise.[22]

He had landed there with his minister companion John Swanson in late July 1844. Swanson had recently been appointed to the Small Isles parish that comprised the islands of Rum, Eigg, Canna and Muck. The duo's vessel, the *Betsey*, a small yacht that required only a single crewman, had been bought by the Free Church so that Swanson could get around the four islands to preach.

A happy geologist, Miller enthused, would be one who, 'with a few thousands to spare, could call Pabba his own'. The 'petrifications' of its shores would fill a museum: 'They rise by thousands and tens of thousands on the exposed places of its sea-washed strata, standing out in bold relief, like sculpturings on ancient tombstones, at once mummies and monuments, – the dead, and the carved memorials of the dead. Every rock is a tablet of hiero-glyphics, with an ascertained alphabet; every rolled pebble a casket, with old pictorial records locked up within.'[23]

Miller's excitement about and the curiosity of other geologists in Pabay and its vicinity are to be accounted for by the attention they were paying at the time to the Lias.

The Lias is a sequence of rock strata consisting of marine lime-stones, sandstones, shales, mudstones and clays that are found in large parts of western Europe, including the British Isles. In Scotland, the Lias is concentrated in the Sea of the Hebrides basin.[24] The importance of the Lias was that it denoted a period – the early Jurassic (roughly between 205 million and 175 million years ago) – the secrets of which in the early to mid-nineteenth century were just beginning to be uncovered in Scotland.[25] It was one of the things that drew Miller to Skye (and Mull). Its 'oozy sea-floor' which 'grew heavy and sank, and on which the belemnite dropped its spindle and the ammonite its shell' imparted to him the idea of '*old* Scotland . . . a land whose hills and islands, like its great aris-tocratic families, have risen from the level in very various ages, and under the operation of circumstances essentially diverse'.[26]

It was along Skye's east coast and at Strathaird that, in Miller's words, was to be found 'the most largely-developed deposit of this formation in Scotland'. Much of it, however, was covered by peat, so that other than along the sides of the channels cut by mountain streams, the sought-for strata were difficult to access. The excep-tion was the Broadford Bay district. And where the Lias was most evident was in the Ob Lusa–Ardnish area, on the eastern edge of the bay. Here, 'from its lower to its upper beds' it was exposed 'in [an] unbroken series along the beach'.

Pabay, though, was the highlight, being 'entirely composed' of the Lias formation, primarily the upper levels. What is more, Pabay's fossiliferous deposits were found in mudstone around a hundred feet thick (although in places on Raasay, as at Hallaig, the same distinctive shale sequence is six times that, and is likely to be where Robert Jameson found those he sent south in 1798).[27]

So important, geologically, were Pabay's Jurassic shale beds, that from mid-century they were designated as the 'Pabba Beds' or 'Pabba Shale'. The term has stuck, although currently, according to the British Geological Survey's lexicon of named rock units, the term used is the 'Pabay Shale Formation'.[28]

It was partly to unlock the testimony of the stones in which they had been held silent for many millennia that Edinburgh-born Archibald Geikie had given up his junior position in an Edinburgh lawyer's office to embark on a career as a field geologist. To engage in scientific enquiry was his aim, but with a strong emphasis on historical understanding. In words that would have chimed with his mentor and greatest inspiration as a geologist, Hugh Miller, Geikie in 1853 had written how 'every stone we tread upon tells a tale of ages that are gone'.[29] In September of the same year, while still in his teens, prompted by Miller and with an invitation from the aforementioned Rev. John Mackinnon, he left Edinburgh on what proved to be a four-hour-long train journey to Glasgow.[30] Armed with his 'stout' hammer with its 'round blunt face and a flat sharp tail', a pocket lens and a notebook, from Glasgow he took a steamboat to Skye. His destination was very specific: Strath parish. And Pabay.[31]

Miller was on Pabay for only a few hours. Seventeen-year-old Geikie by contrast spent several days there. A 'thorough-going empiricist', he relied heavily on observation and therefore needed time to do his job well.[32] And after closely studying its rocks, Geikie concluded that Pabay represented the 'most interesting square mile among the western islands'.[33] He found it difficult to contain his elation not only at the 'prodigious numbers' of fossils but also their 'excellent state of preservation': 'the paleontologist could not wish for a finer display of fossil forms than that shown by these beds', he recorded with obvious delight.[34] He later paid tribute to Miller's importance as an investigator of the Hebridean Lias formations by recommending to the later nineteenth-century authority on British ammonites, Thomas Wright, that one of those he (Geikie) had found on Pabay be named *Aegoceras milleri*.[35]

Geikie was familiar with the fish and reptile fossils found from the Carboniferous period in the south of Scotland and had seen shells and corals found in mountain limestone. Yet here, on Pabay, he enthused, 'were organisms of another stamp', relics of 'another creation' that he had been privileged to witness. And even to smell. So 'richly charged' were some of the beds with organic remains that they emitted 'a strong fetid odour when rubbed or broken'.[36]

Such revelations – both visual and olfactory – were further proof of the contemporary view that the Earth's history comprised a series of catastrophic events and creations that in due course had made a habitat suitable for human life.[37] Pabay contributed material testimony towards such a narrative. Later, however, Geikie was to distance himself from Miller and his Calvinist catastrophism and argue instead that the fossil record supported an evolutionist interpretation of the Earth's history, which, conveniently, validated his contemporaries' faith in the progress of civilisation.[38]

Aware of such discoveries, and of the sheer timelessness of the geological record as it was being revealed by the pioneer geologists, Charles Darwin would later argue, in his *On the Origin of Species* (1859), that evolution was a slow process, taking place over hundreds of millennia. James Ussher's timeline was impossibly short, although several decades were to pass before his chronology was removed from the margins of the text in even the most reputable Bibles.[39]

In 1844 Miller had rhapsodised about how things might have looked when the now-petrified coral beds of what at the time was called Lussay Bay (to the east of Breakish), now Ob Lusa, were forming.

Almost ten years later, across the water, on Pabay, Geikie too – who acknowledged his debt to Miller as a writer on geological matters – gave free rein to his imagination. He conjured up a mental diorama of wispy plants on the sea bed, and the several fauna, ammonites, belemnites and other simple organisms moving gently in Pabay's waters. They represented a lost world, made extinct by the same force – possibly a giant meteorite that had crashed into the sea off Mexico – that is now thought to have wiped out the dinosaurs.[40] Confronted during such spiritual journeying with the sheer immensity of geological time, he would not 'easily efface' the memory of his 'rambles on Pabba'.

Nor, it seems, would Pabay's residents forget Geikie. On Skye itself there were faint memories of some of his predecessors – MacCulloch, Murchison (Geikie's patron after he obtained a position in the Geological Survey in 1855), Sedgwick and Miller. The Genevan professor of mineralogy and geology, Louis Necker, even moved to Skye, where he spent time studying and measuring the Cuillins, living in Portree until he died there in 1861.

There were apocryphal tales of the geologists' bags of specimens being carried on the backs of locals who looked inside, puzzled at their contents – stones – and then emptied them out before refilling them with substitutes when they were close to their destination.[41] And still pocketed their fee.

The first geologists certainly had to suffer for their science. Skye was especially challenging, explained Geikie. The 'most valuable sections' were often on stretches of the exposed coastline 'of some remote loch', 'miles distant from the lowliest hut' and then only accessible by boat. That was if it was calm. Some decades earlier, John MacCulloch had described boats as 'the stage coaches and post-chaises of the country [Skye]'.[42] They 'were convenient enough when we can command the weather', but 'a most detestable species of communication in such a stormy, rainy, uncertain climate'. Professor Robert Jameson and Charles Bell spent several days inside on Skye, waiting for the weather to improve, although it had to be particularly ferocious to deter them altogether from carrying on with their investigations. Adding to their frustration were delays in getting their baggage transported to where they were staying. Skye time and Edinburgh time were very different concepts. On Skye waiting around, not unusually for a day or more – for a horse, a boat or a guide – was the norm. There was some reluctance on the part of locals to escort them, as they tramped for miles over unmapped rain-sodden peat mosses, marched up and down and through steep-sided glens and scaled mountains known only vaguely by name, as a result of which even more days were lost owing to the two men's fatigue and, for Jameson, a sprained back caused by the frequent need to clamber or even jump over large stones and boulders.[43] MacCulloch had been the victim of Skye's thick clouds of midges, the 'torment of this country, the mosquitoes of the

Highlands'. They were certainly no ally of the summertime geologist, as he went about the painstaking business of measuring, recording and collecting.

On Pabay, Geikie was made welcome enough by forty-four-year-old Charles Mackinnon, his wife Flora and their six children. They were at a loss, however, to understand their young visitor's purpose. Hard to fathom was why anyone should be collecting what appeared to be stones from the shore without any intention of selling them. 'Achan! Achan!', Flora Mackinnon would exclaim despairingly when he appeared each evening with 'a fresh cargo of specimens'. Geikie's explanation that these would be put upon shelves and stored in drawers simply confirmed what his hosts had suspected: that they were dealing with an idiot. (It was a conclusion that other natives of Skye had reached about 'a lad [Geikie] wandering about alone and, as it looked, aimlessly, with a hammer in his hand and a bag over his shoulder'.[44] His nickname, he gathered, was Gillen a Clach, or lad of the stones.) Undeterred, he stuck to his task, collecting specimens by day and sorting them in the evenings. This he did in the 'parlour', a room in the Mackinnons' 'hut', with 'four whitewashed walls covered . . . by blackened fir branches with bundles of heather thrown across and lighted by a miserably small window, a foot or so square, formed of brown paper & broken glass'.

Geikie ate humbly if well, on potatoes, oatcakes, milk and tea, with an occasional herring or egg. He slept on a heather bed, in the corner of a barn, with a flickering candle for light. Imprinted indelibly in his memory was the sound of the wind 'moaning' through the 'louvre boards that served for windows'. Through these was to be heard 'the shrieking of the sea-fowl, like the agonised cries of drowning seamen'.[45]

For Geikie's hospitality, food and accommodation however, Charles Mackinnon would accept no money. Instead, despite his uncertain grasp of the English language, he asked Geikie to send him a copy of *Josephus* to read aloud to his children. Apparently, Mackinnon later showed this off proudly. It was the largest book on his shelf.

Whatever its discomforts, Geikie's foray on Pabay was to have a lasting impact. First, there was what it did for Geikie's subsequent spectacular career. Secondly, and partly as a consequence, there was its effect on Pabay.

On his return south, Geikie not only showed to and discussed with Miller the fossils he had collected;[46] it was also with this collection that Geikie made his first contribution to a learned society, the Royal Physical Society in Edinburgh, of which until recently Miller had been president. Young Geikie began his lecture by proudly placing the Pabay fossils upon the table that stood between him and his distinguished audience.[47] Four years later Geikie was invited to present a paper at London's Geological Society where his fossils (now including those he had unearthed on Raasay) were classified and placed in the context of the Lias beds found elsewhere in Britain and Europe.[48] Geikie was triumphant, for, while most of the fossils he had brought from Pabay were of species already known, he had also found four that were new.[49]

Although he had not been the trailblazer, Geikie's lucid, accessible and widely read published work further encouraged the nation's most eminent petrologists and geologists to include Skye – and Pabay – on their travels in the following decades.[50] Geikie himself seems to have returned to the island more than once and, in 1855, visited Scalpay for the first time.[51]

It would be a while yet before tales of the young man who gathered rocks dried up, but the supply of collectable stones was inexhaustible. On 1 August 1864, on a yacht cruise through the Inner Hebrides, a Rev. D. Haughton visited Pabay and 'brought away by diligent quarrying, a good collection of fossils'. His booty was later examined by the paleontologist of the Geological Survey of Ireland, while in December Haughton gave a lecture on his finds at a meeting of the Royal Geological Society of Ireland, at Dublin's Trinity College.[52]

Another of those who came afterwards was Alfred Harker. Between 1895 and 1905 Harker worked on a part-time basis for the Geological Survey of Scotland – and enthused about the quality and abundance of Pabay's 'highly fossiliferous beds'.[53] By 1910 fourteen species of ammonites on Pabay had been identified. Further investigation in the early 1920s, conducted by digging deeper through the shales, and in the cliffs rising above the high-water mark, trebled this number.[54]

Pabay can rightly claim to be Skye's original Jurassic island. (The footprints on Skye from dinosaurs, from the more recent Middle Jurassic, were not discovered until 1982.)

With references to Pabay in Geikie's most popular books – such as *The Story of a Boulder* (1858) and *Scottish Reminiscences* (1904), the plunder continued. By Len's and Margaret's time on Pabay, fossil hunting was somewhat less straightforward than it had been not more than a century earlier. The early collectors had picked up most of the best specimens that lay on the surface. Nevertheless, rich pickings of fossils were still to be had by those who were prepared to spend time searching. Their availability was one of the key selling points made by Len when he began to adver-tise the cottage for holiday letting. With electric light, gas for cook-ing and warmth, and with what by the early 1960s boasted the title of a 'shop', the geologist of the twentieth century could enjoy his or her evenings in a degree of comfort that the intrepid fossil hunter Archibald Geikie would have found astonishing. But possi-bly disappointing. Geikie – a 'smooth, self-seeking, [and] sly', socially ambitious careerist, whose relations with his colleagues were hardly collegiate – liked to be the top dog. Even Len's improved accommodation would have been unlikely to have satis-fied him. Geikie preferred to stay, when he could, in the more salu-brious accommodation enjoyed by Highland landowners when he was in the north.[55]

But the pioneering geologists had done something more than collect fossils. We have seen the frequent comments made about Pabay's fertile appearance. The same was true of Sleat, much of Strath and parts of Strathaird. It was in this part of Skye where, in the words of James Macdonald in his 1811 account of the agricul-ture of the Hebrides, 'we find great tracts of light friable mould upon gravel, and also loam mixed with peat earth, the very best soil for sown grasses and green crops'.[56]

Hugh Miller it was, however, who made the connection between this and the sedimentary strata below. Pabay specifically, he concluded, 'so green, rich, and level', was 'a specimen illustrative of the effect of geologic formation on scenery'. This he contrasted with the neighbouring 'steep, brown, barren' island of Longay, 'composed of the ancient Red Sandstone of the district – differing as thoroughly from it in aspect as a bit of granite differs from a bit of clay-slate'.[57]

The geologists had discovered Pabay's uniqueness; its geology had made it so. It was one of Pabay's attractions, but as we've seen, it also presented challenges.

Chapter 11

'The rabbits must be drastically kept down': furriers' friends, ferocious foes

Early in January 1931, Donald Gunn, one of the gardeners on Scalpay, wrote to George Fraser, the Portree solicitor responsible for overseeing Sir Henry Bell's Skye estate. Gunn's concern was that half of the young trees he had planted only two years earlier had been destroyed. By rabbits. Something must be done to stop them, he urged, 'or they [the rest of the plantation's trees] will have all been eaten up in 3 weeks' time'.[1] Perhaps he was sceptical, but after a delay Fraser sent his assistant, a Mr Macintyre, to Scalpay to make further enquiries. What Macintyre reported was alarming. Without further ado Fraser then wrote to Edward Tappenden, Sir Henry Bell's secretary in London.

It was not only Scalpay's woodland that had suffered from rabbit depredation. The ordinary pasture land had been contaminated by their urine and droppings – thus leaving the island's sheep short of nourishment. There was even an aesthetic dimension: they had attacked a privet hedge in front of Scalpay House. At the rear, older trees – usually ignored by rabbits – had been stripped of their bark too. Indeed, Fraser wrote, they were rampaging through the island, 'searching anything green'. Something had to be done, urgently. For if the rabbits are 'to be allowed as they are at present', Scalpay would 'soon become a rabbit warren and nothing else'.[2]

There was little comfort to be had from knowing that Scalpay was not alone in having to deal with rampaging rabbits. There was a mounting awareness nationwide that 'tree planting is impossible unless means are taken to protect the young plants from the rabbit'.[3] Although efforts had been made to reduce their numbers during the First World War, in 1921 the Game and Heather

(Scotland) Committee declared that, 'with the possible exception of the rat, the rabbit is the most serious four-footed pest that farmers had to deal with'. So alarmed were the country's farmers and agricultural interest groups that in 1937 a select committee was set up by the House of Lords to investigate the scourge and recommend action. Hares were even worse, but fortunately there were fewer of them.

Len Whatley would not have been surprised had he ever seen the correspondence between Gunn, Fraser and others on this rabbit-induced devastation. In April 1950 he had planted three acres of potatoes in the island's best soil. His first planting on Pabay. The crop was minuscule. The reason: extensive rabbit damage. This was despite having been assured that 'rabbits did not touch spuds'. (If only he had had time to add to his reading list the report of the Napier Commission published almost seventy years earlier; one of the members, the Tory MP for Invernessshire, Cameron of Lochiel, had enquired somewhat incredulously of Murdo Nicolson, a Raasay crofter, 'Do rabbits eat potatoes?' He was left in no doubt that they and other game did, with relish.[4]) Not so long afterwards Pabay's voracious feeders turned their attention to the thousand or so fir saplings Len had planted in an effort to create a new shelterbelt and break the force of the wind on growing crops and for wintering his cattle. They destroyed the lot. George Jolly learned the hard way too, losing the best part of 1,000 cabbage plants during one December night.

As Len's father wrote at the time, the rabbits were Pabay's twentieth-century robbers (an allusion to Dean Munro's description of the island's sixteenth-century inhabitants). Having been left for nine years of 'uninterrupted rivalry and passionate courtship', there was now an infestation of thousands of them.[5] On their short exploratory foray onto Pabay in October 1949, Len and Margaret had caught sight of a few rabbit sentinels who scurried into their burrows on their approach, but they had seen nothing to suggest that below ground there lurked a monstrous regiment of them.

On this occasion, however, there was something of a silver lining in this cloud over Len's hopes of successfully farming Pabay. An increase in rabbit prices meant that it would be worthwhile bringing a rabbit trapper to the island. (Coincidentally, Ronald Lockley had taken a rabbit trapper with him to Skokholm when he set up permanent residence on that island in 1927; so absorbed did he become with the rabbits there that in 1964 he also wrote a book about them – *The Private Life of the Rabbit* – which in turn inspired Richard Adams's novel *Watership Down*.) Not only might this help in 'quelling the pest', but their sale might also bring some desperately needed cash.[6]

Within a short time 1,000 rabbits had been killed. But the mammalian tide was not so easily stemmed. To his lengthy list of priority tasks Len now had to add the need for at least two miles of deep-set fencing. Such a serious threat to his plans to cultivate the island by planting a range of crops that included those known to be attractive to rabbits demanded a suitably robust – and more immediate – response. Could the 140-yard long fishing net he had bought to catch dogfish – and the occasional flounder for tea – be used to catch rabbits? The idea was mooted, but dropped. The weary war wore on.

Yet not much more than a century earlier the problem would not have arisen. There were rabbit populations on Scotland's west coast islands, but very far to the south, on Cumbrae and Arran in the Firth of Clyde. Otherwise, observed James Macdonald in his report on the state of agriculture in the Western Isles in 1811, apart from a few 'stragglers', there were 'no rabbit warrens in the Hebrides'.[7] There are still today some Scottish islands that are rabbit-free – Rum and Tiree for instance.

Rabbits, however, had been introduced to Scotland centuries earlier. In the thirteenth century their meat, skins and fur were much in demand.[8] By mid-Victorian times their numbers had soared in those districts where they were to be found, the south west of Scotland for instance.[9] Voracious eaters, they were also prolific reproducers; a single doe (a female rabbit) is capable of yielding as many as eight broods with litters of six or more in a single season. A young rabbit matures in six months.

Welcomed at first as pets and as an additional target for game hunters, even before 1900 the unintended consequences of introducing them had become a serious issue for landowners and tenant farmers. John Mackenzie recalled how in the early nineteenth century his father had introduced to Conon in Ross-shire a few rabbits from England. Seventy years on, 'from this [small] colony,' he continued, 'the whole north is now swarming with the pests.' Sardonically, Mackenzie noted that no one had yet 'suggested a monument to my father for conferring such a benefit to the Highlands!'

Despite a series of measures being taken to destroy them during the First World War, they continued to multiply, and munch virtually anything (although not meat – *leporidae* are vegetarian). As any Skye gardener will wistfully report, reassuring notices in garden centres that certain plants are 'rabbit resistant' cut no ice. Rabbits don't read the signs. Nor, as Len had discovered to his cost, do they eat in accordance with customary expectations.

Scotland's landowners and farmers, in their long war on the nation's pestilential population, resorted to a range of weapons. Snares, guns, netting, ferrets, traps and, from the 1930s, gas, were all used in the attempt to slash rabbit numbers.

A daily chore for Stuart and me on Pabay once we were old enough was to check the wire snares that we had set where netting had been holed or dug under by the rabbits, or on any rabbit runs we could spot. Releasing choking rabbits and then breaking their necks wasn't fun (dead rabbits were easier to deal with, as was shooting them, preferably at a distance). But it was, quite literally, a question of controlling them, or seeing acres of growing crops disappear in the space of a few days. Specialist trappers too were brought over by Len from time to time. As a last resort cyanide gas was used, pumped into the rabbits' burrows, the exits from which were blocked. All in all, an ugly business.

On the other hand, Anthea recalls with pleasure the long walks with her father as he checked his fences and filled any holes rabbits could have used; these were precious times of father–daughter conversation.[10]

* * *

There were in Victorian times those who had seen in rabbits an opportunity to extract additional value from land that was otherwise failing to produce the kinds of returns that had been possible prior to the decline in the prices of mutton and wool.

We know that the returns obtainable from sheep had been falling from the early 1870s. Some were kept on Pabay thereafter, but after shearing in 1885 the bulk of them were sent off, for auction at Inverness. Most of those left were Lord Macdonald's, for the use of the Castle.

The first written reference to rabbits on Pabay that I have managed to find was in 1882, when a John Stewart wrote to the factor Alexander Macdonald as he'd heard that the rights to hunt rabbits on Pabay were to be let.[11] At this time too, Macdonald was in receipt of monies from the sale of rabbits at Manchester Fish Market. So there must have been rabbits somewhere on the Macdonald estates, which included Pabay. In fact, they had become sufficiently problematic at Scorrybreac near Portree a decade earlier, that if their numbers weren't checked, Alexander Macdonald was warned, the hirsel would have had to be reduced to 200 sheep.[12]

But on Pabay, with fewer sheep, there was more room for rabbits to multiply. In fact, the presence even of a limited number of sheep may actually have made life easier for the rabbits, the grazing habits of the former having improved foraging conditions for them.[13]

And there was pressure for more of them. In July 1884, a Newcastle potato seller and game dealer approached Macdonald enquiring whether there was any piece of land 'you would be disposed to let or lease as a rabbit warren'.

It was a timely request.

Nationally, there was a moderate interest in rabbit fur. The main market at the time though was for rabbit meat. Indeed, as recently as 1873 the Parliamentary Committee on the Game Laws was informed that rabbits were 'an everyday dish in the houses of the working classes'.[14] Working-class customers bought nine-tenths of the rabbits sold in British market places. A main attraction was that rabbit meat was relatively cheap compared to other types of butcher fare.

However, the Game Acts that had been passed since the first of these in 1832 meant that forays onto private land for the purpose of catching and killing rabbits – even for the proverbial pot – was deemed to be poaching, punishable by a hefty fine and even imprisonment. Law-abiding consumers therefore were encouraged to buy rather than steal rabbit meat. Consequently, rabbit farming was becoming increasingly common. One Perth game dealer, who was supplied with game from Invernessshire and elsewhere in the north, claimed that each year he dispatched some 80,000 rabbits to England's Midland towns. Accordingly, with regard to Pabay, Alexander Macdonald listened carefully to arguments that rabbits might be a better commercial bet than sheep.

Before long, the island was well on the way to becoming a commercial rabbit warren. Along with the enquiry from Newcastle, in July 1884 a Mr A. Bell, a rabbit trapper from Reston in Berwickshire, expressed a wish to get over to the island to see 'what number of rabbits is there'. Such was the interest in the island's rabbits that in October Macdonald received yet another offer. This time it was from a Mr R.J. Gibson from Broadford. Provided he could have 1,000 rabbits, Gibson was prepared to send over a trapper and pay one shilling and sixpence for each pair. A thousand was a lot, and the price high, but, Gibson pointed out, with rabbits selling in Edinburgh around this time at two shillings and three pence a pair, he was still able – in theory at least – to make a decent profit. He would not offer more though, what with the additional costs incurred in getting to Pabay by boat and the risks of delay in getting dead animals off the island.

As it happened, the agreed number was never achieved, not by Gibson or his trappers anyway. Losing money, Macdonald did his best to improve the quality of Pabay's rabbits. He was unhappy about their small size and 'low condition'. One remedy was to kill as many as possible, William Barron in Armadale advised him. They would, as a result, 'do much better when they are well reduced in numbers and come up a fresh'.[15]

The other way of enhancing the stock was to import higher-grade rabbits from elsewhere. Resort was had to this form of remedial action in 1886, when after Gibson's trapper had completed his February killing, a cargo of rabbits sent by Bookless Bros in Sheffield arrived. This was a fraught process. It had not only involved getting the animals to Skye at a time when the rail links to Kyle of Lochalsh and Mallaig lay in the future. There was delay too as the livestock were kept waiting for a weather window to ship them across to Pabay. Little wonder then, as they lay dazed, weary and hungry in their hampers in Broadford, that Gibson advised Macdonald, 'the sooner they are put on the ground the better after such a long journey as they will not likely take any food that may be given to them'.

For the hard-pressed, land-hungry crofters of Breakish, that the island was being turned over to rabbits was a matter of regret, if not resentment. It was another reason why they were reluctant to go across in the mid-1880s; it was unlikely, in the circumstances, that Pabay would support the four or five families that it had been capable of doing not fifty years earlier.

Unfortunately, it is at this point that the paper trail on Pabay's rabbits dries up. Nonetheless, there is every reason to suppose that the rabbits continued to breed.

* * *

We can pick up the story again thirty years later. Notwithstanding efforts at national level in the 1920s to reduce the UK's rabbit population, on Scalpay estate their cultivation was being encouraged.

It made sense. One consequence of Sir Donald Currie's death in 1909, the interruption of the war years, 1914–18, and the lower level of enthusiasm for the Scalpay estate on the part of his trustees, was a reduction in game stocks. Indeed, as we saw in Chapter 5, by the time Sir Henry Bell bought them, both Scalpay and Pabay were suffering badly from neglect.

As regards rabbits, in Sir Donald Currie's time they had been largely confined to the south-western portion of the island, at the narrows that separated Scalpay from the townships of Dunan and Strollamus.

One of the first suggestions made by Angus Macleod, Sir Henry Bell's new gamekeeper from Rum in 1926, was to clear Scalpay of its present rabbit population and then to re-stock. His reasoning was simple: such was the state of affairs as regards game, 'rabbit will practically be the only shooting available here this season'.[16] At first he had difficulty sourcing a supply of better stock at an acceptable cost, but by March 1927 the keeper had found what he was looking for at Aricarnach, near Luib, on Strollamus estate.[17] The issue was even more pressing on Pabay as the rabbits there were suffering from an outbreak of tuberculosis; by the end of 1927 those that were left were 'a very poor class'. The answer was to kill off the stock entirely and replenish the following spring.[18]

There was a particular problem with Pabay, however. Macleod lived on Scalpay, not Pabay. As he informed Fraser, because he was there only intermittently, the 'Pabay men' were able to trap the rabbits they wanted at will. Worse still, he complained, 'they only pick the best'. Recognising the reality of the situation and conscious of the costs of his own keep on Pabay should he stay there to kill rabbits over a period of weeks, Macleod proposed that he let the 'Pabbay boys' do the trapping and pay them for their efforts.[19] Sir Henry agreed.

Stimulating greater interest in rabbits was the spiralling demand for their pelts. The advent of mass production in the car industry – led by Henry Ford in the USA – had reduced the cost of buying a motor vehicle. As a result, car ownership amongst the middle classes – whose real incomes rose despite the depressed economic conditions of the inter-war years – became increasingly common. By modern standards draughty, and minimally heated, their drivers and passengers had to dress appropriately. Fur wraps and fur coats – made from rabbit pelts – were one means of keeping warm. Aviators too had similar requirements.

In fact, the market for rabbit fur was sufficiently buoyant in 1927 for Mrs Balfour-Graham, of the recently established Scottish Fur Breeders Association, to pronounce that few home industries were 'so promising as in the breeding of rabbit furs'.[20] She was right. Fur made from rabbits was a fashion item, used for hats, fine coats of coney seal, musquash coney – a substitute for mink – and mock ermine. It also had more prosaic applications, in linings for gloves and as trimming for dresses and other garments.[21]

Thus, in the decade following the end of the First World War, the breeding of rabbits for their fur became a substantial business. But not just any rabbit fur would do; quality and colour were of the utmost important if top prices were to be achieved. This required rabbits from carefully selected stock to be housed in hutches, kept scrupulously clean, and well and regularly fed. This ruled out most rabbits bred on Scalpay and Pabay, although attempts were made to introduce strains that could be killed for their fur. The legacy of this was to be seen – literally – into the 1980s on Pabay, where from time to time would be spotted a black or black-belted rabbit.

All this was in addition to the lucrative market for wild rabbit meat, which remained strong during and after the Great War. The figures for Perth station, from where most rabbits killed in Scotland went south by rail, are impressive. In 1925, in the peak season of October to December, 5,000–6,000 rabbits were shipped daily, 36,000 in a typical week, or 150,000 each month.[22]

The opportunity of generating some additional income from rabbit sales from his recently acquired Scalpay estate had not escaped the notice of Sir Henry Bell. Before long rabbits were being killed on all four of the estate's islands. He wrote to Fraser, asking him to encourage Macleod, the new gamekeeper, to try and sell what rabbits he could locally, but failing that, in Edinburgh and Glasgow. As a gesture of goodwill as the new laird, he also instructed Macleod to give some to estate tenants of his choosing, 'and in what numbers you think best'. Bell's generosity was more apparent than real. With rabbits in abundance in the vicinity, none could be sold in Broadford, or hardly even given away. Buyers were to be found in Glasgow, but also Manchester, where they realised the princely sum of three shillings a pair.[23] This though was for Scalpay rabbits. Pabay's could fetch not much more than a shilling a pair.

There is nothing to suggest that Sir Henry was anything other than oblivious to the downside of rabbit cultivation. Less interested than his predecessors in shooting, he may not have been as concerned as they had been in maintaining the heather and foliage that supported the other game on the island.

Given his background in the meat trade he remained confident about the market for lean rabbit meat and possibly some fur too. Consequently, he set his sights on expanding the stock, ordering Macleod in 1930 'not to kill or interfere with the rabbits in any way whatsoever'.[24] In this sense Bell was simply acting in accordance with the dual thinking about the rabbit 'problem' that was exercising the minds of many of those associated with British farming at the time. Undeniably, rabbits did enormous damage. On the other hand, their meat was an affordable food, the provision of which could boost the rents of small farmers (and some larger ones, as on Scalpay, where they might also assist in paying the gamekeeper's wages).[25]

As we saw at the start of this chapter though, things had got badly out of hand. By January 1930 Sir Henry would have had an inkling of what heartbreak rabbits could induce: they had got into the garden and spoiled the 'fine carnations' he had brought from England.[26] The fencing that had been put in to protect the new pine and spruce plantation to the north-east of the garden, while being the recommended three feet six inches high, had only been sunk six inches under the ground, and in places not at all – thereby enabling the rabbits en masse to push or burrow their way in, and eat, damage and ultimately destroy the young trees.[27]

It was only in the following year, ill and close to death, that he began to appreciate that he might have let loose an unstoppable force. He authorised his secretary in March 1931 – barely a week before he died – to inform Fraser that 'the rabbits must be drastically kept down in order not to interfere with the sheep and crops'.[28] This was the message Fraser then relayed to Angus Macleod. Not many months passed before instructions were given for similar action to be taken on Pabay. Otherwise, as on Scalpay, livestock would be at risk.[29]

What followed was a veritable blitz on Scalpay's rabbits (and we must assume the same thing happened, though on a smaller scale, on Pabay). Replacement netting, sunk deeper into the ground than previously, was one feature of what was a multi-faceted defensive strategy, but it was too late to prevent a disastrous outcome for both crops and livestock in 1931. In despair, and to avoid being held responsible for what he saw coming, Donald Robertson, the farm manager, reported the situation to Fraser in May. All the parks, he wrote, 'are as bare as they are in winter', the oats he had planted 'are trimmed off as they come through', while all the clover had gone. As a result, the ewes were weak, more lambs had been lost than at any time previously and Sir Henry's prize Highland cattle (one of whom had perished) were having to be fed on hay brought over from Skye.[30]

Nevertheless, during the course of the summer progress was made. The gamekeeper, Angus Macleod, spent days shooting, ferreting and trapping. By August he was able to report that much of the low ground was rabbit-free. Furthermore, he assured Fraser, those that remained were largely confined to the south side. It was a vast area, but for the time being anyway, he thought he was winning. But the victory was temporary.

*   *   *

As part of the draconian cost-cutting exercise conducted by Sir Henry Bell's son after his father's death, Macleod had been laid off, along with most of the rest of Scalpay estate's employees. But even if Macleod had been retained, his presence would have made little difference. On Skye as in the rest of the United Kingdom, rabbit numbers continued to grow exponentially. The lasting recollection of Pabay of Robert Muntz, in the 1940s the very young son of Captain Muntz, the island's owner at the time, was of 'a lot of rabbits'. Nothing seemed to check their fecundity. By the early 1950s it was believed that Britain's rabbit population was at least 100 million, although some estimates were double that number.

By the mid-1950s, however, the country's rabbits confronted their Armageddon. The killer virus: myxomatosis. A horrific disease, affected rabbits suffered from tumours, swollen eyelids and blindness, seizures, shortage of breath as their nasal passages became inflamed and paralysis, before submitting to what to anyone witnessing it – as we did on Pabay – was a uniquely nasty way to die. The difficulty of trying to spare further agony for a myxomatosis-infected rabbit enduring violent spasms as it writhed and struggled for air, by breaking its neck, is something Stuart still recalls vividly, and with a shudder.

Originating in South America in the 1890s, myxomatosis was deliberately introduced in Australia in 1951 and, in 1952, to France.[31] By the end of 1953 it had been brought across the English Channel, to Kent. By the summer of 1954 myxomatosis had found its way to Kincardineshire, in north-east Scotland. William Milne, a tenant farmer, and his wife, were blamed – and condemned – as 'Mr and Mrs Butcher Milne'.

Other farmers followed in their footsteps, by buying infected carcasses as a means of eliminating rabbits on their land. Driven to distraction by the endless war he had had to wage against them, Len followed suit. By late August what was commonly called 'mixy' was on Skye. But not, as yet, on Pabay. This was despite my parents' efforts to help. On a camping holiday in the south-west of Scotland they came across the carcass of a dead rabbit, packed it up and sent the lethal package to Len. Stuart recalls the excitement when a metal biscuit tin from my mother arrived on Pabay, and his disappointment – and even disgust – when it was opened, revealing its rotting and nauseating contents. Whether this was what had led to the sighting of what appeared to be an ailing animal on Pabay in mid-September is impossible to say (and unlikely), but anyway, it was not enough.

Earlier attempts had certainly failed. In August Henry Hilditch had embarked on a 200-mile search for diseased animals. He found some and brought them to Skye, after which Len took them immediately across to Pabay.[32] However, a month later Henry wrote that 'we [still] were desperate [to] . . . get mixy going on Pabbay'. To this end, Margaret and Dorothy Harrop, who was then staying on Pabay, came across to join Henry in yet another hunt for infected rabbits. If these were let loose it would not be too late in the year for myxomatosis to 'run through Pabay', and thereby transform the stock-feeding situation.[33]

Spreading the disease in this way, however, was to fly in the face of public opinion. On Skye the editor of the *Clarion* was incensed, warning that if the disease had 'been introduced by any farmer, crofter or any other mortal', he would have 'a lot to answer for'.

Hurt caused to the 'humble and timid bunny' he interpreted as the callous act of men driven by a desire for 'filthy lucre', and who assumed that 'the earth entirely belonged to them'. The effect of the calculated spread of myxomatosis would be to deprive hard-pressed families of their weekend dinner.[34]

With the support of Prime Minister Winston Churchill, a clause was included in the 1954 Pests Act that imposed a fine on anyone knowingly spreading the disease. The Act provided grant support for other ways of exterminating rabbits. By the autumn of 1956, more than 16 million acres – including much of the Highlands – had been designated as legal killing fields.[35]

But it was myxomatosis, not well-meaning acts of Parliament that transformed the situation. The rabbit population of the UK was decimated. According to some estimates, 95 per cent of them disappeared.

In the space of less than a year Pabay too was well on the way to being rabbit-free. But not completely. To supplement the killer virus, cyanide gas was employed. Evidently to good effect. Shortly after the last of these interventions, Len's father declared with delight that the rabbits were now 'extinct'. His optimism was premature. By the end of the decade a 'new generation' of rabbits had replaced their forerunners, although their habits seemed different in that they seemed to prefer life above ground and dug fewer burrows.[36]

The war was necessarily resumed. By sheer good fortune, Charlie Campbell, formerly chef at the Lochalsh Hotel, had turned his hand to rabbit trapping. So pleased was Len with his interest in Pabay's rabbits that rather than take payment, he suggested that Campbell sell any that he killed, and reimburse Margaret for his accommodation costs. It was an arrangement that suited both parties well. Within four months some 1,000 rabbits had been disposed of, by a combination of snaring, ferreting and, less often as it reduced their market value, shooting. To complete the task before he returned to the kitchen for the summer season, Campbell systematically applied gas to any burrows he could find. Len too had joined in the rabbit cull occasionally, delighted that a day or two's work could earn him over £6 (for around thirty-six rabbits).

The greater satisfaction was to be had in stemming the rabbit population. In October 1962, he was sure the island 'was greener and grassier' than he had ever seen it. In East Park, the clover was thick on the ground. Warm weather and showers during September had played their part. But so too had the 'low rabbit population'.[37]

It may be coincidental, or perhaps just vanity, but it was at the start of the 1960s that Stuart and I – then just about in our early teens – had been charged with the responsibility of snaring rabbits, and even trusted with an air gun to shoot what we could. In the longer run of course we were tilting at windmills, but for a short time we may have helped to slow the sails.

Chapter 12

The 'sea in-between': boats, beacons and boat-wrecks

On a flat, calm day, the 'sea in-between' Pabay and Broadford and Breakish gleams and glistens like polished glass. This is especially so after days-long gales when, after pounding seashores, cliffs, seawalls, houses, outbuildings and boats, storm winds abate. It is as if the sea has become a spent force, exhausted by its ceaseless thrashing.

We saw in Chapter 7 that, from the outset, Len was left in no doubt about the havoc that the high winds of the Western Isles could leave in their wake. Nor did the frequency or ferocity of these reduce over time. The 1950s were punctuated by a series of vicious winter storms.[1] On Pabay the worst were those that drove in from the south-west, and from the east. With most of the island's structures tucked in at the southern side, much less fearful were gales blowing from the north.

Even so, from whatever direction they came, their impact was difficult, if not impossible, to predict.

In the middle of December 1951, towards the end of the family's second year on Pabay, a storm that swept Scotland hit hardest on Skye, with 90 mph gales putting out of commission ten of the island's telephone exchanges.[2] Within weeks, nature announced the start of the new year of 1952 with another bout of tempestuous weather. Gales of more than 100 mph were recorded. But this time Pabay was in the centre of the tempest's path.

The *Sea Otter* was torn from its mooring, swept along the rocks to the east of the jetty and dashed onto the shore. Its hull staved in, the 'bargain' that Len had painstakingly brought back to life was no longer usable. Nor was the *Shearwater*. Their ruptured hulls lay at the highest point of where the gale-roused tide had driven them, distressing reminders of the sea's fury. The Whatleys' fragile lifeline was broken. So much so that Len had to signal to Broadford by flashing a torchlight that the family was marooned and would have to be rescued.[3]

The frustration for Len was that he had been aware of the destruction the gale was capable of wreaking down at the jetty: he had tried to get down the quarter-mile track to attend to his boats, crawling on his hands and knees as otherwise the gusts would have carried him away. But to no avail. And not for the last time.

All was not lost though, at least not quite. Some time afterwards Len managed to remove the *Sea Otter*'s engine. By applying his remarkable adaptive ingenuity, he and Stan converted and linked it to a generator he had brought to Pabay earlier. It was by so doing that he was able to get illumination into the Nissen huts and barn where the hens were.

Weatherwise, 1952 ended as it had begun. In mid-December, a fierce gale followed a blizzard of such severity that snow drifts reached heights of 15 feet on Skye. A massive hole appeared in Broadford's jetty, from which half-ton rocks were sucked out by the sea. Along the road at Kyle the new car ferry was ripped from its mooring and grounded.

The gale came mainly from the north, and at first it seemed as if Pabay had escaped. It had, but not for long. After a lull, the wind rose again, but from a different direction. It took with it two of the four Nissen huts, one on the higher ground at East Park which, when caught by the sun, had been visible for many miles around. The other was near to the jetty. Only five days earlier, the erectors had finished and departed.[4]

The devastation wreaked by the 1952 gales had taught Len some harsh lessons. But even paying closer attention to how boats were secured was no guarantee of a better outcome. The successor to the *Sea Otter*, the 20-foot *Fern*, was badly damaged in a storm at the end of January 1953. This had nothing to do with any failing on Len's part. So ferociously and ceaselessly had the sea punched at the rubble-built jetty that two stone blocks and the rings to which the boat had been tied had been wrenched away. Still, a bent propeller shaft was a minor problem in comparison to the fifteen fishing boats that had at the same time been lost at Ullapool.[5]

Not dissimilar was another gale-induced calamity in March 1954. With the wind coming from the east, the waves had rolled 'huge' seaweed-covered boulders near the jetty and broken one of the wooden legs designed to support the *Fern* when the tide went out. The jagged end of the snapped support had penetrated the hull. Sea water flooded the engine. Once more the family was marooned. In bitterly cold conditions Len had no choice but to devote two days to repairing the breached hull and stripping down the engine.[6] Boat repairs were something he was getting used to. But they were time-consuming, and costly.

These were times when the realities of island living became stark.

But the family soon learned the importance of being prepared for the worst. Within a year or so of settling on Pabay, Margaret, with Anthea, had left the island for a day on Skye. A storm promptly blew up, and continued for the best part of a fortnight. Len, with his three-year-old son Stuart, was left to fend for the two of them, but with a rapidly dwindling stock of food.[7] As a vegetarian, for Len the protein that was available from island sources – rabbits, shellfish and fish – were no use. Henceforth, bulk buying became the norm, with orders for large quantities of non-perishable goods sent to and delivered by Rose's of Nairn, packed into tea boxes. One cupboard in the kitchen was solidly stacked with tinned food – although Margaret rarely used what was there. Len was not a particularly fussy eater, but he had certain expectations about what was served up – 'Is this pure?' he would ask her – and preferred fresh food. But she did on occasion, out of sight, take a short cut, and could transform what otherwise might for instance be a plain rice dish with the judicious addition of a tin of tomatoes or similar.

The only time I was stranded, to all intents and purposes alone, on Pabay was much later, but the circumstances were similar. Neil, Donald and the family had departed for Broadford ('we'll back in a couple of hours' I was assured), but were unable to get back as the wind had got up. With me on Pabay was Tony, Len and Margaret's sixth child, then barely three years old. Looking after a youngster was a new experience; I was in my mid-teens.

But the much more difficult challenge was to moor Len's recently restored, highly varnished launch (the *Pelagius*, of which he was particularly fond) – something I'd seen being done, but never done myself. She had been left tied alongside the jetty. To avoid her hull being damaged as the rising sea crunched and scraped it against the cemented edge of the stone jetty wall, I had to secure the boat to its mooring, marked by a buoy that connected with the heavy ground chain on the sea bed, some 15 yards off. I managed to get the launch tied to the mooring, but struggled to pull her close enough to the jetty for me to jump from the prow of the boat onto the jetty before the now taut rope jerked the boat back out to its station. After a number of false starts I plucked up the courage to make the leap, just as the launch sprang back from under my feet.

There followed a sleepless night, caused by the howling wind, a power cut, and my new-found child-minding role. I need not have worried about Tony. Like all of the Pabay children, even at such a young age he was remarkably knowledgeable about what had to be done. The next day he instructed me as I completed a full round of feeding for the hens and other animals, before Len and the others returned – impressed by my newly acquired skills in boat management and livestock care.

Not entirely new, however. Len had been keen that at an early age Anthea, Stuart and I should be capable of handling a small boat. On occasion during summer evenings he would take all of us off for a collective rowing lesson – how to work in unison, steer, turn and avoid underwater obstacles. And solo. Anthea recalls the flat-calm day when her father sent her off on her own to row to Broadford – the initial trepidation, her fear as she got halfway across, and the sense of triumph of getting there after two hours at sea. Dorothy Harrop too has memories of Len taking her out fishing, even in rough seas – but demonstrating for her his recently acquired boat-handling abilities.[8] This, Len's capacity to instil a sense of self-belief, can-do confidence based on sound guidance is, for those us who benefited, deeply embedded, part of his lasting legacy.

*　*　*

Pabay is no stranger to shipwrecks. Despite its benevolent appearance from afar, on most sides of the island the flat shale beds are intersected by the sharp-edged reefs alluded to in the Introduction. Like swamp alligators, they are barely covered and, with equally hard to spot skerries, lie ready to grind and puncture the hulls of the vessels of unsuspecting seafarers.

So extensive are the rocky outcrops that, when the tide is out, the island is not far short of double the size it is at high water.

On Pabay's northern edge, even the shallow draught of a rowing dinghy can be too much to guarantee a safe passage close to the shore. This I learned to my cost one summer's evening in the early 1960s when I took a party of increasingly anxious passengers for a trip round the island. We had to travel uncomfortably far out to sea before heading south-west, and the safety of the shoreline.

It was on just this outcrop that in late November 1821 the 77-ton sloop *William & Ann* had run aground whilst on a voyage from Inverness to Liverpool, carrying a cargo of wheat. While the master, Captain Reid, and his crew had been rescued, the 'Island of Papay' was the *William & Ann*'s final resting place.[9] Declared a wreck, it was a sorry end for a vessel with a more interesting career than most small merchant vessels operating around Scotland. Earlier, in 1812, shortly after the outbreak of war between the United States and Britain, under the captaincy of William Eadie, she had been seized by an American naval ship while taking a cargo of coal and glass from the Clyde across the Irish Sea. She was recaptured by the British navy's HMS *Nimrod* on 31 July the following year before returning to her normal role. Reid was by no means the only skipper to have fallen foul of the flattened fingers with their knuckles of rock that stretch out from the north side of Pabay. It is mainly yachtsmen, though, who have been the victims in modern times, fortunately without loss of life.

Pabay's underwater perils were clearly marked on the first reliable marine charts of the Inner Sound: as dark protruding fingers on Murdoch Mackenzie's map of 1775, and as a series of forbidding crosses on that prepared by Joseph Huddart (1741–1816), the distinguished British hydrographer who surveyed Scotland's Hebridean waters and coasts between 1787 and 1791.[10]

As we have just seen however, this kind of information was not enough to warn off the unwary.

By the middle of the nineteenth century the Northern Lighthouse Board (created under the terms of the 1854 Merchant Shipping Act) felt compelled to act. The Board had been adding navigation aids at appropriate locations along Scotland's west coast, including a light-house at nearby Kyleakin. In June 1858, the Board published as widely as it could a 'Notice to Mariners'; this announced that a malleable iron-framed beacon had been erected at the seaward end of the 'reef called Goblach Reef' – now marked on OS maps as Sgeir Gobhlach. This long, unforgiving line of tooth-edged rock stretches out from Pabay's southern shore. (The Gaelic term *sgeir* provides us with another linguistic link with Old Norse – with 'sker' meaning a rock in the sea.[11]) Vessels, the Board ordered, should 'on no account pass between the beacon and the island of Pabba'.[12] The beacon – which became known to seafarers as the Pabay Perch – served too as a guide for anyone approaching the island from Broadford. It does still. To the east of the perch is a single safe channel (although not entirely clear of rocks that sit, barely visible, just beneath the surface at low tide) to the short stone-built jetty that had been constructed during Sir Donald Currie's proprietorship. On this too was secured a barrel-shaped beacon not dissimilar from that on Sgeir Gobhlach, although smaller, which complemented the one Currie affixed to his new landing on Scalpay.

Just how important the Pabay Perch was to mariners was made apparent on 14 August 1888. This was just about the most momen-tous shipping incident to have happened in Pabay's vicinity. Taking care to clear the perch and rocks at Sgeir Gobhlach was John Aitcheson, the mate of David MacBrayne's *Clansman*, a schooner-rigged steam passenger vessel carrying around a hundred tourists and sportsmen from Glasgow to Skye. He was steering a west to southerly course through Caolas Pabba, the narrow channel between the Pabay Perch and Ardnish – the Pabbay Sound.

However, in his account of the accident afterwards, Aitcheson admitted that he had lost sight of the Perch as the crew, preparing to offload some cargo at Broadford, had obscured his view. Travelling at full speed, in the dark – there was no moon, only stars

– just before midnight the vessel ran aground on Sgeir an Roin, a reef off Ardnish peninsula, north of Lower Breakish, that was visible only at half-tide.[13] Panic ensued. The slumbering passengers were abruptly woken by the impact. 'Terrified ladies and gentlemen', according to one report, rushed up on deck, with some of the women 'hysterically shrieking'. The lifeboats were launched, taking women and children to the nearby shore after which they stumbled 'about two miles over bogs and rocks' to Broadford, where they and their fellow passengers passed the night 'as best they could on chairs in the overcrowded hotel and private houses'.

Stuck fast, and lying on her side, neither the *Hansa* nor the *Glencoe* – whose masters were familiar with this stretch of coastline – were able to pull the *Clansman* off the rocks. It looked as if the stricken ship would stay where she was until the next spring tides.

But even the most experienced seamen could find themselves in difficulty as they steered a course through the Sound. Such was the fate of Captain John Mackechnie, master of MacBrayne's largest vessel, the SS *Lochbroom*, when a gale sprang up on a Saturday afternoon late in October 1933 as he was making the short passage from Glenelg to Broadford. With little time or room to take evasive action, the vessel 'struck a rock at the entrance of Broadford Bay', and was so severely damaged that Mackechnie had to run her aground on the beach near the pier.[14] Prudently, on the Queen's visit to Skye on the royal yacht *Britannia* in August 1956, she was moored off Kyle, while the royal party went by car through Broadford to Portree and Dunvegan Castle.[15]

Gales were at the extreme end of the weather spectrum. The fact is that even in moderately poor conditions Pabay could be hard to get to, and leave. Notoriously so. Winds of any severity from the east or north-east made it almost impossible to cross Broadford Bay in a small boat. Getting through the reefs that surrounded much of the island in anything larger was fraught with danger.

It was an issue that had tormented owners, factors and managers of Pabay for decades. In the early 1880s for instance, with Alexander Macdonald intent on tackling once again the age-old problem of Pabay's inadequate drainage, he struggled to engage a ditcher at the price he wanted. Alex MacInnes from Isle Ornsay was blunt in his explanation why he would charge more than Macdonald anticipated: 'I must remind you,' he wrote, 'that Pabbay is such an inconvenient place to go to.' He was unable to persuade anyone to go with him 'for ordinary payment'.[16]

We've seen already that taking seaware from Pabay to Breakish was no easy undertaking. Giving testimony to the Napier Commission in Broadford on 16 May 1883, the fisherman Finlay M'Innes had described how a week earlier he had nearly drowned while trying to do so, whilst on other occasions sea conditions had made it impossible. We should bear in mind that until the appearance of the ubiquitous two-stroke, single cylinder Seagull petrol motor in 1931, all small boats were powered either by oars or sail, this last allowing for much less easy manoeuvrability than an engine. It was the very fact of the island's inaccessibility that had made it such an ideal refuge in the sixteenth and seventeenth centuries for prowling sea raiders.

What suited the early modern maritime marauder, however, was a distinct disadvantage for even the hardiest and most adaptable residents and others on more legitimate business who succeeded them.

*   *   *

The consequences of the recurrent damage to and even loss of his boats were not confined to the loss of Len's time and the cost of repairs and, periodically, replacements. There was also the urgent matter of what to do in the interim. Being boatless even for a few days could create major difficulties. Hiring the Scalpay boat was often the easiest solution, but this incurred additional cost. There was the inconvenience too of waiting until it was available. Naturally enough, Scalpay's needs took priority.

But Len was also increasingly conscious that while the relatively small craft he had had hitherto were perfectly capable of shipping eggs, hens, groceries, children and visitors, they were unsuitable for transporting cattle or sheep. Or indeed for carrying anthracite, bulk fertilisers and heavy equipment.

In the short term, as he established himself on Pabay, he had made do by hiring a small K6 ferry with a turntable for heavy and bulky loads including lime, building and fencing materials and machinery such as a potato spinner and threshing drum. This was owned and operated by William Forsyth in Kyle.

However, this arrangement led to frustration when Forsyth's vessel was otherwise engaged, delayed, grounded at low tide, or unable to get alongside the jetty on Pabay for the same reason. We've seen already that at the lowest tides, there was no water. And furthermore that when the wind was blowing hard from the south or south-east, Pabay's jetty was exposed, providing no shelter for boats unloading or moored there.

Forsyth's craft itself was 'OK' according to Henry Hilditch, but the master was 'just useless'.[17] He was probably right: intending to caulk the hull, in April 1953 Simon the skipper had beached the ferry at the top of the spring tide. Not a bright idea. There the ferry remained, until the next high tides in August, much to the annoyance of Forsyth as well as Len and Henry, who then had to find another boat on Skye with a shallow enough draught to unload at Pabay. And urgently awaiting transportation from Kyle and Broadford were hundreds of fencing posts, several tons of fertilisers and unbagged anthracite and five gallon drums of TVO (tractor fuel). In the wings too, to be brought from Dingwall, was a shorthorn bull.[18]

A more permanent solution was required.

Accordingly, Len's attention turned to an idea he had toyed with earlier. This was to acquire a landing craft, something he had some experience of, having hired one in 1950. Landing craft had been developed in the run-up to the Second World War and were used for beach invasions at several locations, including D-Day (6 June 1944) at Normandy in northern France. The attractions of an LCA (landing craft assault) for Len included its large carrying capacity (up to 50 tons) and shallow draught – five or six inches of water was all they needed. With up to 1,500 LCAs having been constructed, at the end of the war most were surplus to the navy's requirements. One way of disposing of them was to sell them to civilians.

It wasn't long before Len's ruminations became hard fact. In the spring of 1953 he decided that he 'MUST' get the ditches cleared.

That meant getting ditching machinery – that weighed some ten tons in all – over to Pabay.[19]

LCAs, however, were not cheap. The price quoted for one lying at Inverkip on the Clyde was £750. However, following advice from John Campbell, the Irvine puffer owner, who had first-hand knowledge of the current market for commercial craft on Scotland's west coast, and about the LCA in question, Len and Henry offered significantly less. A bargain was struck. The *Jacqueline J* was theirs. Ever wily, Henry Hilditch calculated that part of the cash outlay could be recovered by selling the two 100 HP Perkins diesel engines presently fitted and replacing them with smaller powertrains which Len was sure would provide all the propulsion he needed.[20]

Initially all went well. In October Henry was able to report that Len had bought three heifers from a Breakish crofter. Not only were the two men delighted with the prospect of making a healthy grant-aided profit on the deal, but also with 'the ease with which the cattle went over' – 'just walked onto the LC ... and off the other side'.[21] Even more encouraging, and potentially lucrative, were unsolicited enquiries about the possibility of hiring it out. As MacBrayne's wouldn't take on cargo at places like Mallaig and Kyle (insisting that this should be loaded at Glasgow), there was an opening for a local tramp ship service.

In pursuit of this idea, early in November Len and Henry had committed to taking a full load, including compressors and a heavy steel caravan, from Dornie on the mainland, to Kyle and, via Broadford and Uig, across to Lochmaddy in North Uist. A couple of local men, apparently appropriately qualified, were hired as crew.

Looked at in hindsight it becomes clear that what seemed at the time to be a series of minor hitches was actually indicative of something more seriously wanting in the LCA. Leaking exhaust pipes, rusted bolts, suspect electrical equipment and batteries, the engines playing up and problems with the pumps – all required attention in the days prior to the Uist trip. Somewhat optimistically, Henry Hilditch pronounced that 'These are just the teething troubles of any new Venture!'[22]

Not on this occasion. November came to a close and still the LCA was in Skye. Gales, crew illness and desertions, along with acts of (alleged) sheer incompetence, and further electrical and mechanical problems had further delayed its departure. They had also set Henry off into a raging fit. And no wonder. Expenses were mounting, and he was unable to invoice his customer for goods not yet shipped to their destination.[23] Adding to his frustration was a certain reluctance on the part of the skipper, Lachie Macdonald, to set sail, even though at this time the craft had got as far as Uig. 'Oh, it may be calm at Portree,' he was reported to have said, 'and calm at Uig, but that didn't say what the weather was like at Vaternish Point.'

Eventually, however, the LCA motored out, set – or so it seemed – for the Little Minch crossing. It was a late afternoon in December, as dusk was falling fast. But, fitted with navigation lights that Stan Robinson had fixed some weeks earlier, this seemingly presented no difficulty. The expected time of arrival in Lochmaddy was around nine that night.

Two hours after casting off from Uig, however, the news filtered through that the vessel had disappeared. Henry Hilditch's reaction was incredulity: this was the second 'unsinkable' boat he had known during his lifetime. The first was the *Titanic*.[24] After a couple of days' searching, the *Jacqueline J* was found, not in the middle of the Minch, but on the rocks below the soaring, sheer cliffs at Dunvegan Head in north-west Skye, not far over from Uig. What had occurred was clouded in mystery. Hilditch was now becoming convinced it was something similar to the *Marie Celeste* they were dealing with: wasn't that the ship, he asked rhetorically, that was 'found sailing without a crew and no good reason found why they left'.

All that was known at this stage was that the LCA's men had abandoned the vessel and rowed to dry land at Ardmore, on the Waternish peninsula just north of Stein and below Hallin. Rumours, though, began to circulate that all may not have been what it seemed or, to put it another way, Lachie Macdonald's tardiness about sailing became explicable. The skipper had been seen in Portree and Uig, selling some of the cargo – cement, diesel and tools were mentioned

– in return for drink money. The premature return home of Macdonald and another crewman, Archie Mackinnon from Heaste, in fine fettle and good spirits, further aroused suspicions. Surprise was expressed that Mackinnon had been taken on in the first place: his sea-going experience was limited.[25]

The charge that they had had no intention of crossing the Minch gathered momentum. It couldn't be proved, but what seemed possible was that they had opened some of the water inlets, heard water coming in, and, perhaps, felt the *Jacqueline J* listing, and abandoned her. But without realising that the six buoyancy tanks would keep her afloat. Which explains why she had drifted onto the rocks at Dunvegan Head rather than simply vanishing beneath the waves.

In the days following, several attempts were made to pull the LCA off. Heavy seas however, in a location that was hard to access, and the partial disintegration of the hull, caused a re-think. Lloyds, the insurers, decided that the priority was to salvage the cargo and remove the engines. The hull was to be written off.

Disappointing, yes, particularly if the allegations about the crew's nefariousness were true; had the *Jacqueline J* been scuttled?

But was it a disaster? Not for Henry Hilditch. He confessed to feeling 'a bit of a hypocrite' in accepting commiserations from locals who were aware of the loss of the LCA, and perhaps that he had been duped, whilst rubbing his hands following his calculation that with most of the cargo saved, the insurance money for the hull, and by selling the engines, 'we shall be able to pay off what we owe [on the LCA] ... and have a few pennies left over to go in search of another craft!'[26] His high hopes were dashed, however, when it became apparent that after a north-westerly gale just before Christmas, the engines had broken up while the propellers and oil tanks had been swept out to sea.[27]

For Len, the practical problems remained. Not much more than a year later the *Fern* was out of commission. Without the LCA, he was still dependent on being able to hire for specific loads Forsyth's ferry from Kyle. But this was becoming increasingly unreliable, and even dangerous. Rumour had it that it leaked 'like a sieve'. She did manage a few more trips, but by 1956 the end was in sight.

Two years later the K6 broke loose from its mooring, and within days was driven by a gale onto rocks at Broadford. She was not worth salvaging.[28]

In the meantime, something had to be done about the loss of the LCA's engines, the prospective sale of which had been key if the purchase of the *Jacqueline J* was to work financially. It was this dilemma that persuaded Len and Henry to bid for another vessel. This was MacBrayne's Bridlington-built *Coruisk*, a passenger ferry from the 1930s that was lying unused at Kyle. After a busy round of negotiations, the *Coruisk* was secured for the knock-down price of £250. Henry was convinced they had a bargain and could sell the vessel on, as she stood, for £1,500; alone, the thick hemp fender that skirted round her deck was worth almost what they had paid for the entire boat. Or so he'd been told.

In the event, the *Coruisk* was towed to Pabay, and moored offshore in what was thought to be a secure location. Over time, she was stripped of her assets – the recently refurbished engines of course, as well as the wood-encased, copper-bodied life rafts, the bronze propeller shafts, and the rudder; she was also a useful source of nuts, screws, bolts, pipes and reinforced glass and other small pieces of equipment. Even five years later, Len and Neil MacRae took the *Coruisk*'s propulsion shafts to Kyle and sold them for £30. A bonus on this particular trip was that they had a return cargo, a new bull, who, according to Len, 'rode the swell like a born sailor'.[29]

For family and friends the most memorable of *Coruisk*'s treasures were the pontoon-style life rafts that in the summer warmth could be sat or knelt upon and paddled in the shallower waters of the lagoon in front of the cottage.

But as a seaworthy boat the *Coruisk*'s end came late in December 1955. A combination of an exceptionally high tide, heavy seas and the snapping of a metal cleat to which the main hawser was attached caused her to be driven aground. Notwithstanding efforts to pull her off, she soon became a permanent maritime archaeological fixture lying on the shale beds not many yards from the bungalow.

Meanwhile, another solution to Len's boat dilemma came to light. This took the form of a DUKW, an amphibious six-wheeled vehicle that had been developed in the USA in 1942 and used by the US military during the Second World War, as well as in the subsequent Korean War. For Pabay's purposes a DUKW seemed ideal. Fast-moving and believed to be able to withstand rougher seas than any of Len's boats so far, a DUKW had a carrying capacity of five or six tons by road and just over half that by sea. With its combined sea and land capability, he would be able to 'run it with stuff right to the barn door'.

The chance discovery that a DUKW was available was quickly seized; doubly delightful was that the owner was prepared to bring her by sea to Skye.

Yet as with the landing craft, alarm bells should have begun to ring even as it arrived at Kyle. There were locals too who had their doubts. Neil Mackinnon, Heaste-born and with long experience of the seas around Skye, told me he had been 'horrified' when he heard about it. In his experience of military service in Malaysia, DUKWs were under-powered, hard to manoeuvre at sea, and prone to all sorts of mechanical faults that required constant maintenance.

The gearbox had seized as the engine had overheated – evidently not an unusual problem with this type of craft. The following day, with Henry and Harry Hilditch on board (Len was busy with the harvest), the DUKW was driven down the Kyle slip and into a gale-blown sea for the onward journey to Broadford. At which point the engine failed again. Happily, it was got going – a fuel pipe had been blocked – and the DUKW landed safely in Broadford. Here, 'minor' body repairs and repainting were to be carried out in Sutherland's garage.[30]

With Len anxious to take a delivery of animal feed over to Pabay, and Harry Hilditch impatient to see how the DUKW would sail, with his two sons (David and Duncan) alongside, Harry decided to make the crossing. For Broadford's children – as well as Anthea and Stuart – it was a day to remember. As many as thirty of them had watched goggle-eyed as the vehicle was driven out of the garage, onto the foreshore and into the sea from where, as if by magic, it floated off. Len came out from Pabay and joined Harry part of the way across. He then drove onto the shore, along the track and deposited the two dozen or so sacks of feed in the barn.

Although it was dark, Harry then returned the DUKW to Broadford. The men's spirits were high, so much so that they had talked of having the DUKW painted a 'gay colour', and fitted out with seats from the *Coruisk* so that in the summer visitors could be taken on trips around Pabay.[31]

Their elation was short-lived. The very next afternoon, 25 October, Harry had set off again, taking with him his father Henry and the remaining feed.

The voyage proved to be an equally exciting spectacle for those inhabitants of Waterloo, Breakish and Broadford who happened to be looking out to sea (some, it is said, expecting the worst), as it had been the day before for the village youngsters.

As the DUKW approached the Perch at Sgeir Gobhlach, she disappeared from view. She had hit nothing. Simply, the bilge pumps had seized and the hull had filled with water – which was also coming in through the drain cocks that had been left open. This was bad enough. The sea was rough and spray had been breaking over the front ramps, waterlogging some bales of hay that were on board. Now unstable, the DUKW tipped.

Fortunately, Margaret had seen the last stages of the sinking – and her father's plight; she was in the habit of watching, through a telescope, boats on their way to Pabay. By hanging onto one of the pontoon-style life rafts from the *Coruisk* which they'd had the foresight to put on board, the two men survived until Len came out to pick them up half an hour later – the longest of his life, reflected an exhausted Henry Hilditch afterwards. As he recuperated he was able to reflect too on an uncharacteristic omission on his part: the DUKW was uninsured.

The loss, however, would not be total if it could be salvaged. Despite lying at a depth of seven fathoms at most, even after several searches, neither Len nor Harry nor anyone else was able to locate it – until around 2015 that is, when Royal Navy divers on an exercise came across what was left of the sunken DUKW.

The boat problem endured; in fact, it worsened. All Len had now was a ten-foot dinghy and an outboard motor – with which he made what can only be described as heroic crossings. How else was a business based on the promise of supplying day-old chicks to continue? Even though the dinghy could more easily be pulled out of the water, it met the fate of its predecessors during yet another gale in February 1957 – said by some locals to have been the worst for a century.

Another hull – this time of a motor launch – was found, however, and fitted with the engine salvaged from the *Fern*. But there was little room for complacency. After a late December storm the new boat had filled with water and needed Len to take out and disman-tle the engine – again. Throughout, his stumbling block was lack of cash, so that, as Stuart observed, his father was forced to buy boats that 'were always old, somewhat infirm ... suitable if they were looked after', which wasn't always the case.

Len's hoped-for solution was to lay some light rails at the jetty so that any large-ish boat could be pulled up 'high & dry beyond the tide'. Long enough on his list of 'must do' tasks, there never seemed to be enough time to devote to boat security. It was many years later that the problem was satisfactorily dealt with.

Meantime, Len had little option but to call on the assistance of his island neighbours. The Scalpay boat had the advantage of being close to hand and was capable of carrying livestock.

There were risks in transporting large animals in small boats, as Anthea and Stuart were to discover several years later. This was when both their parents were in hospital (Len was seriously ill and Margaret was heavily pregnant); with no one left who was able to milk the cow, she had to be taken off the island. Helped by Neil MacRae, it was only after a struggle and by sharply twisting her tail that they managed to get the animal aboard.

Eventually they got going, although the sea was now heaving, with wave tops breaking white. However, greatly to Anthea's alarm, Neil on this occasion appeared to be fortifying himself with 'a rapidly diminishing bottle of whisky'. Not the best condition to be in for what followed. Waves were crashing over the boat when the engine cut out. Now wallowing aimlessly and out of control, Anthea was terrified. But so was the cow. The 'next thing we knew she had put a hoof through the boat'. Anthea feared the worst, but Stuart – by now becoming an accomplished boat handler – managed to get the engine running. Mightily relieved, they limped into the pier at Broadford.

For the bulkier loads, however, Len was able to persuade another island dweller to help out. This was Ted Comber, originally from Breakish, who in 1942 with his wife Lilian had moved to a croft on the small island of Soay, which lies near Loch Scavaig to the south of Skye. Better known as Lilian Beckwith, Lilian was the author of several books that drew on her island experiences. Her depictions of fictional characters seemed to locals to be drawn too closely from real life and, under pressure from a hurt and resentful community, the Combers left Soay in 1962 and moved to the Isle of Man.

It was prior to the publication of the first of Lilian's novels, *The Hills is Lonely*, that Len had become acquainted with Comber, as well as his landlord, Joseph or 'Tex' Geddes, who had bought Soay from Gavin Maxwell in 1952. Maxwell, later the author of *Ring of Bright Water* (1960), had earlier tried, and failed, to establish a shark-oil-extraction venture on the island. Nevertheless, as incomers, and multi-talented can-do adventurers seeking to make a living in island environments that others had turned their backs on (most of Soay's crofter inhabitants had left for Mull in 1953), Len, Geddes and Comber had much in common – although the last two shared little in the way of mutual friendship.

Ted Comber was also an experienced seaman, and the owner of a boat that could carry a decent cargo. What was more, he was prepared to help Len out – on a job-by-job basis. His appearance in Broadford early in March 1958 was timely. Some 40 tons of lime and fertilisers were urgently needed on Pabay, with spring preparations under way. With the weather holding, he was also, over a period of days, able to take across the heavy building materials, including concrete slabs, for the extension and bungalow. (On one trip, he was accompanied by two stowaways – Anthea and Stuart – who had hidden in the cabin in a bid to snatch an unplanned visit to their home, and parents.[32]) Comber's willingness to oblige proved invaluable, no more so than after the Nissen hut fire. With the harvest season imminent, Len urgently needed a replacement tractor. Despite being busy with boatloads of tourists at Glen Brittle, Comber took time out to motor to Kyle, where a crane loaded the tractor onto his boat, before he then motored to Pabay with Len to deliver it to its final destination.[33]

Hugh Miller, the stonemason, geologist, writer and Christian evangelical, in 1843. One of the earliest photographs ever taken, this shows Miller – in his prime and bursting with inquisitive energy – the year prior to his visit to Pabay. In 1844 he revealed to the world the extent of the island's rich fossil beds. (Hugh Miller, David Octavius Hill and Robert Adamson, National Galleries of Scotland, Elliot Collection, bequeathed 1950)

Archibald Geikie as a young man. Geikie was in his late teens when he went on his first geological excursion to Pabay in 1853. Later knighted, Geikie, who was dubbed the 'lad of the stones' whilst on Skye, played a major part in bringing the attention of geologists to Pabay. (Courtesy of the British Geological Survey)

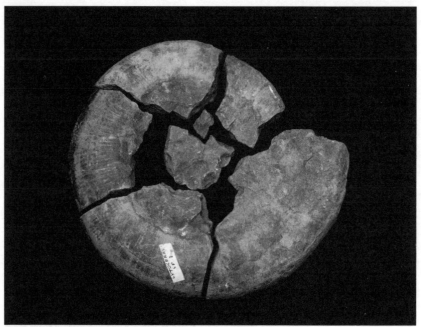

Above. Outer whorl of an ammonite – Lytocerus – in seven pieces. 30cm diameter. This fossil was found in Pabay's 100-foot-deep, outcropping Jurassic shales, which in the 19th century were much investigated by geologists after their abundance was revealed by John MacCulloch and Hugh Miller. Pabay continues to attract geology students and their teachers from universities across the UK. (Museums Collections Unit, University of St Andrews)

Right. Contemporary engraving of a Pabay ammonite discovered by Sir Roderick Murchison, 1828. (James Sowerby, *The Mineral Conchology of Great Britain* (London, 1812–46), Vol. VI (1829), 556)

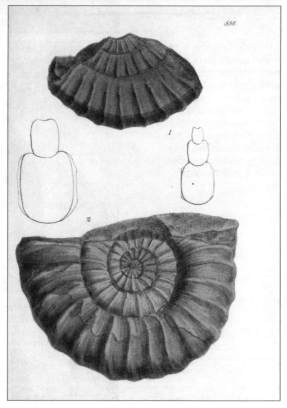

The *Sea Otter*, which Len restored in 1950 after he had bought what had been a waterlogged hull and engine from Colonel Swire in Orbost, near Dunvegan. (Whatley Collection)

The *Sea Otter*, wrenched from her mooring and destroyed in the gales of January 1952. Behind lies the *Shearwater*, also badly damaged. These were the first of several boats that Len lost during the family's time on Pabay. The jetty was exposed to easterly and south-easterly winds. The mainly heavy, clinker-built boats Len bought were almost impossible to take out of the water, for protection, if bad weather threatened. (© Stan Robinson Collection)

Above. The *Jacqueline J* at Broadford jetty. This was the landing craft Len bought in 1953, but which was mysteriously abandoned by her crew whilst taking plant and equipment to Lochmaddy in December that year. She subsequently broke up under Dunvegan Head. (© Stuart Whatley Collection)

Left. The DUKW, 1955, bought by Len partly so that bulk cargoes of items such as fertilisers could be taken direct from Kyle or Broadford to the barn or Nissen huts on Pabay. Unfortunately she sank on her second voyage to the island. (Whatley Collection)

Restoring the last large boat – 27 feet long and clinker built – Len bought for Pabay. He enjoyed the aesthetic pleasure of the restoration work and the companionship of David Illingworth, on the left, a skilled boat builder, and Ned Rimmer, on the right. (© Christopher A. Whatley)

Arrangements of this kind, however, were necessarily temporary, and barely served Pabay's needs. Len continued his search for a fit-for-purpose boat of their own – at a price he could afford. After seeing an advertisement in the *Oban Times* he and Henry made tracks for Lochailort where they found what Len was looking for. It was a converted lifeboat – the *Dolina*, covered in the bow area and over the Kelvin engine, capable of carrying five tons, including cattle. The price was reasonable too – £170.

In the coming months and years, the new boat performed even better than anticipated. The weather was now much less of a concern, as she could handle seas that would have been impossible in a dinghy. (Even so, of wooden, clinker-built construction, heavy and under-powered, she was not easy to steer when the wind was driving from the south-west, and alarmed even sea-hardy passengers.) Livestock could be moved – in small numbers – in accordance with market demand, rather than when third-party transport could be arranged. And directly, by sea to Kyle and then onwards by lorry to the sales at Dingwall and Inverness. The problem of the lack of a secure berth on Pabay was overcome by stationing the new boat in Broadford, with Neil MacRae now hired to make the runs to Pabay as required. This he did, along with building work at Dunollie, as well as being caretaker at the village hall (where he also acted as MC when dances were on).[34]

As a result, Len could focus fully on farming, building work and his new creative pursuits. Having said that, he had come to love the sea and had mastered the tides, swells, wind and dramatic changes in local weather conditions that in 1950 he had had to read up on in books. An image locked into my mind for over fifty years now is of a crossing to Broadford made early one clear blue morning on a gently undulating marble-smooth sea. Len was standing erect in the stern of the *Pelagius*, hand gently on the tiller, his foot tapping as he whistled the tune of the 'Bluebell Polka' – well known after Jimmy Shand's recording of it in 1955. A man content, at one with his world.

He was certainly cheered a short time later, when the boat situation was even further improved. The current small car ferry at

Kylerhea was being replaced by a bigger vessel. The Scalpay owners proposed that they and Len purchase the old ferry boat. Len had a look at what he said was the best bargain he had ever seen. Going for £120, with a diesel engine and capable of carrying up to ten tons, she was ideal for shipping sheep, cattle, feed and fertiliser. A deal was struck for joint ownership, with Pabay being paid for Neil's time, and for fuel, whenever it was used on Scalpay business.[35]

Even better for everyday purposes was the purchase of yet another boat in May 1965. Twenty-seven feet long, clinker-built and with a lockable cabin and wheelhouse, she was much more secure than the *Dolina* when lying overnight at Broadford.

It was just as well. *Dolina*'s timbers were rotting. Her end – not entirely ignominious for a boat that had been the best yet – was to be cut in half, turned upside down and become a henhouse.[36] The same fate eventually befell the *Coruisk*.

Ironically, just at the time when Len was on the verge of leaving Pabay, he had a surfeit of seaworthy craft. Six, in fact. They ranged from the recently acquired launches to a Klepper Aerius sailing canoe with outriggers, and the small rowing dinghy that Anthea, Stuart and I had more than once overhauled and painted. No longer was Len dependent on a single vessel as a lifeline, or Seagull outboard motors with their rope-pull starter motors which all too often coughed, spluttered but failed to ignite. (By the time the island was sold, however, the Klepper had gone. Ned Rimmer, a worker on Pabay, had left her at low water one evening, from where the light craft had been lifted to disappear forever in yet another gale. The small dinghy suffered a similar fate.)

With the assistance of David Illingworth, an experienced boat builder (amongst his other abilities) who had recently appeared on Pabay, in 1965 Len revelled in the aesthetic pleasure of fitting out the newest boat, its engine 'a joy', that ran 'with a very satisfying Scandinavian tonk-tonk'.[37] Pleasing too was that her Saab diesel engine was many times more fuel-efficient than her petrol- and paraffin-gulping predecessors.

It was almost as if Pabay had its own mini Armada. All so different from fifteen years earlier, when Len had had to make do with one waterlogged hull and a small dinghy. It had been the steepest of learning curves. To get to this point he had bought fourteen boats, which gave him a success rate of much under 50 per cent.

One of those he had in 1965 however was a relatively recently acquired 14-foot teak dinghy, complete with outboard motor. Entirely serendipitously, this was the boat in which Len and Margaret had been taken for their first exploratory trip to Pabay, in the autumn of 1949.

Chapter 13

For sale: 'Len Whatley's Kingdom'

With the opening of a new decade in 1960, the priorities on Pabay began to shift. Farming, of course, was still central. Poultry continued to be key. But not eggs. Egg prices were half what they had been in the early days. Crofters had seized the opportunity there was to sell eggs to tourists, periodically flooding the market. Squeezed margins on egg sales were unavoidable, so much so, in Henry Hilditch's opinion, that if Pabay just produced eggs, 'it would be out of business'.[1] To be fair, he had foreseen the likelihood of a glut of eggs some years before, based on his observation that after the First World War 'thousands' of ex-servicemen had spent their gratuities on poultry farms. Before long, supply had outstripped demand, forcing the closure of many of the fledgling farms.[2]

Len therefore directed his energies towards day-old chicks, chickens and table birds, and to improving the productivity of the poultry operation. By importing four-week-old chicks from Cantray Home Farm near Inverness, the leading Scottish breeding station, he anticipated reducing stock mortality to less than 0.5 per cent.

Cattle and sheep numbers remained steady, with none of the attrition that had marred the later 1950s. By contrast, in 1963 a record number of calves were born. Sales of beef calves at six to twelve months had by now become a relatively stable element on the island's balance sheet.

On the arable side, the annual cycle of liming, some ploughing, rotavating, harrowing, sowing, fertilising and harvesting was now well established – although predictions of what would need to be done – or could be completed, on a day-to-day basis rarely panned out. Donald Fletcher was proving to be an invaluable asset for the farm. Neil MacRae was the other stalwart, not only on the boat, but also helping out when Len had additional jobs to do – like putting up the housing for the diesel generator and dipping and dosing the sheep.[3]

And as had so often happened in the past, volunteers – seeking only board and accommodation – turned up and did stints of a few weeks or more. Particularly fortuitous was the appearance of Christian Aikman, from Hull. A poultry expert, she had picked Pabay from the list of accredited poultry stations and written to Len asking if she could come and gain some experience before she took up a post as a government poultry inspector. She arrived in October 1959 and stayed for at least six months, during which time she ran the entire operation, even plucking and packing the chickens in polythene bags ready for dispatch to Broadford.[4] Henry was on cloud nine.

Initially, at least, Len's back held up. But he was often in pain, and had difficulty sleeping.[5] To provide some relief Stuart recalls occasions when he and Anthea were asked to pull on their father's legs, to stretch his spine; this was to supplement a fortnight's traction administered by a London specialist.

His discomfort became even more severe if he had to exert himself unduly. This happened on those occasions the tractor slipped off the tracks or when a cow yet again meandered into a ditch, prompting a physically exhausting rescue mission. In fact, so debilitating had Len's condition become that he went off Skye to consult with osteopaths in Glasgow and London. Ominously, in October 1960 he returned encased in a plaster waistcoat, with instructions to keep it on for a month. It was not until December that his straitjacket was removed. The best treatment at the time was considered to be rest, and long periods lying on his back. He did his best to take it easy, but then forgot. The consequence was further setbacks, as in April 1961. On this occasion, he had been forking the last load of silage from off the back of the tractor, and 'felt my back give badly'. He was immobilised for three days. He tried to restrict his working hours to seven a day and would deny that he did any heavy lifting. But in virtually the next sentence, take pride in his achievement – with two men helping him – in cutting 'a full winter's quota of peat . . . between 9.30 & 5'.[6]

Yet with the departure of the Jollys the family could begin to feel firmly ensconced in the newly completed bungalow. Len and Margaret were able to rent out, for holiday purposes, either the original cottage or the extension or, depending on what workers had to be accommodated, both.

The opportunity was timely. Entirely coincidentally, around a week after George and Sally left, Len flew back (to Glasgow, where he caught the train for Mallaig) from London where he had seen another specialist about his back. He looked well. But he had with him 'a whole list of things he must and must not do'.[7] From this it was clear that a 'reorganisation of Pabay . . . [was] a must'. Heavy tractor work was out, let alone strenuous manual tasks. What previously he and Margaret had thought of as supplements to the farming operation would now have to become core business. In fact, at the start of the 1960s, the generous, open-ended farm subsidies that had been available during the later 1940s and through the 1950s were coming under Exchequer scrutiny owing to fears about inflation. Common Market assistance lay some years ahead. Activities that had been more or less successful earlier – sheep farming for example, and even poultry production – by the mid-1960s were becoming less so. As agricultural production became more concentrated in larger units, the smaller holdings (and poorer land) of the Highlands and the north-west region – which of course included Pabay – suffered relative decline.[8] It was a good time to move in a different direction.

Letting was at the heart of this. The omens were promising. Tourism in the Highlands, often talked about but lacking government investment, had been left to develop largely unaided.[9]

However, visitor numbers to Skye had risen during the 1950s. Under the Conservative Government, the tourist trade was being taken more seriously than in the past, with the establishment, for example, of the Highland Tourist Development Company.[10] This, though, was of little direct assistance to Len and Margaret. A provider of loans for hoteliers who wished to expand their facilities, Harry Hilditch at Dunollie was one of the company's first beneficiaries. Len and Margaret could only look on enviously as, 'just like that', Henry and Harry Hilditch found themselves in receipt of a low-cost loan of £7,500.[11]

Of more immediate relevance for Pabay was the growing demand for self-catering accommodation for a clientele interested in the countryside and outdoor pursuits like bird-watching, and perhaps a bit of history.[12] The elite visitors to Skye of the Victorian and Edwardian eras were being supplanted as the era of large-scale tourism got under way. With its geology and early Christian associations, Pabay – like Eigg and other Hebridean islands at the time – had much to offer the discerning visitor.[13] And on the horizon was a Sunday ferry service to Skye, which, despite vociferous opposition led by the Rev. Angus Smith of Snizort, in the north of the island, began running in June 1965.[14]

Accordingly, Donald's priority now was to finish the extension and then turn his attention to putting in dormer windows to extend the size of the bedrooms of the original cottage. Critically, in order to satisfy the toilet requirements of more delicate visitors, he was to instal an internal WC. The lack of an indoor water supply was recognised as a serious barrier to entry to the tourist trade. There were parts of Skye – Waternish for example – where fewer than 10 per cent of houses were so supplied, and whose owners therefore felt unable to offer overnight accommodation.[15]

For her part, Margaret sought out second-hand furniture at sales. It was a task that she, who like her father was blessed with a built-in aptitude for haggling, relished.

On the assumption that the most likely source of the kind of paying guests they preferred (and who would be interested in an island holiday) would be readers of the *New Statesman, The Dalesman* and *The Times*, this was where Len and Henry placed advertisements.

Within weeks, the first and only guest for 1961 had disembarked. But much to everyone's delight, before Christmas, three weeks at £12 a week had been booked for the following August. With deposits paid in full.[16] In fact, what very soon became apparent was that Len and Margaret could sell weeks in August several times over; the trick – soon accomplished – would be to extend the season, from June to September, and even to secure some bookings over Easter.

Repeat visits though demanded a high level of visitor satisfaction. Increasingly irritated by the frequency with which Air Force jets on practice flights swooped low over the island, the sudden booming roar of their engines alarming livestock and terrifying unsuspecting guests in search of peace and tranquillity, Len protested to RAF Kinloss. His complaint was referred to Whitehall, leading him to remark wryly that 'any day now they will be passing me on to Moscow'.[17]

But there were other ways too of making money. Margaret became a serial competitor for prizes offered by newspapers and magazines – and won both money prizes (£2, for instance, for a rag doll submitted to *Farmers Weekly*) and bits and pieces of mainly kitchen equipment, some useful, others not.[18]

To capitalise on having potential customers so close at hand, she stepped up her baking. Her offerings included fresh bread (now even better than before, following lessons learned from a baker holidaymaker) and cakes, as well as a range of other produce. The milk and cream she used were produced by a Guernsey cow, 'Daisy', bought in the spring of 1963 for £65, with the surplus being sold to Dunollie.[19] Knitting operations too were scaled up. The 'Pabay Knitwear' brand was launched, with ties Len designed doing especially well. Less so the matching socks.

Launched too were Pabay stamps. Len's request that the GPO make deliveries direct to Pabay as well as collect mail had been turned down, a blow for the island's developing craft sales business.

So he became Pabay's postmaster, with his own stamps. Stamps from Herm, in the Channel Islands, had been available since 1949 – in addition to the normal postage stamp – introduced in part to encourage tourism. However, they were also eagerly sought by stamp collectors. Len and his brother Allan checked out Pabay's legal position, which was the same as for Herm. On neither island was there an official GPO service, so local stamps were permitted. The only stipulation was that Pabay stamps could not be placed on the front of envelopes, only on the back. On postcards, they had to be on the left side.[20]

No time was lost. In 1962 a two pence stamp was issued. Designed too were Pabay envelopes and postcards. For keen collectors, a set of four stamps, each with a different design (thistle, ragwort, ling and flax) could be had for two shillings and nine pence, directly from Pabay but also in shops in Broadford and Kyle, and nearby youth hostels. Very soon, what Len called 'the stamp and envelope lark' became a 'nice sideline', with orders coming in from as far afield as Sweden and Canada.[21] He was right to be pleased. It was not long before some 25,000 Pabay stamps were being sold each year.[22]

Len also spent more time painting. On one of his medical trips off Skye he had seen how popular landscape paintings could be, selling in some cases for 'nothing less than 10 guineas'. Dunollie he envisaged as one outlet for his work, as well as direct sales from Pabay, with potential purchasers being those either staying or who had come for the day on boat trips from Broadford. Those accommodated on the island were able to hire Neil and the launch for sea trips or, if they declared themselves capable and keen, to go off on their own in smaller craft.[23]

By the start of 1963 Len was beginning to think seriously about another sideline from the mid-1950s, but which had been brought to a halt with the Nissen hut fire: pottery.[24] He was by this time selling pots made by David Lane, of Cam Pottery in Cambridge, whose hand-thrown, mainly domestic stoneware Len had greatly admired. Indeed, he had invited Lane to Pabay to pass on some of his experience.

What he soon realised however, was that if Lane's had been Pabay pots, 'we would have sold many more'.[25] Consciously or otherwise, he had recognised the importance for tourists to Skye (and the same was true elsewhere in the Highlands and Islands) of being able to source and buy what was perceived to be local – that is particular to the locality, wholesome (uncorrupted by mass production) and if possible traditional.[26] Craft goods, including hand-thrown pottery, fitted the bill.

Around the same time, Len had been gifted, and had devoured, Bernard Leach's *The Potter's Craft*. The book not only espoused Leach's philosophy and belief in the importance of the artist-craftsman, following the lead of William Morris in the later nineteenth century; it was also an invaluable source of practical advice on clay preparation, and making, decorating and firing pots.

Before long, he was in production, albeit still on a small scale. But then, disaster struck.

In the autumn of 1963 Len suffered a major heart attack. Gravely ill and struggling with further spasms in his chest, after a lengthy delay he was taken to the new Mackinnon Memorial Hospital in Broadford, where he spent several weeks being treated, and began the lengthy process of recuperation. By a fortunate coincidence, Margaret too was admitted some weeks later (in October) to give birth to what would be her last child, Anthony (Tony) Graham Whatley. (Now there were six: Anthea, Stuart, Rachel, Alison, Michael – and Tony.) Even though the maternity ward was still under construction, Len was able to get around in his wheelchair to see her, and the couple spent time together in the day room – looking across the bay to Pabay.[27]

With the onset of the heart attack, instructed by Margaret, Donald Fletcher had had to make a hasty evening crossing to Broadford in search of the local GP. It was not the first time that a medical emergency had revealed how vulnerable the family were to crises of this kind. For island dwellers in the Hebrides the inability of doctors to attend in emergency owing to adverse sea conditions – especially during the winter months – was an age-old problem.[28]

Len and Margaret had endured a bad scare in February 1955 when Stuart's temperature rose – and kept on rising – and he developed severe earache. High winds had caused the *Fern* to drag her anchor, leaving only a dinghy to make the crossing to Broadford. Stan Robinson made it across, but only after what one onlooker described as 'a bad tossing'. He found the doctor who, however, refused to go back with him unless Stan could guarantee he would be brought back that night. Impossible. Hopes the next day that the larger Scalpay boat might help out were dashed as it was a local fast day. To breach this risked bringing a rebuke from the minister and the kirk session. In the event, Stuart recovered.[29] But for his parents these had been four days of anxiety, that in other circumstances could have had serious consequences.

Not life-threatening, but equally distressing, was when young Michael (Len and Margaret's second son) got his finger badly crushed on a trailer catch whilst being taken with his sister Alison on the tractor by Donald to feed a blind calf. Len and Margaret were home from hospital, but Margaret was still recovering from giving birth to Tony. Len could only do his best to stem the blood, frantic in his impotence, as for a day or more the sea was too rough to get to Broadford, or for a doctor to come to Pabay. Real or imagined, pain – and anxiety – intensify when relief is denied by an angry sea.

Donald Fletcher's capacity for emergency crossings to Broadford had first been tested in February 1962, when it appeared that Margaret had gone into labour prematurely. This time, even though it was during the night, a doctor and nurse did go over, but without having to do anything other than diagnose a coughing fit as the cause of Margaret's abdominal discomfort.[30] Michael Norman Whatley was born more or less on his due date, safely, in Broadford Hospital just over two weeks later, on 13 March.

After Len's heart attack and its coinciding with Margaret's confinement, Anthea had had to return from Redditch, in the English Midlands, where she had set up a hairdressing business, to look after her siblings.

In preparation for the time she would be giving birth and preoccupied with the care of the infant (and with her four-year-old daughter Alison to care for), Margaret – practical as ever – had arranged for the family to have temporary use of Liveras House, in Broadford, near to the hospital. For the children (Rachel, Alison and a very young Michael), it was an eye-opener: round the clock electricity, a refrigerator – and, for the first time in their lives, home-made ice cream.

But it was Len's need for more immediate access to medical help, and the younger children's wants, that marked the beginning of the end as far as life on Pabay was concerned.

Even prior to this, in 1962, Len had contemplated giving up. Farming losses in the previous two years had been such that the income from house lettings and associated sales (from craft goods, artwork and stamps) had become crucial if the family were to remain on the island. There were now five children to support. Margaret's parents were ageing. Henry had been hospitalised with a thrombosis, and although he had recovered, his wife Margaret was ailing. Soon Alison, who had been born in January 1959, would be approaching school age. And now there was Michael – and before long, Tony. Boarding with their grandparents, as the three older children had done, was out of the question. With Len's back limiting what farm work he could do, and now with concerns about his heart health, he and Margaret had to consider even more seriously whether staying on Pabay was a viable option.

After much anguished deliberation and discussion, they decided to go. The following spring (in 1965), Pabay was advertised for sale, at offers over £17,500.

It was ironic that just at this time, the world outside was beginning to take notice of what the Whatleys had accomplished. Compounding the irony was that Len had followed as closely as he could George Henderson's *Farming Ladder* principles and practices, building steadily from a sound base. There were only two rungs on Henderson's ladder that a farmer with faith, commitment and hard work should fear: 'ill health and accident'. For Len, both rungs had proved to be rotten.

'Len Whatley's Kingdom' is how an obviously impressed feature writer from the *Sunday Post* – then selling not far short of three million copies a week – described Pabay. He was not alone in appreciating the wrench Len would feel if he had to pull up the roots he had sunk so deeply into the island's soil. Satisfied visitors too helped spread the word, including one man who, after spending two holidays on Pabay, wrote a piece extolling the island's virtues and Len's and Margaret's achievements for the *Wolverhampton Express and Star*.

Putting the island up for sale was one thing. The 1960s was a difficult decade in Britain, as the country staggered from one crisis to another. Labour disputes, strikes, alarming balance of payments deficits, the value of the pound sterling and credit controls were headline news.

Although there was no obvious dip in enthusiasm for island ownership, the means of acquiring one had become more difficult. Henry Hilditch expressed 'some satisfaction' that the new Labour Government under Harold Wilson was committed to moving from a 'free for all' towards the 'more orderly society' he had long advocated.[31] But he and Len were at the same time painfully aware of the immediate consequences of the Labour Chancellor of the Exchequer James Callaghan's tax rises, public expenditure cuts and restrictions on bank lending.[32] Between 1964 and 1970 the bank rate rarely fell below 7 per cent.

Finding a purchaser in such circumstances was unlikely to be straightforward.

And so it proved. If there was any compensation it was that while no one was prepared take the plunge and buy Pabay, many of the viewers turned out to be good customers for the craft goods Len and Margaret continued to put on sale.[33]

Meanwhile, they began the drawn-out evacuation process. By the time a 'greatly excited' Alison started school in the autumn of 1965, Margaret and the children had found accommodation, albeit temporarily, in the former school house in Breakish, within sight of their former island home. The Director of Education had been persuaded that offering the house to the Whatleys at a low rent – roughly £1 a week including rates – was preferable to having to supply Pabay with a teacher for Alison, who was now six and school-ready.[34]

Despite the worsening condition of his back, Len remained for much of the time on Pabay, with the bulk of the hard work, including tidying the place up for prospective purchasers, being done by Donald, and Ned Rimmer. (Ned had first become acquainted with Skye – and Pabay – through his work as a ground surveyor with the Ordnance Survey when the trig point on the island had been put in, after which he joined up with the Combers on Soay as a crewman on the *Northern Dawn*, lobster fishing off Barra. What had also drawn Ned to Pabay was Anthea, then in her mid-teens, stunningly attractive, with a sparkling personality to match her good looks.) Moveable items such as pieces of furniture and equipment that might be useful in future were transported to Breakish.

There were poignant moments. One of these was late in 1965 with what Len hoped – vainly as it happened – would be the sale of his last batch of calves. There were seventeen of them, which had to be shipped to Broadford. With the ferry boat shared with Scalpay out of action, they were taken over in the Pabay boat in three separate lots, to be picked up by a lorry at midday.

The first tranche arrived and were penned into the coal yard by the pier, although not before Len had exhausted himself by running along the shore to get hold of a calf that had slipped away. One of the calves from the second boatload, however, broke free entirely, raced to the shore and 'started to swim back to Pabay', or so it looked to those concerned. Ned tried to head it off with the boat, but once he moved away, off again went the calf, swimming further out. Meantime, the other calves had escaped, and also headed for the shore. There followed several hours of pandemonium that closely resembled a Carry On film. With rain lashing down, futile attempts were made to capture the first fugitive, which after swimming for well over an hour had come ashore back at Broadford, bolted up the hill behind Corry pier and ended up crashing around the minister's manse garden. The rest rampaged through the village.[35] Leaving wasn't easy.

At the same time, the family had to find somewhere else to settle permanently, and where they could live without being so reliant on Len's being fit for strenuous physical work. Breakish was one possibility. With the primary school about to close, the building could be turned into a craft shop and pottery. There was potential for a campsite at nearby Lusta. Initially though, the island habit was a hard one to break. Raasay was soon to be connected by MacBrayne's with a regular ferry service from a new pier at Sconser, so rumours that the big house there might soon come onto the market were followed up. So too were some deserted cottages. This could work, given Margaret's interest in catering of some kind, perhaps a bed and breakfast business, although she was keen too to carry on knitting.

But what they lighted upon was a large, rambling and somewhat run-down property at Edinbane, at the end of Loch Greshornish, in the north-west of Skye near Dunvegan. The two-storey building was reputed to have been a coaching inn, dating from c.1543. Set in three acres of ground, Edinbane Lodge, as it was called, reflecting its use as shooting accommodation, boasted nine bedrooms, three bathrooms and four public rooms. Available for sale, too, was some of the existing furniture – including (unthinkable on Pabay) fitted carpets. The Lodge required some work to make it habitable, but the only major undertaking would be the addition of a septic tank, as currently waste water was simply running into the fast-flowing River Choishleader, which ran directly into Loch Greshornish.[36] For the burn, the owners also had fishing rights. It would be some time, though, before the Whatleys would acquire these.

They had become aware of the Lodge entirely by chance. Two partners, Norman Young, a hairdresser from Redditch, with whom Anthea was working (having left Pabay for this purpose), and Douglas Sanderson, had toyed with the idea of moving to Skye. Prior to this they had plied their trade in a salon in Portree and, through Anthea, had visited Pabay and become acquainted with the family – the female members especially, who welcomed free hairdos. Keen – or so they thought – to settle on Skye, the two men had put in an offer for Edinbane – not realising that in Scotland acceptance of this was a binding contract. Their enthusiasm cooled, however. They wanted out, and would sell to Len for £3,500, the sum they had offered the present owner – a member of the Hilleary family, long-time proprietors of Edinbane Estate.

But without selling Pabay, Len could do nothing. Family finances were so tight that for a time it looked like Stuart, who had gone to Chile to teach English for a 'gap year', would be stranded. Although Henry had been able to pull strings at the Peace Pledge Union, which contributed to the cost of the outward journey, there wasn't enough to pay his return air fare. Previously important income earners – the calves Len had specialised in – now produced little. Again, this was largely as a result of the Government's credit-tightening in 1966. Farmer-purchasers of the calves from the south, who then turned them into beef cattle, no longer had the where-withal to buy either the calves or the necessary feed. At Broadford the price paid for two-year-olds fell from £59 in 1965 to £32 the following year.[37] Should Len sell at a loss, or hold onto them over the winter in the hope that prices would rise by the following spring, and meantime bear the cost of buying in feed? There was no easy answer. Both lost money. And compounding the problem, Ned – now integral to day-to-day operations on Pabay – had to take time off, having been hospitalised with a prolapsed disc.[38]

The timing was doubly unfortunate as the previous summer Neil MacRae had been paid off – a bitter, fraught and unhappy ending to what had been a keystone relationship. The denouement had followed Ned being invited by Len to use the newly refurbished launch ('all spick and span like a new pin') to take parties from Broadford on evening cruises – advertised on posters Stuart had designed. Neil was miffed, to say the least, and not best pleased to be told this after two years of trying to do the same thing, although he had attracted few customers. The reason, allegedly, was that he hadn't set regular times. By contrast, Ned had been taking parties of twelve out (more actually, but Board of Trade regulations set the total at this number), with customers travelling from as far as Inverness for the privilege.[39]

But, despite gnawing worries about money, the years of uncertainty – as Pabay remained unsold and Len and Margaret's relationship was strained when she moved, with the children, to Breakish – were far from being years lost. Len's eagerness to advance his skills in ceramics was heightened as he adjusted to life with a suspect heart and chronic back pain. In anticipation of being freed from the burdens of island farming, and as he spent even more time making pots, his earlier optimism was fully restored. 'I am in great form,' he told his brother, 'no aches or pains & working well.'[40]

Coincidence had played its part too. An acquaintance of Ned Rimmer's was the aforementioned David 'Dave' Illingworth, who in the early 1960s had a workshop at Morar Pottery, near Mallaig. In due course Illingworth was introduced to Len, who not only benefited from the former's knowledge of pot making, but also his other skills. Illingworth, designated a 'Renaissance man' in one obituary after his death in 2009, had been a precision engineer, watchmaker, jeweller and prawn fisherman – in Morecambe Bay – but it was his ability as a boat builder that endeared him to Len. Indeed, in the spring of 1965 he was persuaded to come across and stay – as did Ned and, for a time, Alan Browne. (Ironically, with Stan and Rosa Robinson and their three children having come back for a visit, and the holiday accommodation fully let, the summer of 1965 was probably Pabay's busiest ever.)

Gentle and charismatic, Illingworth was an autodidact who had recently become a convert to the Glasgow-born psychiatrist Ronald D. Laing's radical views on the nature and treatment of mental illness (his orthodoxy-challenging book, *The Divided Self*, had been published in 1960). Illingworth was also a poet – who introduced me to the work of the Russian poet Yevgeny Yevtushenko, the first work of literature I ever took seriously. A disciple of the anti-authoritarian educationalist A.S. Neill, he was contemptuous of the state education system and, at a critical juncture in my life, persuaded me that there was more to learning than passing examinations and gaining academic qualifications. This was heartening, as I had none, other than the single 'O' level in Art that I had left school with. For a lad in his mid-teens, as I was, it was a glorious time. I wrote a card from Pabay to my mother expressing my delight that I was 'taking folk out fishing, for pay', and catching plenty too. Watching as the three men renovated the hull and engine of the last boat Len would buy (and playing a minor part by making some slatted seating for it), and relishing stimulating conversations about the meaning of life, Bach's fugues (one of Len's musical enthusiasms), art and artists, crafts and plans for the future, I almost succumbed to Len's invitation to join him on Pabay and work for him.

But I'd discovered Glasgow's clubs – the Elizabethan and the Maryland; live music – Maggie Bell, the Beatstalkers and the Poets; pubs – and women. Pabay in these respects was wanting. I sensed too that on Pabay or even at Edinbane, opportunities for doing something else with my life would be limited. Indeed, it was Len who had on more than one occasion persuaded me that I had talents that belied the unflattering reports my teachers sent me home with at the end of each school year, or the short testimonial provided by the headmaster who had recently brought my school career to a close: I was pleasant, a regular attender, and just might pass all of two 'O' grades (in English and Art). He was over-optimistic.

As important from Len's perspective, and for life post-Pabay, was the presence of Lotte Glob, Illingworth's young Danish wife. She was born in 1944, the daughter of an eminent Danish archaeologist. Early on – after a spell aged nineteen spent in County Cork, Ireland – she developed an abiding affection for Scotland's rugged landscape. This, and her determination to find employment as a ceramicist, took her to Morar, where Illingworth guided – and subsequently married – her.[41]

Glob had been tutored by some of Denmark's leading artists, including the ceramicists Gutte Erikson and Erik Nyholm.[42] Although in the mid-1960s she was just out of her teens, watching her throw was, for Stuart, 'magical', and mesmerising. Stuart by this time was becoming increasingly interested in pottery, even though, after his return from Chile, he had matriculated at Glasgow University for a science degree. Before the end of the decade he had changed tack and enrolled at Glasgow's School of Art, for a diploma course in drawing and painting. During the vacations, he not only took over some of his father's roles on Pabay but, with him, also continued to make and fire pots.

For just prior to this, as the Pabay venture drew to a close, Stuart and his father had one particularly successful firing in a modest-sized kiln. Astonished when they calculated that the pots they had produced might sell for the princely total of £20 (just under £400 today), they became even surer of the direction they should take once they got to Edinbane. For Stuart, painting no longer looked like the best way to make a living. So confident was Len that this endeavour might work that he offered to buy the dilapidated coach house in the grounds at Edinbane. It would require to be redesigned and refurbished, but it could be converted into a pottery workshop.

Despite having set their hearts on Edinbane by the end of 1965, Len and Margaret seemed no further forward a year later; and by now they were also committed to buying the coach house. There had been an encouraging number of enquiries about Pabay – over a hundred – and several visits by potential purchasers, but no one had been prepared to take the plunge. Concern was growing that with the island being more or less on a care and maintenance basis, once more – as had happened during the 1940s – its condition as a sustainable farming unit would deteriorate, and further deter would-be purchasers.

Margaret, normally so resilient, began to struggle. For one thing, she was less sanguine than Len was about his state of health. Paradoxically, now she was off the island she felt isolated. She missed the companionship that Pabay had engendered. Unable to drive a car at this stage (she had never had to learn), she was cut off from the people she knew – even though they were only three miles along the road in Broadford – in a way that she had never known on Pabay, where everyone on the island, even campers, was within a couple of hundred yards of each other.

The children – Alison, Michael and Tony – were now cooped up inside the house. On Pabay they would disappear for entire days, safe and secured by the ring of sea. Increasingly, they got on her nerves. Len, the pacifier and her lifetime's companion, was on Pabay, and his trips to Breakish were intermittent. Once, on the edge of depression and barely able to muster the strength to fulfil orders for jumpers (which would normally have delighted her), she broke into her own narrative in a letter she was writing, to complain that the children were 'arguing like mad & screaming'. Why, she wondered; was it some failing on her own part, had she somehow been 'inefficient'?[43] Her father-in-law Herbert had recently been to stay and had been niggled about a particularly fraught incident involving the children – reawakening for her the sense of disapproval she had first felt back in 1947, when she had had to reveal that she was pregnant with Anthea. Despite her many accomplishments and ability to get things done smoothly and preferably with little 'fuss', she was understandably unhappy. In the circumstances, her ego was easily bruised.

Nevertheless, it seemed that the log-jam might be broken through by yet another serendipitous event.

At the start of 1965 Donald (Don) and Judith (Judy) Maclachlan were a young, newly married couple living in Richmond, Surrey. Don was a senior research chemist with G.V. Planer, scientific equipment manufacturers. Judy was a book illustrator. That summer they set off for a holiday in Scotland, in a bubble car that

broke down at Darlington. Worse, overnight their tent and camping gear were stolen. Undeterred, they continued their journey
north by train, and picked up at Kyle the prize-wining catamaran
that Donald had designed and built in his living room. This had
been sent on in advance of their arrival. Sailing from Loch Carron,
they landed on Pabay.[44] And were warmly welcomed, once
Margaret, back on Pabay for the summer, had in her canny fashion
eyed up and approved the somewhat discomfited sailors – who
had assumed Pabay was deserted.[45]

Although the Maclachlans were younger than Len and
Margaret, the two couples had much in common. Judy was a
talented painter. Len was intrigued by Don's hand-built boat. And
enthused by the new experience of sailing and fishing from it. So
too was Stuart, whose interest in and admiration of multi-hulled
craft has never waned. That Donald had been a pacifist who had
refused to do National Service was another melding point. His
verve (he could talk ten to the dozen), kaleidoscopic knowledge
and slight eccentricity provided another unexpected tonic for Len.
For their part, Don and Judy were so struck by the invigorating
atmosphere on Pabay, and the beauty of their surroundings, they
stayed for longer than they had anticipated, accommodated in the
cottage extension. Plans were laid for a return visit to Pabay.
Before long though, these were revised. They had now decided to
come to Skye and live and work, in Don's case, building boats
full-time.

Their move had not come altogether out of the blue. Raised in
Glasgow (although born in the London borough of Hillingdon, in
1935), Donald had a fondness for Scotland, especially the
Highlands. As a schoolboy, he had often cycled north – all the way
from London. (In 1963, I cycled the much shorter distance from
Glasgow to Broadford, over a three-day period – and thence by
boat to Pabay – a trip sufficiently arduous that I went home by
train, and thereafter abandoned the bicycle as a means of getting
to Skye.) Judith too savoured the north-west and the landscapes
that were often features of her work. Indeed, it was while she was
working as a temporary warden at the youth hostel in Achiltibuie
in Wester Ross that the pair had met.[46]

So firm had the friendship between the two couples on Pabay become that within a few months they had found a solution that met their respective needs. Don and Judy were to sell their Richmond flat. They would then pay for part of the value of Edinbane Lodge and live there. The balance Len would provide, with a £1,000 bank loan. Once Pabay was sold, he and Margaret and the children would leave Breakish and move to Edinbane, at which point the Maclachlans would find somewhere else to live. Meanwhile Don would busy himself by building a bigger boat – a trimaran. This he did, similarly to his original craft, by turning the dining room into a temporary boat yard.

The financial aspect of the arrangement was further eased by renting out part of the Lodge to another family. This was the Welfords, a household of six from Weymouth on England's south coast, whom Len had invited to come to Pabay for a visit at Easter 1966. Daphne Welford was a maths teacher and had been Len's first serious love in the late 1930s. He hadn't seen her since the outbreak of war with Germany, when she had met and fallen in love with a serviceman, Peter Welford, and, who knows, may have hankered to build anew on memories of an intense but unfulfilled relationship. (Was it significant that Len, who had had his own recent skirmish with death, was particularly keen to get hold of *Love and Death*, by Dorset-born Llewelyn Powys, the story of a dying man's rekindling of a poignant love affair from his youth?[47]) Sensing the possibility that the closer proximity of an old flame might cause it to reignite, Margaret put on a brave face, as inwardly she seethed.

The Welfords had already been thinking of relocating to Scotland, and had looked seriously at Laide, near Durness, north-west Sutherland. However, like the Maclachlans, they had been captivated by what their son Alex has called the 'atmosphere, life-style and philosophy' that from the outset on Pabay had infused the Whatley household. So they decided instead to divert to Skye.[48] The process was complicated, as Daphne remained in her senior teaching post in Weymouth, but facilitated by the availability of temporary accommodation at the Lodge. Peter, her husband, older than her, was a gifted musician and secured a post at Portree High School.

What was projected as a short-term arrangement – for a year – turned out to be rather lengthier. Despite putting the sale of Pabay into the hands of the agents who recently – in 1966 – had successfully sold Eigg, there were still no takers. The sale saga even caught the attention of the national press. In June 1967, for instance, the *Daily Record* published a lengthy valedictory article headed 'Farewell to a Paradise Island'. This paid tribute to Len, 'king of the Priest's Island' for bringing Pabay into the twentieth century and ended by concluding that 'whatever the new regime, Pabay will flourish'.[49] At least one local worthy was less impressed. Days after the article appeared, Stuart overheard one of the paper's readers in Broadford Co-op: 'Ah Morag, you'll have heard they're leaving. I always said they wouldn't last long.'

The *Record*'s piece helped to raise Pabay's profile – even if the picture of Margaret, Stuart, Alison and Michael walking by the shore, which accompanied the article, had been taken in Breakish rather than on Pabay, which it purported to show. But it did the trick, and the following month the *Sunday Telegraph* also ran with the Pabay story, with Margaret now assuming a new identity: Mrs Leonard Watting.

Prior to this, however, a much more eye-catching proposition was on the cards. During 1966 the Society of Friends – or Quakers – was actively engaged in establishing co-operative communities, the 'requirements of human happiness and human welfare ... [being] incompatible with a system of private ownership and private enterprise'.[50] Highland Scotland was thought to be a desirable location for one such community, which might include from one hundred to three hundred people who would pool their skills for the communal good.

By the end of the year Skye was firmly in the sights of the group concerned, led by Sydney (or Bransby) Clarke, a thirty-eight-year-old Carlisle journalist.[51] One of Clarke's associates had acquired a shipment of 20,000 seeds of Russian-bred blueberries, and Skye seemed to offer ideal growing conditions.[52] Sleat was one option. Raasay was another. Raasay though was going to cost a lot more than the hundreds of pounds the Quakers could raise.

News of the Quakers' scheme attracted the news media across

the nation, including the BBC. Henry Hilditch was immediately on the case. Contact made and, enthused by the sale particulars Len had drawn up, Clarke immediately wrote to the newly created (in 1965) Highlands and Islands Development Board (HIDB) in Inverness, asking for financial help. Although he had not yet seen the island, Clarke outlined what he would do if they acquired it. 'Being a vegetarian community' the beef cattle would be sold, although the Guernsey cow would be kept (and supplemented by others) for milk, butter and cheese. Poultry too was to be retained, but with the focus on 'good laying' free-range birds. Committed as the Quakers were to self-sufficiency (as Len and Margaret had been at the start), they would concentrate on vegetable growing and large-scale market gardening, along with cane fruit – and blueberries.

In the belief 'that the island at one time was well wooded', they would extend the shelter belts in order to 'give us a modest source of wood for crafts' and saleable timber. Pabay, Clarke declared, seemed 'to meet our requirements as fully as any site in the region is likely to'; its availability 'an opportunity we don't want to miss'.[53] Accordingly, he submitted a note of interest. With his wife Graylene and two young children, in June he even pitched a tent on the island, and began sowing seeds nearby, having brought with them a small library of books that included one on tisanes – drinks made by boiling plants.[54]

This, however, is about as far as the scheme got. Hand-scribbled notes on Development Board memoranda show that officials were dubious about supporting 'these "get away from it all" people'. Back to nature 'is not development', although 'with religion' such a scheme 'might be OK on Skye', one official had written caustically. The bottom line though was that the Friends had insufficient funds. The Board could only assist in offering loans for buying property where applicants' contributions were substantial, the proposal was fully worked out and viable, job-creating and likely to generate enough money to repay the loan with interest.[55] Such an outcome seemed unlikely on Pabay – although the Board took many months to tell Len and Margaret, who throughout 1967 were hopeful of, and increasingly desperate for, a sale.[56] Exasperated, and doubly disappointed as an arrangement with a private buyer for Pabay who was willing to allow the Quakers to farm there had also fallen through, Clarke protested, railing at the absence of affordable places to lease or rent in the Highlands. His island idyll was over.[57]

* * *

The protracted wait for a buyer ended in 1970. A couple, Edward (Ted) and Anne Gerrard from Harpenden, Hertfordshire, had seen an advertisement for Pabay in *The Times*. Divorcees, they had been looking for somewhere they could build a new life – ideally on an island. Although they were both engravers, Ted (who had also been a champion bicycle racer) had a lifelong interest in migratory birds. They had looked at Bardsey Island, two miles off the north-west coast of Wales, renowned for the richness and variety of its bird population, including Manx shearwaters, and its position on significant migration routes. Although nothing came of this, they were not deterred. On learning about Pabay, Ted and his stepson had immediately driven north, hired a man to take them across to Pabay – in dismal, wet weather – and driven home the following day. This was after having struck a deal with Len in Dunollie Hotel. In no position to refuse an offer that was even less than the £15,000 that was now Pabay's asking price, there and then Len settled on £14,000.[58]

He had hardly struck gold, but at least he was now debt-free and able to repay – after fifteen years – Sarah Campbell, and the Bank of Scotland. He and Margaret could also take outright possession of Edinbane Lodge and the coach house.

Pabay no more. At least that was how it seemed at the time, with all eyes now on Edinbane. In fact, another link with Pabay had been severed that year, with the death of Henry Hilditch, for so long the lynchpin without whom it is doubtful that the island adventure would have lasted so long.

Rarely did things happen easily for Len and Margaret. For one thing, the Maclachlans were still in the Lodge at Edinbane. And if Len's and Stuart's pottery plans were to be realised, they had a major task on their hands in converting the coach house. So, for a time, Len, Margaret and their four younger children crammed themselves into a caravan, near what was to become the pottery.

Len was now able to concentrate full-time on refurbishing the Lodge. With Phil Ebdon, a Londoner who had come to Skye with his wife Rowena, and Alex Welford and Stuart during their long vacations, he made rapid progress. Before long he was able to move Margaret and the children into the house. And, in March 1972, Edinbane Pottery was formally opened, building on the skills Len had managed to hone by setting up a mini pottery in the coach house during its transformation.

Family members recall the joy and sense of fulfilment he felt throwing pots, which he soon learned to do in volume. With Stuart now having graduated from art school, the venture flourished, Len providing the brain and experience, and Stuart – initially anyway – the brawn (and understanding) required for mixing and preparing clay, and loading, firing and emptying the kiln. Probably more conscious of the fragile state of his health than those around him, Len insisted that Stuart deal with the business side of the operation, in preparation for what would come later.

Later came very soon. The family had settled comfortably into the Lodge. Margaret relished the space she now had, the large kitchen and the opportunities there were for a more active social life in the village; having passed her driving test, she could roam even further, including to the shops in Portree. Len seemed as happy as he had ever been. In the last letter I wrote to him I joked about his new-found status as laird of Edinbane. (On Pabay he had barely had time to write, but now he picked up his pen and wrote long, lucid letters, interspersed with wry observations on the politicians we loved and loathed, and about life in general.) He had even become a grandfather, as both Anthea and Stuart began their own families.

Len used the garden ground at the Lodge for playing all sorts of games with the children, relatives and friends – badminton was a favourite, and croquet reminded him of his childhood in Birmingham, where he'd played this with his father and mother on their stamp-sized back lawn. Now having vastly superior television reception than had been possible on Pabay (where only one channel could be picked up and watched, and then through a fuzzy mist), he watched avidly the unfolding of the Watergate scandal that broke in 1972 and brought down President Nixon in August 1974. Notwithstanding his parents' distaste of violence of any kind, he became an enthusiastic fan of boxing, above all Cassius Clay, better known as Muhammad Ali, drawn to him by his ring skills and personality but also as Ali had been stripped of his titles owing to his objection to the Vietnam War and refusal to be drafted into the army. A fellow CO.

He was able, too, to take up pursuits he had enjoyed as a younger man. With more room available, he bought a billiard table, on which he played – very well – both billiards and snooker.

After Christmas in 1974 and just before Hogmanay, towards the end of a game with his sons Stuart and Michael, he decided to slip upstairs and lie down. And there, on his bed, he died. He was fifty-five, but he had done and achieved more in those five and a half decades than most people over much longer lifetimes.

His obituary in the recently established *West Highland Free Press* was succinct. Generous, modest and mainly content, his 'great joy' was creating and attempting to make 'simple and beautiful things'. This, the writer, his brother-in-law Harry Hilditch, wrote, 'was the key to his . . . life'.[59] It was fitting that in the weeks following, Stuart sent each member of the family a piece of his father's pottery, a tactile memorial to its maker's ability to handcraft 'beautiful things'. Its provenance was from the early days on Pabay: Len's efforts to clean John Blackadder's ditches. But it reflected too his natural inquisitiveness, his generosity about imparting his knowledge, skills, insights and values, his enthusiasm for new pursuits and resourcefulness.

Chapter 14

An island 'full of woods':
forward to the past

At first sight, the Gerrards seemed even less likely to succeed on Pabay than Len and Margaret. As well as having limited financial resources, they had no previous experience of farming. In fact, when I spoke with her early in 2018, reflecting back on their years in Pabay, Anne remarked that they had been 'greenhorns when we started, and greenhorns at the end'.[1] And dependent upon them were three rather than two school-age children: Richard, Nigel and Gillian.

As with the Whatleys, the Gerrards' first years were challenging, although they had the compensation of better housing to move into. The rabbits had returned with a vengeance, and continued to breed in profusion, and eat. As in the past, sheep – blackface initially – managed to slip into the open ditches. To begin with, the couple had no tractor. As had happened in the 1950s, Nissen huts they erected were torn away by the wind that blew unchecked across the island. For a time, they resorted to cutting seaweed and, like their predecessors, quickly recognised the cash-generating potential of winkle-picking, which became a family pursuit. They carried on the stamp business, refreshing the range with pictures of the island's birds, and seaweed. Anne earned £4 a week from the GPO for acting as the postmistress. She was also an artist, embroiderer and flower arranger.

Recent history repeated itself in other ways too, with Ted approaching the Department of Agriculture for advice about what activities might be supported. Less interested in arable farming than Len, his best option seemed to be to increase the number of sheep on the island; the minimum number required by the Department was 150 breeding ewes. Accordingly, as Len had in the early days, Ted embarked on a massive programme of drain and ditch clearance, with a maze of new ones cut in order to extend the area able to carry sheep. But not just any sheep.

He and Ann bred Shetland ewes with Gotland rams, a Swedish breed that produce a fine, long and dense fleece. Unusually, they ate seaweed, a commodity in abundance on Pabay. Critical, though, was a buoyant market during the late 1960s and 1970s for sheep-skin jackets and coats. The headquarters and manufacturing centre for what had become a global fashion item in the hands of design-ers like Oscar de la Renta and Ralph Lauren – and much loved by rock stars like Eric Clapton and Jimmy Hendrix – was Antartex, in Alexandria, near Loch Lomond.[2] It was here that Pabay's pelts were sent, with the meat being sold abroad.

But fashion is cyclical and, as demand for sheepskin dropped off, Ted turned his attention to salmon fishing (rights to which, as proprietor, he had), evading the Royal Navy's fishery protection vessels' interest in his use of illegal gill nets and benefiting from the enthusiasm of Duncan Hilditch (Harry Hilditch's son, who had taken over the business from his parents) at Dunollie Hotel for local salmon. Maritime activities of this kind were made easier by a long-overdue improvement at the jetty: with instruction in the use of explosives from men of the Royal Artillery, Ted fash-ioned a storm basin to the west of the existing jetty in which boats could be safely sheltered.[3] The difference this made for boat secu-rity on Pabay was immense – allied to Ted Gerrard's use from the start of a dory, a small, lightweight boat with a shallow draught that was stable and easily handled. It is telling that Ted's boat is still around (albeit in a yard near Portsoy, on the other side of Scotland).

However, even had this work been completed earlier, it was too late and too small to be of any assistance to a Royal Navy torpedo boat that had been beached on Pabay during a winter storm in 1972. Although the debacle was hushed up, the *Daily Mirror* mischievously ran with a short notice that Gerrard had managed to get hold of the vessel's flag.[4]

Throughout the Gerrards' time on the island, which came to an end in 1981, Ted scrupulously studied and recorded Pabay's bird-life. This proved to be another revelation, inasmuch as he was able to demonstrate the existence of a previously unknown flock of Greenland white-fronted geese that during the winter roosted on Pabay before flying to Scalpay and the adjoining coastline of mainland Skye during the daytime. He had time, too, to wrestle with the question of how birds navigate when migrating long distances, sometimes following complex routes.

In part, it was his search for an explanation (which challenged received wisdom) that took him and his wife away from Pabay, on a voyage by yacht bound for the Sargasso Sea, but which reached only as far as Madeira, where they stayed for the next twenty-one years.[5]

So again, in 1979, Pabay was put on the market, this time for the asking price of £150,000. Islands were now much more fashionable than they had been when Len and Margaret had been selling up – although they would become even more so later. Along with the island were to go Ted and Anne Gerrard's flock of 'seaweed-eating sheep', and the findings of a report that shellfish farming would be viable.

The new residents were members of the Philip family. The purchaser, the corporate title of which was Avalon Marine, was Michael Philip, who had been a district commissioner in what before gaining independence in 1963 had been the British Crown Colony of Kenya, in East Africa, formerly the British East Africa Protectorate. With his brother Alastair, Michael also had a 1,000-acre farm on the Mau escarpment, on the western side of the Rift Valley, long favoured by colonialists – 'white settlers'.[6]

During the 1950s and early 1960s, however, Kenya was the locus of 'one of the bloodiest and most protracted wars of decolonisation' in the history of Britain's declining empire, with the removal of the settlers a prime aim of the Mau Mau insurgents. Even though Jomo Kenyatta, the African nationalist president of what from 1964 was the Republic of Kenya, was keen to placate the fears of the settler population, conditions in what from 1964 was the Republic of Kenya became uncomfortable for Europeans who declined to take up Kenyan citizenship. Large swathes of farmland were redistributed amongst members of Kenyatta's Kikuyu elite.[7] The 'White Highlands' had been Kikuyu territory before they had been brutally cleared during the British occupation.

However, with British Government funding of £12.5 million that allowed the Kenyan Government to buy back colonialists' land at market prices, Philip gave up what had been a prosperous farming venture; he was one of nearly 20,000 settlers who left.[8] By 1978, the brothers, their wives and sons had returned to the United Kingdom. After taking over a small nine-acre farm near Scarborough, Michael Philip, the wealthier of the two brothers, who had originated in Muchalls in Kincardineshire, decided, in the words of his nephew Rod, that he 'wanted a bit of Scotland'. With Pabay's ownership registered under Geneva-based Avalon Marine, there were tax benefits too.[9]

Why Michael Philip opted for Pabay at first sight seems strange. Kenya was equatorial. In the temperate climate of the Central Highlands and the Rift Valley, growing conditions are excellent.[10] It was what drew Europeans there in the first place. In fertile soils, Kenyan farmers nowadays grow and export vegetables, fruit and fresh cut flowers, in abundance. On Pabay, as we've seen in the case of George Jolly, vegetable cultivation was difficult, and impossible to make a living from.

In Kenya, the Philip's farm – Manungan Hill – was surrounded by land as far as the eye could see; on Pabay it was the sea that fringed the farm.

Yet in conversation with Rod Philip – born in Kenya and who worked for his uncle there and on Pabay during his twenties – similarities emerge between the Philip family's experience of farming in Africa and Skye that belie the roughly 7,000-mile distance between the two locations. Both were in their way isolated: at Manungan Hill they were 30 miles from their nearest neighbours in Kenya. On Pabay it was the two and a half miles by what at times was a turbulent sea that separated them from other people. In both places, stocking up on vital supplies involved a significant journey, by land and sea respectively. Both were served by basic electricity generator systems that kicked into action when the first light was switched on, and closed down when the last light went off.[11]

Perhaps most important of all, both ventures were in their way pioneering, and physically demanding, requiring, as we've seen with Len, determination and a level of resourcefulness that can be hard for an outsider to appreciate.

What is striking when looking at Pabay's progress not only over decades, but also back to the early nineteenth century, and at John Blackadder's prescription for turning the island into the productive farm he and others hoped it could be, is how few and slight the gains were, the fleeting nature of success, and how often the same challenges came up and had to be confronted.

It is true that the Philips benefited from the invaluable 90-foot-long storm harbour blasted out of the rock by Ted Gerrard. They inherited, too, the herd of Gotland sheep, in which there was still some potential. The market for their fleeces remained active; there was even a possibility that Hunters of Brora might spin at least some of it into woollen yarn.

Aware that there was little or no sale for dark-coloured Gotland lambs, they introduced Cheviot sheep, which after cross-breeding produced saleable stock. And the new residents had the advantage too of numbers: Alastair Philip and his wife, and their two fit sons, Rod and Harvey, sometimes with a third brother, Ian, comprised the island's workforce. Furthermore, there was less financial pressure than there had been during the Whatley and the Gerrard years. Michael Philip paid an annual salary for managing the island to his brother Alastair, who was also able to dip into his savings as necessary. Modest wages and largely in-kind payments kept Alastair's sons reasonably content. When required they resorted to the adult equivalent of pocket-money generation on a Hebridean island: whelk-gathering. The Philips too kept the stamp business going.

However, in order to increase stock numbers to the optimal 250 ewes it was reckoned Pabay could carry, they needed to improve the quality and extent of the grassland. This, in turn, required vast amounts of lime to be brought to the island – from the same quarry at Torrin that Len had used – and spread, not always with purpose-built equipment, but partly by hand. To ship it to Pabay, as well as for getting lambs off as required by autumn, they used a landing craft – Ted Gerrard's, restored – supplemented by the Raasay ferry.

Len's fencing too had seen better days and had to be replaced and extended. There was also a kind of continuity in how they communicated with mainland Skye. Initially the Philips used a flag signalling system that the Gerrards had devised, graduating thereafter to a VHF ship-to-shore radio. Other improvements included adding an upper floor to the extension and fitting a dormer window onto the back of the original cottage. A new, bigger diesel-powered 15 kW generator meant that for the first time it could be centrally heated – round the clock if need be. They improved and extended the original cottage too – adding a second bathroom as well as a further two bedrooms upstairs.

In part, the upgraded fencing was to deal with what for all of Pabay's owners in the second half of the twentieth-century was the ongoing saga of the rabbit war. 'Swamped' is how Rod Philip described feeling, as he scaled up his weaponry from a .22 rifle to a shotgun before resorting to the use of a spotlight in the dark, along with a smart sheepdog with which one night he managed to kill over 100 rabbits. Even though there were further outbreaks of disease, these were never severe enough to wipe out entirely Pabay's rabbit stock, through which traces of the fashionable breeds introduced by Sir Henry Bell continued – as in the 1950s – to be revealed in sightings of belted and black and ginger-coated animals. Disease-free, however, rabbit meat proved to be a welcome food supplement, along with fish.

Previous chapters have demonstrated that Pabay is no place for the faint-hearted. Alastair's wife Clarice (Peggy) felt 'imprisoned' there, and after three years the couple began their evacuation to mainland Skye by buying Corry Lodge estate – around 80 acres of land that had once been the farm of which in the early Victorian era Pabay had been an appendage – for grazing cattle. Quite unexpectedly, however, Peggy collapsed and died – on Pabay – after a heart attack. As with Len's island dance with death a quarter of a century earlier, the tragedy hastened another family's departure.

Interest, once Pabay had been put on the market, was even more intense than in 1979. The media this time focused on the fact that Pabay now was inhabited by two unmarried brothers, and the differential between property prices in London, and on Skye. In the former a garage could cost £250,000; Pabay was advertised for £150,000, much the same as Michael Philip had paid for it eight years earlier. Interest though doesn't always equate with serious intent – as Len had found out in the later 1960s. To discourage time-wasters – it was claimed there were 1,700 enquiries – the Philips charged £50 to take more serious viewers across to Pabay for a look. Within three months they had a worthwhile offer – of well over the £270,000 being asked for Corry and Pabay combined. Michael Philip now turned westwards and purchased the estate of Inversanda, Ardgour, Argyll.

We know that Pabay's spell was powerful, its fertile appearance from spring through to autumn an enticement for the unwary. It was early in the year when David Harris, a successful building contractor, and his wife Mary, from Hertfordshire in the south of England, had come to inspect Pabay. Something of an impulse buy, they were clearly not the first southerners to have felt an affinity with the recumbent emerald jewel in Broadford Bay; like Margaret Whatley in 1949, they had seen few weeds, and felt positive about what could be done with the island. And like Len and Margaret, they had little or no inkling of what David calls the 'logistics' of island living; the instances he cites are getting a pint of milk (straightforward enough in Farnham, Hertfordshire but not so easy on an island without a cow), or – rather more difficult – moving a large quantity of diesel across, let alone greater amounts of essential materials.[12]

Whilst for a time they carried on with the Gotland sheep, these were subsequently shipped to their farm at Corry. Unlike some of their predecessors, however, the Harrises weren't constrained by the need to make Pabay pay its way.

Their enthusiasm was trees, and their intention was to turn Pabay into something of an Inner Hebridean arboretum. Over two seasons 10,000 were planted. But conscious of what Pabay had once been – 'full of woods' – the Harrises have planted only species known to flourish in the west of Scotland: oak, ash, holly, willow and Scots pine. The downside of this commendable effort to work with history and the natural environment is that most of the cultivable ground, upon which so much time and laborious effort had been expended by three families over the near half-century since Len Whatley planted his first potatoes in 1950, along with the pasture land that had fed the island's livestock, was ploughed up and made ready for tree planting. But the Harrises' predecessors' endeavour wasn't wasted: the nitrogen and nutrients from the several hundreds of tons of lime and other fertilisers that had been laboriously spread and ploughed in over the decades gave the saplings a head start.

Although David Harris is hardly a frequent visitor to his island, in conversation with him the depth of his attachment to Pabay becomes apparent. He is still as excited about arriving on Pabay as he was on that spring day twenty-eight years ago. During even relatively short stays he has (like many of his predecessors) become aware of the way light changes by the hour, and even more so the weather – slight shifts in the direction and strength of the wind. He soon understood the advantages of a flat-bottomed boat, the only way of overcoming the 18-foot tide that otherwise cuts off the island's people for several hours each day owing to low water at the jetty. But even with such a versatile craft he has learned that it is still the sea that largely governs when he can cross to or from Broadford, and when it is best to wait.

Just like Hugh Miller, Thomas Ratcliffe Bartlett – and Len Whatley – he has become mesmerised by the place, using terms like 'magical' and 'special' to describe his feelings, while explaining too, to paraphrase his own words, that he has found on Pabay things about life that remain undiscovered elsewhere.

To his credit, Harris seems aware that he's standing on the shoulders of those who have gone before, and by exploiting what's useful from the modern world, above all money made elsewhere, has connected with and reinforced some of what's there.

He's had Len's pre-fab bungalow pulled down and replaced by a strikingly modern, two storey house – which took an incredibly short four months to put up; it had taken Len – often working on his own – three years to build the bungalow. But the contemporary house is built on Len's foundations. Harris's introduction of solar panels is innovative, but the wind-powered generator that with solar power now produces three kilowatts of electricity represents a more efficient and effective fuel-saving return than what Len put in in the early 1950s: the 24-volt Freelight. The farm steading – the barn, bothy and yard as originally built for Sir Donald Currie well over a century ago – has been renovated and upgraded instead of being removed. Pabay stamps are still being designed and sold. Geologists continue to visit, although one hopes when they leave they won't be laden with the fossil-heavy bags their predecesors delighted in taking away.

* * *

There isn't any livestock on the island. No cattle graze there now; a tradition dating back 500 years at least has ended. Nor do sheep, let alone the pigs, geese, ducks and hens that Len Whatley introduced with such optimism in the 1950s, when the island was alive with the sound of their respective calls.

Pabay's purpose now is fundamentally different from what it has been for centuries. No longer a place to make a living, albeit one that for long periods was barely above subsistence level, on Pabay what human life there is – and that sporadically – depends on livings made elsewhere. Government assistance aimed at increasing national food production allied to what was literally back-breaking hard work sustained the Whatley family during the 1950s and 1960s. State priorities, however, have shifted: big farming has marginalised marginal farms, and people with the tenacity and toughness of Len and Margaret or those who came after them are few and far between. With the recognition by Government that trees and wood are a vital resource, tree planting attracts Forestry Commission grants and Woodland Trust assistance, while various payments are available for managing existing woodland.

Nigel Smith, Ted Gerrard's stepson, who was employed by the Harrises for five years during the 1990s – and who did much of the tree planting – has watched as the consequences of such radical changes in land use have materialised. Even the composition of the island's wildlife is changing. Nick Henson's comprehensive list of the fifty-nine winter birds he had spotted early in 1956 no longer applies; geese, lapwings and skylarks – whose short, sharp whistling sounds were the aural backdrop to a fine Pabay summer – have disappeared.

But so too, remarkably, have the rabbits. In the woodland's nursery phase, the Harris children were put to work weeding between the trees, and Nigel Smith used an industrial strimmer to keep the thistles and other unwanted foliage down. However, without cattle and sheep to keep them short, grasses, rushes and other weeds have created an environment sufficiently uncongenial even for Pabay's hardy rabbits. Viral haemorrhagic disease – a rabbit killer that reached Scotland in 1995 – played its part too, although on Soay, to the south of Skye, the rabbit cull has been attributed to the infiltration of mink.[13] Even in determining the causes of common animals' decline, islands differ. Otters, always resident on Pabay in the past but rarely seen, are now there in large numbers.

Scalpay also has lost its rabbit population, although their role as island pests has been assumed by voles. As with Pabay, Scalpay's cattle have been disposed of, while the Walfords have retained only a small flock of sheep. The buildings associated with the once-thriving home farm and splendid walled garden now house deteriorating boat hulls, an array of rusting farm machinery and equipment and, in one store, a ghoulish collection of stags' antlers. Michael Walford raises from seed much of the stock of trees he is currently engaged in planting out, as well as managing the garden – but on his own, with the assistance of a single full-time farm manager supplemented as the need arises by part-time workers mainly from overseas. In short, the Scalpay estate, once the pride and joy of Sir Donald Currie, is running down, with little sign in the foreseeable future of a return to the thriving condition in which he and his successor Sir Henry Bell sought to put it, let alone when it was home to almost a hundred people.

Last year Stuart and I, with one of his sons, Richard, returned to Pabay – in my case after an absence of fifty years.

When we were in our early teens we could walk round the island comfortably in little under an hour and a half. This time we struggled for the best part of four hours through rough, boot-dragging grass, rushes and heather to make it back to the jetty where we were being picked up in the fast RIB that would return us to Kyleakin. And that was hurrying, slipping and stumbling as we detoured along the rock-strewn shore. The rabbit-, cattle- and sheep-clipped clifftop paths we once skimmed over are heavily overgrown. Even the Norsemen would struggle now to get far onto the island, but anyway they'd have no need to, with not a sign left of the productive land that had attracted them as they sailed through the Sound.

We saw the improvements to the housing stock effected by the island's owners since Len and Margaret left; more, bigger and well-finished. We were impressed by how spick and span the farm buildings are. But at the same time, it felt strangely disconcerting being in a farmyard into which we had once helped herd loudly protesting, liberally defecating cattle and sheep, or nervously nudged the bull into his pen, and watched as Len and Margaret chased, caught and broke the necks of hens before proceeding to strip them of their feathers. It has become a polished showpiece, with the uneven cobbles of the yard laid in the 1890s having been replaced by a smooth, tiled surface. The barn doors had obviously been renewed too and looked in A1 condition. But inside there was no trace of the starlings we'd once spent hours shooting – as pests – from the rafters, or the great, golden, warm-centred bales of hay that had been stored there and upon which we clambered and hid, or of the workbench and array of tools Len had used to saw, drill, make and repair, and where we'd fashioned our crude toy wooden boats. The whole place was eerily silent and almost antiseptically free of farmyard smells.

It is as if those human beings who inhabited, laboured and sometimes prayed on Pabay over the centuries were a mirage. On the south side, the chapel remains that were to be seen until relatively recently are now hard to find. Just about visible are what's left of the walls of one of the cottages that formed the settlement that was deserted following the potato famine; the ridges of the lazy beds have disappeared under the unchecked growth of the last three decades.

Signs that Len and Margaret toiled there for the best part of two decades are fast disappearing. The fate of the land Len brought back into use and cultivated we know about. A few squint posts and some dangling strands of wire are all that are left of the fencing operations he spent so long on during the early 1950s. The upturned section of the hull of the *Coruisk* that was used as a henhouse is still standing, just. The hard-packed earthen floor remains, but the chickens are long gone. The hulls of a couple of his wrecked boats that were still to be seen on the south-eastern shore in the 1980s – including the former lifeboat he restored in the mid-1960s – have now been swept off to their sea grave. Wild yellow flag irises that flourish on Pabay, as elsewhere in the Western Isles, watch over the spread-eagled

remains of the hull of Len's beloved varnished launch, the *Pelagius*.
Lying just above the water line near the jetty where she once proudly
floated, the dismembered timbers are no longer able to bear the
weight of the Kelvin engine that has broken from its mounting.
Rusted, but still identifiable, it lies heavy amongst the sea- and rain-
washed debris of what was once the very best of boats, a symbol of
the beautiful things men can build, but of their fragility too in
exposed locations like Pabay's.

What endures are the rocks, and the fossils – which, just as we had
done as boys, we delighted in spotting, picking up and pocketing. It
is ironic that creatures that swam in Pabay's warmer waters many
millions of years ago have left a more secure mark than those human
beings who have been there during the last couple of centuries.

Without either animal husbandry or people on it, the former
links between Pabay and the community on mainland Skye too are
being weakened.

Local connections are no longer being sustained, other than
temporarily, when tradesmen or the boat across might be required.
The services offered by the vet, doctors or the schools are redundant. It is largely indirectly, in the shape of local employment and
the multiplier effects of the wages generated from time to time by
the Harrises' needs, that Pabay now feeds the local economy.

In these respects, Pabay has shared the fate of so many other small
Scottish islands. The number of Scotland's inhabited islands fell by
more than half between 1861 and 2011, but it was those with the
smaller populations – of less than fifty people – where the losses have
been most severe.[14] Perhaps the most vividly remembered of these
departures happened on St Kilda, whose people left – at their own
request – in 1930. The process by which formerly thickly populated
smaller islands were deserted, however, began long before this and
continues to the present. In 1841, the island of Isay I can see from
Stein housed fifteen families in 'considerable comfort', and had its
own general store. A decade later they had gone; the street of cottages,
which still stand in remarkably good order, albeit roofless, is now
heavily overgrown. Sheep aren't even being taken over for summer
grazing, nor are they on the Ascrib islands, the narrow rocky chain
off the opposite edge of Waternish peninsula.

North Rona, the most northerly of the Western Isles, was emptied of its last people in 1884; Mingulay, which lies south of Barra, in 1912; Cora, off Gigha at the southern end of the Inner Hebrides, in the 1940s, shortly before the Monachs, a group of islands to the west of North Uist, the last residents of which left in 1948.[15] And despite the access provided by Calum MacLeod's hand-built road in the north of Raasay, the adjoining island of Eilean Fladday was abandoned in the 1970s.

The pattern of population decline and the disappearance of livestock seems set, although there have been periods of remission like that witnessed by Anne Cholawo on Soay before it suffered Pabay's fate: virtual abandonment as people who had long been the island's mainstay either died or gave up, in 1951 petitioning the government to be relocated, which they were, to Mull.[16] This final flurry of endeavour was in the second half of the twentieth century – the main focus of this book – when, like Soay, Pabay as a people-supporting island not only held on but flourished and enriched immeasurably the inner lives of those fortunate enough to have been involved. Even this qualitative reward, however, has less allure nowadays than was once the case; younger people are rarely prepared to tolerate the privations of relative isolation or take on the challenges that against the odds their mothers and fathers and grandparents rose to. They want – and need – more than islands can offer.

Though not everywhere. There are exceptions, like Muck, one of the four Small Isles to the south of Skye. Muck is slightly bigger than Pabay and more productive. Substantial government investment in the harbour, reasonably reliable transport links (a vital precondition of island viability) and a determined and mutually supportive community that hasn't quite fallen below the optimum number required to be sustainable have combined not only to stem but to turn the tide of depopulation. Community ownership – as for example on Gigha and Eigg, can have a regenerative impact too.[17] But by and large it is Scotland's larger islands – Orkney, Shetland, Mull, Arran and Skye, with populations that have reached critical mass levels, that have done best.[18]

The harsh realities of trying, not to tame nature – that's futile – but to work with nature in more unforgiving environments can

test even the most enthusiastic and physically able small island
dwellers beyond endurance. Self-sufficiency is an admirable aim,
but on an island like Pabay, impossible to attain, or it has been
hitherto. Island living, as we've seen, is expensive, and fraught with
difficulties beyond the comprehension of Britain's increasingly
urbanised population (only 2 per cent of Scotland's inhabitants are
island-dwellers). Over 75 per cent of Scotland's people were town-
dwellers in 2001; the drift away from the countryside has not only
been rapid but is also more marked in Scotland than anywhere else
in Western Europe, other than in England.[19] Earned incomes from
the traditional sources of farming and fishing are invariably insufficient to balance household budgets, let alone satisfy twenty-first-
century lifestyle aspirations. Wi-Fi connects (in some locations)
but doesn't quite overcome the gulf the way bridges, causeways
and timetabled ferries do.

Consequently, ownership of many of Scotland's most desirable
islands has become the privilege of those with surplus capital to
invest, and who seek not to subsist on them, but rather to gain the
less tangible rewards of island ownership that include having a
unique holiday getaway, and to avoid wintering there.

Across the smaller islands of Skye and much of the Hebrides,
therefore, the tragic procession of leavings goes on.

Epilogue

Three families have lived on and tried to make a living from Pabay over the past seventy years. Eventually, they've left, exhausted, but not defeated. Richer for their experiences, and no poorer materially than when they arrived. Pabay hasn't been the end, but a stepping stone to something else: for the Gerrards, a voyage to and life on Madeira before returning to live in Broadford; for the Philips, Inversanda estate, although Rod and Linda, his wife, went off to Banffshire, as a builder and architect respectively.

Sometimes, however, that something else has happened on Skye. In this sense, Pabay has left a legacy that would have pleased those politicians and policy-makers who, like Thomas Johnston, sought to stem the outflow of people from the Highlands and Islands and create a sustainable economic and social environment free from the poverty and distress that had blighted so much of Skye's history in the nineteenth and early twentieth centuries.

Len's and Margaret's eldest son Stuart not only succeeded his father at Edinbane Pottery, but has built it up to become one of Skye's leading craft outlets. Open all year round, it has become a magnet for visitors to Skye, particularly during sequences of rainy days, when business booms. If ever Skye were to become independent, the pots that he posts off to customers elsewhere in the UK and overseas would make a healthy contribution to the island's balance of payments.

Over what is now almost half a century, Stuart has continually employed one or more assistants (there were five at one time) and trained apprentice potters, some of whom have set up elsewhere on Skye or in the Highland region – and further afield.[1] Specialising in wood-fired and salt-glazed stoneware, his stature in Scottish potting circles is such that he became a frequent demonstrator and exhibitor at Scottish Potters Association conventions. His wife Julie's paintings – along with those of his son Len – are to be seen in galleries on Skye and elsewhere. Two of his younger sons, Brian and Richard, are still on Skye, both in the building trade, with impressive reputations for the quality of their work. Benefiting from his father's familiarity with boats and the love of the sea that owes its origins to Pabay, Christopher, Stuart and Julie's youngest son, has begun to make a living as a sailing instructor.

Donald Maclachlan, the research scientist and boat-builder who appeared on Pabay out of the blue with his young artist wife Judith in 1965, and then helped ease Len and Margaret's move to Edinbane, also stayed on Skye. Judy's artwork attracted critical acclaim, and buyers, and she eventually opened a gallery at Camus Lusta, near Stein, where the couple settled after Edinbane.

For Don, boat design was relegated to second place when, in 1971, after learning of a gap in the market that intrigued him, he began to manufacture (at the couple's home, in Stein) electronic pressure-measuring equipment – transducers – for research engineers. So swift was the uptake that with the help of G.V. Planer, his former employer, he formed Gaeltec Ltd. The Highlands and Islands Development Board too provided assistance, so that by 1974 he was able to employ additional staff – who moved into a custom-built workshop in Dunvegan in 1977. By the mid-1980s the company was providing employment for twenty-seven people, including science and software engineering graduates – for whom work opportunities were all too rare on Skye – and winning awards for its success in export markets. By the following decade Gaeltec's miniature catheter tip pressure transducers were being used mainly by clinicians to investigate and treat a variety of ailments, and being sold worldwide.

Although Donald died suddenly in 2007, Gaeltec is still thriving.[2] His son Donald is still on Skye and through his business, DLM Stonecraft, has established himself as one of the island's leading stone masons. It was Donald who restored the internal stone walls of my house at Stein, and who has rebuilt part of the garden wall.

After Edinbane, Alex Welford, who experienced a 'personal revolution ... catalysed by the Whatley family's practice of self-determination and independence, and their background of pacifism and socialism', found himself on Raasay, assisting his then partner Lyn Rowe in setting up the Outdoor Centre there. Although their relationship failed, after an interlude teaching English in Germany (where his new partner and future wife, Assi, a potter working at Edinbane, came from), Alex drew on some of the seafaring experience and resourcefulness he had acquired on Pabay to set up Bow & Stern, initially a one-man business selling and servicing marine equipment. Hard going for the first years of the 1990s, the business survived, and he was able to exploit the demands created by the nascent fish farming industry, not only on Skye but from farms in the Western Isles and mainland sea lochs.

He developed a relationship with Malakoff & Moore in Orkney, makers of Voe Boats – aluminium workboats – not only selling but also fitting the craft with Bow & Stern's engines, and subsequently servicing them. A neat twist in this account is that he supplied David Harris with a boat which, with his knowledge of what could be a rough and wet crossing to Pabay, he had advised should be fitted with a small cabin or cuddy near the bow. Twenty-five years on David Harris not only still uses the boat, but loves it. Bow & Stern too continues to trade, although in new hands, Alex having sold up in 2004 – the multi-national nature of the fish farming business making it less likely to use the services of local suppliers.[3]

As a lad, Ted Gerrard's stepson, Nigel Smith, was struck by the clarity of the water around Pabay as he was taken across to school in Broadford.[4] Helping his parents harvest seaweed and pick winkles had fostered his fascination with the maritime environment. After leaving school, it was in this that he worked initially, farming oysters in Scalpay Sound, for instance, until effluent from a nearby salmon farm forced him to give up. Some years later, on holiday with his wife Moira in the south of France, he took a trip in a glass-bottomed boat. Although the water there was murky, Nigel recognised that with such a craft he could share with visitors the sea life that flourished in the clearer waters around the Kyle of Lochalsh (although he also considered Loch Ness).

In 1998, after two years of preparation that included raising (with difficulty) the requisite capital of £140,000, working with Alistair Salmon to design the UK's first boat with underwater windows, and Sandy Morrison to build it, and battling with the Maritime and Coastguard agency for a safety certificate, he launched *Seaprobe Atlantis*.⁵ Such has been the success of the venture that Smith was able to commission a larger boat that accommodates fifty-five passengers; he has now been in business for twenty years.

*   *   *

This book owes its existence to my Aunt Margaret, and it is right that it should end with her. With Len's death, she was now the sole parent – and support – for her children, who were still at Edinbane: Alison, Michael and Tony. With the pressure this created on one hand and rebounding from the death of the husband she had known from her early teens on the other, she became something of a merry widow.

Exuding positivity and having rediscovered the high spirits that had endeared her to so many visitors to Pabay, she became a familiar face at ceilidhs that at the time were a feature of the social life of north-west Skye. And met Charles (Charlie) Mackinnon, a native of Waternish, who had spent much of his life at sea before returning to his family's croft and, in the evenings, working as a part-time barman. In December 1979, they married. Margaret, the incomer from the south who had felt apprehensive amongst the Gaelic-speaking revellers on the crossing to Skye in the winter of 1949 had, at the age of fifty-one, integrated to the point that not only had she married a Gael, but also one who could be overtly anti-Sassenach. He was happy, however, with her interest in and enthusiastic support for Gaelic music, made manifest in their regular attendance at the Mòd, the peripatetic annual festival of Gaelic song, dance, literature and culture.

By May 1980 Margaret and Charlie had turned Edinbane Lodge into a thriving hotel, bar and restaurant, and built a new extension which for several years was north Skye's premier venue for traditional music and dancing.[6] Committing themselves from the outset to all-day opening that began with breakfast for guests – and with diners able to stay until after one in the morning, for them seven years was enough, and the couple sold up in 1987.

This was the catalyst for their move to Waternish. Charlie ran the croft while Margaret returned to the craft work she had begun on Pabay. Soon, even while living in the caravan that was her temporary home before the couple were able to inhabit the croft house, she set up Dunhallin Crafts and became a leading light in the Skye and Lochalsh Arts and Crafts Association. She was one of a number of representatives of Skye's voluntary organisations – in her case Help the Aged – who was presented to the Queen and the Duke of Edinburgh on their Golden Jubilee tour of Scotland in 2002. By now thoroughly immersed in the life and society of north-west Skye, she devoted her organisational skills to the Duirinish and Bracadale Agricultural Association's annual Dunvegan show. With her forthright attitude, and ability to drive a hard bargain, she was able to attract a range of sponsors, and relished handing out the prizes. Her name lives on, in the shape of the Margaret Mackinnon Memorial Cup, which is awarded at the show in Dunvegan for the best horse, sheep or cow.

Margaret passed away after a lengthy illness on Christmas Eve in 2005. It was appropriate that this was in Edinbane's Gesto Hospital, the Friends group of which she had been a founder member. Her funeral, four days after Christmas, was one she'd have enjoyed picking over, in her roguish way.

In Dunvegan's bleak, chilly, faintly damp-reeking parish church, mourners – close family and friends but also acquaintances and admirers drawn from the community she'd become part of – endured the admonitions of a Presbyterian minister who ill-advisedly and perhaps due to his unfamiliarity with her, said too little about Margaret and too much about sin.

The procession to and proceedings at the exposed and shelter-less graveyard at Trumpan followed the traditional Skye form.

On a day of biting cold wind, accompanied by unrelenting sheets of rain thrashing in off the sea, her coffin was slowly and sombrely borne by black-coated pall-bearers to the graveside, where family members were called on by name and in order of precedence to take one of the eight cords with which she would be lowered into the ground of her adopted island.

It was only back in Stein Inn, where the funeral party gathered, that warmth was restored to our chilled bodies through the sharing of fond memories of a wonderful woman.

A well-known figure on Skye, with strong views, some of them unpalatable, Charlie Mackinnon was not everyone's idea of the considerate husband. To his credit, however, he had found the most fitting burial plot in Trumpan graveyard for his late wife. Margaret's substantial, polished black marble headstone stands tall on an elevated spot in the graveyard. Nothing blocks it from the broad sweep of the open sea lying between Waternish Point and Dunvegan Head, and across to the islands of the Outer Hebrides. It is in its way an apt location, silent but eloquent testimony to the end of a journey that had begun in the dislocation of the Second World War in the English Midlands.

But it is on Pabay, where, in the hearts and minds of those who knew her and are still with us, she brought joyfulness to our lives, and still belongs.

Acknowledgements

B ooks like this cannot be written without the generous assistance of many people. I am not simply being courteous by mentioning them. Although their contributions have taken many forms, each in its own way has been important, and deserves recognition.

Alison Beaton, Skye and Lochalsh Archive Centre, Portree, has not only been a model archivist – friendly, efficient and resourceful during all of my visits – but has also provided me with pointers about other people who she felt might be able to help. Sue Geale, Museum Manager, Museum of the Isles, Clan Donald Centre, Armadale has, despite the multiple demands of her role, gone out of her way to find relevant source material. Thanks are due too to her colleague Sarah Addison. Other archivists and librarians who have gone that extra mile on my behalf are Caroline Brown, University of Dundee; Caroline Lam of the Geological Society's Library, London; Claire Daniel, Sam Maddra and Katie McDonald, University of Glasgow Archive Services; Claire Sillick and Robin Urquhart of the National Records of Scotland; Catriona Foote, Special Collections, University of St Andrews Library; and Neil Hooper of the James MacLaren Society.

For assisting with some of the images I wish to thank Peter Best; David H. Caldwell; Simon Larson, photographer, Isle of Skye; Jessica Burdge, Collections Curator, Museums Collections Unit, University of St Andrews; Sharon Kelly and Jan Merchant of Dundee University Archives (who between them digitised most of the black and white photographs); Laura Lloberas, National Galleries of Scotland; Maggie Wilson, National Museums of Scotland; and Allen Linning and family. Staff in institutions such as the National Library of Scotland and the Highland Archive Centre in Inverness have dealt with my enquiries and, where they could, supplied me with relevant material.

A growth area in recent years has been the interest in genealogy. Researching family history demands a certain specialist knowledge, and I am fortunate to have been able to call on the consummate skills of both Sylvia Valentine and Kirsty Wilkinson (of the research service My Ain Folk). Sylvia also worked on the sasines for me; a vital contribution.

The nature of this book is such that I have had to delve into unfamiliar subjects and disciplines. On archaeology and Scotland's first settlers I have benefited from the advice of Professor Caroline Wickham-Jones. Professor Rob Duck of the University of Dundee has guided me through the early days of the Scottish geologists, and kindly read and commented on relevant sections of this book. Dr Michael Taylor, University of Leicester and the National Museum of Scotland, has also improved my understanding of nineteenth-century geology and the contributions of Hugh Miller and Sir Archibald Geikie, and has been generous in sharing his research and writing with me. Professor Christopher Smout has done the same in relation to climate change and the environment. Catriona MacDonald of the University of Glasgow, whose family roots are in Harris and North Uist, has been a constant source of encouragement, as well as of suggestions of books I should read – including those of a more literary and even lyrical nature; their influence has fed back into my text.

This book has been written from a more personal perspective than I have been used to; for her gentle but firm guidance on how best to do this, I am grateful to Fiona Watson. Annie Tindley, University of Newcastle and Scotland's Land Futures, has been enthusiastic from the start, as has Andrew Mackillop of the University of Glasgow. In the early stages I learned much from Madelaine Bunting about how to blend personal and contemporary observations with historical narrative. Kirsty Gunn has also offered advice and, above all, encouragement and a belief that I could write this kind of book. Dawn Mullady read and commented on some chapters at draft stage, from a non-specialist perspective.

My wife Patricia has read drafts and spotted slips and infelicities, as well as performing the invaluable service of introducing me to Sylvia Valentine, her PhD student.

A pleasure – and unexpected bonus – in writing a book like this has been the opportunity to meet and speak with people who have been involved with Pabay, both directly and indirectly, and through members of their family. Descendants of Sir Donald Currie, onetime owner of Pabay (through his possession of Scalpay estate) include Fiona Lorimer, a granddaughter; Alastair J. Riddell; and Robert Molteno, the family's historian, who was kind enough to read my chapters on the Currie years. Mary Jeffrey-Jones, great granddaughter of Currie's successor, Sir Henry Bell, allowed me to see her mother's recollections of her grandfather, and has permitted me to use some of her pictures of Scalpay from the 1920s. Her brother-in-law, Professor Ian Robert Manners, of the University of Texas, Austin, shared with me his notes on Sir Henry Bell's background, and also read and commented on my draft chapter on Bell. Frederick Muntz, grandson of Captain Gerald Muntz, Pabay's owner during the 1930s and until 1947, was able to supply me with copies of letters in his possession, and shared his early reminiscences of Pabay. The present proprietors of Scalpay, Michael and Veronica Walford invited me across to see them, Scalpay House and the adjoining grounds. Nick Broughton, in Breakish, long-time farm manager on Scalpay, took me over, put me in touch with Pabay's more recent owners and has given me access to his photographic collection. Anne and Ted Gerrard talked with me about their time on Pabay, as did Rod and Linda Philip (who also provided photographs), Rod having lived and worked on Pabay during the 1980s. I have been fortunate enough to speak too with David Harris, Pabay's present owner – who's had the island for longer than anyone since the lords Macdonald. I have had immensely enjoyable conversations with locals who have observed Pabay and its people both close up and from afar over the decades, including knowledgeable characters like Neil Mackinnon of Heaste. Nigel Smith, formerly of Pabay, proprietor of *Seaprobe Atlantis*, shared his thoughts and arranged to take me across to the island. David Wyatt remembered some of the boat names I'd forgotten.

Doing research for a book in which my own family features has presented new challenges but also created the opportunity to reflect on the past and share long-forgotten memories, even if these were sometimes vague and occasionally contested. My cousin Anthea has been a passionate ally of the project and has provided all sorts of material, including her own notes and some pictures. Her brother Stuart, proprietor of Edinbane Pottery, has also been helpful throughout, as a source of information and pictures, as well as being a touchstone on matters such as boats, rabbits and pottery. My four other cousins, Rachel, Alison, Michael and Tony have all played their part, as has Michael's wife Carole. Allan Whatley, their uncle and my late father, was an assiduous collector of letters, diaries, photographs and ephemera of all kinds; this and his typewritten notes on the family's history have been hugely helpful. In the Notes section this material has been classified as the Whatley Collection. I have benefited enormously too from the accounts, notes, and insights of family friends: Dorothy Harrop, Judith Maclachlan, Alex Welford, Stan 'Robby' Robinson, and others – not least Fiona Davis, George Jolly's daughter.

Helen Bleck has been an assiduous editor, while Andrew Simmons and his colleagues at Birlinn have managed the book production process with consummate skill. Last but not least I should thank Hugh Andrew and his fellow directors for the faith they have had in this project since it was first mooted; without their continued support, this book would not have been written, or published.

Notes

INTRODUCTION

1. See Michael Bartholomew, *In Search of H. V. Morton* (London, 2004).
2. William Donaldson, *The Jacobite Song: Political Myth and National Identity* (Aberdeen, 1988), 3–4.
3. Allan I. Macinnes, 'Jacobitism in Scotland: Episodic Cause or National Movement?', *Scottish Historical Review*, 86:2 (October 2007), 225–52; see too Murray Pittock, *Culloden* (Oxford, 2016).
4. Moray Watson, 'The Idea of Island in Gaelic Fiction', *The Bottle Imp*, 21 (2017), 1–7.
5. In conversation with David Harris, 25 May 2018.
6. *Illustrated London News*, 1 April 1976.
7. Mairi Hedderwick, 'Foreword', in Richard Clubley, *Scotland's Islands: A Special Kind of Freedom* (Edinburgh, 2014).
8. Daniel Maudlin, *The Highland House Transformed: Architecture and Identity on the Edge of Britain, 1700–1850* (Dundee, 2009), 26–43.
9. *Press & Journal*, 9 August 1963.
10. J.A. MacCulloch, *The Misty Isle of Skye: Its Scenery, Its People, Its Story* (Stirling, 1936 ed.), xi.
11. Charles Jedrej and Mark Nuttall, *White Settlers: The Impact of Rural Repopulation in Scotland* (London, 1996), 9–28.
12. Murray Watson, *Being English in Scotland* (Edinburgh, 2003), 28.
13. H.V. Morton, *In Search of Scotland* (London, 1929; 1930 ed.), 206.
14. *Express and Star*, 26 January 1965.
15. *West Highland Free Press*, 29 September 2017.
16. Ronald Black (ed.), *An Lasair: Anthology of 18th Century Scottish Gaelic Verse* (Edinburgh, 2001), 367–71.
17. Alexander R. Forbes, *Place-names of Skye and Adjacent Islands* (Paisley, 1923), 12–13.
18. Scotland's Places, Ordnance Survey Name Books, Inverness-shire, 1876–8, Vol. 11, OS1/16/11/40.
19. See, for example, Ian Armit, *The Archaeology of Skye and the Western Isles* (Edinburgh, 1996).
20. Allan Kennedy, *Governing Gaeldom: The Scottish Highlands and the Restoration State, 1660–1688* (Leiden, 2014), 4–5.
21. Highland Council Archives, Inverness, CH2/622/1, Strath Kirk Session Minutes, 1886–95, 4 March 1887.
22. Donald D. MacKinnon, *Memoirs of Clan Fingon* (Tunbridge Wells, 1899), 18.

23. The maps referred to here are all available online, and held by the National Library of Scotland (http://maps.nls.uk/).

CHAPTER 1

1. Patrick Barkham, *Islander: A Journey Around our Archipelago* (London, 2017), 9.
2. Michael Robson, *St Kilda: Church, Visitors and 'Natives'* (Isle of Lewis, 2005), 176–8.
3. Adam Nicolson, *Sea Room: An Island Life* (London, 2002), 3.
4. Youssef Mezrigui, 'The Shangri-la Society in D.H. Lawrence's *The Man Who Loved Islands*', *International Journal of Language and Literature*, 4, 1 (June 2016), 250–3.
5. *Sunday Telegraph*, 30 July 1967.
6. *The Scotsman*, 16 April 1927.
7. Allan I. Macinnes, *Clanship, Commerce and the House of Stuart, 1603–1788* (East Linton, 1996), 59.
8. Michael Lynch, *Scotland: A New History* (London, 1991), 167.
9. National Records of Scotland [NRS], Register of Deeds, RD4/1771/1, f.294, Minute of Sale, 1751.
10. 'Sgiathanach', 'Lachlan Mackinnon or 'Lachlan Mac Thearlaich Oig', the Skye Bard', *The Celtic Magazine*, 3 (January 1876), 91–4.
11. All of this information is derived from extracts from birth and marriage records held by Scotland's People. I am grateful to Sylvia Valentine for finding this material on my behalf.
12. Whatley Collection [WC], Henry Hilditch [HH] to Herbert Whatley [HW], 23 March 1952.
13. Roger Hutchinson, *A Waxing Moon: The Modern Gaelic Revival* (Edinburgh and London, 2005), 21.
14. Roger Hutchinson, *Calum's Road* (Edinburgh, 2008).
15. See R. Andrew McDonald, 'The Galley-Castles and the Norse-Gaelic Seaways: Movement, Mobility and Maritime Connectivity in Medieval Atlantic Scotland, *c.* 1000–1500', in Paula Martin (ed.), *Castles and Galleys: A Reassessment of the Historic Galley-Castles of the Norse–Gaelic Seaways* (Isle of Lewis, 2017), 8–15.
16. Neil Oliver, *Vikings: A History* (London, 2012), 132.
17. R. Andrew Macdonald, *The Kingdom of the Isles: Scotland's Western Seaboard, c. 1100–c. 1336* (East Linton, 1997), 253.
18. MacKinnon, *Memoirs of Clan Fingon*, 19–20.
19. Donald McWhannell, 'Sailing-Times in the Norse–Gaelic Seaways', in Martin (ed.), *Castles and Galleys*, 44.
20. McDonald, 'Galley-Castles', 19.
21. <http://en.wikipedia.org/wiki/Rubha_an_Dùnain> (accessed 20 July 2017); *West Highland Free Press*, 1 December 2017; see too <www.macaskillsociety.org> (accessed November 2018).
22. NRS, GD362/1, 'Journal of Skye by JB, 1799'.
23. W.H. Murray, *The Islands of Western Scotland: The Inner and Outer Hebrides* (London, 1973), 141–2.
24. McWhannell, 'Sailing-Times', 50.
25. Barbara E. Crawford, *Scandinavian Scotland* (Leicester, 1987), 11–26.

26. See Alan Macniven, 'The Ruins of Danish Forts? Exploring the Scandinavian Heritage of Hebridean Galley-Castles', in Martin (ed.), *Castles and Galleys*, 59–92.
27. The Papar Project (2005), 'The Hebrides', <http://www.paparproject.org.uk/hebrides5.html> (accessed 31 July 2016).
28. John MacCulloch, *The Highlands and Western Isles of Scotland . . . in Letters to Sir Walter Scott, Bart* (London, 1824, 4 vols), 3, 405.
29. Isobel Macdonald, *A Family in Skye* (n.d., typed copy, Highland Archive Centre, Inverness), 20–1.
30. H.V. Morton, *In Search of Scotland* (London, 1929; 1930 ed.), 220.
31. Donald Gillies (ed.), *Annals of Skye, 1939–40* (Nethy Bridge, n.d.), 13 April, 6 May 1940.
32. *The Scotsman*, 16 April 1927.
33. Herman Moll, 'The north part of Great Britain called Scotland' (1714).
34. Martin Martin, *Description of the Western Isles of Scotland circa 1695* (Edinburgh, 1999), 94.
35. MacCulloch, *Highlands and Western Isles*, 3, 406.
36. The Hon. Mrs Murray, *A Companion and Useful Guide to the Beauties in the Western Highlands of Scotland, and the Hebrides* (London, 2nd ed., 1805), 105.
37. MacCulloch, *Highlands and Western Isles*, 3, 404.

CHAPTER 2

1. Alan McKirdy, John Gordon and Roger Crofts, *Land of Mountain and Flood: The Geology and Landforms of Scotland* (Edinburgh, 2007), 163–97.
2. Richard Tipping, 'Living in the Past: Woods and People to 1000 BC', in T.C. Smout (ed.), *People and Woods in Scotland: A History* (Edinburgh, 2003), 22.
3. H.J.B. Birks, *Past and Present Vegetation of the Isle of Skye: A Palaeoecological Study* (Cambridge, 1973), 173.
4. T.C. Smout (ed.), *Scottish Woodland History* (Edinburgh, 1997), 5–6.
5. Tipping, 'Living in the Past', 27.
6. K. Hardy and C.R. Wickham-Jones, 'Scotland's First Settlers', *History Scotland* (Winter 2001), 22–7.
7. See K. Hardy and C. R. Wickham-Jones, 'Scotland's First Settlers: the Mesolithic seascape of the Inner Sound, Skye and its contribution to the early prehistory of Scotland', *Antiquity*, 76 (September 2002), 825–33; Skye and Lochalsh Archive Centre [SLAC], Martin Wildgoose to Jeff Harris, 21 October 1999.
8. See Robert A. Dodgshon, *No Stone Unturned: A History of Farming, Landscape and Environment in the Scottish Highlands and Islands* (Edinburgh, 2015), 8–10.
9. F.W.W. Green and R.J. Harding, 'Climate in the Inner Hebrides', in J. Morton Boyd (ed.), *Natural Environment of the Inner Hebrides* (Edinburgh, 1983), 132.
10. National Records of Scotland [NRS], GD362/1, Journal of Skye by JB, 1799.
11. Joan Blaeu, *Atlas of Scotland* (Amsterdam, 1664), 127, 133.
12. J.A. MacCulloch, *The Misty Isle of Skye: Its Scenery, Its People, Its Story* (Stirling, 1936 ed.), 102.

13. Colin Martin, 'Early Harbours and Landing-Places on Scotland's Western Seaboard', in Martin (ed.), *Castles and Galleys*, 118.

14. Allan I. Macinnes, *Clanship, Commerce and the House of Stuart, 1603–1788* (East Linton, 1996), 67.

15. Donald D. MacKinnon, *Memoirs of Clan Fingon* (Tunbridge Wells, 1888), 21–2.

16. Steve Murdoch, *The Terror of the Seas? Scottish Maritime Warfare, 1513–1713* (Leiden, 2010), 135–6.

17. Thomas Pennant, *A Tour in Scotland and Voyage to the Hebrides, 1771* (Edinburgh, 1992 ed.), 11.

18. A.M.W. Stirling, *Macdonald of the Isles: A Romance of the Past and Present* (London, 1914), 169.

19. University of Edinburgh, Centre for Research Collections, Robert Jameson Notebooks, 1373/4, Journal of a Tour Through the Hebrides, begin 22 May 1798, Part 2, 2, 4 August 1798.

20. Mairi Stewart, 'Using the Woods, 1600–1850 (1) The Community Resource', in Smout (ed.), *People and Woods*, 101–2.

21. Birks, *Past and Present Vegetation*, 174.

22. Brian Fagan, *The Little Ice Age* (New York, 2000), 48–9.

23. Karen Cullen, *Famine in Scotland: The 'Ill Years' of the 1690s* (Edinburgh, 2010), 49–53.

24. Syd House and Christopher Dingwall, '"A Nation of Planters": Introducing the New Trees, 1650–1900', in Smout (ed.), *People and Woods*, 139–42.

25. Alex Woolf, *From Pictland to Alba, 789–1070* (Edinburgh, 2007), 12–13; James E. Fraser, *From Caledonia to Pictland: Scotland to 795* (Edinburgh, 2009), 50; see too Peter G.B. Mitchell and Hector I. MacQueen (eds), *Atlas of Scottish History to 1707* (Edinburgh, 1996), 53–6.

26. Fraser, *Caledonia*, 115.

27. Barbara E. Crawford, *Scandinavian Scotland* (Leicester, 1987), 165.

28. Aidan MacDonald, 'The Papar and Some Problems: a Brief Review', in Barbara E. Crawford (ed.), *The Papar in the North Atlantic: Environment and History* (St Andrews, 2002), 20.

29. Crawford, *Scandinavian Scotland*, 164–7.

30. Ann MacSween, *Skye* (Edinburgh, 1990), 36.

31. Woolf, *Pictland*, 13.

32. Crawford, *Scandinavian Scotland*, 103.

33. Alan Macniven, 'What's in a Name? The Historical Significance of Norse Naming Strategies in the Isle of Islay', in Christian Cooijmans (ed.), *Traversing the Inner Seas* (Edinburgh, 2017), 38–45.

34. T. Ratcliffe Barnett, *Autumns in Skye, Ross & Sutherland* (Edinburgh and London, 1946 ed.), 90–1.

35. Whatley Collection [WC], Len Whatley to Allan and Evelyn Whatley, 31 December 1950.

36. William Wall, *The Islands* (Pittsburgh, 2017), 101.

37. T.S. Muir, *Ecclesiological Notes on Some of the Islands of Scotland* (Edinburgh, 1885), 37.

38. See *Royal Commission on the Ancient and Historical Monuments of Scotland: Ninth Report with Inventory of Monuments and Constructions in the Outer Hebrides, Skye and the Small Isles* (Edinburgh, 1928).

39. Alan Macquarrie, 'Early Christianity in Scotland: The Age of Saints', in Colin

MacLean and Kenneth Veitch (eds.), *Scottish Life and Society, A Compendium of Scottish Ethnology: Religion* (Edinburgh, 2006), 15–41.

40. Papar Project, 'The Hebrides'.
41. Alexander R. Forbes, *Place-names of Skye and Adjacent Islands* (Paisley, 1923), 263.
42. Fraser, *Caledonia*, 115.
43. Macdonald, *Kingdom of the Isles*, 17–19.
44. William Reeves, 'Saint Maelrubha: His History and Churches', *Proceedings of the Society of Antiquities of Scotland*, 3 (1857–9), 260.
45. Fraser, *Caledonia*, 205–6, 252–3.
46. Reeves, 'Saint Maelrubha', 290.
47. <http://www.applecrossheritage.org.uk/christian.html> (accessed 19 July 2017).
48. Rev. D.M. Lamont, *Strath: In Isle of Skye* (Glasgow, 1913), 38–9.
49. Ratcliffe Barnett, *Autumns in Skye*, 92–3.
50. Otta Swire, *Skye: The Island and its Legends* (Edinburgh, 2015 ed.), 6.
51. M. Lynch (ed.), *The Oxford Companion to Scottish History* (Oxford, 2001), 103.
52. Saint Adamnan, *Vita Sancti Columbae*, ed. William Reeves (Dublin, 1857), 138–9.
53. Derek Cooper, *Skye* (London, 1970), 57.
54. Fraser, *Caledonia*, 79.
55. Swire, *Skye*, 9–11.
56. Lizanne Henderson and Edward J. Cowan, *Scottish Fairy Belief* (East Linton, 2001), 21.
57. Crawford, *Scandinavian Scotland*, 43.
58. Lamont, *Strath*, 50–2.
59. Macinnes, *Clanship*, 65.
60. Quoted in I.F. Grant and Hugh Cheape, *Periods in Highland History* (London, 1987), 110–11.
61. Macinnes, *Clanship*, 68–9.
62. Michael Robson (ed.), *Curiosities of Arts and Nature: the new annotated and illustrated edition of Martin Martins' classic A Description of the Western Islands of Scotland* (Port of Ness, 2003), 132.
63. A.R.B. Haldane, *The Drove Roads of Scotland* (Newton Abbot, 1973 ed.), 70–1.
64. 'Sgiathanach', 'Lachlan Mackinnon', *The Celtic Magazine*, 3 (January 1876), 92.
65. Donald D. MacKinnon, *Memoirs of Clan Fingon* (Tunbridge Wells, 1888), 51.
66. NRS, GD374/129, Case for Opinion, Charles Mackinnon of Mackinnon, 1763; Answers for Sir James Macdonald and his Curators, defenders, to the Petition of Charles Mackinnon of Mackinnon, February 1763.
67. Macinnes, *Clanship*, 222.
68. Alexander Nicolson, *History of Skye* (Portree, 1930; 1995 ed.), 239; Stirling, *Macdonald*, 167.
69. James Macdonald, *General View of the Agriculture of the Hebrides, or Western Isles of Scotland* (Edinburgh, 1811), 752.
70. Hull History Centre, Bosville-Macdonald Family Papers, DDBM/27/3, Survey and Valuation of Lord Macdonald's Estate, 1800. I am indebted to Sue Geale for this reference.

71. Macdonald, *General View*, 22.
72. Clan Donald Centre, Armadale, Museum of the Isles [MI], GD221/1032, Sir John Murray to John Campbell, 25 August 1807.
73. *The Scotsman*, 6 December 1851.
74. John A. Love, *Rum: A Landscape Without Figures* (Edinburgh, 2001), 140.
75. Hugh Miller, *The Cruise of the Betsey* (Edinburgh, 1889 ed.), 143.
76. Papar Project, 'The Hebrides', 5–6.
77. Anna Ritchie, *Viking Age Scotland* (London, 1993), 35–7; Papar Project, 'The Hebrides', 5–6.
78. Woolf, *Pictland*, 52–7.
79. Crawford, *Scandinavian Scotland*, 40.
80. Aidan MacDonald, 'The *papar* and Some Problems: a brief Review', in Barbara E. Crawford (ed.), *The Papar in the North Atlantic: Environment and History* (St Andrews, 2002), 22.

Chapter 3

1. See Andrew Porter, *Victorian Shipping, Business and Imperial Policy: Donald Currie, the Castle Line and Southern Africa* (Woodbridge and New York, 1986).
2. Museum of the Isles [MI], Armadale, Macdonald Papers, GD 221/2840/12, John Robertson to A. Macdonald, 31 July 1884.
3. MI, GD221/2335/1–4, Letters to A. Macdonald, 4 July, 11, 13, 14 October 1881.
4. *The Scotsman*, 4 June 1894.
5. *New Statistical Account of Scotland*, Vol. 14 (Edinburgh 1834–45), 303.
6. SLAC, D293/1/2, Particulars of the Islands of Scalpay and Pabay in the Parish of Strath and County of Inverness, October 1922 (and 1894).
7. *The Scotsman*, 18 May 1893; Ewan Cameron, *Land for the People? The British Government and the Scottish Highlands, c. 1880–1925* (East Linton, 1996), 77.
8. *Inverness Courier*, 23 March 1894.
9. See Willie Orr, *Deer Forests, Landlords and Crofters: The Western Highlands in Victorian and Edwardian Times* (Edinburgh, 1982), 12–27.
10. Clifford Gulvin, *The Tweedmakers: A History of the Scottish Fancy Woollen Industry, 1600–1914* (Newton Abbot, 1973), 48.
11. J. Neville Bartlett, *Carpeting the Millions: The Growth of Britain's Carpet Industry* (Edinburgh, 1978), 54–60.
12. Orr, *Deer Forests*, 167.
13. See Eric Richards, *Patrick Sellar and the Highland Clearances* (Edinburgh, 1999).
14. The phrase is taken from James Hunter, *Set Adrift Upon the World: The Sutherland Clearances* (Edinburgh, 2015).
15. *Dundee Advertiser*, 17 December 1892.
16. Ronald Black (ed.), *To the Hebrides, Samuel Johnson's Journey to the Western Islands of Scotland and James Boswell's Journal of a Tour to the Hebrides* (Edinburgh, 2007), 125.
17. John MacAskill (ed.), *The Highland Destitution of 1837* (Woodbridge, 2013), 84, 97–100.
18. Alexander Fenton, *The Northern Isles: Orkney and Shetland* (East Linton, 1997), 275.

19. James Hunter, *A Dance Called America: The Scottish Highlands, the United States and Canada* (Edinburgh, 1994), 110–12.
20. MI, GD221/771, John Campbell, to John Campbell WS, 4 April 1803.
21. MacAskill, *Highland Destitution*, 54.
22. MacAskill, *Highland Destitution*, 53–7.
23. A. Gibson and T.C. Smout, 'Scottish Food and Scottish History', in R.A. Houston and I.D. Whyte (eds), *Scottish Society, 1500–1800* (Cambridge, 1989), 72–3.
24. James Hunter, *Scottish Exodus* (Edinburgh, 2007), 188; MI, GD221/416/1, Note on Kilchrist near Broadford, 27 March 1766.
25. National Records of Scotland [NRS], HD20/71, Comparative Table of Destitution in Skye, 1847–50.
26. NRS, HD20/86, Local Committees, Broadford, papers relating to Skye, Raasay and other islands, 1846–50.
27. Hunter, *Dance*, 116.
28. NRS, HD10/25, Letters, Donald Macinnes to Captain Fishbourne, 11 September 1848.
29. James Hunter, *The Making of the Crofting Community* (Edinburgh, 1986), 59.
30. Stephen P. Walker, 'Agents of Dispossession and Acculturation. Edinburgh Accountants and the Highland Clearances', *Critical Perspectives on Accounting* (2003), 823–5, 832.
31. Hunter, *Making of the Crofting Community*, 120.
32. Thomas M. Devine, *Clanship to Crofters' War: The social transformation of the Scottish Highlands* (Manchester, 1994), 63.
33. Philip Gaskell, *Morvern Transformed: A Highland Parish in the Nineteenth Century* (Cambridge, 1968), 106.
34. T.C. Smout, 'Tours in the Scottish Highlands from the eighteenth to the twentieth centuries', *Northern Scotland*, 12 (1982), 111; *Nature Contested: Environmental History in Scotland and Northern England Since 1600* (Edinburgh, 2000), 131.
35. Gaskell, *Morvern Transformed*, 81–108.
36. *Edinburgh Evening Courant*, 22 March 1828.
37. Scotland's People, Census 1841, Strath Parish, Skye, Island of Scalpay.
38. NRS, HD1/19, Highland Destitution: Registers, 1840–52, Lord Macdonald's estate.
39. NRS, HD20/86, Applicants for relief (Strath), 5–11 March 1848.
40. Roger Hutchinson, *Calum's Road* (Edinburgh, 2008), 7–9.
41. NRS, HD4/5, Passenger List, Highland and Islands Emigration Society, 1852–7.
42. Devine, *Clanship*, 187–91.
43. *Inverness Courier*, 23 April 1857.
44. Archibald Geikie, *Scottish Reminiscences* (Glasgow, 1904), 397.
45. Scotland's People, Census 1861, Strath Parish, Skye, Island of Scalpay.
46. Walker, 'Agents', 826.
47. Rob Gibson, *The Highland Clearances Trail* (Edinburgh, 1983), 60.
48. *Inverness Courier*, 23 April 1828, 6 December 1855, 5 February 1857, 23 March 1894.
49. Hutchinson, *Calum's Road*, 29.
50. Alexander Nicolson, *History of Skye* (Portree, 1995 ed.), 261.
51. Orr, *Deer Forests*, 7–9; Cameron, *Land*, 88–9.

52. Gaskell, *Morvern Transformed*, 77.
53. MI, GD 221/4324/1D, Minute of Agreement, 1861.
54. Andy Wightman, *The Poor Had No Lawyers: Who Owns Scotland (And How They Got It)* (Edinburgh, 2011), 165.
55. Smout, *Nature Contested*, 133.
56. Martin Martin, *A Description of the Western Islands of Scotland ca 1695 and A Late Voyage to St Kilda, Martin Martin; Description of the Occidental i.e. Western Islands of Scotland, Donald Munro* (Edinburgh, 1999), 320.
57. Thomas Pennant, *A Tour in Scotland and Voyage to the Hebrides, 1771* (Edinburgh, 1992 ed.), 288.
58. Smout, 'Tours', 110.
59. Orr, *Deer Forests*, 30.
60. John A. Love, *Rum: A Landscape Without Figures* (Edinburgh, 2001), 153–4.
61. Devine, *Clanship*, 66–7.
62. Osgood Hambury MacKenzie, *A Hundred Years in the Highlands* (Edinburgh: 2005 ed.), 72.
63. Gaskell, *Morvern Transformed*, 58–9.
64. Hayden Lorimer, 'Guns, game and the grandee: the cultural politics of deer-stalking in the Scottish Highlands', *Ecumene*, 7 (4), (2000), 409.
65. Lorimer, 'Guns, game and the grandee', 410–11.
66. Wendy Ugolini, 'Scottish Commonwealth Regiments', in Edward M. Speirs, Jeremy A. Crang and Matthew J. Strickland (eds), *A Military History of Scotland* (Edinburgh, 2012), 489–90.
67. Orr, *Deer Forests*, 39–40.
68. Mary Miers, *Highland Retreats* (New York, 2017), 81, 157.
69. NRS, HD19/17, Relief Officer's letters, receipts, Strathaird, Broadford, 1849, Donald M'Innes to Captain Smith, 25 February 1849.
70. *Manchester Weekly Times*, 2 October 1858.
71. John Morrison, *Painting the Nation* (Edinburgh, 2003), 103.
72. Smout, 'Tours', 107–10.
73. SLAC, PL, SL/D293/1/19, G.M. Fraser to Messrs Bischoff Coxe & Co, 6 June 1932; J. Mackintosh to G.M. Fraser, 7 June 1932.

Chapter 4

1. *Dundee Courier*, 25 May 1909.
2. *Aberdeen Journal*, 17 October 1894.
3. Andrew Porter, *Victorian Shipping, Business and Imperial Policy: Donald Currie, the Castle Line and Southern Africa* (Woodbridge and New York, 1986), 266–7.
4. *The Scotsman*, 5 August 1896.
5. Porter, *Victorian Shipping*, 46.
6. <http://www.oxforddnb.com/view/article/32671> (Sir Donald Currie; accessed 21 March 2017).
7. *The Scotsman*, 14 April 1909.
8. <http://www.oxforddnb.com/view/article/32671>.
9. T.M. Devine, *The Scottish Nation, 1700–2000* (London, 1999), 453–5.
10. *Dundee Courier*, 22 November 1907.
11. *The Scotsman*, 15 August 1894.

12. James Hunter, *The Making of the Crofting Community* (Edinburgh, 1986), 128–30.
13. *Greenock Telegraph & Clyde Shipping Gazette*, 27 May 1885.
14. National Records of Scotland [NRS], GD1/36/2/5, papers relating to crofter unrest, 1883–4.
15. Roger Hutchinson, *Martyrs of Glendale and the Revolution in Skye* (Edinburgh, 2015), 50–6; Scotland's People, Census, 1881, Strath.
16. Norman Macdonald and Cailean Maclean, *The Great Book of Skye* (Portree, 2014), 162–3.
17. Hunter, *Making of the Crofting Community*, 133–5; see too Hutchinson, *Martyrs*.
18. Roger Hutchinson, *Calum's Road* (Edinburgh, 2008), 13.
19. Museum of the Isles [MI], GD221/4502, Offer, the lotters of Breakish, 1812.
20. Osgood Hanbury MacKenzie, *A Hundred Years in the Highlands* (Edinburgh, 1995 ed.), 152.
21. MI, GD221/2254, 2257, claims from Neil Ross and Samuel Campbell, 14, 16 February 1881.
22. Napier Commission, Evidence from Broadford, 16 May 1883, 262–3, 309.
23. See William P.L. Thomson, *Kelp-Making in Orkney* (Stromness, 1983), 19–25.
24. 'Highland and Island Crofters', *The Scotsman*, 15 December 1877.
25. Hunter, *Making of the Crofting Community*, 121; Macdonald and Maclean, *Great Book of Skye*, 153–4.
26. *The Scotsman*, 4 October 1899.
27. MI, Macdonald Papers, GD 221/2593/10/1, Angus McEwan to A. Macdonald, 31 March 1885.
28. Hunter, *Making of the Crofting Community*, 138.
29. Hutchinson, *Martyrs*, 158–65.
30. NRS, GD1/36/2/5, Alexander Boyd to the Chief Constable, Inverness, 30 June 1884.
31. See MI, GD 221/3129, Lady Macdonald to Mr Macdonald, February 1886.
32. *The Scotsman*, 6 November 1880.
33. Hunter, *Making of the Crofting Community*, 161–2.
34. Ewan Cameron, *Land for the People? The British Government and the Scottish Highlands, c. 1880–1925* (East Linton, 1996), 39.
35. *Dundee Evening Post*, 16 October 1901; *Greenock Telegraph & Clyde Shipping Gazette*, 25 August 1888; *Hampshire Advertiser*, 29 December 1906.
36. *Dundee Courier*, 22 November 1907.
37. *The Scotsman*, 6 November 1880.
38. Syd House and Christopher Dingwall, '"A Nation of Planters": Introducing the New Trees, 1650–1900', in Smout (ed.), *People and Woods in Scotland*, 154–5.
39. *The Scotsman*, 21 April 1909; Peter J. McEwan, *The Dictionary of Scottish Art and Architecture* (Ballater, 1988), 353.
40. Alan Calder, 'Dunn and Watson: The Scottish Commissions', *James MacLaren Society Journal*, 6 (Winter, 2008–9), 4.
41. In conversation with Michael and Veronica Walford, 28 April 2018.
42. SLAC, D293//1/15, Inventory of Furnishings in Scalpay House, July 1925.
43. Neil and Rosie Hooper, 'A Visit to Scalpay House', *James MacLaren Society Journal*, 6 (Winter, 2008–9), 17.
44. *Arbroath Herald*, 27 July 1905.

45. *The Scotsman*, 14 January 1901.
46. Scotland's People, Census 1901, Strath, Skye, Island of Scalpay.
47. MI, GD221/3050/13, A. McSwan to A. Macdonald, 13 October 1885.
48. Charles W.J. Withers, *Urban Highlanders: Highland–Lowland Migration and Urban Gaelic Culture, 1700–1900* (East Linton, 1998), 110–11.
49. Napier Commission, Vol. XXXXII, Appendix A, 50.
50. MI, GD221/2547, Donald MacKinnon to Alexander Macdonald, [?] December 1882.
51. 'Highland and Island Crofters', *The Scotsman*, 15 December 1877.
52. NRS, GD1/36/2/5 (1), Simon Fraser (Broadford Police Station) to Chief Constable, Inverness, 28 November 1883.
53. MI, GD221/4753, List of Breakish crofters who have applied to the Crofters Commission, 7 March 1889.
54. *Arbroath Herald*, 27 July 1907.
55. Calder, 'Dunn and Watson', 6–7.
56. *Inverness Courier*, 7 September 1897.
57. *The Scotsman*, 25 June 1897.
58. See Mary MacPherson, *Memoirs of Kyleakin* (Perth, 1950).
59. On Bullough, see John A. Love, *Rum: A Landscape Without Figures* (Edinburgh, 2001), 230–49.
60. *Arbroath Herald*, 27 July 1905.
61. Macdonald and Maclean, *Great Book of Skye*, 60–1; Charles Jedrej and Mark Nuttall, *White Settlers: The Impact of Rural Repopulation in Scotland* (London, 1996), 84.
62. Forbes, *Place-names of Skye and Adjacent Islands*, 143.
63. *The Bystander*, 25 April 1906.
64. University of Glasgow Archives, UGD 100/7/1/22, Notice of sale and particulars for the *Iolaire*, January 1922; *The Scotsman*, 3 August 1948.
65. Isobel Macdonald, *A Family in Skye* (n.d., privately printed; copy in Highland Council Archives, Inverness).
66. *Glasgow Herald*, 25 May 1899.
67. Macdonald, *A Family in Skye*, 35.
68. *The Scotsman*, 1 September 1906.
69. *The Scotsman*, 19, 21 April 1909.
70. *Chronicle of the [Molteno] Family*, Vol. 7, 2 (April 1920), 31.
71. *Dundee Courier*, 22 May 1920.
72. *Western Times*, 1 May 1909.
73. *The Scotsman*, 3 August 1948.

Chapter 5

1. Camille Dressler, *Eigg: The Story of an Island* (Edinburgh, 2007 ed.), 115–30.
2. *Surrey Mirror*, 20 March 1931.
3. R.H. Campbell and T.M. Devine, 'The Rural Experience', in W.H. Fraser and R.J. Morris (eds), *People and Society in Scotland, II, 1830–1914* (Edinburgh, 1990), 66.
4. James Hunter, *The Making of the Crofting Community* (Edinburgh, 1986), 184–92.
5. Ian Fraser Grigor, *Highland Resistance: The Radical Tradition in the Scottish North* (Edinburgh and London, 2000), 182–3.

6. Ewan Cameron, *Land for the People? The British Government and the Scottish Highlands, c. 1880–1925* (East Linton, 1996), 166.

7. Grigor, *Highland Resistance*, 192–7.

8. SLAC, D293/1/1, Sir Henry Bell to G.M. Fraser, 20 May 1925.

9. Hunter, *Making of the Crofting Community*, 205.

10. SLAC, D293/1/21, G.M. Fraser to J.D.E Muntz, 8 August 1932.

11. Ian Robert Manners, 'Scalpay – A Brief History' (typescript, October 2011), kindly copied for me by Mary Jeffrey-Jones.

12. SLAC, D293/1/2, B. Coxe to G.M. Fraser, 19 November 1931.

13. SLAC, D293/1/1, Sir Henry Bell to G.M. Fraser, 10 April 1928.

14. SLAC, D293/1/19, G.M. Fraser to Col Lord Arthur Browne, 4 August 1932.

15. Ian Robert Manners, 'The Bell Family: A [Slightly] Revisionist History' (typescript, 14 May 2010), copy from Mary Jeffrey-Jones.

16. Much of this section is derived from Manners, 'The Bell Family'.

17. *Surrey Mirror*, 20 March 1931.

18. Matthew Brown (ed.), *Informal Empire in Latin America: Culture, Commerce and Capital* (London, 2008).

19. See Gordon Bridger, *Britain and the Making of Argentina* (Southampton, 2013).

20. Colin M. Lewis, *Argentina: A Short History* (Oxford, 2002), 3.

21. Mira Wilkins, *The History of Foreign Investment in the United States to 1914* (Harvard, 1989), 309.

22. *Surrey Mirror*, 12 November 1909.

23. Nesta FitzGerald, granddaughter of Sir Henry Bell, 'Reminiscences', kindly lent by Mary Jeffrey-Jones, NF's daughter.

24. *Surrey Mirror*, 20 March 1931.

25. *Surrey Mirror*, 6 December 1929.

26. SLAC, D213/1/17, R.C. Ballantyne to Sir Henry Bell, 27 July 1925; G.M. Fraser to R.C. Ballantyne, 7 August 1925.

27. SLAC, D213/1/17, R.C. Ballantyne to Sir Henry Bell, 11 November 1925.

28. SLAC, D213/1/17, Edward Tappenden to G.M. Fraser, 28 May 1926.

29. SLAC, Christine MacPhee to G.M. Fraser, 3 June 1926; R.C. Ballantyne to G.M. Fraser, 23 June 1926

30. SLAC, D213/1/17, Sir Henry Bell to G.M. Fraser, 11 November 1926.

31. SALC, D293/1/5, Sir Henry Bell to G.M. Fraser, 28 March 1927.

32. SLAC, D293/1/7, G.M. Fraser to Col Macdonald, 23 August 1926.

33. SLAC, D293/1/5, Sir Henry Bell to G.M. Fraser, 15 September 1926.

34. SLAC, D293/1/7, G.M. Fraser to Sir Henry Bell, 31 August 1926.

35. Macdonald and Maclean, *Great Book of Skye*, 188.

36. SLAC, D293/1/7, K. Macdonald to G.M. Fraser, 13 April 1927.

37. Macdonald and Maclean, *Great Book of Skye*, 383.

38. SLAC, D293/1/5, D. Robertson to G.M. Fraser, 3 September 1928.

39. Alexander Fenton, *Scottish Country Life* (Edinburgh, 1976), 19–23.

40. Museum of the Isles [MI], GD221/2533/4, Alex McInnes to Alexander Macdonald, 7 November 1882.

41. SLAC, D293/1/1, D. Robertson to G.M. Fraser, 16 February 1929.

42. SLAC, D293/1/2, G.M. Fraser to Bischoff, Coxe, Bischoff & Thompson, 12 May 1931.

43. SLAC, D293/1/3, Sir Henry Bell to G.M. Fraser, 19 February 1929.

44. SLAC, D293/1/1, Sir Henry Bell to G.M. Fraser, 28 December 1928.

45. SLAC, D293/1/3, Major Bell to G M Fraser, 23 September 1928.
46. SLAC, D213/1/17, L. MacLean to G.M. Fraser, 15 April 1926.
47. SLAC, D293/1/10, Angus McLeod to G.M. Fraser, 30 June 1926.
48. SLAC, D293/1/10, G.M. Fraser to Messrs C. and D. MacTaggart, 2 March 1932.
49. SLAC, D293/1/106, Donald Macinnes to G.M. Fraser, 11 July 1932; Donald Robertson to G.M. Fraser, 15 August 1932.
50. SLAC, D293/1/14, G.M. Fraser to A. McLeod, 13 March 1929; G.M. Fraser to Edward Tappenden, 6 March 1929.
51. MI, GD221/3248/13, A. McSwan to A. Macdonald, 17 September 1886.
52. SLAC, D293/1/10, Angus McLeod to G.M. Fraser, 4 November 1926.
53. SLAC, D293/1/10, Angus McLeod to G.M. Fraser, 20 March 1931.
54. SLAC, CI/5/19/2/1/75, file on Scalpay Island Side School, 1925–31.
55. SLAC, D293/1/7, Sir Henry Bell to G.M. Fraser, 29 November 1929.
56. SLAC, D293/1/2, G.M. Fraser to Bischoff, Coxe etc., 13 May 1931.
57. SLAC, D293/1/7, G.M. Fraser to Sir Henry Bell, 27 August 1929.
58. James Hunter, *The Claim of Crofting: The Scottish Highlands and Islands, 1939–1990* (Edinburgh, 1991), 35.
59. SLAC, D293/1/2, Particulars of the Estate of Scalpay, May 1931.
60. SLAC, HCA, D293/1/7, G.M. Fraser to Major Bell, 5 June 1931.
61. Madeleine Bunting, 'Island Mythologies', *The Bottle Imp*, 21 (July 2017), 2–3.
62. SLAC, D293/1/20, G.M. Fraser to Bischoff, Coxe, etc., 1 September 1931; Macdonald and Maclean, *Great Book of Skye*, 112.
63. SLAC, D293/1/106, Donald Robertson to G.M. Fraser, 8 September 1932.
64. Ewan A. Cameron, 'The Highlands since 1850', in Anthony Cooke et al. (eds), *Modern Scottish History, 1707 to the Present, Vol 2: The Modernisation of Scotland* (East Linton, 1998), 61.
65. SLAC, Messrs Bischoff, Coxe, etc. to G.M. Fraser, 16 July 1931.
66. SLAC, D293/1/19, John Paterson to G.M. Fraser, 3 July 1932.
67. SLAC, D293/1/19, G.M. Fraser to Bischoff, Coxe, etc., 6 June 1932.
68. Macdonald and Maclean, *Great Book of Skye*, 183, 189, 330–1.
69. SLAC, D293/1/19, L.H. Smith to G.M. Fraser, July 1932.
70. SLAC, D293/1/21, G.M. Fraser to Messrs Maclay, Murray and Spens, 27 August 1932.
71. SLAC, D293/1/106, Major Henry Bell to G.M. Fraser, 11 August 1932.
72. *The Scotsman*, 13 July 1938.
73. Information from Robert Muntz, 24 January 2017; *The Scotsman*, 26 October 1939.
74. *The Scotsman*, 3 October 1941.
75. Scotland's People, Marriages, Strath, 1940.
76. G.M. Fraser to Captain Muntz, 16 April, 20 May 1943 (copies of letters kindly given me by Frederick Muntz).

Chapter 6

1. Rev. Murdo Macleod MacSween, 'The Parish of Strath', in Hugh Barron (ed.) *The Third Statistical Account of Scotland, XVI, Inverness* (Edinburgh, 1985), 537. The chapter was revised and updated by the Rev. A. MacVicar in July 1966.

2. Whatley Collection [WC], HH to HW, 25 March 1966.

3. Henry Hilditch, 'An Autobiography' (typescript, 1944), 106–7.

4. From notes written in Henry Hilditch's *Holy Bible*.

5. William Hetherington, *Swimming Against the Tide: The Peace Pledge Union Story, 1934–2014* (London, 2015 ed.), 6–9.

6. *Peace News*, 17 December 1970.

7. WC, HH to HW, 23 May 1962.

8. *Birmingham Daily Post*, 11 October 1939.

9. Andrew Rigby, *A Life in Peace: A Biography of Wilfred Wellock* (Bridport, 1988), 78–80.

10. Hilditch, 'An Autobiography', 118.

11. *Fife Free Press & Kirkcaldy Guardian*, 12 February 1944.

12. WC, HH to HW, 28 March 1960.

13. Material for this section is drawn from 'My Father's Book', a compilation by Allan Whatley of letters, notes, cards, autobiographical and biographical writings.

14. John Bew, *Citizen Clem: A Biography of Attlee* (London, 2017 ed.), 62.

15. Whatley Collection [WC], Francis Hurley to Herbert Whatley, 26 June 1916.

16. Arthur S. Peake, *Prisoners of Hope: The Problem of the Conscientious Objector* (London, 1918).

17. For a contemporary account, see Mrs Henry Hobhouse, *'I Appeal Unto Caesar'* (London, 1917).

18. WC, A. Lambert to Herbert Whatley, 24 May 1916.

19. WC, Allan Whatley, 'I Never Knew it Would Happen', autobiographical notes, 1919–63 (typescript, 1992).

20. Correspondence from Alex Welford, 2 April 2018.

21. WC, Allan Whatley, 'The Gang Rambles, 1933–1946' (typescript, 1972).

22. WC, Allan Whatley, '1940 to 1946' (typescript collection of Second World War work experiences, n.d.).

23. *Birmingham Mail*, 29 September 1944.

24. WC, Allan Whatley, 'I Never Knew'.

25. Rigby, *A Life*, 84.

26. Keith Gressen, 'The New Thinking', *The Nation*, 13 November 1917.

27. WC, H. Allan Whatley, Diary, 1940–46.

28. *Birmingham Daily Post*, 11 April 1945.

29. *The London Gazette*, 2 January 1948.

30. See *Community Education. Being a Description of the Work of Residential and Non-Residential Colleges for Adult Education* (London, 1938; Educational Settlements Association).

31. Rigby, *A Life*, 113.

32. John Martin, 'Doubleday, Henry (1810–1902)', *Oxford Dictionary of National Biography*, Oxford University Press, 2004; online edition, October 2007 <http://www.oxforddnb.com/view/article/65575> (accessed 21 September 2017).

33. WC, HH to HW, 7 February, 21 September 1959.

34. Highland Council Archives, Inverness, C1/10/5/14, Crofting Counties Scheme, Correspondence, 1936–55, Memorandum prepared for meeting of the Crofting Counties, Inverness, 19 April 1950.

35. *Birmingham Daily Post*, 13 August 1956.

36. Tex Geddes, *Hebridean Sharker* (Edinburgh, 2012), 7–8.

37. WC, Allan Whatley, 'Pabay: Isle of Skye, as told to and recorded' (typescript, 1995), 5.
38. Frank Fraser Darling, *Island Years, Island Farm* (Dorset, 2011 ed.), 24.
39. John Morrison, *Painting the Nation: Identity and Nationalism in Scottish Painting, 1800–1920* (Edinburgh, 2003), 77–110.
40. Madeleine Bunting, *Love of Country: A Hebridean Journey* (London, 2016), 7.
41. Madeleine Bunting, *The Plot: A Biography of An English Acre* (London, 2009), 127.
42. *Dundee Courier*, 15 August 1932.
43. See Anne Cholawo, *Island on the Edge: A Life on Soay* (Edinburgh, 2016).
44. R.M. Lockley, *Dream Island Days: A Record of the Simple Life* (London, 1930; 1943 ed.), 9.
45. R.M. Lockley, *Inland Farm* (London, 1943).
46. WC, Len Whatley to Allan and Evelyn Whatley, 31 December 1950.
47. Lockley, *Inland Farm*, 9.
48. *Illustrated London News*, 1 April 1975.
49. Lockley, *Dream Island Days*, 21.

Chapter 7

1. See Donald A. Maclean, *The Weather in North Skye* (Inverness, 1977).
2. Whatley Collection [WC], Len Whatley to Herbert and Mary Whatley, 8 January 1950.
3. National Records of Scotland [NRS], GD362/1, 'Journal of Skye by JB, 1799'.
4. University of St Andrews Special Collections, J.D. Forbes Collection, msdep7/ incoming letters, 1836 (26), J.D. Forbes to Jane Forbes, 1 July 1836
5. University of St Andrews Special Collections, J.D. Forbes Collection, msdep7/ Journals, 15, Highlands, 1836.
6. *Evening Telegraph*, 5 August 1930.
7. Whatley Collection [WC], Allan Whatley, 'Pabay: Isle of Skye, as told to and recorded' (typescript, 1995), 19.
8. Information provided by Stan Robinson, 18 January 2018.
9. WC, HH to HW, 7 May 1953.
10. Stan Robinson, 18 January 2018.
11. WC, HH to HW, 11 March 1954.
12. T.C. Smout, 'The Improvers and the Scottish Environment: Soils, Bogs and Woods', in T.M. Devine and J.R. Young (eds), *Eighteenth-Century Scotland: New Perspectives* (East Linton, 1999), 211–3.
13. Robert A. Dodgshon, 'Budgeting for Survival: Nutrient Flow and Traditional Highland Farming', in S. Foster and R.C. Smout (eds), *The History of Soil and Field Systems* (Aberdeen, 1994), 83.
14. Frank Fraser Darling, *Island Years, Island Farm* (Dorset, 2011 ed.), 195.
15. John Kings and Brian Giles, 'The Midlands', and Marjory Roy, 'The Highlands and Islands of Scotland', in Julian Mayes and Dennis Wheeler (eds), *Regional Climates of the British Isles* (Routledge, London and New York, 1997).
16. Louise C. Ross, Gunnar Austrheim et al., 'Sheep grazing in the North Atlantic region: A long-term perspective on environmental sustainability', *Ambio*, 45, (September 2016), 1–21.

17. WC, HH to HW, 14 March 1953.
18. Raymond O'Malley, *One-horse Farm: Crofting in the West Highlands* (London, 1948), 182–5.
19. *Clarion of Skye*, April 1952, 6.
20. H.J.B. Birks, *Past and Present Vegetation of the Isle of Skye: A Palaeoecological Study* (Cambridge, 1973), 18.
21. Thomas Pennant, *A Tour of Scotland and Voyage to the Hebrides* (Birlinn: Edinburgh, 1998), 307.
22. *Sunday Post*, 12 July 1964.
23. F.H.W. Green and R.J. Harding, 'Climate in the Inner Hebrides', in J. Morton Boyd (ed.), *Natural Environment of the Inner Hebrides* (Royal Society of Edinburgh: Edinburgh, 1983), 132.
24. James Hunter and Cailean Maclean, *Skye: The Island* (Edinburgh, 1986), 17.
25. See Richard Cavendish, 'Britain Abandons the Groundnuts Scheme', *History Today*, 51, 1 (January 2001).
26. Matteo Rizzo, 'What was left of the groundnut scheme? Development disaster and labour market in southern Tanganyika, 1946–1952', *Journal of Agrarian Change*, 6.2 (2006), 205–38.
27. I.F. Grant, *Highland Folk Ways* (London, 1961), 65.
28. *Clarion of Skye*, January 1952, 7; Macdonald and Maclean, *Great Book of Skye*, 443.
29. Donald Gillies (ed.), *Annals of Skye, 1939–40* (Nethy Bridge, n.d.), 13 April 1940.
30. *Aberdeen Press and Journal*, 2 February 1949.
31. R.A. Dodgshon, 'Coping with Risk: Subsistence Crises in the Scottish Highlands 1600–1800', *Rural History*, 15 (2004), 1–25.
32. Martin Martin, *A Description of the Western Islands of Scotland circa 1695* (Edinburgh, 1999), 96.
33. H.V. Morton, *In Search of Scotland* (London, 1929; 1930 ed.), 222–3.
34. Information from Dorothy Harrop, 27 May 2018.
35. Anne Cholawo, *Island on the Edge: A Life on Soay* (Edinburgh, 2016), 92–4.
36. WC, Len Whatley to Allan and Evelyn Whatley, 31 December 1950.
37. O'Malley, *One-horse Farm*, 1.
38. O'Malley, *One-horse Farm*, 198.
39. WC, Donald Anderson (Librarian, Inverness) to Len Whatley, 5 March 1953.
40. John A. Burnett, *The Making of the Modern Scottish Highlands 1939–1965* (Dublin, 2011), 15.

Chapter 8

1. Ewan A. Cameron, 'The Modernisation of Scottish Agriculture', in T.M. Devine, C.H. Lee and G.C. Peden (eds), *The Transformation of Scotland* (Edinburgh, 2005), 190.
2. Communication from Stan Robinson, 10 April 2018.
3. T.C. Smout, *Exploring Environmental History: Selected Essays* (Edinburgh, 2009), 190–1.
4. SLAC, SL/D103/1, Department of Agriculture, Portree, Progress Inspection, 23 October 1951.
5. Whatley Collection [WC], Len Whatley to Herbert Whatley, n.d.
6. WC, HH to HW, 20 February, 23 March 1952.

7. WC, HH to HW, August 1952.
8. WC, Len Whatley to Allan and Evelyn Whatley, July 1952.
9. WC, HH to HW, 7 May 1953.
10. Comunication from Stan Robinson, 28 February 2018.
11. WC, HH to HW, 10 July 1952.
12. WC, Scrap book, Pabay, Skye (1), undated cutting.
13. Communication from Stan Robinson, 10 April 2018.
14. WC, HH to HW, 5 April 1952.
15. WC, HH to HW, 4 August 1952.
16. WC, HH to HW, 20 February 1952.
17. WC, HH to HW, 5 September 1952.
18. WC, Christopher Whatley to Evelyn Whatley, 12 June 1960.
19. Communication from Stan Robinson, 22 November 2017.
20. WC, HH to HW, 1 April 1952.
21. Communication from Stan Robinson, 28 February 2018.
22. G.J. Riekie, P.N. Williams, A. Raab, and A.A. Meharg, 'The potential for kelp manufacture to lead to arsenic pollution of remote Scottish islands', *Chemosphere*, 65, 2 (October 2006), 332–42.
23. Quoted in Krisztina Fenyo, *Contempt, Sympathy and Romance: Lowland Perceptions of the Highlands and the Clearances during the Famine Years, 1845–56* (East Linton, 2000), 48.
24. WC, Notes on Pabay, provided by Dorothy Harrop, 2017.
25. Communication from Stan Robinson, 28 February 2018.
26. WC, HH to HW, 14 March 1953.
27. WC, HH to HW, 22 February 1953.
28. WC, HH to HW, 29 April 1956.
29. WC, HH to HW, 18 October 1959.
30. Donald Gillies (ed.), *Annals of Skye, 1939–40* (Nethy Bridge, n.d.), January 1939.
31. Communication from Stan Robinson, 11 May 2018.
32. Murray Watson, *Being English in Scotland* (Edinburgh, 2003), 33.
33. WC, HH to HW, 22 February 1953.
34. Cameron, 'Modernisation', 199.
35. George Henderson, *The Farming Ladder* (London, 1944), Preface.
36. WC, HH to HW, 11 April 1954.
37. James Hunter, *The Claim of Crofting: The Scottish Highlands and Island 1930–1990* (Edinburgh, 1991), 54.
38. Communication from Stan Robinson, 18 January 2018.
39. Michael Flinn (ed.), *Scottish Population History from the Seventeenth Century to the 1930s* (Cambridge, 1977), 463–4.
40. Marjory Harper, *Emigration from Scotland between the Wars: Opportunity or Exile?* (Manchester, 1998), 56–9.
41. Gordon Pentland (ed.), *The Autobiography of Arthur Woodburn (1890–1978)* (Edinburgh, 2017), 132–3.
42. Ewan A. Cameron, 'The Highlands since 1850', in Anthony Cooke et al. (eds), *Modern Scottish History, 1707 to the Present, Vol 2: The Modernisation of Scotland* (East Linton, 1998), 62.
43. Andy Wightman, *The Poor Had No Lawyers: Who Owns Scotland (And How They Got It)* (Edinburgh, 2011), 2–3.
44. Ian Levitt, 'The creation of the Highlands and Islands Development Board, 1935–65', *Northern Scotland*, 19 (1999), 88; David Torrance, *The Scottish Secretaries* (Edinburgh, 2006), 159, 165.

45. Thomas Johnston, *Memories* (London, 1952), 174, 176.
46. Torrance, *Scottish Secretaries*, 199–203.
47. *A Programme of Highland Development*, Cmd. 7976 (HMSO, 1950).
48. *The Scotsman*, 24 April 1948.
49. John A. Burnett, *The Making of the Modern Scottish Highlands 1939–1965* (Dublin, 2011), 178.
50. Levitt, 'Highlands and Islands Development Board', 93.
51. House of Commons Parliamentary Papers Online, *Agriculture in Scotland: Report of the Department of Agriculture for Scotland for 1952*, Cmd. 8792 (HMSO, 1953), 11.
52. See for example, Cabinet Papers (50), 135, Marginal Land, 23 June 1950.
53. WC, HH to HW, 20 February 1952.
54. WC, HH to HW, 19 January 1954.
55. *Aberdeen Press and Journal*, 6 March 1950.
56. *Dundee Courier*, 17 November 1955.
57. Communication from Stan Robinson, 28 February 2018.
58. WC, HH to HW, 10 December 1954.
59. WC, HH to HW, 15 January 1955.
60. Communication, Stan Robinson, 28 February 2018.
61. WC, HH to HW, 2, 4 May, 5 June 1955.
62. Philip Clarke, 'Poultry production through the ages', *Farmers Weekly*, 11 February 2014, 2.
63. WC, HH to HW, 23 October, 9 November 1952.
64. WC, HH to HW, 22 April 1953; *Dundee Courier*, 30 April 1934, *The Scotsman*, 4 June 1949.
65. WC, HH to HW, 8 June 1953.
66. WC, HH to HW, August 1952.
67. WC, HH to HW, 23 November 1953.
68. WC, HH to HW, 28 June 1953.
69. Hunter, *Claim of Crofting*, 56.
70. WC, HH to HW, 5 July 1953.
71. WC, HH to HW, 6 January 1954.
72. WC, HH to HW, 14 February 1954.
73. WC, HH to HW, 15 January 1955.
74. WC, HH to HW, 14 March 1953.
75. WC, HH to HW, 2 May 1955.
76. Information kindly provided by Anthea Beszant. For information on those involved in the First World War see livesofthefirstworldwar.org website, hosted by the Imperial War Museum.
77. National Records of Scotland, Statutory Register, Marriages, 1920, 587/4, viewed (by Anthea Beszant), 23 October 2017; Register of Sasine Abridgements, 1138 (4), 20 September 1956.
78. WC, HH to HW, 12 January 1957.
79. WC, HH to HW, 15 March 1956.
80. N. Henson, 'Winter birds on Pabay, Skye', *Glasgow Bird Bulletin*, 5, 3 (November 1956), 25–30.

Chapter 9

1. Whatley Collection [WC], HH to HW, 10 January 1956.
2. WC, Len Whatley to Allan Whatley, 26 May 1961.
3. WC, HH to HW, 12 October 1955.
4. Communication from Stan Robinson, 10 April 2018.
5. *The Scotsman*, 29 December 2010.
6. WC, HH to HW, 9 April, 20 August, 4 September 1957.
7. WC, Allan Whatley, 'Pabay: Isle of Skye, as told to and recorded' (typescript, 1995), 112.
8. WC, HH to HW, 9 March 1959.
9. Communication from Fiona Davis, 3 June 2018.
10. Stana Nenadic, *Lairds and Luxury: The Highland Gentry in Eighteenth-century Scotland* (Edinburgh, 2007), 194–5.
11. Robert A. Dodgshon, *From Chief to Landlords: Social and Economic Change in the Western Highlands and Islands, c. 1493–1820* (Edinburgh, 1988), 87–8.
12. WC, HH to HW, 1 February 1957.
13. WC, HH to HW, 30 March 1958.
14. WC, HH to HW, 13 May 1958.
15. WC, HH to HW, 27 February 1958.
16. WC, HH to HW, 7 June 1959.
17. WC, HH to HW, 13 May, 9 November 1958.
18. Communication from Fiona Davis, 3 June 2018.
19. WC, HH to HW, 26 November 1959.
20. WC, HH to HW, 26 July 1959.
21. WC, HH to HW, 21 September 1959.
22. WC, HH to HW, 18 June 1961.
23. See Gary C. White et al., *Capture-recapture and removal methods for sampling closed populations* (Los Alamos, 1982).
24. *Aberdeen Evening Express*, 15 December 1961.
25. '"Ecologists' Statistician", George Mann Jolly (1922–1998)', *Wildlife Society Bulletin*, 27, 1 (1999), 238–9.
26. WC, HH to HW, 20 August 1958.
27. WC, HH to HW, 19 April 1959.
28. WC, HH to HW, 26 July 1959.
29. WC, HH to HW, 22 September 1960.

Chapter 10

1. Whatley Collection [WC], HH to Allan Whatley, 30 January 1956.
2. See <http://www.bgs.ac.uk/discoveringGeology/time/Fossilfocus/belemnite.html> (accessed November 2018). British Geological Society website.
3. *New Statistical Account of Scotland*, Vol. 14, (Edinburgh, 1834–45), 302.
4. B.R. Bell and J.W. Harris, *An Excursion Guide to the Geology of the Isle of Skye* (Glasgow, 1986), 28.
5. University of Edinburgh, Centre for Research Collections [UE, CRC], GEN 521/2, Sir A. Geikie, 'Notes on the Lias District of Skye', 1853.

6. Alan McKirdy, John Gordon and Roger Crofts, *Land of Mountain and Flood: The Geology and Landforms of Scotland* (Edinburgh, 2007), 60–2.

7. <https://doi.org/10.1093/ref:odnb/14304> ('James Hutton'; accessed 16 December 2017). This is the Oxford Dictionary of National Biography website.

8. Archibald Geikie, *Life of Roderick Murchison* (London, 1875), 105.

9. David R. Oldroyd, *The Highlands Controversy: Constructing Geological Knowledge through Fieldwork in Nineteenth-Century Britain* (Chicago, 1990), 21–2.

10. David A. Cumming, 'John MacCulloch's "Millstone Survey" and its consequences', *Annals of Science*, 41:6 (1984), 567–91.

11. Thomas Pennant, *A Tour in Scotland and Voyage to the Hebrides, 1771* (Edinburgh, 1992 ed.) 284.

12. Derek Flinn, 'John MacCulloch, M.D., F.R.S., and his Geological Map of Scotland: His Years in Ordnance', *Notes and Record of the Royal Society of London*, 36, 1 (August 1981), 83–7.

13. John MacCulloch, *A Description of the Western Islands of Scotland, including the Isle of Man* (Edinburgh and London, 3 vols, 1819).

14. UE, CRC, Notebooks of Robert Jameson, 1373/4, Journal of a Tour Through the Hebrides, Part 2, 11 August 1798.

15. Thomas Wright, *A Monograph on the Lias Ammonites of the British Islands* (London, 1878), 352.

16. Alan McKirdy, *Skye: Landscapes in Stone* (Edinburgh, 2016), 16–24.

17. The material in this paragraph is condensed from David Stephenson and John Merritt, *Skye: A Landscape Fashioned by Geology* (Perth, 2006).

18. K.M. Goodenough, *The Geological Assets of Broadford and Strath: Statement of Significance and Identification of Opportunities* (Report CR/06/0785N, British Geological Survey, Nottingham, 2006).

19. See Simon J. Knell and Michael A. Taylor, 'Hugh Miller: fossils, landscape and literary geology', *Proceedings of the Geologists' Association*, 117 (2006), 85–98.

20. Hugh Miller, *The Cruise of the Betsey* (Edinburgh, 1889 ed.), 149.

21. Geological Society Archives, LDGSL/839/37, Notebook, Skye, Roderick Murchison, 1827.

22. For early descriptions and images of Pabay's fossils see James Sowerby, *The Mineral Conchology of Great Britain* (London, 1812–46), Volume VI (1829).

23. Miller, *Cruise*, 149.

24. S.P. Hesselbo and A.L. Coe, 'Jurassic sequences of the Hebrides Basin, Isle of Skye, Scotland', in I.R. Graham and A. Ryan (eds), *Field Trip Guidebook* (Dublin, 2000), 42–58.

25. N. Morton and J.D. Hudson, 'Field guide to the Jurassic of the Isles of Raasay and Skye, Inner Hebrides, NW Scotland', in P.D. Taylor (ed.), *Field Geology of the British Jurassic* (Geological Society, London, 1995), 209.

26. Miller, *Cruise*, 4–5.

27. L.F. Spath, 'On the Liassic Succession of Pabay, Inner Hebrides', *Geological Magazine*, 59, 12 (1922), 548–51.

28. See <http://www.bgs.ac.uk/lexicon/lexicon.cfm?pub=PABS> (accessed November 2018).

29. David Oldroyd, 'Some youthful beliefs of Sir Archibald Geikie, PRS, and the first publication of his "On the Study of the Sciences"', *Annals of Science*, 54:1 (1997), 72, 78–84.

30. Sir Archibald Geikie, *A Long Life's Work: An Autobiography* (London, 1924), 32.
31. Michael A. Taylor, *Hugh Miller: Stonemason, Geologist, Writer* (Edinburgh, 2007), 101.
32. Oldroyd, *Highlands Controversy*, 337–40.
33. UE, CRC, GEN 521/2, Sir A. Geikie, 'The Upper Lias of Pabba', 1853, 23.
34. UE, CRC, GEN 521/2, Sir A. Geikie, Notes on Skye, 1853, 22–4.
35. Wright, *Monograph*, 344.
36. Archibald Geikie, 'Exhibition of a Collection of Liassic Fossils from Pabba and Skye', *Proceedings of the Royal Physical Society of Edinburgh*, I (1854–58), 6.
37. Taylor, *Hugh Miller*, 62–3.
38. Michael A. Taylor, '"Miller's most important geological discovery"; Archibald Geikie (1835–1924) as pupil and memorialist of Hugh Miller (1802–56)', forthcoming. I am grateful to the author for letting me see a proof copy of this paper.
39. Martin Rees, in *The Daily Telegraph*, 2 January 2018.
40. McKirdy, Gordon and Crofts, *Land*, 71–2.
41. Sir Archibald Geikie, *Scottish Reminiscences* (Glasgow, 1904), 394–5.
42. MacCulloch, *Description*, III, 405.
43. UE, CRC, Jameson Notebooks, 2, 15 July to 14 August 1798.
44. Geikie, *Reminiscences*, 396.
45. UE, CRC, Geikie, 'Upper Lias', 25.
46. Geikie, *Long Life's Work*, 34.
47. Geikie, 'Exhibition', 6.
48. Thomas Wright, 'Notes on the Fossils collected by Mr Geikie from the Lias of the Isles of Pabba, Scalpa and Skye', *Quarterly Journal of the Geological Society*, 14 (January 1858), 24–36.
49. Archibald Geikie, *The Story of a Boulder* (Edinburgh, 1848), 25.
50. See Morton and Hudson, 'Field guide', 209.
51. Geikie, *Long Life's Work*, 42.
52. *Saunders's Newsletter and Daily Advertiser*, 26 December 1864.
53. Lyall I. Anderson, 'Before the Scottish Survey: Alfred Harker the Geologist', *Proceedings of the Geologists' Association*, 125 (2014), 350–8; Alfred Harker, 'The Geology of the neighbourhood of Broadford, Skye', *Proceedings of the Geologists' Association*, 22, 4 (1911), 204–9.
54. Spath, 'Liassic Succession', 548–51.
55. Michael A. Taylor, 'Autobiography and documentable fact in the family background and religious affiliation of Archibald Geikie (1935–1924)', forthcoming; thanks again to Dr Taylor for letting me see this paper pre-publication.
56. James Macdonald, *General View of the Agriculture of the Hebrides, or Western Isles of Scotland* (Edinburgh, 1811), 22.
57. Miller, *Cruise*, 149–50.

Chapter 11

1. SLAC, D293/1/10a, Donald Gunn to G.M. Fraser, 8 January 1931.
2. SLAC, D293/1/10a, G.M. Fraser to Edward Tappenden, 4 March 1931.
3. *The Scotsman*, 14 September 1935.

4. Roger Hutchinson, *Calum's Road* (Edinburgh, 2008), 23.
5. Whatley Collection [WC], H.W. Whatley, 'Life on an Island' (typescript notes, n.d.).
6. WC, Len Whatley to Allan and Evelyn Whatley, 31 December 1950.
7. James Macdonald, *General View of the Agriculture of the Hebrides, or Western Isles of Scotland* (Edinburgh, 1811), 488.
8. Peter Bartrip, 'The Arrival, Spread and Impact of Myxomatosis in Scotland during the 1950s', *Scottish Historical Review*, LXXXVIII (April 2009), 137.
9. T.C. Smout, *Nature Contested: Environmental History in Scotland and Northern England Since 1600* (Edinburgh, 2000), 123–4.
10. WC, Allan Whatley, 'Pabay: Isle of Skye, as told to and recorded' (typescript, 1995), 55.
11. Museum of the Isles [MI], GD221/2501, John Stewart to Alexander Macdonald, 26 September 1882.
12. MI, GD221/1947, W. MacLeod to Alexander Macdonald, 6 May 1872.
13. Louise C. Ross, Gunnar Austrheim et al., 'Sheep grazing in the North Atlantic region: A long-term perspective on environmental sustainability', *Ambio*, 45, (September 2016), 8.
14. *The Scotsman*, 8 March 1873.
15. MI, GD221/3248/15, William Barron to A. Macdonald, 25 September 1886.
16. SLAC, D293/1/10, Angus Macleod to G.M. Fraser, 3 August 1926.
17. SLAC, D293/1/10, Angus Macleod to G.M. Fraser, 2 March 1927.
18. SLAC, D293/1/10, Angus Macleod to G.M. Fraser, 10 February, 28 December 1927.
19. SLAC, D293/1/10, Angus Macleod to G.M. Fraser, c.14 December 1927.
20. *Dundee Evening Telegraph*, 4 August 1927.
21. *The Scotsman*, 17 November 1928; *Daily Telegraph*, 14 June 1930.
22. *The Scotsman*, 28 November 1925.
23. SLAC, D293/1/10, Sir Henry Bell to G.M. Fraser, 12 October 1926; Angus Macleod to G.M. Fraser, 26 October, 20 November 1926.
24. SLAC, D293/1/10a, Angus Macleod to G.M. Fraser, 18 March 1931.
25. *The Scotsman*, 17 November 1928.
26. SLAC, D293/1/5, Donald Gunn to G.M. Fraser, 27 January 1930.
27. SLAC, D293/1/7, G.M. Fraser to Major Frank Scott, 23 August 1930.
28. SLAC, D293/1/10a, Edward Tappenden to G.M. Fraser, 13 March 1931.
29. SLAC, D293/1/2, Robert Whyte to G.M. Fraser, 26 October 1931.
30. SLAC, D293/1/10a, Donald Robertson to G.M. Fraser, 7 May 1931.
31. See Peter W.J. Bartrip, *Myxomatosis: A History of Pest Control and the Rabbit* (London, 2008).
32. WC, HH to HW, 3 August 1955.
33. WC, HH to HW, 14 September 1955.
34. *Clarion of Skye*, November 1955, 11.
35. Bartrip, 'Arrival, Spread and Impact of Myxomatosis', 142–53.
36. WC, HH to HW, 22 November 1959.
37. WC, Len Whatley to Allan Whatley, 25 October 1962.

CHAPTER 12

1. See Alastair Dawson et al., 'Weather and Coastal Flooding History: The Uists and Benbecula', School of Geosciences, University of Aberdeen (2011), Appendix 1.
2. *Aberdeen Evening Express*, 3 December 1951.
3. *Express and Star*, 26 January 1965.
4. Whatley Collection [WC], HH to HW, 17, 22 December 1952.
5. WC, HH to HW, 2 February 1953.
6. WC, HH to HW, 11 March 1954.
7. *Sunday Post*, 12 July 1964.
8. WC, Notes on Pabay, Dorothy Harrop, 2017.
9. <http://canmore.org.uk/event/834631> (accessed November 2018).
10. Joseph Huddart, *Memoir of the Late Captain Joseph Huddart* (London, 1821), 43, 49.
11. See Alison Grant, 'Gaelic Place-Names: Viking Influence on the Gaelic Place-Names of the Hebrides', *The Bottle Imp*, 21 (June 2017), 1–5.
12. *Bell's Weekly Messenger*, 12 June 1858.
13. *Greenock Telegraph*, 25 August 1888.
14. *Aberdeen Press and Journal*, 30 October 1933.
15. *Birmingham Daily Post*, 13 August 1956.
16. Museum of the Isles [MI], GD221/2511/3, Alex MacInnes to A. Macdonald, 15 September 1882.
17. WC, HH to HW, 1 April 1952.
18. WC, HH to HW, 11 April 1953.
19. WC, HH to HW, 8 June 1953.
20. WC, HH to HW, 28 June 1953.
21. WC, HH to HW, 25 October 1953.
22. WC, HH to HW, 5 November 1953.
23. WC, HH to HW, 30 November 1953.
24. WC, HH to HW, 7 December 1953.
25. In conversation with Neil Mackinnon, 25 March 2018.
26. WC, HH to HW, 19 December 1953.
27. WC, HH to HW, 6 January 1954.
28. WC, HH to HW, 9 November 1958.
29. WC, Len Whatley to Allan Whatley, 26 May 1961.
30. WC, HH to HW, 12 October 1955.
31. WC, HH to HW, 22 October 1955.
32. WC, HH to HW, 13 March 1958.
33. WC, HH to HW, 20 August 1958.
34. WC, HH to HW, 20 January 1960.
35. WC, HH to HW, 20 March 1962.
36. WC, HH to HW, 3 January 1965.
37. WC, Len Whatley to Allan Whatley, 11 June 1965.

CHAPTER 13

1. Whatley Collection [WC], HH to HW, 21 March 1960.
2. WC, HH to HW, 16 February 1954.

3. WC, HH to HW, 22 October 1960.
4. WC, HH to HW, 10 October 1959.
5. WC, HH to HW, 3 November 1960.
6. WC, Len Whatley to Allan Whatley, 26 May 1961.
7. WC, HH to HW, 9 November 1961.
8. John Bryden, 'Scottish Agriculture, 1950–1980', in Richard Saville (ed.), *The Economic Development of Modern Scotland 1950–1980* (Edinburgh, 1985), 141, 156.
9. John A. Burnett, *The Making of the Modern Scottish Highlands 1939–1965* (Dublin, 2011), 205.
10. David Torrance, *The Scottish Secretaries* (Edinburgh, 2006), 235.
11. WC, HH to HW, 1 November 1959.
12. Sir Kenneth Alexander, 'The Highlands and Islands Development Board', in Saville, *Economic Development*, 226.
13. Camille Dressler, *Eigg: The Story of an Island* (Edinburgh, 2007 ed.), 148–9.
14. *Aberdeen Press and Journal*, 12 July 1965.
15. *Clarion of Skye*, June 1956, 3.
16. WC, HH to HW, 9 November 1961.
17. WC, Len Whatley to Allan Whatley, 25 November 1962.
18. WC, HH to HW, 4 January 1962.
19. WC, Len Whatley to Allan Whatley, 2 July 1963.
20. WC, HH to Allan Whatley, 12 November 1962.
21. WC, Len Whatley to Allan Whatley, 2 July 1963.
22. *Daily Record*, 23 June 1967.
23. WC, 'Pabay' brochure, *c.* 1964.
24. WC, HH to HW, 4 January 1963.
25. WC, Len Whatley to Allan Whatley, 2 July 1963.
26. Jedrej and Nuttall, *White Settlers*, 16–17, 83–7.
27. WC, Len Whatley to Allan Whatley, 29 November 1963.
28. *Highlands and Islands Medical Services Committee. Report to the Lord Commissioners of Her Majesty's Treasury, Volume I* (1912), 6–8.
29. WC, HH to HW, 6 March 1955.
30. WC, HH to HW, 11 February 1962.
31. WC, HH to HW, 10 September 1966.
32. See Glen O'Hara, '"Dynamic, Exciting, Thrilling Change": the Wilson Government's Economic Policies, 1964–70', *Contemporary British History*, 20:3 (2006), 383–402.
33. WC, Len Whatley to Allan Whatley, 11 June 1965.
34. WC, HH to HW, 17 July 1965.
35. WC, HH to HW, 5 October 1965.
36. WC, HH to HW, 22 December 1965.
37. WC, HH to HW, 10 September 1966.
38. WC, HH to HW, 12 November 1966.
39. WC, HH to HW, 17, 18 July 1965.
40. WC, Len Whatley to Allan Whatley, 30 August 1966.
41. <https://balnakeil.wordpress.com/the-original-far-north-project/> (accessed 10 December 2018).
42. Giles Sutherland, 'Lotte Glob – 50 Years in Clay: A Major Retrospective', *Ceramic Review*, 250 (July/August 2011), 1–2.
43. WC, Margaret Whatley to Allan Whatley, n.d.
44. WC, Len Whatley to Allan Whatley, n.d.

45. Conversation with Judith Maclachlan, 2 February 2018.
46. 'Obituary: Donald F.A. Maclachlan', Imperial College, London, Alumni, 11 July 2007.
47. 'A Point of View: Does aetheism have to be anti-religious?', <http://www.bbc.co.uk/news/magazine-34054057> (accessed November 2018).
48. Correspondence from Alex Welford, 2 April 2018.
49. *Daily Record*, 23 June 1967.
50. *The Friend*, 11 February 1966.
51. *Scottish Daily Mail*, 18 February 1967.
52. National Records of Scotland [NRS], HDB9/21, Quaker Settlement in the Highlands, [?] to Deputy Chairman, HIDB, 8 December 1966 (owing to the sensitivity of the file, the names of writers and recipients have been redacted).
53. NRS, HDB9/21, Sydney Clarke [?] to HIDB, 18 February 1967.
54. *Sunday Telegraph*, 30 July 1967.
55. NRS, HDB9/21, internal memorandum, 6 March 1967; [?] to Sydney Clarke, 13 March 1967.
56. WC, Margaret Whatley to Allan and Evelyn Whatley, n.d. (December 1967).
57. *Scottish Sunday Express*, 15 October 1967.
58. *Illustrated London News*, 1 April 1975.
59. *West Highland Free Press*, 10 January 1975.

Chapter 14

1. In conversation with Anne and Ted Gerrard, 27 March 2018.
2. *New York Times*, 25 November 1977.
3. *Birmingham Post*, 25 May 1979.
4. *Daily Mirror*, 20 November 1972.
5. See Ted Gerrard, *The Boffin Bird* (2009) and *The Cuckoo Paradox* (2015).
6. See Brett L. Shadle, *The souls of white folk: White settlers in Kenya, 1900s–1920s* (Manchester, 2016).
7. Daniel Branch, *Defeating Mau Mau, Creating Kenya* (Cambridge, 2009), 201.
8. Caroline Elkins, *Britain's Gulag: The Brutal End of Empire in Kenya* (London, 2005), 2–3, 362.
9. *Glasgow Herald*, 6 July 1988.
10. Paolo Paron, David O. Olago, and Christian T. Omuto (eds), *Kenya: A Natural Outlook: Geo-Environmental Resources and Hazards* (Oxford, 2013), Chapter 5 especially.
11. The information on the Philip family's time on Pabay was gleaned in conversation with Rod and Janet Philip, 22 April 2018, and subsequent email communications.
12. In conversation with David Harris, 25 May 2018.
13. D. Chasey and R.C. Trout, 'Rabbit haemorrhagic disease in Britain', *Mammalia*, 59 (1995), 599–603; Anne Cholawo, *Island on the Edge: A Life on Soay* (Edinburgh, 2016), 240–1.
14. Michael Anderson, *Scotland's Populations from the 1850s to Today* (Oxford, 2018), 80–1.
15. *The Scotsman*, 8 April 2016.
16. Anderson, *Scotland's Populations*, 90.

17. Andy Wightman, *The Poor Had No Lawyers: Who Owns Scotland (And How They Got It)* (Edinburgh, 2011), 144–53.
18. <www.scottish-islands-federation.co.uk/island-statistics/> (accessed November 2018); Anderson, *Scotland's Populations*, 84.
19. Anderson, *Scotland's Populations*, 35, 96.

Epilogue

1. *West Highland Free Press*, 9 July 1993.
2. <http://www.gaeltec.com/about-us/> (accessed 15 January 2018).
3. Communication from Alex Welford, 31 May 2018.
4. In conversation with Nigel Smith, 7 May 2018.
5. *Press and Journal*, 23 June 2014.
6. *Press and Journal*, 22 May 1980.

Index